The Road and the Car in American Life

The MIT Press   Cambridge, Massachusetts, and London, England

The Road and the Car in American Life

John B. Rae

Copyright © 1971 by
The Massachusetts Institute of Technology

This book was designed by The MIT Press Design Department.
It was set in Linotype Baskerville
by The Colonial Press Inc., Clinton, Massachusetts.
It was printed and bound by Halliday Lithograph Corp.
in the United States of America.

ISBN 0 262 18049 9   (hardcover)

Library of Congress catalog card number: 70-148972

Contents

Tables

Figures

Illustrations

This study of the social and economic effects of highway transportation in the United States was made possible by a research grant from the Automobile Manufacturers Association, Inc., giving the author full responsibility for the selection and interpretation of the material.

Acknowledgments

This book was undertaken as a study of the economic and social impacts of automotive highway transportation. It was not planned to commemorate any particular occasion, but it seems most appropriate that it should be published in the year that the American automobile industry has selected to celebrate the seventy-fifth anniversary of its founding, dating that event from the appearance of the first motor vehicles on the streets of Detroit. Without the automobile industry there would be no automotive highway transportation and indeed little highway transportation of any kind to write about.

My primary indebtedness is to the Transportation Research Department and the Transportation Research Committee of the Automobile Manufacturers Association. Included here are the members who initiated this study and gave it their constant encouragement: John J. Cummings, until 1970 Manager of the Transportation Research Department; George A. Elgass, Chrysler Corporation; Earnest W. Elliott, Chrysler Corporation; A. J. Goldenthal, Ford Motor Company; W. W. Hotchkiss, American Motors Corporation; John N. Stewart, General Motors Corporation. They provided the financial support for the research that has gone into this book, they and their associates generously assisted me in collecting and compiling information, and they left me completely free to organize, evaluate, and interpret the data according to my own judgment. The responsibility for the facts that appear in the book and for the interpretations placed on these facts is entirely mine.

I owe thanks to many other members of the Automobile Manufacturers Association: in particular, Thomas C. Mann, President of the Association; Stanley S. Roe, Director, Economics Division; Peter E. Pekkala, Manager of the Economic Research

and Statistics Department; Earl R. Kreher of the same department; and Robert C. Lusk, Director of Educational Services.

So many others have contributed to this book that it is difficult to decide how to list them. The names that follow are in no
special order, and if any have been omitted, the lapse is inad-
vertent, and I apologize for it.

I owe much to J. Allen Davis, former general counsel of the
Automobile Club of Southern California for making available
materials from his own rich collection and enabling me to use
the Club's excellent library. Dr. Richard G. Lillard of California
State College at Los Angeles introduced me to Mr. Davis and has
been helpful in other ways. I have had full cooperation from
John McDonald, Director of Engineering and Technical Services; Paul Fowler, Traffic Engineer; Vince Desimone, Transportation Planning Engineer; and John E. Rempert, Highway Engineer and a former student of mine at M.I.T.

I am much indebted to William L. Hall, Regional Director,
Highway Safety Programs Office, Federal Highway Administration, who not only provided valuable data on highway development but also read several chapters of the manuscript and
offered useful criticism. His son, Dr. Jerome W. Hall of the
University of Maryland, a former student at Harvey Mudd
College, also helped with information that would have been
difficult to secure otherwise.

Professor E. Neal Hartley, Archivist of the Massachusetts Institute of Technology, and Miss Eleanor L. Bartlett, Archive
Librarian, were instrumental in locating and enabling me to use
studies of the impacts of Route 128. The Transportation Center
Library at Northwestern University gave me full cooperation
through Dr. John A. Bailey, Director of the Transportation Center, and B. Jacobson, Librarian. I wish to acknowledge also the
help of my good friend Dr. Harold A. Williamson of North-

western University and his son, Dr. Harold A. Williamson, Jr., of the University of Illinois.

It should go without saying that no one gets very far in any area of American automotive history without the help of Dr. James J. Bradley, Curator of the Automotive History Collection, Detroit Public Library—help that is given freely and generously. Willing assistance also came from Dr. Henry E. Edmunds, Director of the Ford Archives, and Richard Ruddell, Manager, Educational Affairs Department, Ford Motor Company.

In addition, invaluable advice and assistance came from John M. Kaiser, Assistant to the Traffic Commissioner, New York City; Robinson Newcomb of Robinson Newcomb Associates; George Young of Spencer-Roberts and Associates; and G. P. St. Clair of the Highway Research Board. Information on highway travel overseas was willingly supplied by the British and Japanese Consulates-General in Los Angeles. Valuable suggestions came from William D. Hart, Transportation Economist, National Highway Users Conference, Inc., and Ram Kirpalani, whom I met while he was studying transportation economics at the University of Southern California.

Another former Harvey Mudd College student, Bruce Goeller, deepened my understanding of urban transportation problems by inviting me to participate in a conference on the subject held by the RAND Corporation during the summer of 1967.

My daughter Helen has patiently typed my drafts. The final manuscript was done by Mrs. Glenn E. Thompson, secretary of the Department of Humanities, and Mrs. Ivan White, secretary of the Department of Physics, at Harvey Mudd College. My wife, Florence Rae, has once again been my indexer. Mrs. Charles Lofgren prepared some of the charts and tables.

John B. Rae
August 1970

I The Road Yesterday

1 The Highway in History

Travel and transport by road are functions of civilized society. Primitive tribes, in hunting expeditions or folk wanderings, doubtless followed reasonably well-defined trails, worn by the passage of people or animals seeking the easiest routes for their journeys and following the natural contours of the land. But these were not roads in the sense of being purposely built in order to assist the movement of traffic. The first roads were likely to be tracks of this kind with the worst obstacles removed, and with some attempt to provide a firm surface on soft ground and perhaps a bridge or ferry service where fords were inadequate; this kind of effort presupposes an organized society that has the requisite skill and labor force and for which trade and travel have acquired some importance.

The appearance of wheeled vehicles provided an additional and extremely important incentive to the conscious design and construction of highways. Hilaire Belloc, who was not only a prominent figure in English literature but also a profound student of highway history, has advanced the thesis that the vehicle was prior to and responsible for the road, because the concentration of weight on the wheels demanded a "made" surface.[1] There were certainly vehicles before there were identifiable roads. The wheel and axle came into use at least five thousand years ago. Existing archaeological evidence places the origin of wheeled vehicles in the region south of the Caucasus Mountains and extending over eastern Turkey and northern Persia, sometime before 3000 B.C.[2] This is a region of steppe and desert, but sufficiently timbered to provide the necessary material, over which vehicles could move without undue difficulty, just as cov-

1 Hilaire Belloc, *The Highway and Its Vehicles* (London: Studio, Ltd., 1926), pp. 1, 5.
2 See Stuart Piggott, "The Beginnings of Wheeled Transport," *Scientific American*, vol. 219, no. 1 (July 1968), pp. 82–90.

ered wagons much later rolled over the American plains without having to follow a fixed route.

The emergence of wheeled transport was a major step in human progress, illustrated at the time by the remarkably rapid diffusion of the technology under primitive conditions. By about 2500 B.C. it had spread across Europe as far as Denmark. In the meantime the more advanced civilizations of the Sumerians and the Hittites developed carts and chariots on a more sophisticated level than the first crude vehicles of the people to the north. There could have been multiple invention. The case for diffusion is somewhat more convincing, but the surviving evidence is so fragmentary that it is impossible to be absolutely certain. Before 2000 B.C. the streets of Babylon had stone tracks to accommodate carts with a five-foot wheelbase. A thousand years later we read that the Canaanite general Sisera had 900 iron chariots (Judges 4:3), surely the earliest panzer force on record.

These vehicles of antiquity have left an ineradicable impress on our civilization. Their wheelbases, as the Babylonian streets indicate, were generally about five feet, and almost invariably within a range of four to seven feet. The dimensions were determined by simple factors: the most efficient hauling arrangement was a double team harnessed abreast; in a war chariot enough width was needed for two men to act side by side—one to drive, the other to wield the weapons; and four to seven feet gave the breadth needed for stability without going to excessive and cumbersome size.[3] The gauge of the vehicles determined the width of roads and streets, and roads and streets once built are expensive and difficult to change. To this day we conform, not only on highways but on railroads as well, to the approximate span of the first primitive vehicles used by man.

By contrast, the early American civilizations never produced a wheeled vehicle, and this fact was reflected in their road sys-

3 Belloc, *Highway and Its Vehicles,* pp. 4, 5.

tems. It also strengthens the supposition that the wheel-and-axle was a conscious invention spread by diffusion except to the American continent, which by then was out of touch with the rest of the world. The Mayans built elaborate elevated causeways with vertical stone sides and a loose fill in between.[4] They ran straight between ceremonial centers and were intended primarily for religious functions, but their existence probably stimulated other uses. The empire of the Incas was bound together by a network of roads extending 2,000 miles through modern Ecuador and Peru.[5] They were expertly engineered but designed only for foot traffic or occasionally for pack animals.

It was therefore possible, if exceptional, for an organized highway system to develop independently of wheeled vehicles. And since it is entirely possible that the highway vehicle of the future may dispense with wheels, perhaps Belloc's definition should be broadened to state that the character of the highway is determined by the kind of traffic it must carry and the specific techniques available for carrying it. In effect, this is a restatement of the principle laid down by the great highway engineer John Loudon McAdam: "Roads must be built to accommodate the traffic, not the traffic regulated to preserve the roads." [6]

On this basis the "amber roads" that crossed Europe from the Mediterranean to the northern coasts of Germany must rank among the first regular highways. They began as trails followed as early as 2000–1500 B.C. by traders in search of the amber that is found along the Baltic coast. By the sixth century B.C. they were well-established trade routes of sufficient importance so that even though there was no central government to supervise them,

4 H. J. Spindler, "The Indian Trail," in Jean Labatut and W. J. Lane, eds., *Highways in Our National Life: A Symposium* (Princeton, N. J.: Princeton University Press, 1950), p. 59.
5 Hermann Schreiber, *History of Roads* (London: Barrie and Rockliff, 1961), p. 186.
6 Charles L. Dearing, *American Highway Policy* (Washington, D.C.: The Brookings Institution, 1941), p. 20.

the local people seem to have been willing to maintain the roads at difficult sections—corduroying in soft ground, keeping the surface firm near fords, and even providing grooves for cart wheels in mountain areas.[7] Similar grooves, including passing tracks, were cut in mountain roads in ancient Greece.

The amber roads, like most highways of the ancient world—and indeed most highways until modern times—were not used for heavy loads because there were no vehicles capable of carrying such loads over long distances economically. Nevertheless, they offer an interesting piece of evidence that even under the conditions of those days travel by land was sometimes preferred even when the alternative of water transport was available. These journeys must have been incredibly difficult and dangerous, but they apparently were considered less risky than a voyage in the clumsy ships of the day across the Bay of Biscay and through the navigational hazards of the North Sea. Although the traffic on the roads was small in bulk, it was high in value and in historical significance.

This was a piecemeal and only partially organized effort at road development. Comprehensively planned highway systems were a product of the rise of large empires because good roads were essential in order to maintain political and military control over extensive territories. These roads were designed primarily for the passage of troops and messengers, but merchants and other travelers inevitably sought them out as relatively easy and well-protected routes. There was one outstanding exception: the Inca roads were prohibited to all but official traffic. Other empires were more generous toward commerce. The Maurya dynasty of India built a highway network which came to be so heavily used that when the great Asoka became emperor in 256 B.C., he found it necessary to encourage water traffic in order to reduce con-

7 Schreiber, *History of Roads*, p. 6.

gestion on the roads.[8] The Royal Road of Persia, built in the reign of Darius I (521–485 B.C.), was a remarkable feat of highway engineering in that for its 1,500-mile length from Susa to the Aegean it followed the most efficient route and bypassed most of the principal cities on the way.[9] This arrangement, however, was not adopted in order to expedite traffic; its purpose was to ensure that a local revolt would not automatically disrupt the empire's main artery. Along this road traveled the couriers who gave the United States Post Office its motto. As described by Herodotus:

> Along the whole line of road there are men stationed with horses, in number equal to the number of days which the journey takes, allowing a man and a horse to each day; and neither snow, nor rain, nor heat, nor darkness of the night stays these messengers from completing their appointed distance as swiftly as possible. (Herodotus, *The History,* Book 8.)

The culmination of highway development in the ancient world was, of course, the network constructed by those skillful and indefatigable engineers, the Romans. They built 50,000 miles of main highways and probably twice that extent of secondary roads, solid and substantial so that they continued to serve western Europe for over a thousand years after the splendor of Imperial Rome disintegrated. Beyond all question the highway system was a major contributor to the long Roman hegemony. Some legends about Roman roads are unfounded. They were never absolutely straight; Roman road builders preferred straight lines when they could get them, but they never completely ignored natural obstacles. Nor did all roads lead to Rome; they crisscrossed the empire to serve the needs of the marching legions and carried a good deal of commerce as well. There is no need to exaggerate the Roman achievement; the facts are impressive

8 *Ibid.,* p. 20.
9 *Ibid.,* pp. 11, 13.

enough. Besides their skill in road construction, the Romans developed a concept of an integrated highway system on a level of sophistication that would not be matched until modern times. They differentiated between main and secondary roads and recognized that their empire needed a comprehensive and interconnected road network.

The main highways were built and maintained by the Roman government. They produced the legend of the straight Roman road because their primary function was strategic, and consequently they took the most direct route possible; since cost was a secondary consideration, they could be driven across or through natural obstacles.[10] The secondary roads were primarily commercial. They were the responsibility of local authorities, and their quality varied according to the wealth of the province or municipality that supported them.

Good roads increase mobility; this is a self-evident proposition. In the Roman world, as in all civilizations down to the twentieth century, the potentialities of road transport were severely limited by the inadequacies of the vehicles. Nevertheless, wealthy Romans were able to make substantial land journeys by coach, something no other society could achieve until the eighteenth century. In addition, the oxcart, clumsy and inefficient as it was, could function just well enough on Roman roads that it was usable for local hauling of moderately heavy loads. The highway system, in fact, generated sufficient use so that ancient Rome had traffic congestion like any modern city. Regulations aimed at relieving congestion in the Forum and along the Appian Way were no more effective than their twentieth-century successors.

After the fall of Rome there was a long period in which the development of highways was virtually at a standstill. It was not through lack of ability to build good roads; where they had the

10 M. P. Charlesworth, "Roman Empire Highways," in Labatut and Lane, eds., *Highways in Our National Life,* p. 34.

opportunity, medieval engineers showed themselves to be skillful enough, and in fact their techniques were better adapted to the climate of northern Europe than the massive solidity favored by the Romans. The trouble was the absence of central governments with the resources to build and maintain highways and the power to protect them. So road building and trade declined. Roman roads remained the mainstay of western Europe for a thousand years, but they deteriorated badly for lack of maintenance. It was only with the rise of national monarchies in the later Middle Ages that renewed attention was given to highway improvement. Even then, however, the responsibility for maintaining roads was usually given to local authorities, who almost uniformly discharged this responsibility in a way that persisted in the Western world until well into the nineteenth century. The men of the community were required to work on the roads for a specified number of days each year; as could be expected, this chore was ordinarily done reluctantly and badly. The Middle Ages also saw the concept of the "King's Highway" come into existence—a public highway open to all who wished to use it on their lawful occasions. But the "King's Highway" for some centuries meant only a right of passage, and not an actual nationally maintained road. Paradoxically, the era that saw a retrogression in roads also saw an advance in vehicles. Medieval wagons adopted the pivoted front axle, and the introduction of horseshoes and horse collars made it possible to replace the ox with the far more efficient horse as a draft animal.[11]

The first attempts to create recognizably modern highway systems came in the latter part of the seventeenth century, and they were stimulated by the need to provide better accommodation for wheeled traffic. The pioneers were England and France. In the former, an increased reliance on carts and coaches for

11 See Marjorie N. Boyer, "Medieval Pivoted Axles," *Technology and Culture,* vol. 1, no. 2 (Spring 1960), pp. 128–138.

transport produced a demand for better roads, to which the government responded by putting the matter into the hands of private enterprise through the chartering of turnpike trusts. The results were mixed. Some turnpike companies were well managed, others were not. By 1830 Britain had 104,770 miles of public roads, of which 22,000 miles were turnpikes.[12] The overall effect was less, perhaps, than had been hoped for, but there was improvement in the road system, and the decay of the British turnpikes was due much more to railroad competition than to any inherent unsoundness in the idea of supporting roads by user charges. France, as a major land power, had to have good roads for its armies to move on, and these roads had to be capable of carrying heavy wheeled traffic in the form of guns and caissons. It was not just happenstance that made Nicholas Joseph Cugnot the designer of the first known self-propelled highway vehicle. He was a French artillery officer, and the steam-powered contraption that he tested in 1769 was intended for military use.

To meet France's highway requirements, the famous Finance Minister of Louis XIV, Jean Baptiste Colbert, invoked the *corvée,* forced labor on the roads. It was, as we have seen, a virtually universal system for getting roadwork done. The difference was that in France the obligation was now rigorously enforced and supervised, and this feature became so unpopular that it was one of the grievances leading to the French Revolution. The importance of the French highway network is reflected in the organization early in the eighteenth century of a special body of engineers, the Corps des Ponts et Chaussées, from which emerged the world's first college for the formal academic training of engineers, the École des Ponts et Chaussées, founded in 1747 specifically to provide a body of men skilled in the construction and maintenance of roads and bridges.

12 John Copeland, *Roads and Their Traffic 1750–1850* (New York: Augustus M. Kelley, 1968), p. 62.

The climax of this highway renaissance was reached with the work of John L. McAdam (1756–1836) and Thomas Telford (1757–1834) in introducing new techniques of highway design and construction. Telford, a brilliant civil engineer who also did outstanding work in bridge and canal construction, was referred to in his day as "the Colossus of Roads." The British A-5 from London to Holyhead and the A-74 from Glasgow to Carlisle both follow routes initially laid out by Telford. McAdam's name was incorporated into the language as a descriptive term for improved road surfaces. They ushered in a colorful if short-lived era in highway transportation. With smooth roads and easier grades it was possible to design horse-drawn vehicles capable of carrying passengers and mail on regular schedules and at higher speeds than had hitherto been feasible—in this situation the causal relationship ran from highway to vehicle. The macadamized road gave the stagecoach its heyday; it also made the movement of freight by wagon a little easier.

This era, to repeat, was short-lived. The steam locomotive running on rails appeared before McAdam and Telford died, and in a very short time the railroad proved too powerful a competitor for all but local short-range highway traffic. A railroad train could travel faster than any stagecoach, and it could haul heavy freight far more economically than could horse-drawn wagons. As road use declined in importance, highway construction and improvement slowed down, until at the turn of the twentieth century a new technology came along to revive interest in road transport.

Highway Travel in Early America

When European settlers arrived on the North American continent, they found no great empire with an organized road system like that of the Incas. Overland travel was restricted largely to Indian war and hunting parties following forest trails established by long usage. These trails showed a remarkable sense of terrain. "An Indian overland trail," says an eminent historian of American travel, "always led the traveler to his destination in less time, or with fewer physical obstacles to overcome, than any other course that could be selected between the two points which it connected." [13] These trails became routes for trade and migration for the early colonists, but as settlement expanded, more was needed in the way of highway facilities. Most colonial traffic was waterborne, as was natural for a group of settlements strung along the seaboard; nevertheless, water transport could never completely replace roads.

Colonial governments followed the English practice of putting the responsibility for maintaining roads on local authorities, and with about the same lack of success. Colonial roads were generally of poor quality; in the northern sectors, in fact, it was likely to be easier to move by sleigh in winter than by wheeled vehicle in other seasons. Work on the roads was provided by adopting the European practice whereby men paid their highway taxes by labor on the roads. The results were no better in America than in Europe.

An expanding society, however, generated an increasing need for good highway transportation. As early as 1707 there was regular freight service by wagon by a road across New Jersey from Perth Amboy to Burlington, in effect linking New York and Philadelphia. Because this service was a monopoly operating on a franchise from the colonial government, it raised a chronic issue of transportation policy: that is, the extent to which regulation or control by public authority is desirable. To protests against the monopoly Governor Cornbury replied:

At present, everybody is sure, once a fortnight, to have an opportunity of sending any quantity of goods, great or small, at reasonable rates, without being in danger of imposition; and the

13 Seymour Dunbar, *A History of Travel in America* (New York: Tudor Publishing Co., 1937), p. 19.

sending of this wagon is so far from being a grievance or monopoly, a trade has been carried on, which was never known before, and in all probability never would have been.[14]

This statement is almost a classic defense of the "chosen instrument" policy, which was based on the contention that granting such a privilege to a single operator made possible the establishment of a service that either would not exist or would be poorer in quality if it was subject to unrestricted competition. If the volume of traffic in this case was sufficient for only one wagonload a fortnight, the governor's position had some validity.

The use of carts and wagons in the colonies increased substantially during the eighteenth century, with a marked acceleration in the latter half. Boston had 22 wheeled vehicles owned by its citizens in 1768 and 145 in 1798; Philadelphia went from 38 in 1760 to 827 in 1794.[15] This growth naturally stimulated a demand for highway improvement, which was resisted by the operators of packhorse trains—an example of another familiar historical phenomenon. Before the Revolution the outstanding American contribution to highway transportation was the Conestoga wagon, developed in Lancaster County, Pennsylvania, about 1750 and destined for a long and distinguished career as a carrier of goods. It held loads up to three tons, and it was flared at both ends to keep the cargo in place on heavy grades. Its wheels were four inches or more across, which helped on the primitive road surfaces it normally had to use. On an improved road a Conestoga, pulled by four to six horses, could make fifteen to twenty miles a day[16]—or about two miles an hour.

The Conestoga is also credited with helping to establish movement of traffic on the right as the rule of the road in America,

14 *Ibid.*, p. 176.
15 *Ibid.*, p. 192.
16 J. A. Durrenberger, *Turnpikes* (Valdosta, Ga.: published by the author, 1931), p. 118.

instead of the left as in Britain. The teamster was always on the left of the wagon, either astride the near wheelhorse, or walking, or riding on the "lazy-board," an oak board that pulled out between the two left wheels, from which the driver could guide the horses and operate the brake. The wagon therefore had to be on the right of the road for the driver to have a clear view ahead, and the lighter vehicles found it easiest to use the well-marked and firmly packed ruts made in dirt roads by the big Conestogas. New Jersey officially adopted right-hand operation in 1813.

There was not much improvement in the roads themselves, and there was not likely to be while highway policy remained predominantly in local hands. Moreover, the general economic structure of the colonies provided little incentive to build through highways; the populous sections along the seaboard had adequate water transportation, and in the thinly settled interior neither the resources nor the traffic as yet existed to justify an expensive road system. The most ambitious pre-Revolutionary road projects were undertaken *ad hoc* for military purposes: Braddock's Road from Cumberland, Maryland, to the Forks of the Ohio (Pittsburgh), following for some distance the route later taken by the National Road; and Forbes's Road across southern Pennsylvania to the same place. Both were trails hacked laboriously through the wilderness, just wide enough and firm enough to let cannon and supply wagons pass. They were not kept up after they had served their immediate functions, but for half a century they remained the only routes across the Appalachians that could accurately be termed roads.

Turnpikes and Internal Improvements

When the United States became an independent nation, its need for a highway system was recognized in the constitutional provision giving Congress power to establish post offices and post roads. The strict constructionist school of thought subsequently maintained that this clause did not permit the federal government actually to build roads but merely to designate highways constructed by state and local authorities as mail routes. This attitude probably had some effect in retarding the adoption of a national highway program; the limited resources of the government at that time were undoubtedly a stronger deterrent. The first positive step toward such a program was an act of 1802, passed in anticipation of the admission of Ohio to the Union, providing that 5 percent of the revenue from the sale of public lands in Ohio should be devoted to highway construction, with two-fifths of this amount to be allocated to roads connecting the Ohio and Potomac Rivers. In 1808 Albert Gallatin, in his *Report on Roads and Canals,* proposed a sweeping expansion of this policy by recommending that the income from the public domain be used to finance a comprehensive national transportation network. There was, however, no immediate response.

In the meantime, the country and its internal commerce continued to grow so that there was increasing pressure for roads capable of handling more than local traffic. It was calculated that in 1816 it cost as much to move a ton of goods thirty miles by land as it did to bring the same goods all the way from Europe.[17] In this situation the several states adopted the British policy of chartering turnpike companies so that highway financing could be secured from private sources. In those days, moreover, charging tolls was the most effective method of making through traffic bear its share of highway costs—a motivation repeated in the toll roads of the mid-twentieth century. Long-distance traffic was in fact the chief source of revenue for these early turnpikes except a few of the toll roads situated near the large centers of population.[18] To this the point might be added

17 G. W. Taylor, *The Transportation Revolution* (New York: Rinehart and Co., 1951), p. 132.
18 Durrenberger, *Turnpikes,* p. 118.

that there was a reciprocal relationship between highway and traffic; the long-distance traffic could hardly have existed unless the improved roads represented by the turnpikes had been there to enable it to move.

A few states (Virginia, Connecticut, Maryland) began to charge tolls on some of their roads in the 1780s in order to finance improvements, but the turnpike boom really began with the chartering of the Philadelphia and Lancaster Turnpike by the Commonwealth of Pennsylvania in 1792 as the first private turnpike corporation in the United States.[19] The project was so attractive that its first stock issue of a thousand shares at $300 each was oversubscribed. The road itself took two years to build: sixty-two miles long, thirty-seven feet wide of which twenty-four were laid in stone, at a total cost of $465,000, or about $7,500 a mile. The Philadelphia and Lancaster Turnpike could have had an additional distinction. In 1804 Oliver Evans proposed to the company to operate steam wagons on its road and submitted what would now be called a cost-effectiveness study.[20] He estimated that one such vehicle could carry one hundred barrels of flour at three miles an hour on level roads and one on hills, making the trip from Columbia to Philadelphia in two days, whereas it would take five horse-drawn wagons to haul the same load and they would need three days. In summary, the "steam waggon" would show a profit of $5 a day against $18.33 for the five horse wagons together. Neither the turnpike company nor the state legislature, however, responded favorably.

Pennsylvania subsequently chartered over eighty turnpike companies whose combined mileage of completed road reached

19 T. H. MacDonald, "History of the Development of Road Building in the United States," *Transactions of the American Society of Civil Engineers,* vol. XCII (1928), p. 1188.
20 Grenville and Dorothy Bathe, *Oliver Evans: A Chronicle of Early American Engineering* (Philadelphia: Historical Society of Pennsylvania, 1935), pp. 98–99.

a maximum of 2,400 miles in the 1830s. New York's system was still more extensive, including 278 companies with a capital of $11 million and about 4,000 miles of road in the 1820s, when the opening of the Erie Canal checked the New York turnpike boom.[21] New England reached a peak of 3,764 miles of turnpike in 1838, for an estimated cost of $6,500,000,[22] leaving behind names that still persist like the Newburyport and Worcester Turnpikes in Massachusetts. Virginia adopted a comprehensive policy in 1816 for supervising turnpike construction through a Board of Public Works, whose chief engineer in later years was Claudius Crozet, a graduate of France's École Polytechnique and the first Professor of Engineering at the United States Military Academy.[23]

The states regulated the turnpike companies closely. Tolls were fixed, and standards of construction were established. In general, these roads were reasonably well built, although Mc-Adam's methods did not appear until fairly late in the turnpike era. In the 1840s and 1850s plank roads became popular. The first one of which there is a record was built in Toronto, Canada, in 1835. They were cheap and easy to ride on; their drawback was that the wood decayed so that a plank road normally had to be completely rebuilt within seven years.[24] The turnpikes were not especially profitable; 2 or 3 percent was an average return. The revenues never came up to expectations; coach companies usually made special arrangements whereby they obtained a substantial discount, and ordinary toll collections were freely evaded —with some help from the law, as in Massachusetts, where exemptions were granted to people going to and from gristmills or

21 Durrenberger, *Turnpikes*, pp. 55, 61.
22 E. C. Kirkland, *Men, Cities and Transportation*, Vol. I (Cambridge, Mass.: Harvard University Press, 1948), p. 38.
23 Robert F. Hunter, "Turnpike Construction in Antebellum Virginia," *Technology and Culture*, vol. IV, no. 2 (Spring 1963), pp. 177–200.
24 MacDonald, "Development of Road Building," p. 1194.

church, on military duty, on journeys within the town where the toll gate was, or "on the common and ordinary business of family concerns." [25]

During this period, extending roughly to 1850, turnpike construction overshadowed public highway development, even though a considerable zeal for "internal improvements" stimulated a fair amount of road activity on the part of the federal government. The most important consequence of this activity was the National Road, begun in 1811 to implement the act of 1802, previously mentioned, allocating 2 percent of the public land revenues in Ohio to connect the new state with the seaboard. Progress was slow until the War of 1812 demonstrated an urgent need for good internal communications—immense difficulties were encountered in moving military forces and equipment to the theaters of war in the Old Northwest. Consequently in 1816 work was pressed vigorously so that the road was opened to traffic two years later between Cumberland, Maryland, where it connected with turnpikes to Baltimore and Philadelphia, and Wheeling on the Ohio, a distance of 130 miles. Two years later it was decided to continue the road across Ohio, and it eventually extended across Indiana also. The last federal appropriation was made in 1838, to complete construction in Indiana and grading in Illinois, but, significantly, the Illinois section was deliberately left unsurfaced because the government by this time thought it might substitute a railroad for a highway.

The road was built to a width of sixty feet, with a stone base fifteen inches thick and a gravel surface rolled firm; in later years some sections were macadamized.[26] Construction costs averaged

25 Kirkland, *Men, Cities, and Transportation,* p. 43.
26 MacDonald, "Development of Road Building," p. 1191. MacDonald points out that although McAdam's technique was publicized after 1816, improved American roads even before this time were constructed on generally similar lines.

$6,000 a mile. The route is easy to identify; it was subsequently followed very closely by U.S. 40.

The National Road (or Cumberland Road) achieved immediate importance as an artery of commerce, but throughout its life it was plagued by political troubles, or at least the opposition to federal support for the highway was expressed in political and constitutional terms. In 1822 President Monroe vetoed a bill that would have permitted the federal government to impose tolls in order to pay for the upkeep of the road, on the ground that this was an invasion of the rights of the states in which it lay. Since federal support continued for another sixteen years, the importance of the Cumberland Road veto can be exaggerated; nevertheless, in the ensuing years responsibility for maintenance gradually devolved on the states.

There was federal support for highways in other forms. During the 1820s three grants of land were made to assist the construction of roads in Ohio and Indiana.[27] They were modest, averaging a section per mile, and were important chiefly as foreshadowing the more generous grants made later for canals and railroads. One of these grants did produce a road in Indiana from Lake Michigan through Indianapolis to Madison on the Ohio River; the land yielded $240,000.

Congress also contributed to highway construction by subscribing to stock in various turnpike companies. This policy ran into presidential disapproval when Andrew Jackson in 1830 vetoed a subsidy of this kind for a road from Maysville to Lexington, Kentucky, on the ground that the entire project was

27 General Land Office, *Statement of Land Grants Made by Congress to Aid in the Construction of Railroads, Wagon Roads, Canals, and Internal Improvements* (Washington, D.C.: Government Printing Office, 1915), p. 22. Six other wagon road grants, on a more generous scale, were made between 1863 and 1869 for roads in Michigan, Wisconsin, and Oregon. The results in terms of providing highway facilities were unimpressive.

within a single state, although its sponsors argued that the road was intended as a link in an interstate route leading south from a junction with the National Road in Ohio. Jackson's action did not terminate all federal aid to roads at this time; indeed, it would probably have been of little significance if other factors had not been present to diminish interest in highways.

As in Britain, the early nineteenth-century surge of road activity in the United States was brought to a halt by the emergence of the railroad—canal competition played its part also, but it was minor compared with the role of rail transport. In the existing state of transportation technology, the highway was outclassed by the railroad in both cost and speed, and it would recover its status only when a technological breakthrough in the vehicle was achieved. Yet highway transportation remained a vital factor in the national scene. For example, the role of wagons and wagon roads in the growth of the American West not only constituted a colorful episode in American history but was more significant economically than is generally appreciated.[28] For hauls of less than fifteen miles, the wagon remained competitive with rail transport because of its greater flexibility. Indeed, the increased volume of traffic generated by the building of canals and railroads created a demand for short hauls by road that more than offset the loss of long-distance business.[29] Moreover, while local transport constitutes a less glamorous subject for the historian than the building of great waterways and trunk line railroads, or even through highways, it was a matter of acute importance to those who had to depend on it. As the historian of the Virginia turnpikes remarks: "Most American farmers, and many townsmen, were not fortunate enough to live on a waterway or a railroad line. To these people, the quality and cost of

28 For this story see W. Turrentine Jackson, *Wagon Roads West* (New Haven, Conn.: Yale University Press, 1964); and O. O. Winther, *The Transportation Frontier* (New York: Holt, Rinehart and Winston, 1964).
29 Taylor, *Transportation Revolution,* p. 156.

common road transportation was a matter of everyday concern." [30]

This highway renaissance of the late eighteenth and early
nineteenth centuries made a definite contribution to the economic growth of the country. By present-day standards the "improved" roads of that era were only fair, but they were enough
of an advance to speed up travel and reduce transportation costs.
The Virginia historian just quoted estimates that the turnpikes
reduced freight costs from 20 or 25¢ a ton-mile to 15¢, certainly
a meaningful differential for the movement of freight. Five cents
a ton-mile, indeed, must have created a substantial volume of
freight shipment that could not have moved at all at the higher
rates.

Passenger travel was stimulated in two ways. An improved
highway network covering a large part of the country enabled
coach lines to operate at higher speeds over more territory and
with greater regularity; it also permitted the development of
better vehicles, such as the famous Concord coach, sturdy and
capable of making fast trips and at the same time incorporating
greater comfort for the occupants. As early as 1784 a prominent
Yankee, Levi Pease, was running regular service between Boston
and New York. In 1789 the coaches left every Monday, Wednes-
day, and Friday between May 1 and November 1, and twice a
week in winter. The 210-mile trip took six to nine days, later
reduced to four. In the 1820s a mail coach service made the run
in forty-one hours, without overnight stops; the fare was $11.[31]

By that time stage lines fanned out from every important city.
Between Boston and Providence, where connections could be
made by steamboat to New York without having to make the
long trip around Cape Cod, there were fifteen to twenty trips a

30 Hunter, "Turnpike Construction in Antebellum Virginia," p. 177.
31 Durrenberger, *Turnpikes*, p. 26; Kirkland, *Men, Cities, and Transportation*, p. 55.

day over the Boston Post Road covering fifty miles in about five hours, at a cost of $3.[32] On the National Road the coach time between Cumberland and Wheeling, 130 miles through difficult mountain country, was twenty-four hours. There is an interesting comparison for turnpike travel between Pittsburgh and Philadelphia. Stage coaches made the 300-mile journey in six days, wagons in twenty. The coach fare was $20, with a charge of 12½¢ a pound for baggage in excess of fourteen pounds; the freight rate on the wagons was $5 a hundredweight.[33]

There was one other feature of highway improvement that is usually ignored; yet it is a feature of travel by road that is duplicated by no other transportation medium. Because the roads were better, there was a stronger incentive for people to own their own vehicles. The wealthy had coaches; people of moderate means used two-wheeled, one-horse buggies ("the wonderful one-hoss shay"). In one year, 1814, 16,660 one-horse vehicles and 5,330 private coaches passed through a turnpike toll gate at Roxbury, Massachusetts, on the edge of Boston. When the railroad began to cut down this kind of travel, one of its devotees extolled its merits in terms that, except for the speed, reflect what the automobile would later offer to the many as well as the few:

After all, its old-fashioned way of five or six miles an hour, with one's own horses and carriage, with liberty to dine decently in a decent inn, with the delight of seeing the country and getting along rationally, is the mode to which I cling, and which will be adopted again by the generations of after times.[34]

32 Dunbar, *History of Travel,* p. 743.
33 Durrenberger, *Turnpikes,* p. 34.
34 Kirkland, *Men, Cities, and Transportation,* Vol. I, p. 49.

2 The Rebirth of the Highway

From just before the middle of the nineteenth century until its end, both highway transportation and highway development were eclipsed by the expansion of the railroad. The problem was not in the road itself; there was adequate knowledge of how to build good roads. The limitation was in the available vehicles. Except for short runs, horse-drawn carriages and wagons could not compete effectively with rail transport. As was pointed out in the previous chapter, there was no actual decline in either the need or the demand for road transport. On the contrary, because the railroad permitted overland traffic to move more efficiently and economically than had ever before been possible, its effect, as with most technological innovations, was to create more business —in this case to create traffic that had not previously existed.

Some attempts were made to harness steam power to highway use. Steam vehicles, in fact, operated on roads before they did on rails, beginning with Cugnot's carriage of 1769. This experiment failed, but others followed, and at the beginning of the nineteenth century Richard Trevithick in Britain and Oliver Evans in the United States showed the way to practical steam locomotion.

The bulk and weight of the early steam engines and the inadequacy of the roads made it easier to apply steam power to railway locomotives than to highway vehicles. Nevertheless, nineteenth-century Britain saw an interesting series of experiments with steam-powered omnibuses. The results were mixed. The vehicles were prone to mechanical breakdowns, there were some bad accidents from boiler explosions, and since the engines were coal-fired, it was never possible to prevent smoke from being a nuisance. On the other hand, there were several examples of successful operation on regular schedules at speeds of ten to twelve miles an hour.[1] The breakdowns and accidents were unavoidable in a new technology and were certainly no worse than contemporary railroad experience. The steam omnibuses died out, not because of any inherent and irremediable defects, but because they were driven off the roads by discriminatory tolls and adverse legislation. In this respect they offer an unusual case study in the potential consequences of ill-advised political interference with technological change.

One commentator on British highway policy says, "The early period of the steam road-coach had ended by 1840, its development having been effectively stultified by the excessive tolls imposed by the local road authorities upon an otherwise flourishing and technically successful industry." [2] The writer was somewhat overenthusiastic about both the financial and the technical success of steam omnibuses, and some sympathy is due local authorities faced with the novel problem of unusual wear and tear on their roads caused by these heavy vehicles, but it is apparent that the measures taken against steam road vehicles were needlessly severe. Behind the severity was the hostility of the stagecoach operators and, as time went on, of the railways, who saw in the steam omnibuses a competitor for their passenger business—an attitude with a certain amount of prophetic insight.

Nevertheless, the experiments with steam-powered highway transport continued until in 1866 Parliament passed the Locomotives on Highways Act, the so-called "Red Flag Law," stipulating that all self-propelled vehicles on public highways must be limited to a maximum speed of four miles an hour and must be preceded by a man on foot carrying a red flag. The law was amended in 1878 to eliminate the flagman, but it retained the

1 John Copeland, *Roads and Their Traffic 1750–1850* (New York: Augustus M. Kelley, 1968), pp. 170–171.
2 D. C. Field, "Mechanical Road Vehicles," in Charles Singer *et al.*, *A History of Technology*, vol. V (New York and London: Oxford Press, 1958), p. 420.

speed limit and required two people to be in the vehicle while it was in operation, with a third to go ahead and give warning at danger spots like intersections and curves or help to control frightened horses.

This act remained in force until 1896. Herbert Austin, later Lord Austin, one of the great British automotive pioneers, claimed in later years that it had little effect in retarding British automobile progress because in those days no one was building vehicles capable of going over four miles an hour anyway.[3] Maybe so—but what of those thirty years, or perhaps fifty, of enforced technological stagnation? If steam omnibuses could make scheduled runs in the 1830s at average speeds of ten to twelve miles an hour, as they did, then by the 1890s it should have been possible to attain still better performance. It is difficult to avoid the conclusion that Britain lost an opportunity to take the lead in the development of self-propelled highway vehicles.

Similar experiments with steam power on highways occurred in the United States, but on a less intensive scale than in Britain and with poorer prospects of success. The superiority of the railroad for long-distance travel gave it a pronounced advantage under American conditions, and this advantage was accentuated by the deterioration of the country's road system. The stagecoach and the wagon had a brief surge of glory just after the middle of the century when Justin Butterfield's Overland Mail ran between St. Louis and San Francisco, and figures like Ben Holladay operated extensive stage lines throughout the West for both passengers and freight. But the roads they used were crude tracks, and as soon as the railroads appeared, the stages were reduced to feeders carrying local traffic.

The result was that there was little incentive to spend money

3 Samuel B. Saul, "The Motor Industry in Britain to 1914," *Business History*, vol. V, no. 1 (December 1962), p. 40.

on building trunk roads in any area where rail transport was available. France maintained its national highways reasonably well, but elsewhere roads suffered from indifference. In the United States the spread of the railroad network appeared to remove any need for a national highway system, or even state systems. Roads might still be needed for strictly local traffic, but this was a responsibility that could be left to local authority, as it always had been, and if local authority did the job badly, why, that too was the way it always had been.

Local authority continued to use the statute-labor system (working off road taxes) until the twentieth century. The following account, written in 1889 by a leading American geologist of the period, is worth giving at length because it is an illuminating description of how the system functioned—and it may be taken as an accurate description for other times and other places as well:

In most rural districts of the United States the common roads are built and maintained in the most ignorant and inefficient manner. In no other phase of public duties does the American citizen appear to such disadvantage as in the construction of roads. Generally road-making and the so-called road-mending are performed not by a tax of money but by an impost on the labor of the county. The voting part of the population is summoned each year to give one or two days to working out the road-tax. The busy people and those who are forehanded may pay their assessment in money: but most of the population find it more convenient to attend the annual road-making picnic in person. Theoretically the gangs of men are under the supervision of a road-master. More commonly some elder of the multitude is by common consent absolved from personal labor and made superintendent of operations.

Arriving on the ground long after the usual time of beginning work, the road-makers proceed to discuss the general question of road-making and other matters of public concern, until slow-acting conscience convinces them that they should be about their task. They then with much deliberation take the mud out of the road-side ditches, if, indeed, the way is ditched at all, and plaster the same on the centre of the road. A plough is brought into requisition, which destroys the best part of the road, that which is partly grassed and bush-grown, and the soft mass is heaped up in the central parts of the way. The sloughs or cradle-holes are filled with this material, or perhaps a little brush may be cut and heaped in, making a very frail support for the wheels. An hour or two is consumed at noonday by lunch and a further discussion of public and private affairs. A little work is done in the afternoon, and at the end of the day the roadmaking is abandoned until the next year.[4]

Under the circumstances it is understandable that a highway authority of the period should describe the roads of the United States as "inferior to those of any civilized country." [5] This neglect of the roads would have been more understandable if the need for highway transport had been lessening, but it was not. In 1878, for instance, the United States had fifteen million carriages, carts, and wagons on its roads and streets.[6] Nor were the roads bad because of any lack of knowledge of how to make them better. A steam-powered stone crusher was invented in 1858 by Eli Whitney Blake, and the steam road roller was introduced from Britain a few years later. Brick and asphalt surfacing began to be used for city streets in the early 1870s.[7] The manufacture of Portland cement in the United States started at this same time, but it was not until 1893 that the first concrete street surface was laid in Bellefontaine, Ohio.

The Bicycle and the Good Roads Movement

Between the end of the Civil War and 1870 several spokesmen campaigned vigorously for highway improvement, conspicuously Henry F. French, a New Hampshire attorney who became president of the newly founded Massachusetts Agricultural College

4 N. S. Shaler, "The Common Roads," *Scribner's Magazine*, vol. 6, no. 4 (October 1889), p. 477.

5 Philip P. Mason, *A History of American Roads* (Chicago: Rand McNally, 1967), p. 35.

6 Albert C. Rose, "From Railroad to Automobile," in Jean Labatut and W. J. Lane, eds., *Highways in Our National Life: A Symposium* (Princeton, N. J.: Princeton University Press, 1950), p. 84.

7 T. H. MacDonald, "History of the Development of Road Building in the United States," *Transactions of the American Society of Civil Engineers*, vol. XCII (1928), pp. 1194–1195.

(now the University of Massachusetts); J. R. Dodge, statistician of the United States Department of Agriculture; and Governor William Claflin of Massachusetts.[8] The results were negligible. Although country districts were in the worst plight, the farm population by and large was reluctant to take on the heavy expense of paving rural roads. Given the inefficiency of wagon transport, the advantage to be gained from better road surfaces was far from obvious, especially when, as Jeremiah Jenks, a prominent advocate of road improvement, stated as late as 1889, "A very large proportion of our people have never seen a really good road for hauling purposes, and have in consequence no clear idea of the gain that would come from good roads." [9]

Before serious attention could be given to the highway situation, something had to come along to get people out on the roads in large numbers and create an awareness of the flexibility and convenience of travel by road. This requirement was met by the bicycle, a device whose significance in the history of transportation has never been properly appreciated. It not only was instrumental in stimulating the building of up-to-date roads but also contributed a number of important technical features to the automobile—the pneumatic tire will do as an example.

The bicycle as a vehicle for general use dates from the introduction of the geared, low-wheeled "safety bicycle" by James Kemp Starley of Coventry, England, in 1885.[10] Some years earlier an American Civil War veteran, Colonel Albert A. Pope, began to import British bicycles into the United States and in 1878 became the pioneer American bicycle manufacturer, using the

8 Philip P. Mason, *The League of American Wheelmen and the Good Roads Movement, 1880–1905* (Ann Arbor, Mich.: University of Michigan Press, 1958), pp. 65–67.
9 MacDonald, "History of Road Building in the U.S.," p. 1195.
10 H. B. Light, "The Rover Story," *Rover News*, vol. 1, no. 2 (January 1961), p. 3. Starley called his bicycle the "Rover." The company later turned to automobiles and still exists as part of the British Leyland Motors Corporation.

trade name Columbia. The safety bicycle had far greater utility than the high-wheeled velocipedes that preceded it and, what was especially important, could be ridden by women as well as men. It touched off a bicycle boom that sent people in multitudes out on the highways—such as they were.

The bicyclists had other problems besides the actual condition of the roads; in fact, they provided a preview of what would happen when the motor vehicle came along. They were greeted with suspicion and hostility. They were frequently regarded as a menace to public safety, accused of "scorching," the term of those days for speeding, and in rural areas there was complaint that bicyclists frightened horses. The bicyclists were harassed by local ordinances imposing unrealistic speed limits and other restrictions just as the early motorists were. For example, a bicyclist was frequently required to dismount when approaching a horse and if necessary to lead the animal to safety out of sight of the bicycle.[11] Moreover, the decline of highway travel had produced a near-disappearance of good roadside facilities for food or overnight stops.

The worst difficulty remained the roads themselves. The bicycle offered an opportunity for low-cost individual travel, but it was an opportunity severely curtailed by poorly surfaced, unmarked, indifferently maintained roads. So the bicyclists became the spearhead of a campaign for highway improvement. Bicycle clubs were initially formed to promote and plan trips and hold races, and they very soon became involved in trying to protect their members from petty local harassment and in promoting conditions that would increase the enjoyment of bicycling. Better roads naturally were a primary objective.

This was by no means an exclusively American phenomenon. In Britain, for instance, the bicycle organizations established a Roads Improvement Association in 1886, which joined with the

11 Mason, *League of American Wheelmen*, pp. 35–37.

automobile clubs in 1901 to agitate for a central highway authority and state grants for road improvement.[12] In the United
States the League of American Wheelmen was founded in Newport, Rhode Island, in 1880, "to ascertain, defend and protect
the rights of wheelmen, to encourage and facilitate touring." [13]
As part of this program the League energetically campaigned for
better roads.

The League, however, found that it had inadequate public
support. It suffered from being considered a group of "idle
rich," probably with some justification at first. The fact that it
was organized in socialite Newport has significance. At that time
an American-made bicycle cost $150 to $200, an expensive luxury
for anyone of limited means.[14] Widespread use had to wait a few
years until quantity manufacturing brought prices down to a
low of $30. In addition, the membership of the League of Ameri-
can Wheelmen was geographically limited. At the time it was
founded, three-fifths of its members came from New York and
Massachusetts, and only 12 percent from west of New York State.
Moreover, while the bicycle was a boon to city dwellers, it did
nothing to solve the problem of the farmer. Consequently, the
first efforts of the League of American Wheelmen to secure highway legislation were humiliatingly defeated, with the result that
the League changed its policy. Instead of agitating directly, it
supported, and sometimes organized, other groups for good roads,
and it intensified efforts to educate the public more thoroughly
on the benefits of highway improvement.

By the 1890s these efforts at stirring up public opinion were
producing results. Moreover, powerful allies had joined the
movement. The railroads were becoming convinced that improved roads would extend the area from which they could draw

12 Rees Jeffrey, *The King's Highway* (London: Batchworth Press, 1949),
p. 2.
13 Mason, *League of American Wheelmen*, p. 37.
14 *Ibid.*, pp. 44–45.

traffic, especially in country regions where it was unprofitable to build branch lines for a limited volume of local traffic. Even at this expanding stage of railroad development, there was accumulating evidence of an overabundance of branch lines in many parts of the country. There was also a hope that all-weather highways would relieve seasonal congestion on the railroads by enabling farmers to deliver their crops to rail points for shipment at other times than the few periods in the year when existing roads were passable.[15]

More important, in the 1890s the scandalous condition of rural roads at last began to stir public opinion, particularly the farm population. Perhaps the efforts of the League of American Wheelmen and other proponents of good roads were beginning to bear fruit. More likely, the long period of agrarian unrest was now approaching a climax, reflected in the Farmers Alliances and the Populist movement; and since the railroads had been a prime target of farm discontent, highway transportation had the merit of offering a possible alternative means of moving goods. It took time for this feeling to develop because many farmers continued to be afraid that road improvement would add more to their tax burdens than it was worth. Nevertheless, events moved fast. A National League for Good Roads was founded in 1892, and a year later a Good Roads Convention was held in Washington, D.C.

Their efforts resulted in the creation of an Office of Road Inquiry in the Department of Agriculture in 1893. Its initial appropriation was only $10,000, and its functions were purely educational, but it was a step toward the goal of the Good Roads advocates: "lifting our people out of the mud." [16] The first head of the Office of Road Inquiry, which would in time become the

15 For a discussion of the arguments for road improvement, see Mark Reinsberg, "The Heyday of Highway Benefits," *Interstate Commerce Practitioners' Journal,* vol. 30, no. 9 (June 1963), pp. 1143–1168.
16 MacDonald, "History of Road Building in the U.S.," pp. 1195–1196.

Bureau of Public Roads, was General Roy Stone, an enthusiastic proponent of good roads. Another significant forward step, of tremendous influence in demonstrating the potential benefits of highway transport, was the initiation of Rural Free Delivery around Charleston, West Virginia, on October 1, 1896.[17] Within a year there were RFD routes in twenty-nine states, and by 1900 the RFD network was nationwide. The Good Roads movement brought state as well as federal action. Legislation for highway improvement was enacted by New Jersey in 1891, and other states soon followed.[18] In general, these initial state programs provided for two major reforms in highway policy. First, some of the responsibility for improving and maintaining roads was transferred from local authorities to larger units, usually counties. Second, the states established standards for highway construction and required the employment of professional engineers so that trunk roads at least were built and maintained by somewhat more sophisticated techniques than shoveling mud from the ditches into the middle of the right-of-way.

The creation of the Office of Road Inquiry meant that there was an agency responsible for collecting factual data on the nation's highway system so that it became possible to evaluate the assertions regarding the condition of American roads. In general, the criticisms seem to have been justified. A road census completed in 1904 showed 2,151,570 miles of highway in the United States, of which 153,662 miles, about 7 percent, could be classified as "improved." Of the improved roads, 38,622 miles were surfaced with water-bound macadam (small stones), 108,233 with gravel, and the rest varied—sand, shell, even some plank.[19] There were just 141 miles surfaced with something better than water-bound macadam: 123 miles of brick surface, of which 104 were in Ohio,

17 *Automotive Information,* vol. 4, no. 7 (March 1967), p. 6.
18 Mason, *History of American Roads,* p. 46.
19 MacDonald, "History of Road Building in the U.S.," p. 1197.

and 18 miles of bituminous macadam or asphalt, 16 in Ohio. The remaining 93 percent of the road mileage was plain dirt, uncomfortably dusty in good weather and usually impassable in bad.

The Office of Road Inquiry also made some effort to calculate the volume of highway transport and the economic burden of carrying it on poor roads. In 1895 it estimated the total tonnage hauled on public roads for the year to be 313,349,227, for a cost of $946,414,665.[20] The average load was calculated as 2,002 pounds, and the average cost of carriage by wagon as 25¢ per ton mile. The Office (that is, General Stone) estimated that two-thirds of the cost of highway transport could be saved by road improvement through reducing wear and tear on draft animals and wagons, permitting heavier loads to be hauled, and reducing the time required to make trips. Richard T. Ely, the eminent economist, was more conservative in his estimates; he placed the annual saving at $100,000,000.[21]

Toward a National Highway Policy

The highway legislation of the 1890s was minor in scope. As far as it had significance, it was as the prelude to a national highway policy, and it indicated quite clearly the basis on which Congress would be willing to support such a policy. The telling factor was a growing awareness of the potential benefits that better roads might bring to the farmer. This was by far the most powerful of the arguments for highway improvement at the turn of the century. There was still little disposition to provide federal aid for a general-purpose highway network, but there was a mounting body of sentiment for "farm-to-market" roads. The farm organizations, notably the National Grange, were propo-

20 Charles L. Dearing, *American Highway Policy* (Washington, D.C.: The Brookings Institution, 1941), p. 237.
21 Mason, *League of American Wheelmen*, p. 94.

nents of the Good Roads movement, and the farmers themselves were more willing to support it when it became likely that some of the cost of road programs would be borne by state or federal authority rather than laid entirely on local taxpayers.

The 1890s also saw the motor vehicle appear on the American scene, to become a factor of rapidly increasing importance in the development of highway policy. The pioneer motorists repeated the experiences of their bicycling predecessors: they were very frequently subjected to harassment and hostility, and they found few roads fit for automobile traffic. When Alexander Winton drove one of his first cars from Cleveland to New York in 1897, via Buffalo, Rochester, Utica, Syracuse, and Albany, the trip took ten days (July 28 to August 7) over roads described by Winton as "outrageous." Four years later, Roy D. Chapin, the future founder of the Hudson Motor Car Company, did a little better when he drove a curved-dash "Merry Oldsmobile" from Detroit to the 1901 Automobile Show in New York in seven and a half days. He crossed Ontario to Niagara Falls and then followed Winton's route, except that in upstate New York he used the towpath of the Erie Canal for 150 miles because it was better than the roads. The Apperson brothers of Haynes-Apperson drove one of their cars from Kokomo, Indiana, to New York in the same year in a less publicized but certainly equally difficult journey, which took about the same time as Chapin's. Admittedly, the vehicles were primitive and service facilities were nonexistent, but the evidence of bad roads is still overwhelming. Under the circumstances the completion of three transcontinental automobile trips in 1903 (the fastest took fifty-three days) approaches the miraculous.

Thus the motor vehicle added to the pressure for road improvement. The motorist had an even stronger incentive than the bicyclist to get the country out of the mud; a mired car was more of a problem than a stuck bicycle. The automobile, however, was still a minor factor in transportation when the first specific proposal for a federally supported highway program appeared in Congress. This was a bill introduced in 1902 by Representative Walter F. Brownlow of Tennessee to establish a Bureau of Public Roads in the Department of Agriculture and provide $20,000,000 in matching funds to aid in building roads. Urban areas were expressly excluded from this measure. There was no action on the Brownlow bill, but it foreshadowed the course that would eventually be taken.

In the decade after 1902 there was a rapid growth of automotive transportation that not only accentuated the need to do something about country roads but also indicated that this new device had potential utility for the farmer. The merging of forces was symbolized by the American Automobile Association, founded in 1902, holding a joint Good Roads Convention with the National Grange in 1907.[22] Immediately afterward the Model T Ford appeared, designed expressly to take hard pounding on country roads and to have the simplicity and reliability needed for service in which the owner would have to be his own mechanic. In addition, the motor truck was beginning its revolution in rural transport. By 1913 Congressman Stanton Warburton of Washington could state:

> There is nothing that promises so much in reducing the cost of transportation for the short hauls, such as thirty, forty, or fifty miles, as the auto truck. No sooner are hard surfaces completed to large centers than the auto truck appears on the road as the freight carriers for the distances I have mentioned.[23]

This was acknowledgment that a new era in transportation was emerging and that the concept of the farm-to-market road might have to be revised from what it had been when all that was in prospect was movement by wagon. The new era was on the

22 D. L. Cohn, *Combustion on Wheels* (Boston: Houghton Mifflin Co., 1944), p. 12.
23 Reinsberg, "The Heyday of Highway Benefits," p. 1160.

way, but it had not yet arrived, and the focus of political attention remained on local rural roads. In the year that Congressman
Warburton made this statement about trucks, Congress accepted
at least a limited responsibility for the nation's highways by
appropriating $500,000 for the improvement of roads on which
rural mail was carried.[24]

The concept of a truly national road system was dramatized
by Carl Graham Fisher, an Indianapolis businessman who helped
promote the Indianapolis Speedway and founded the Prest-O-
Lite Company (automobile headlights). In 1911 he proposed the
creation of a hard-surfaced coast-to-coast highway, to be named
the Lincoln Highway. The idea attracted enthusiastic support
from the automobile industry and the motoring public; among
its most active advocates were Roy D. Chapin and Henry B. Joy,
head of the Packard Motor Car Company. The Lincoln Highway
Association was formally organized in 1913, and segments of the
route were eventually opened and marked. However, the heavy
cost and the difficulties of having to deal with a variety of state
and local authorities resulted in the disbanding of the Association after the passage of the Federal Aid Road Act of 1916.

This act, landmark as it was in the history of American highway policy, showed a continuing ambivalence on the direction
that such a policy ought to take; that is, should federal aid be
used to develop a system of arterial routes, or should it go primarily to providing better communications for the farm population? In the debate on the act one group of Congressmen argued:

The railway station is the terminus for roads; neither freight
nor passengers will ever be carried long distances over roads as
cheaply as they could be over railways, and it is an idle dream to
imagine that auto trucks and automobiles will take the place of
railways in the long-distance movement of freight or passengers.[25]

24 Mason, *History of American Roads*, p. 51.
25 Dearing, *American Highway Policy*, p. 81.

The act as passed appropriated $75 million to be spent under the direction of the Secretary of Agriculture over a five-year period for the improvement of rural post roads.[26] Federal subsidies, in other words, were not specifically restricted to farm-to-market roads, but neither was there any suggestion of developing a network of trunk highways. The money was to be spent through state highway departments—an important provision because it compelled states without highway departments to organize them. The federal funds were granted on a matching basis, up to 50 percent of the cost of road improvement on projects approved by the Bureau of Public Roads, but not at that time to exceed $10,000 per mile.

The Federal Aid Road Act of 1916 was recognition of the fact that better roads were essential to the national welfare and that highway improvement was therefore a national as well as a local responsibility. Before it had time to become effective, the United States became involved in the First World War so that the projected program could not go into operation under the conditions for which it had been planned. The war, however, made it abundantly evident that the country urgently needed a coherent network of trunk highways and not just a piecemeal improvement of local roads. The railroad system, especially in the Northeast, was brought almost to a halt by monumental traffic congestion. Freight cars piled up at the seaports waiting to be unloaded, and others had to be stacked on sidings and in yards waiting their turn to move up. Finally the government had to take over the railroads in order to avert the threatened paralysis.

When this situation materialized, the country had to face the fact that there was no alternative system of transportation ca-

26 MacDonald, "History of Road Building in the U.S." p. 1201. The administration of the program was vested in the Bureau of Public Roads, the successor to the original Office of Road Inquiry. There were several changes of name. The agency became the Bureau of Public Roads in 1918.

pable of providing relief for the railroads. In an effort to find a remedy the Council for National Defense created a Highway Transport Committee in November 1917, with Roy D. Chapin at its head. Up to this time trucks destined for France were shipped by rail from their midwestern factories to the ports of embarkation. Chapin, in cooperation with the Army, undertook to relieve some of the strain on the railroads by having the trucks move under their own power and carry a payload in the process.

This operation required sending out teams of engineers to locate and mark feasible routes and enlisting the aid of state and local authorities to keep the selected roads open and fit for truck traffic. The first truck convoy went from Detroit to Baltimore at the end of 1917 in what a contemporary engineering journal called a "daring adventure"—driving these heavy vehicles across the Alleghenies in winter on unimproved roads.[27] Of the thirty trucks that began this first trip, twenty-nine reached Baltimore, and before the war ended, 18,000 trucks had made their own way to the seaboard, giving an impressive demonstration of what highway transportation was capable of even in adverse conditions.

At the end of the war further action was imperative. The 2 million motor vehicles of 1915 became almost 10 million in 1920, all attempting to use a road system of demonstrated inadequacy. There was, in consequence, a great expansion of highway construction by state and local governments, but with all the good intentions in the world these could not have given the country a coherent highway network. That could be achieved only by federal action, and this action produced the Federal Highway Act of 1921, which provided that federal aid should be concentrated upon "such projects as will expedite the completion of an adequate and connected system of highways, interstate in char-

---

27 F. L. Paxson, "The Highway Movement, 1916–1935," *American Historical Review,* LI, no. 2 (January 1946), p. 243.

acter." [28] Each state was required to designate 7 percent of its road mileage as "primary," and this mileage alone was eligible for federal aid, matching state funds on a fifty-fifty basis. The first appropriation under this law was $75 million for the fiscal year 1922, a significant comparison with the provision made in 1916 to spend the same amount over five years.

The 7 percent figure came to approximately 200,000 miles of road, and by 1923 the Bureau of Public Roads, under Thomas H. MacDonald, an able engineer who would be chief of the Bureau for many years, had planned a tentative network of arterial highways serving every city of 50,000 or more.[29] In another two years a satisfactory mechanism for securing cooperation among the states was created, and the country's first genuine national highway system, which would eventually total some 350,000 miles,[30] was in progress. These roads initiated the uniform method of route marking that became universal in American highway practice—even numbers for east-west routes, odd for north-south.

28 *U.S. Statutes at Large,* 67th Congress, 1st sess., p. 212.
29 Paxson, "The Highway Movement," p. 246.
30 Spencer Miller, Jr., "The Modern Highway in America," in Labatut and Lane, eds., *Highways in Our National Life,* p. 97.

3　The Automotive Revolution

All the improvements of highway engineering and all the co-ordinated highway networks in the world would have had little meaning without the revolution represented by the mass-produced motor vehicle, which made possible the utilization of roads to an extent and in ways never before possible in the history of the human race. The nature of this revolution is even now imperfectly understood. It was the product of two separate technological innovations, each a major step in itself. One was the development of the self-propelled highway vehicle; the other, the introduction of the technique of mass production.

Where did it begin? The dream of a vehicle moving by its own power goes back through the centuries. Seven hundred years ago Roger Bacon foresaw carriages made so that "without animals they will move with unbelievable rapidity," and almost three centuries later Leonardo da Vinci left a design for a self-propelled vehicle. It was never built and could not have been because Leonardo's ideas were far ahead of the techniques and skills of his day. In any event, it would not have worked because the gear train, as shown in Leonardo's drawing, would have had the wheels turning in opposite directions.

The dream first achieved reality with the steam carriages mentioned in the previous chapter. They were still not the automotive revolution—just its forerunners. There had to be development and refinement to realize the first essential step toward a new era in transportation: a vehicle capable of providing the flexible personal mobility that no other mode of travel could offer. This goal was reached late in the nineteenth century when a variety of odd-looking contraptions began to appear almost furtively on the streets of European and American cities. There have been the usual endless arguments, as with most great inventions, about who did it first. For our purpose it does not really matter. Uninterrupted development of the automobile can be safely dated from the work of Karl Benz and Gottlieb Daimler in Germany in 1885. If necessity is the mother of invention, presumably the speed with which an invention is adopted is a fair measure of the degree of necessity, and by this standard the need for a workable motor vehicle was urgent. In less than ten years there was a full-fledged automobile industry in France as well as Germany, with firms like Panhard and Levassor issuing regular catalogs; and the prototype of the modern automobile had been designed to replace the buggy with an engine stuck underneath.

In view of what was going to happen, it is one of the great paradoxes of history that the United States was well behind Europe in the development of the motor vehicle, both in quantity and quality. The first American cars were essentially repetitions of what had already been done in Europe—repetitions, but not copies. The American pioneers, beginning with the Duryea brothers in 1893,[1] had surprisingly little information about what was going on in Europe and had to work out their problems for themselves. Consequently, the Americans were still laboriously building experimental powered buggies while the French and Germans were producing operational automobiles on a commercial scale.

It was probably just as well that there should have been some indigenous American development, even if it involved a good deal of needless waste effort. If the American automotive pioneers had simply borrowed an existing European technology, they or their business associates and successors might also have been disposed to accept the European view of the automobile as primarily an article of luxury for the wealthy. Instead they, at any rate enough of them, had their own independent ideas about the

1 The story of the American automobile industry even now comes close to being encompassed in a single lifetime. J. Frank Duryea, who built the car that made its first run on September 20, 1893, died in February 1967 at the age of ninety-seven.

function of a device that they could regard as their own creation, at least as far as the United States was concerned.

The direction of these ideas was indicated soon after the turn of the century when Ransom E. Olds introduced the curved-dash buggy that became famous as the "Merry Oldsmobile" and Henry Ford began to implement his dream of "a car for the great multitude." The motor vehicle in America was to be for the use of the many rather than the enjoyment of the few. Was this just because American conditions differed from European? In part, yes. For the man bold enough to believe that the horseless carriage could be more than a plaything, the United States offered a larger potential market than any European country—but it was a potential rather than an actual market. The United States had a growing economy, a large population, and a higher standard of living than existed elsewhere, but these conditions did not automatically create a glowing opportunity for anyone who chose to manufacture motor vehicles. The opportunity existed only for those with the vision to see it and the ability to grasp it.

What could have happened is illustrated in a penetrating study of the early British automobile industry by Samuel B. Saul. The author charges the pioneer British manufacturers with a lack of commercial acumen and "a passion for technical perfection and individuality for its own sake," and he quotes the influential journal *Autocar* as endorsing this attitude as late as 1912 by saying: "It is highly to the credit of our English manufacturers that they choose rather to maintain their reputation for high grade work than cheapen that reputation by the use of the inferior material and workmanship they would be obliged to employ to compete with American manufacturers of cheap cars." [2] Professor Saul acknowledges that Britain did not enjoy

2 Samuel B. Saul, "The Motor Industry in Britain to 1914," *Business History*, vol. V, no. 1 (December 1962), p. 41.

the same mass market as the United States and therefore could not adopt American production methods unreservedly. The point is well taken in that the potential American market was undoubtedly greater, but "potential" remains the governing word. There was no mass market for automobiles until it was created by men who were willing to experiment with new techniques of production in order to do so. The first British manufacturer to attempt the same thing was William R. Morris, later Lord Nuffield, and he did not have a car on the market until 1913, by which time the largest producer of automobiles in the United Kingdom was Henry Ford.[3]

It was by no means inevitable that American automobile development should have followed the course that it did. There was ample opinion in those early days that the car was strictly an item of luxury. Woodrow Wilson, as president of Princeton University, deplored the motor car as likely to stimulate socialism in the United States by inciting the poor to envy of the rich. In this attitude Mr. Wilson was reflecting the frequent propensity of the intellectual to express his concern for the common man by undertaking to determine what the common man should go without. As it turned out, he was wrong about the automobile, but he was wrong only because there were enough other individuals in the United States with the foresight to see what the motor vehicle might become and the willingness to take enormous risks to reach their goals.

The steps that in our own day have made it possible for four-fifths of all American families to own at least one automobile constitute an astounding feat of production and organization. Henry Ford is usually credited with conceiving a "car for the great multitude" and then making it possible, and properly so,

3 P. W. S. Andrews and Elizabeth Brunner, *The Life of Lord Nuffield* (Oxford: Basil Blackwell, 1955), p. 59; Graham Turner, *The Car Makers* (London: Eyre and Spottiswoode, 1963), p. 20.

but it does not diminish the credit due Ford to acknowledge that others made vital contributions as well. Ransom E. Olds produced the first really successful low-priced car. Henry M. Leland demonstrated that quality and precision were fully compatible with interchangeability. William C. Durant envisioned a great automobile company with an offering for every range of the market; the organization needed to achieve the goal was provided by Alfred P. Sloan. Walter Chrysler, one-time Kansas farm boy, took a bankrupt company and made it one of the Big Three. The list could be extended; this is just a sample of the men who gave the American automobile industry its distinctive form.

Their immediate objective was to build and sell motor vehicles, as many as possible, but this was not all. Henry Ford saw his car for the great multitude as a means of freeing the farmer from his age-old isolation, and the others similarly were motivated by more than a desire to make money. In any event, what they accomplished was an industrial miracle, with multiple effects on the economy and the society of all of contemporary civilization.

Growth of the Automobile Industry

The remarkable growth of the American automobile industry has been told many times. For the first part of the twentieth century, until the outbreak of the Second World War, it has been summarized by the Federal Trade Commission:

The rapid popular acceptance accorded the motor vehicle in the United States is shown by the number of units manufactured during the period 1899–1937. Fewer than 4,000 motor vehicles were produced in 1899, while five years later the census reported a yearly production in excess of 22,000 units, and by 1914, or fifteen years later, yearly production passed the half-million-unit mark. In 1919 production of motor vehicles was 1,683,916 units, and for the next ten years production continued to increase, irregularly from year to year, until by 1929 the all-time peak in yearly production of 5,294,087 units was attained. The force of the depression was soon felt by the motor-vehicle industry for by 1931 yearly production had dropped to 2,295,063 units, and

Table 3.1   Growth of the Motor Vehicle Industry, 1899–1937

This tabulation of index numbers of production of motor vehicles and the value of products (using 1929 as a base) by census years concisely shows the industry's remarkable growth in productive capacity, particularly during the period from 1899 to 1929.

Year	Index of Production (1929—100)	Value of Products (1929—100)
1899	less than 0.1	0.1
1904	0.4	0.7
1909	2.0	5.0
1914	11.0	14.0
1919	32.0	64.0
1921	30.0	45.0
1923	74.0	85.0
1925	79.0	86.0
1927	63.0	77.0
1929	100.0	100.0
1931	43.0	42.0
1933	35.0	30.0
1935	74.0	64.0
1937	89.0	83.0

Source: Federal Trade Commission, *Report on the Motor Vehicle Industry* (Washington, D.C.: Government Printing Office, 1939), p. 7.

by 1933 to somewhat less than 2,000,000 units. Improved economic conditions were reflected in the almost 4,000,000 units produced in 1935, and the 4,732,426 units produced in 1937.[4]

This record is amplified in Tables 3.1 through 3.3. Impressive as these figures are, they tell only part of the story. The rise of the automotive industry in less than thirty years from one hundred fiftieth to first among American industries had of necessity a profound impact on the entire American economy. By the 1920s motor vehicle manufacturing absorbed 20 percent of the output of steel in the United States, 80 percent of the rubber, and 75 percent of the plate glass.[5] Beyond the straightforward de-

4 Federal Trade Commission, *Report on the Motor Vehicle Industry* (Washington, D.C.: Government Printing Office, 1939), pp. 8–10.
5 Wilfred Owen, *Automotive Transportation. Trends and Problems* (Washington, D.C.: The Brookings Institution, 1949), p. 61.

Table 3.2　Relative Importance of Motor Vehicle Manufacture, 1899–1937

Industry and Year	Wage Earners (average for the year)	Wages	Value Added by Manufacture	Cost of Materials	Value of Products
Motor Vehicles and Motor Vehicle Bodies and Parts:	Rank	Rank	Rank	Rank	Rank
1899	—	—	—	—	150
1904	—	—	—	—	77
1909	20	—	17	—	21
1914	15	7	6	7	7
1919	7	5	3	2	2
1925	3	1	1	1	1
1931	2	2	2	2	4
1935	1	1	1	1	1
1937	2	2	1	1	1
Motor Vehicles:					
1914	22	16	12	9	8
1919	9	7	6	4	3
1925	10	8	4	2	1
1931	12	12	8	3	2
1935	8	6	4	2	1
1937	8	4	5	1	2
Motor Vehicle Bodies and Parts:					
1914	34	25	38	49	47
1919	18	13	20	29	25
1925	8	6	8	8	9
1931	11	9	9	7	11
1935	4	2	6	5	5
1937	4	2	4	5	5

Source: FTC, *Report on the Motor Vehicle Industry*, p. 9.

mand for increased quantities, the automobile industry was responsible for significant changes in both the quality of the materials it required and the techniques of producing them. The production of alloy steels in the United States was begun largely in response to the needs of the automobile industry, because there had not been enough demand previously to make it worthwhile for the steel industry to make it. Similarly, the continuous-

Table 3.3   Wages and Value of Products, Motor Vehicle Industry, 1899–1937

| Census Years | Motor-Vehicle and Motor-Vehicle Bodies and Parts Industries | | | Motor Vehicles — Value of Products (percent of United States total) |
	Wage Earners' Annual Average (percent of United States total)	Wages Paid (percent of United States total)	Value Added by Manufacture (percent of United States total)	
1899	*	*	*	*
1904	0.2	0.3	0.3	0.2
1909	1.1	1.4	1.4	0.9
1914	1.8	2.5	2.9	2.1
1919	3.8	4.7	4.6	3.9
1921	3.1	3.9	4.1	3.8
1923	4.6	6.0	5.7	5.2
1925	5.1	6.7	6.5	5.1
1927	4.4	5.7	5.3	4.6
1929	5.1	6.3	6.3	5.3
1931	4.4	4.9	4.9	3.8
1933	4.0	4.8	4.5	3.5
1935	5.3	7.2	5.8	5.2
1937	5.6	7.5	6.0	5.1

* Less than 0.1 percent.
Source: FTC, *Report on the Motor Vehicle Industry*, p. 10.

strip mill for making sheet steel cheaply and in quantity was introduced to supply the requirements of automobile bodies,[6] and the production of plate glass by continuous process was begun by the Ford Motor Company in order to meet a need that existing techniques could not satisfy.[7] The automobile also transformed the petroleum industry from being mainly a producer of illuminants and lubricants to being primarily a producer of gasoline. Here again the change was both qualitative and quantitative. The enormously increased demand for gasoline provided a powerful incentive not only to step up output but to develop better refin-

6 G. S. Armstrong and Co., *The Automotive Industry* (New York: G. S. Armstrong and Co., 1953), p. 38.
7 Charles E. Sorensen with Samuel T. Williamson, *My Forty Years with Ford* (New York: W. W. Norton and Co., 1956), p. 172.

ing techniques so as to secure a greater yield of gasoline from the same amount of crude oil. In addition, the desire for improved performance in automobile engines stimulated efforts to make more efficient fuels, the outstanding example being the development of ethyl gasoline early in the 1920s.

Moreover, the increasing millions of motor vehicles required services of various kinds and created demands that opened new business opportunities. The individual features of this process will be discussed in detail later, but it is worth looking at the aggregate picture first. In 1963 one out of every six business enterprises in the United States was directly dependent on the manufacture, distribution, servicing, and use of motor vehicles.[8] The governing word in this situation is "directly." Only businesses directly dependent on the automobile are counted. Motels, for instance, are included, but not hotels; restaurants are excluded, even drive-ins and roadside restaurants manifestly located to attract automobile trade.

In addition, in this same year, 1963, over thirty categories of industry produced $8.8 billion worth of articles that went into motor vehicles.[9] The employment figures show a striking comparison. Data compiled for the period 1963 to 1966 show 13.5 million people employed in "Highway Transport Industries": manufacturing of motor vehicles and parts; petroleum refining; automotive sales and service; state and local roads; trucking firms; taxicab companies, intercity bus lines, school bus systems, and bus terminal and service facilities.[10] Of this total, 865,000 were engaged in the manufacture of vehicles and parts; in other words, fourteen times as many people were employed in operating, supplying, and servicing automobiles as in making them. This is

8 *1968/Automobile Facts/Figures* (Detroit: Automobile Manufacturers Association, 1968), p. 33, based on U.S. Department of Commerce, *Census of Manufacturers and Census of Business, 1963.*
9 *Ibid.,* pp. 36–37.
10 *Ibid.,* p. 38.

actually a conservative estimate because the totals do not include construction workers employed by private highway contractors or about 150,000 employees of local and suburban transportation systems, which except in a few large cities now means chiefly bus services.

People on Wheels

It would be possible to keep adding statistics to drive the lessons home, but there is more to the story than the physical growth of an industry, phenomenal as it has been. The mass production of motor vehicles meant mass consumption—this, after all, is the only reason for instituting mass production—and mass use. The implications of this feature of the automotive revolution have been far-reaching; to the extent that they can be evaluated, this too will be done in detail later. Meanwhile, what was the general picture when the automobile came into general use in American life?

There were 8,000 motor vehicles registered in the United States in 1900 and over 32 million in 1940, of which over 27 million were passenger cars.[11] This was a 4,000-fold increase in forty years. During the same period the population of the United States rose from 76 million to 132 million, an increase of about 74 percent. These are round figures. Table 3.4 compares the growth of population with motor vehicle registrations and show a startling change in the ratio of cars to people.

Because the growth rates and the total numbers we are considering are so spectacular, it would be easy to get absorbed in the statistics and miss an underlying and significant meaning. The development of a practical motor vehicle would by itself have revolutionized highway transportation. For the first time in all history there was a fast, efficient, and economical means of moving people and goods by road. Even if the passenger car had

11 *Ibid.*, p. 19.

Table 3.4   Private Automobile Registrations and Population, 1900–1969

Year	Auto Registrations*	Population†	Ratio of Cars to People
1900	8,000	75,994,575	1:9,499
1910	458,377	91,972,266	1:201
1920	8,131,522	105,710,620	1:13.0
1930	22,972,745	122,775,046	1:5.3
1940	27,372,397	131,669,275	1:4.8
1950	40,190,632	150,697,361	1:3.7
1960‡	61,430,862	179,323,175	1:2.9
1969‡	86,709,830	201,422,000	1:2.3

* Excludes publicly owned automobiles.
† Resident population.
‡ Includes Alaska and Hawaii.
Sources: U.S. Department of Commerce, Bureau of the Census; U.S. Department of Transportation, Bureau of Public Roads.

remained an item of luxury, the impact of the motor truck and the bus would still have been profound. Truck transport offered a flexible, low-cost method of moving freight, with the particular advantage of being able to serve communities that lacked convenient access to a railroad. The bus provided comparable cheapness and flexibility for passenger travel, similarly capable of reaching communities without rail facilities. It also proved useful in city transit systems because of its maneuverability and its ability to operate economically on routes of low-density traffic.

If, therefore, the twentieth century had seen roads and streets traversed by trucks and buses, along with an occasional private car, this would still have been a radical transformation of highway travel from the slow, plodding, cumbersome movement of previous millennia. This, indeed, is largely the story of road transport in western Europe between the First and Second World Wars. The British Ministry of Transport describes how during this period bus service became of major importance to the working population and reduced the isolation that was the greatest drawback of rural life. This report continues: "It was in the carriage of goods, however, that the motor vehicle exerted its greatest influence. Not only could it offer the flexible door-to-door service which the railways had never been able to provide, but it was itself adaptable to a multitude of specialized purposes." [12]

This description can be applied equally well to the development of commercial highway transport in the United States and Canada during the same period, except that it was on a larger scale. But in the American situation there was something more, and very different. This was the mass-produced, low-priced automobile, distributed in millions as no such item of property had ever been distributed before. Consider the registration data again. In 1920, 8 out of the 9 million registered vehicles were private passenger cars, or 89 percent; 23 out of 26 million in 1930, or 88 percent; 27 out of 32 million in 1940, or 84 percent. Since then the proportion of passenger cars has remained consistent at about 83 or 84 percent of the total. [13]

The shifting percentages are not especially significant. What counts is that the private passenger automobile in these quantities represents a new era in transportation because it provided personal mobility of a completely novel kind and on a completely novel scale. Mass production of motor vehicles dates from Henry Ford's introduction of the moving assembly line in 1913. In just about fifteen years the use of the automobile had become so widespread that it would have been possible to move the entire population of the United States by car at one time. (This was and still is a theoretical possibility. It has never actually been done, even though it may be easy to get the impression on holiday weekends that it is being attempted.)

One historian has defined the significance of this new mobility by stating that the great achievement of the automobile was "to

12 *Traffic in Towns*, Report of the Steering Group and the Working Group appointed by the Minister of Transport (London: Her Majesty's Stationery Office, 1963), p. 10.
13 *1968/Automobile Facts/Figures*, p. 19. The totals exclude military vehicles.

free the common man from the limitations of his geography." [14]
Yet, although the common man was the principal beneficiary of
the automotive revolution, this was not a case of the poor man
coming to enjoy a luxury formerly limited to the rich. The rich
themselves had never enjoyed anything like this before.

The Initial Effects

It took time for the full impact of the automotive revolution
to develop, but from the beginning the motor vehicle had recog-
nizable and distinctive effects on American life. One of the first
features to emerge is that the American automobile from the
beginning had a utilitarian function. Elwood Haynes built his
first car in 1894 because as superintendent of an oil company he
had to travel extensively around the countryside of Ohio and
Indiana, and he believed that a mechanized vehicle would serve
his needs better than a horse and buggy—making him the first of
a long line of Americans to reach the same conclusion.

The concept of the motorcar as a rich man's plaything died
slowly; it would not finally be laid to rest until the point was
reached when over half the automobile output in the country
consisted of Model T Fords. Yet the utilitarian potentialities of
the motor vehicle were evident almost from the beginning. The
Post Office was experimenting with motorized carriage of mail as
early as 1896, and three years later it conducted systematic tests
with motor vehicles for collecting mail.[15] The tests showed that
cars could cover a mail route in half the time required for horse-
drawn vehicles. By the turn of the century electric cabs had been
introduced in New York, and department stores there and in

14 J. R. T. Hughes, "Eight Tycoons: The Entrepreneur and American History," quoted in R. M. Robertson and J. L. Pate, *Readings in United States
Economic and Business History* (Boston, Mass.: Houghton Mifflin Co., 1966),
p. 431.
15 Automobile Manufacturers Association, Inc., *Automobiles of America*,
2nd rev. ed. (Detroit: Wayne University Press, 1968), p. 20.

other eastern cities were beginning to use trucks for deliveries. The next few years saw the appearance of motor-driven ambulances (1900) and fire engines (1903).

It was only to be expected that, once a practical motor vehicle appeared, it should be adopted for uses like these. What is more striking is the speed with which the private passenger automobile displayed the multipurpose usefulness that it has retained ever since—a vehicle capable of being employed for pleasure or business trips interchangeably. If we look at the people who bought cars in the early days, it is quite evident that many of them were looking for something more than a plaything.

The first independent automobile dealership on record was established by William E. Metzger in Detroit in 1898. Among other cars he sold Mobile steamers, and the first twenty were disposed as follows:

4   to   "capitalists"
4   to   physicians
2   to   manufacturers
4   to   merchants
1   to   a broker
1   to   a printer
1   to   a plumber
3   to   "general businessmen" [16]

Some of these categories are a little vague—it would be interesting to know, for instance, what distinguished a "capitalist" from a manufacturer, merchant, or "general businessman." We can assume that the printer and the plumber were owners of their establishments rather than journeymen workers. Nevertheless, the utilitarian implications are strong. The physicians unquestionably bought cars for professional use; medical men appear prominently among the early purchasers of motor vehicles, because

16 Ralph C. Epstein, *The Automobile Industry* (Chicago and New York: A. W. Shaw Co., 1928), p. 95.

awkward as cars were in those days they still got the doctor around farther and faster than the horse and buggy enshrined in the "country doctor" tradition.

Alexander Winton had a somewhat more elaborate breakdown of his first twenty sales. They were:

2   mechanical engineers, Pennsylvania
2   railroad car manufacturers, Pennsylvania
1   oil pipe manufacturer, Pennsylvania
1   capitalist, Pennsylvania
2   coal operators, Pennsylvania
1   coal dealer, Pennsylvania
1   brewer, Pennsylvania
1   engineer, New Jersey
1   locomotive manufacturer, New Jersey
1   physician, New York
1   electric manufacturer, Ohio
1   piano manufacturer, Missouri
1   flour miller, Minnesota
2   hosiery manufacturers, Ontario
2   dry goods merchants, Ontario[17]

This list has several interesting features. The buyers are definitely an upper-income group, but as with Metzger's customers, they do not suggest people who were buying cars merely for joyriding. The geographical dispersal is surprisingly wide (these cars were sold in 1898). Of twenty cars built in Cleveland, only one went to an Ohio purchaser—the "electric manufacturer, Ohio," who happened to be James Ward Packard. The others were spread from New York and New Jersey on one side to Minnesota and Missouri on the other.

Some years later, in 1906, another automobile manufacturer wrote a letter to *The Automobile,* explaining that he was plan-

17 *Ibid.,* p. 96.

ning to build 20,000 "runabouts" in the following year and stated:

The assertion has often been made that it would be only a question of a few years before the automobile industry would go the way the bicycle went. I think this is in no way a fair comparison and that the automobile, while it may have been a luxury when first put out, is now one of the absolute necessities of our later day civilization. The bicycle was a recreation and a fad. The automobile, while it is a recreation, is in no way a fad.[18]

The letter was signed "Henry Ford."

In this same year the disastrous earthquake in San Francisco provided a dramatic demonstration of the desirability, indeed the necessity, of having a flexible means of transportation that could be relied on in an emergency. It also demonstrated that the so-called "pleasure" car could be instantly converted to serve vital community needs. The two hundred private automobiles in San Francisco were impressed into public service, and the San Francisco *Chronicle* observed:

That the automobile played an all but indispensable part in saving the western part of San Francisco, and at the same time has proved invaluable in the serious business of governing the city through its greatest stress, is conceded by every man who has had his eyes open during the ten days or so that have elapsed since the earthquake. . . . Men high in official service go even further and say that but for the auto it would not have been possible to save even a portion of the city or to take care of the sick or to preserve a semblance of law and order.[19]

In addition, Walter White, head of the White Motor Company, organized a truck convoy to carry supplies to the stricken city, one of the first of many demonstrations that motorized road transport could function when other means of access were closed.

All this came before mass production and the widespread distribution of car ownership, and before there was a road system

18 *The Automobile*, XIV (January 11, 1906), p. 107.
19 James J. Flink, *America Adopts the Automobile, 1895–1910* (Cambridge, Mass.: The M.I.T. Press, 1970), pp. 46–47.

capable of making highway travel, either for pleasure or business, practical for any but short distances. In other words, even when it could function only within a markedly restricted scope, motorized highway transportation rapidly made its way into national life as something capable of meeting needs more effectively than they could be met otherwise, and in fact meeting needs that could not be met in any other way. Some people saw what was happening, but not many as yet. Henry Ford, as his letter shows, was aware of the prospect in 1906, and he acted accordingly. It is sometimes forgotten that one reason for the phenomenal success of the Model T was that it was designed to operate on rough, rutted roads. When mass production of motor vehicles was introduced, it preceded any major improvement in the highway network. The historical principle that the highway is built for the vehicle, rather than vice versa, holds good for the automobile.

A New Era Begins

Nineteen fourteen was a historic year. It saw the outbreak of the First World War, with all its fateful consequences. It also saw the Ford Motor Company in complete assembly-line production and introducing the five-dollar day. This may seem a matching of events of unequal import; it is not. A perceptive French student of the American scene, Father R. L. Bruckberger, has stated that by these steps, especially the five-dollar day, Henry Ford contributed far more to the emancipation of the worker than Lenin did through bloody revolution three years later.[20] Ford's was a peaceful revolution, which achieved its goal by the simple device of making every worker a potential customer, and, says Bruckberger, "one cannot be a customer and a proletarian at the same time, any more than, at the same time and in the same equation, one can be both a master and a slave."

20 R. L. Bruckberger, *Image of America* (New York: Viking Press, 1959), pp. 196–197.

One incident of 1914 passed unnoticed and would certainly have appeared trivial beside the earth-shaking events of that fateful year—but it was a sign of change. The production of motor vehicles in the United States for the first time exceeded the output of wagons and carriages.[21] Old Dobbin, like it or not, was on the way out. To take a longer view of the replacement of the horse by the motor vehicle, the production of horse-drawn vehicles in the United States reached a peak of 570,000 in 1899, declined steadily to 342,000 in 1919, and never again exceeded 200,000.[22] The number of nonfarm horses dropped from 3.2 million in 1910 to 1.7 million in 1920.

The war itself dramatized the arrival of a new day in transportation. Right at the start came the dramatic episode of the Marne, when the taxicabs of Paris were commandeered to rush troops from the city to strike the flank of the advancing German armies. (A present-day visitor to Paris may wonder why the taxicabs were used to carry troops instead of being used themselves as lethal weapons.) More important by far was the unglamorous service of motor trucks in carrying supplies where rail transport did not exist. Throughout the crisis of Verdun, the only supply route open to the defending French armies was a single secondary road—not even a Route Nationale—and it took an endless line of trucks moving along this route to save the city.

At home in the United States the war, as described in Chapter 2, showed that motorized highway transportation could have made a major contribution to the war effort if there had been even a moderately adequate road network. The War Department has been unfairly criticized for neglecting motor transport. The tale is repeatedly told of how in 1900 a German army officer was compiling a book entitled *Mechanical Traction in War*, and

21 Epstein, *Automobile Industry*, p. 10.
22 L. N. Moses and H. F. Williamson, Jr., "The Location of Economic Activity in Cities" (Unpublished manuscript. Transportation Library, Northwestern University, 1966), p. 20.

when he inquired what was being done in the United States, he was informed by General John M. Wilson, Chief of Engineers, U.S.A., that "road traction engines" had not been seriously considered as a means of military transportation "because the want of good roads in the countries where our military operations have heretofore been carried out preclude their successful operation." [23]

This was not bureaucratic stuffiness; General Wilson was stating the plain facts of the case. Curiously, however, he seems to have been unaware that in 1899 the Army did purchase some electric vehicles for general transportation purposes. To the extent that American military forces were inadequately equipped and organized for the kind of war that was being waged in Europe, this was simply a reflection of the generally casual attitude that most Americans at that time had toward military preparation.

When the war ended, the motor vehicle was definitely established in American society. The production achievement was in full career, and the methods of the automobile manufacturers were being eagerly studied and imitated by other American industries and by other industrialized and industrializing nations seeking to duplicate this formula for the creation of wealth. The transportation implications of the automobile, however, had not really made themselves felt. For this, the two developments that went into high gear in the 1920s were necessary: widespread distribution of automobile ownership and substantial highway improvement.

The First Appraisals

After about ten years of remarkable expansion in the distribution and use of motor vehicles, some serious efforts began

23 See Christy Borth, "The Automobile: Power-Plant and Transport-Tool of a Free People," *Centennial of Engineering, 1852–1952* (Chicago, Ill.: Museum of Science and Industry, 1953), p. 441.

to be made at evaluating the impact of this novel phenomenon on the country's economic and social structure. At the end of the 1920s a commission appointed by President Hoover made a thorough survey of contemporary changes in American life, published under the title *Recent Social Trends in the United States.* Of the automobile it had this to say:

It is probable that no invention of such far reaching importance was ever diffused with such rapidity or so quickly exerted influences that ramified through the national culture, transforming even habits of thought and language. . . .

This phenomenal growth involved a displacement of earlier vehicles, such as the horse carriage and the bicycle. It also involved habituation to the use of the automobile of classes in the population who formerly owned no vehicle of private transportation. Within the space of a few years, for vast numbers motor travel ceased to be a novelty and came to be regarded as a necessity. . . .

In no inconsiderable degree the rapid popular acceptance of the new vehicle centered in the fact that it gave to the owner a control over his movements that the older agencies denied. Close at hand and ready for instant use, it carried its owner from door to destination by routes he himself selected, and on schedules of his own making; baggage inconveniences were minimized and perhaps the most important of all, the automobile made possible the movement of an entire family at costs that were relatively small. Convenience augmented utility and accelerated adoption of the vehicle.[24]

Thus we see the automotive revolution as it appeared in 1933, forty years after the Duryea car and twenty years after the first Ford assembly line. Perhaps the most appropriate comment on this appraisal is the interpretation given by a Washington taxi driver to the inscription "The Past Is Prologue" over the main door of the National Archives: "It means you ain't seen nuthin' yet."

24 Malcolm M. Willey and Stuart A. Rice, "The Agencies of Communication," *Recent Social Trends in the United States* (New York: McGraw-Hill Book Co., 1933), pp. 172–177.

4 The Automobile and Highway Policy

The new era in highway transportation ushered in by the automobile necessitated a comprehensive reformulation of highway policy. With motor vehicles coming onto the roads in increasing millions, there was irresistible pressure for an extensive program of highway construction and improvement at all levels of government. The roads and streets of the past simply would not do. Even where they were in good condition, they had still been designed for slow-moving and normally low-density traffic; they simply could not stand up under the wear and tear of fast-moving motor vehicles. Working out the technical problems, such as determining the most suitable surfacing for given conditions, was largely a matter of accumulating the necessary engineering data by study and experience. Resolving fundamental questions of policy was much more difficult, especially because at the beginning of the automobile era some of the major issues were either not recognized or not understood.

There are three basic categories of roads and streets. First, there are those whose primary function is to provide access to property. Second, there are those designed to carry local traffic from one part of a community to another or between nearby communities. Third, there are the arterial highways intended for through traffic, intercommunity and for the most part long-distance. However, the nature of highway travel being what it is, almost any road or street may be used for all three purposes. With slow-moving vehicles there was no great need to differentiate between highway functions. Local and through traffic could use the same roadway without serious interference, and there was not, and did not have to be, any great qualitative difference between main and secondary roads.

The automobile brought a very different situation. Motor vehicles operate over a much wider range of speeds than their predecessors did, and they can provide efficiently and economically a greater variety of services than had been possible with any previous method of road transport. But to realize these advantages it is necessary to distinguish between types of traffic and consequently to differentiate roads by function. Where traffic is light, roadways can still be multipurpose, carrying through and local, fast and slow traffic. Once the flow of vehicles reaches any appreciable volume, however, a functional separation becomes desirable. To mingle conflicting flows of traffic invites confusion, congestion, and danger. In other words, once the motor vehicle comes into general use, the highway system has to be planned accordingly; this is nothing more than a restatement of McAdam's principle that "Roads must be built to accommodate the traffic," with the difference that in an automobile age the road should be designed for a particular kind of traffic rather than for all traffic indiscriminately.

Adapting to the Automobile

In 1933 Rosemary and Stephen Vincent Benét began a poem:

The old rutted roads have been turned to macadams,
But Quincy and Braintree remember the Adams.[1]

This couplet sums up the initial response to the automobile in the United States—and everywhere else for that matter. The Federal Highway Act of 1921 was the first recognition in American highway policy of the desirability of functional specialization, at least for arterial routes. But the arterial network thus provided would account for only 7 percent of the nation's more than 3 million miles of roads and streets, and it would be over ten years before it approached being the "adequate and connected system of highways, interstate in character" that the law contemplated.

1 From: *A Book of Americans* by Stephen Vincent Benét, Holt, Rinehart and Winston, Inc., Copyright, 1933, by Rosemary and Stephen Vincent Benét. Copyright renewed © 1961 by Rosemary Carr Benét. Reprinted by permission of Brandt & Brandt.

Meanwhile, the rest of the highway network was very much in the condition described by the Benéts—the old roads patched up to make them more or less passable for motor vehicles. Actually, much of the country's basic road plant already existed when the Office of Road Inquiry made its study in 1904. There was a substantial jump from the 2.35 million miles[2] of that year to the 3.16 million miles of 1921, the first year in which the Bureau of Public Roads compiled complete statistics. This apparent 34 percent increase, however, represents insufficient data in the first survey, changes in the method of recording the data, and new construction in regions that were still sparsely populated in 1904.[3]

Even if all that was to be done was to rebuild the existing road system so as to make it suitable for automobile traffic and to increase its capacity, it was an immense task. For the state and local authorities who were going to have to do most of it, the acute problem was finance. If the necessary funds were found, adequate techniques of highway construction were available— not the best that might have been applied, but adequate.

The remedy, to a considerable extent, was provided by the automobile itself. As early as 1900 revenues were being raised from automobiles in the form of fees for registrations and drivers' licenses, but these could never have been great enough to support a major highway program. The impost on individual vehicles would have had to be so heavy as to inhibit severely the ability of ordinary people to buy and operate automobiles and so would have defeated its own purpose. The breakthrough was the adoption of gasoline taxes, beginning with a one-cent-a-gallon levy by Oregon in 1919, as a device that related highway revenue to

2 This was total mileage. The figure given in Chapter 2 was for rural mileage only.
3 Charles L. Dearing, *American Highway Policy* (Washington, D.C.: The Brookings Institution, 1941), p. 113.

highway use. In time, such taxes have become the principal source of highway revenues to the extent that highway transportation now effectively pays for its roads. (See Figures 4.1 through 4.3.)

As Tables 4.1 and 4.2 show, gasoline and other highway user taxes have grown steadily from being a very modest proportion of the total funds available for road construction and maintenance to being the principal source of such funds. They have never provided for all highway expenditures, and this is as it should be. Contrary to the notion that sometimes is publicly propounded, society does not provide roads and streets for the exclusive benefit of the operators of motor vehicles. It provides roads and streets because they are required for social needs, which existed long before the automobile appeared and would

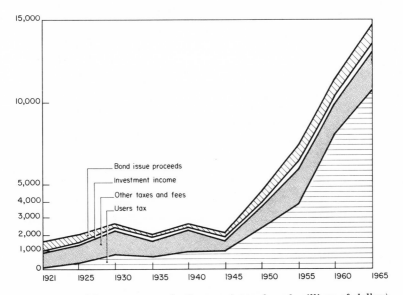

Figure 4.1 Highway revenues (in five-year intervals and millions of dollars)
Source: U.S. Department of Transportation, *Highway Statistics Summary to 1965*, Table HF-201.

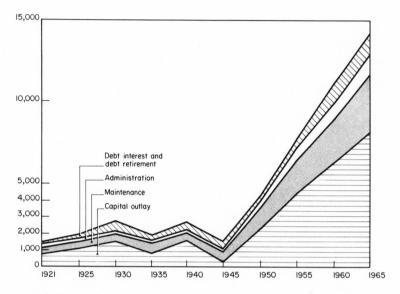

Figure 4.2   Highway expenditures (in five-year intervals and millions of dollars)
Source: U.S. Department of Transportation, *Highway Statistics Summary to 1965*, Table HF-202.

continue to exist even if the automobile had never been invented. Our era differs in that the motor vehicle has greatly enhanced the ability of highway systems to meet these needs. It seems only reasonable that modern highway programs should take this factor into account.

Consider the basic functions of roads and streets as they have just been described. Those whose primary purpose is to give access to property obviously benefit chiefly the owners whose property they serve, and the cost of supporting such roads is a proper charge on the property. Similarly, roads and streets intended principally for local use, to meet community needs, are properly the responsibility of the community they serve. The most appropriate and most equitable application of user taxes

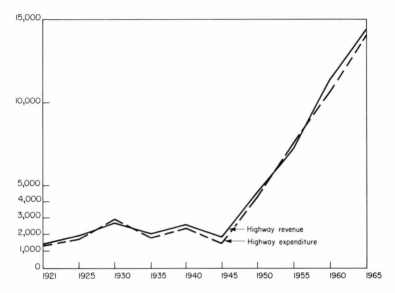

Figure 4.3 Comparison of highway revenues and expenditures (in five-year intervals and millions of dollars)
Source: U.S. Department of Transportation, *Highway Statistics Summary to 1965*, Tables HF-201, HF-202.

is to the highways designed for through traffic: in other words, the highways whose users are more obviously beneficiaries than any other identifiable group. These distinctions are not hard-and-fast and cannot be because of the unavoidable multipurpose character of most roads and streets, but without them intelligent highway planning and effective allocation of funds become impossible.

At any rate, from user taxes and other sources a vast amount of road construction and improvement was begun during the 1920s. As the tables show, very little of this effort went into an increase of aggregate highway mileage. Between 1921 and 1930 the total mileage of all roads and streets increased by just about 100,000, or 3 percent, and this was more than was added during

Table 4.1   A Comparison of Highway Revenues and Expenditures, 1921–1965 (in five-year intervals and in millions of dollars)

| Highway Revenues | | | | | Highway Expenditures | | | | | |
Imposts on Highway Users*	Other Taxes and Fees†	Investment Income	Bond Issue Proceeds	Total	Year	Total	Capital Outlay‡	Maintenance§	Administration‖	Debt Interest and Retirement
123	872	61	353	1,409	1921	1,385	836	359	83	107
387	1,158	39	380	1,964	1925	1,851	1,039	464	118	203
823	1,478	47	387	2,735	1930	2,852	1,522	677	115	538
783	1,086	23	171	2,063	1935	1,998	920	540	99	439
1,135	1,335	37	212	2,719	1940	2,688	1,450	610	128	500
1,162	662	48	57	1,929	1945	1,696	373	796	127	500
2,432	1,424	95	655	4,606	1950	4,471	2,297	1,432	298	453
3,934	2,043	183	1,185	7,345	1955	7,355	4,334	1,881	455	685
8,206	1,800	260	1,219	11,485	1960	10,762	6,290	2,640	810	1,022
10,700	2,227	371	1,073	14,371	1965	14,243	8,380	3,232	1,259	1,372

* Includes motor fuel and vehicle taxes, tolls, and parking fees.
† Includes property taxes and assessments, general fund appropriations, and miscellaneous taxes and fees.
‡ Includes capital outlay on rural, municipal, state, territorial, and unclassified roads.
§ Includes maintenance on rural, municipal, state, territorial, and unclassified roads.
‖ Includes expenditures on administration, research, highway police, and highway safety.

Source: U.S. Department of Transportation, *Highway Statistics: Summary to 1965*, Tables HF-201, HF-202, pp. 61–76.

Table 4.2 Highway Taxation, 1913–1931

Trends of Motor Vehicle License and Gasoline Tax Collections*

| Year | Motor Vehicles Registered | | Motor Vehicle Licenses, Fees, etc. | | | | Gasoline Tax | | | |
	Number (in thousands)	Index (1925 = 100)	Total Collections Amt. (in thousands of dollars)	Index (1925 = 100)	Aver. per Car Amt.	Index (1925 = 100)	Total Collections Amt. (in thousands of dollars)	Index (1925 = 100)	Aver. per Gal. Amt. in Cents	Index (1925 = 100)
1913	1,258	6	8,192	3	$ 6.51	50	—	—	—	—
1914	1,711	9	12,382	5	7.24	55	—	—	—	—
1915	2,446	12	18,246	7	7.46	57	—	—	—	—
1916	3,513	18	25,865	10	7.36	56	—	—	—	—
1917	4,792	24	37,501	14	7.83	60	—	—	—	—
1918	5,853	29	51,477	20	8.79	67	—	—	—	—
1919	7,144	36	64,697	25	9.06	69	—	—	—	—
1920	8,380	42	102,546	39	12.24	94	—	—	—	—
1921	10,463	52	122,479	47	11.71	90	5,302	4	—	—
1922	12,238	61	152,048	58	12.42	95	11,923	8	—	—
1923	15,092	76	188,971	73	12.52	96	36,814	25	—	—
1924	17,592	88	225,492	87	12.82	98	79,734	55	—	—
1925	19,954	100	260,620	100	13.06	100	146,029	100	2.26	100
1926	22,001	110	288,282	111	13.10	100	187,603	128	2.38	105
1927	23,133	116	301,061	116	13.01	100	258,967	177	2.76	122
1928	24,493	123	322,630	123	13.17	101	304,872	209	3.00	133
1929	26,501	133	347,844	133	13.13	101	431,312	295	3.22	142
1930	26,524	133	355,705	136	13.41	103	493,865	338	3.35	148
1931	26,124	131	355,037	136	13.59	104	525,986	360	3.44	152

* U.S. Department of Agriculture, Department Bulletin, no. 1279, pp. 81, 83 and 84; and U.S. Bureau of Public Roads, Tables Miscellaneous A-1; MV-2; and g-1 (MSS). From *Recent Social Trends*, p. 1359.
Source: *Recent Social Trends in the United States*, Report of the President's Research Committee on Social Trends. Copyright 1933 by the Research Committee on Social Trends, Inc. Used with the permission of McGraw-Hill Book Company.

Table 4.3   A Comparison of Improved and Unimproved Highway Mileage, 1921–1965 (in five-year intervals and in thousands of miles)

Year	Improved Mileage	Unimproved Mileage	Total Mileage
1921	447	2713	3160
1925	626	2620	3246
1930	854	2405	3259
1935	1255	2055	3310
1940	1557	1730	3287
1945	1721	1598	3319
1950	1939	1374	3313
1955	2273	1145	3418
1960	2557	989	3546
1965	2776	914	3690

Source: U.S. Department of Transportation, *Highway Statistics: Summary to 1965*, Table M-200, p. 119.

the next ten years. The significant change is in the mileage of surfaced highway, which almost doubled between 1921 and 1930 and again between 1930 and 1940. A landmark was reached in 1945, when the mileage of improved road in the United States exceeded the unimproved for the first time. The term "improved" or "surfaced" has to be treated with some caution; even in 1945 over a million of the 1.7 million miles so classified were surfaced with soil, sand, gravel, or stone.[4] (See Table 4.3 and Figure 4.4.) But these roads did have made surfaces and adequate drainage so that they were usable for automobile traffic in most weathers.

The extent of the changes that took place during the first stages of modern highway development in the United States appears in data given by the President's Committee on Social Trends. Between 1904 and 1930 the mileage of improved roads increased by 330.5 percent, while the total road mileage was rising 40 percent; the proportion of surfaced road grew from 7.1

4 U.S. Department of Transportation, *Highway Statistics: Summary to 1965* (Washington, D.C.: Government Printing Office), p. 120.

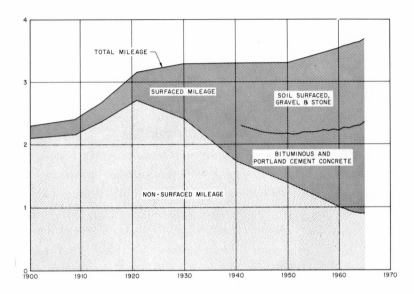

Figure 4.4   Total road and street mileage in the United States, 1900–1965
(in ten-year intervals and millions of miles)
Source: Federal Highway Administration, courtesy of Mr. William R. Hall.

to 23 percent and the proportion of "high type surface" (paved
road) from 0.1 to 18.1 percent.[5]

This was a marked and much-needed improvement of a road
system that had been notoriously inadequate even for preautomobile traffic, and since most of the work was begun after 1920,
it was a creditable achievement to have done so much in so short
a time. The cost of the achievement at first glance looks heavy.
The Committee on Social Trends notes that expenditures on
rural roads accounted for 17.5 percent of the increase in all taxes
between 1913 and 1930 and 25 percent of the increase in state
and local taxes for the same period.[6] This, however, can fairly

5 M. M. Willey and S. A. Rice, "The Agencies of Communication," *Recent
Social Trends in the United States* (New York: McGraw-Hill Book Co., 1933),
p. 175.
6 Clarence Heer, "Taxation and Public Finance," *ibid.*, p. 1358.

be regarded as a price the American people had to pay for previous neglect of rural roads, and there were compensating factors. User taxes contributed 60 percent of the increase in expenditures for highways between 1913 and 1930; beyond this direct recompense there were substantial economic benefits from highway improvement, which will be discussed in later chapters.

This qualitative advance, however, fell short of providing a highway system capable of permitting a smooth and efficient flow for a growing volume of motor vehicle traffic. Except among a few highway experts there was little appreciation or understanding of the fundamental difference between a road system built so that it could be used by motor vehicles and a road system specifically designed for automobile traffic. The Highway Act of 1921 acknowledged the desirability of a national network of arterial highways, and the primary federal-aid roads met an urgent need. They were, however, constructed on the conventional pattern, with no control of access and predominantly two-lane. Some stretches of multilane road were built in heavily traveled areas after 1924, seldom as divided highways and frequently with three lanes.

The highway designers of the period had to work with the knowledge and the resources available to them, and in the 1920s the concepts of the kind of roads required for motor vehicle traffic were just emerging. Hilaire Belloc, who was not an engineer but whose grasp of highway problems showed sheer genius, proposed in 1924 that Britain construct "a very few great arterial roads joining up the main centres of population." [7] They were to be wide (Belloc mentioned 100 feet), as straight as possible, and with no intersections at grade. Limitation of access is implied rather than precisely stated, and there is no suggestion of separate roadways for opposing streams of traffic, but essentially Belloc is envisioning the modern express highway. Some specific

7 Hilaire Belloc, *The Road* (London: T. Fisher Unwin, 1924), pp. 196–198.

elements of a road system designed for motor vehicles were pro-posed even earlier. A French engineer, Eugene Henard, published a proposal in 1906 for grade-separated intersections and inter-changes on the general principle of the cloverleaf.[8] An American patent for the same idea was issued to Arthur Hale in 1916.

One of the first tangible applications of these concepts on any substantial scale was the beginning of the Italian *autostrade* late in the 1920s. In the United States there was recognition of the desirability of special-purpose roads, but it took the form of metropolitan parkways seeking to alleviate congestion by pro-viding roadways exclusively for noncommercial vehicles. The most important of these parkway systems was developed, appro-priately, in the largest metropolitan area, in Westchester County and Long Island outside New York City. It was conceived aston-ishingly early, in 1906, when the Bronx River Parkway Commis-sion was created, although the parkway itself was not completed until 1923.[9] It and the other Westchester County parkways that followed pioneered both in the design of express highways and as models of recreational development. A description of them reads:

When built, these four-lane, 40-foot wide highways were far ahead of their time. The four parkways—Bronx River, Hutchin-son River, Saw Mill River, and Cross County—cost $60 million. They stretch in elaborate curves to make up a 75 mile parkway network. . . .

Bronx River Parkway . . . was acclaimed as an engineering marvel. Grade separations had been specified at most road inter-sections, and a 40-foot roadbed provided room for four 10-foot lanes. The width of the park and parkway ranged from 200 feet to 1,700 feet.

The other three parkways were patterned after the Bronx River Parkway. Hutchinson River Parkway was opened to traffic in 1928, Saw Mill River Parkway in 1929, and the Cross County Parkway in 1931.

8 Spencer Miller, Jr., "The Modern Highway in America," in Jean Labatut and W. J. Lane, eds., *Highways in Our National Life: A Symposium* (Prince-ton, N.J.: Princeton University Press, 1950), p. 105.
9 *Ibid.,* p. 108.

The system included a series of open areas for recreational purposes that covered more than 17,000 acres, including 9 miles of beaches and shoreland. In effect, planners worked out two interlocking and overlapping systems—one for parks, parkways, and recreation and another to provide pleasant automobile transportation throughout the county. . . .

The parkways, though still attractive, are not capable of carrying heavy-volume and high-speed traffic. The problem of maintaining and improving the parkways that became apparent in the 1940's was accentuated further during the 1960's.

With the transfer of the parkways to the State in 1961, an extensive modernization and repair program was begun. The program includes widening and straightening the parkways. Among other programs to meet today's traffic needs, dividing strips will be added between opposing lanes.[10]

The same report continues with a brief reference to the parkways of Greater Boston, which antedate the automobile, having been started in 1877 on the advice of one of the first great American city planners, Frederick Law Olmsted. The account states:

Between 1877 and 1930, 78 miles of parkways were constructed in the Boston metropolitan area at a cost of more than $39 million. Early Boston park commissioners sought to make parkway routes interesting and pleasant. Rights-of-way extended from a minimum of 200 feet up to 1,200 feet, with a roadway 40 feet wide. . . .

Designed primarily to move traffic—though not the heavy volume of today—Boston's early parkways were a pleasant means of travel between parks. With rapid metropolitan growth, the parkways tended to become commuting links between suburbia and downtown activities.

The Boston parkways were four-lane roads for the most part, but without median dividers or grade separation.

In the 1920s, however, the parkways were just a small sample of what might be done. The high cost of such roads militated against their general adoption. Parkways were constructed only in the high-density traffic areas on the outskirts of large cities, where the benefits they offered in expediting traffic could be clearly seen; they were seldom extended into central city areas

10 U.S. Department of Commerce, *A Proposed Program for Roads and Parkways* (Washington, D.C.: Government Printing Office, 1966), pp. 105–107.

where land acquisition was more expensive. It was still too early in the history of automotive transportation for any general understanding to have developed that express highways offered benefits that more than offset their cost.

Under the circumstances it would have been somewhat miraculous if the primary roads had been built at that time as superhighways; it is just a little regrettable that the miracle did not occur, at least in regions of heavy traffic volume. Another policy deficiency, less justifiable and probably more serious, was the exclusion of cities and towns from the federal aid program, even if they were on the primary routes. The result was that the arterial highways disgorged their traffic onto city streets that had never been intended to handle it. Cities and towns had to take on this burden along with their own local traffic problems, sometimes with help from their states but with none from the federal government although their main streets were actually part of the primary road system. Through traffic normally was routed straight through the town or city center. If conditions became intolerable, bypasses were improvised on less heavily traveled side streets, frequently inadequately marked so that the motorist avoided downtown congestion at the risk of getting lost in the suburbs.

The Depression Years
The depression period of the 1930s produced conflicting ideas on highway policy. The initial reaction of public authorities was to reduce expenditures, and the curtailment of road construction was an obvious step. A decline in highway revenues was a further incentive in this direction, with the special feature that the sharpest decline was at the local level:[11] property taxes, in other words, were harder hit than user taxes. The use of the automobile, in fact, declined surprisingly little; from the peak of the

11 Sigvald Johannesson, "Highway Finances and Related Problems," in Labatut and Lane, eds., *Highways in Our National Life*, p. 212.

boom in 1929 to the bottom of the depression registrations dropped by only about 10 percent, from 26.5 million to 23.9 million.

Against this pressure to reduce expenditures was the fact that road building was a time-honored method of relieving unemployment—a much better one than digging ditches or raking leaves, because it made a lasting contribution to the capital resources of the society. Consequently, after the New Deal administration came into power, allocations for roads and streets as relief measures offset the decline in "regular" highway expenditures to the extent that by 1939 relief and recovery accounted for 80 percent of all federal expenditures for roads and 40 percent of the total outlay on highways from all sources. The actual figures are: all expenditures for roads, $2,371,317,000; total federal expenditures $1,171,422,000; relief agencies, $947,192,000.[12] Between 1933 and 1942 federal relief agencies spent $4 billion on roads and streets.[13] There was also a major change in national highway policy. In 1934 federal aid was at last made available for the urban segments of primary roads. More important, in 1936 federal aid was extended to secondary "feeder" roads: that is, roads classified as Rural Free Delivery routes, farm-to-market roads, or school bus routes. By the end of the decade these secondary federal aid highways came to 80,000 miles, and the relief agencies accounted for another 600,000 miles of road and street improvement.[14]

All this was certainly to the good, but was it good enough? While the improvement of secondary roads was unquestionably desirable, it can be argued that an opportunity was missed for a

12 Dearing, *American Highway Policy*, p. 61.
13 G. P. St. Clair and C. A. Steel, "Financing Highways in the United States," paper prepared for the Fifth Pan American Highway Congress, Lima, Peru, 1944.
14 *Highway Statistics: Summary to 1965*, p. 167; Charles L. Dearing and Wilfred Owen, *American Highway Transportation* (Washington, D.C.: The Brookings Institution, 1949), p. 107.

major step forward in the trunk highway network. As late as 1950 the 350,000 miles of primary state highway, 11 percent of the total rural road mileage, carried 74 percent of the rural traffic.[15] Only 5.5 percent of all rural roads had a traffic volume exceeding 500 vehicles a day. If the policy objective was to create a more effective national highway system, then better results would have been achieved if more of the federal effort had gone into the arterial roads where traffic volume was heaviest.

While the United States was black-topping country roads, Germany was building its *autobahnen*, the world's first genuine freeway system,[16] ostensibly for the same purpose as the American highway program—that is, to relieve unemployment. Admittedly, conditions in the two countries were different. Germany had no such mass use of automobiles as the United States, so that there was less need for improvement of secondary roads. The *autobahnen* may or may not have been planned with military use in mind.[17] The fact remains that Germany got a modern system of trunk highways at a time when costs were minimal, and the United States did not.

It could have been done, or at least a substantial start could have been made, without unduly sacrificing secondary road improvement. The technology was well understood, both from the work of the Germans and Italians and from the parkway experi-

15 Miller, "The Modern Highway in America," in Labatut and Lane, eds., *Highways in Our National Life*, p. 97.
16 Some clarification of terms is in order. The Bureau of Public Roads distinguishes between "freeway" and "expressway." Both are divided highways; the freeway has complete grade separation and complete control of access, while the expressway has limited control of access and may have some intersections at grade. A parkway may be either a freeway or an expressway; its distinguishing characteristic is that it excludes commercial vehicles. Local usage, however, frequently disregards the BPR's definitions. The highways designated as expressways in most cities are actually freeways.
17 A British historian, A. J. P. Taylor, in *The Origins of the Second World War*, 2nd ed. (New York: Fawcett World Library, 1968), p. 280, suggests that economic recovery was genuinely the motive for building the *autobahnen*.

ments at home. All that was needed was a policy decision and the allocation of funds. But the pressures that determined American highway policy worked in other directions. Insofar as relief was the purpose of road activity, "make-work" projects were considered to be more effective if they were local and small-scale, with, among other things, a minimum of "labor-saving" construction machinery. They were certainly more politically effective that way. There would undoubtedly have been an outcry against spending money on superhighways while men were out of work, even though the building of a network of such roads might well have been a far greater stimulus to the economy than what was actually done.

Beyond the relief consideration, there was a deeper-seated force urging improvement of local roads. A prominent American historian of the period explained it thus:

From about 169,000 miles in 1925, the federal aid system grew to 226,000 miles. Its trunk routes passed near to the homes of most Americans, yet touched only a small fraction of the three million miles of roads. The backwardness of these was emphasized as the farmer's car pushed through the mud and then speeded up on the hard surface of the arterials.[18]

This was a powerful voice demanding greater emphasis on secondary roads, too powerful for any popularly elected government to ignore, and in this depression decade only the federal government had the resources to act. Nor is the farmer to be criticized for seeking to have his particular needs satisfied, because no other group in American society has had its living conditions more thoroughly transformed for the better by the combination of motor vehicles and good roads. What the writer quoted here is really saying is that once people have experienced good roads, they will never again be content with bad ones.

What was done during the 1930s was a useful contribution to

18 F. L. Paxson, "The Highway Movement, 1916–1935," *American Historical Review*, vol. 51, no. 2 (January 1946), p. 250.

the nation's total highway network, and much of it would have had to be done sooner or later. The program, however, was uncoordinated, directed at specific needs and responding to specific pressures rather than fitting into a comprehensive national highway system. The most regrettable omission, to repeat, was that nothing was done at the national level to begin work on a system comparable to the present interstate highways.

One of the difficulties in the way of developing a really first-class highway system was that depression conditions encouraged diversion of highway revenues to other purposes. The gasoline tax in particular was almost too successful. It was a lucrative source of revenue, easy to collect, and its yield was far less affected by the depression than either property or income taxes. There was accordingly a strong temptation for legislative bodies to see in it a relatively easy source of funds for other than highway purposes. State after state yielded to the temptation as other revenues shrank. Between 1934 and 1939 the percentage of user taxes diverted to other purposes ranged from 13.8 to 16; the amounts rose from $122 million to $182 million annually.[19] If the diverted funds had been strictly allocated to meeting the emergency situations created by the depression, the practice would be easier to defend, but the data make it quite clear that most of the money simply went into general funds.

Since pressure for diversion of highway revenues is a recurring phenomenon, this previous experience is worth considering. To begin with, the practice involves unsound principles of taxation. A leading American transportation economist, Charles L. Dearing, in commenting on the policies of the 1930s, observes that there are two types of diversion. One is the borrowing or

19 Dearing, *American Highway Policy*, pp. 177–178. For a detailed account of controversy over diversion in one major state, see J. Allen Davis, "Raids on the Gas Tax," manuscript, Los Angeles, Automobile Club of Southern California, 1960.

appropriating for other purposes of funds collected specifically for highways; the other is the imposition of highway user taxes in order to raise revenue for nonhighway purposes.[20] The first, he says

in effect constitutes a breach of faith with road users. Either the user rates have been fixed so high that they produce more revenue than is required to maintain the road plant in satisfactory condition, or the plant is being permitted to deteriorate because of the diversion of road funds to other purposes.

The second involves discriminatory taxation. A user tax is equitable if the amount collected is immediately related to the service rendered. It is not equitable if it is imposed as a special tax on one section of the public with no corresponding benefit. Like any sales tax, gasoline and other highway user taxes are regressive in their incidence: that is, they bear most heavily on those least able to pay. They are therefore justified only if the payer gets a direct return for his money; that is, better roads that save travel time, promote safety, and reduce costs.

There are practical objections too to the diversion of highway funds. At the most elementary level, it is manifestly impossible to maintain an orderly program of improvement and maintenance if revenues are uncertain. A greater drawback was described in opposition to a proposal for diversion of California highway funds in 1933: "Experience in other States has demonstrated that whenever the door is opened to diversion of gas tax revenues to general purposes, the result is inevitably an increase in the rate of gas tax imposed." [21]

The diversion of highway taxes was energetically resisted on a scale which indicates that the opposition consisted of much more than a so-called "special-interest" group. Even before the depression, Minnesota (1920) and Kansas (1928) adopted anti-diversion amendments to their constitutions; since then twenty-

20 Dearing, *American Highway Policy*, pp. 178–179.
21 J. Allen Davis, "Raids on the Gas Tax," p. 39.

eight other states have followed.[22] In addition, the Hayden-Cartwright Act of 1934 provided that federal aid could be reduced by as much as one-third to states that diverted highway revenues.[23] These deterrents, however, have not prevented continued attempts to use road taxes as a convenient means of raising money for other purposes.

The Beginning of Modern Highways

One of the paradoxes of the 1930s was that, while national policy subordinated the development of trunk highways to the improvement of local roads, local activities provided the first full-fledged examples of through highways designed for high-speed motor vehicle traffic. First in point of time were Connecticut's Merritt and Wilbur Cross Parkways, which differed from the metropolitan parkways previously mentioned in that they were designed for long-distance rather than local traffic.

Planning for the Merritt Parkway began in 1926, with the idea of doing something to relieve the congestion on the Boston Post Road, U.S. 1, which carried its traffic straight through the densely populated communities stretching from New York along the Connecticut coast. Construction began in 1934, financed by a local bond issue, state aid, and the Public Works Administration, and the road, continuing New York's Hutchinson River Parkway northeastward, was completed for thirty-seven miles to the Housatonic River in 1937.[24] From there it was continued as the Wilbur Cross Parkway another thirty miles to Meriden, just south of Hartford. In order to finance the extension, both the Merritt and Wilbur Cross Parkways were made toll roads on a limited basis; toll gates were established so that through traffic

22 *Highway Statistics: Summary to 1965,* p. 87.
23 Public Law No. 393, 73rd Congress, H.R. 8781.
24 Wilfred Owen and Charles L. Dearing, *Toll Roads and the Problem of Highway Modernization* (Washington, D.C.: The Brookings Institution, 1951), p. 14.

had to pay, but local traffic could enter and exit at intermediate interchanges without charge.

The two parkways excluded commercial traffic. They were divided highways with grade separation and complete access control, and they provided one of the earliest demonstrations of the advantages of this kind of construction for arterial highways. Ten years after the Merritt Parkway was opened, the Connecticut State Highway Department was able to show that the average trip time for the full length of the Parkway was 67 minutes compared with 109 minutes on U.S. 1, and the fatality rate on Route 1 was four and a half times as great as on the Parkway.[25]

The first major express highway designed for all kinds of traffic was the Pennsylvania Turnpike, began by the Commonwealth of Pennsylvania as a project for relieving unemployment. The concept grew from the existence of an abandoned railroad right-of-way stretching across the state between Harrisburg and Pittsburgh. It was a relic of a railroad power struggle in the 1880s, when the Pennsylvania Railroad promoted the West Shore Railroad to parallel the New York Central between New York and Buffalo, whereupon the Central retaliated by chartering the South Pennsylvania Railroad in 1883 to invade the heart of its rival's territory. However, Morgan intervention produced a settlement in 1885 whereby the New York Central acquired the West Shore and agreed to discontinue the South Pennsylvania project. By that time much of the grading had been done, and nine tunnels had been bored through the mountains; then for fifty years the right-of-way lay there unused.

A proposal to use this partly prepared route for a toll road was introduced into the Pennsylvania legislature in 1935, and after a study financed by the Works Progress Administration, thereby emphasizing the relief objective, the Pennsylvania Turnpike Commission was created in 1937 with the necessary legal

25 *Ibid.*, p. 15.

authority to issue bonds and build and operate the highway.[26] At that time, however, there was so little understanding of the advantages of the controlled-access highway that few people believed that motorists would be willing to pay tolls to use one if alternative but conventional toll-free routes were available. The Turnpike Commission was unable to sell its bonds, and initial construction had to be financed by a grant of $29.2 million from the Public Works Administration and a loan of $40.8 million from the Reconstruction Finance Corporation.

With this assistance it was possible to open 160 miles of the Pennsylvania Turnpike, between the present Carlisle and Irwin Interchanges, on October 1, 1940. It used seven of the nine railroad tunnels, saving 9,000 feet of vertical climb compared with the alternate routes and permitting grades to be held to a maximum of 3 percent. One consequence was that the Pennsylvania Turnpike became particularly attractive to truck traffic. Tests on adjacent twenty-five-mile sections of the Turnpike and the old Lincoln Highway (U.S. 30) showed that a truck with a gross weight of 50,000 pounds required 50 percent more fuel on the old road than on the Turnpike and took ninety-three minutes on it as compared with forty-one on the Turnpike.[27] Increasing gross weights increased the Turnpike savings exponentially. For truck operations, therefore, the Turnpike toll charges were an investment rather than a cost.

Across the country there was another small but significant beginning, also stemming from local initiative—namely, the construction of the first freeway in Los Angeles. Of all major American cities, Los Angeles is the one most closely identified with the automobile, yet it entered the automobile era just as poorly

26 *Ibid.*, p. 7. It is necessary to understand that the limited-access highways required special legal sanction. Under the common law definition of a "public highway," owners of abutting property have the right of access. Special provision therefore had to be made to permit access control.
27 Owen and Dearing, *Toll Roads*, p. 9.

equipped as any other. As late as 1924 its downtown streets were narrow and disconnected.[28] A study made that year resulted in the building of a gridiron pattern of arterial streets and boulevards, whose effectiveness was diminished by lack of control over commercial development with direct access to the roadway, as well as by failure to relate street capacity to traffic volume.[29] This 1924 study was foresighted enough to suggest segregation of traffic by types, without proposing any way of doing so, along with some grade separation for intersections and elevated highways in congested areas.

In 1937 two reports were made on the increasingly complex traffic situation in Los Angeles, both very similar. A Regional Planning Commission recommended elevated highways, a radial freeway system, and bypass routes; the Automobile Club of Southern California proposed "motorways" to be incorporated into downtown buildings, and steps to eliminate interference between streams of traffic.[30] This must have been one of the very earliest proposals to suggest multipurpose utilization of freeway space.

The principal champion of the freeway was Lloyd Aldrich, who became Los Angeles city engineer in 1933. He grasped the essential element of transportation for a modern metropolis: the time required to complete a journey is more important than the distance traveled. He believed that the solution for Los Angeles was a system of trunk routes built on the pattern of the New York parkways, and he finally persuaded P. G. Winnett, the president of Bullock's department store, to raise $100,000 from the business community for a study along these lines.[31] The result was a re-

28 Paul T. McElhiney, "The Freeways of Metropolitan Los Angeles," Ph.D. thesis, School of Business Administration, University of California at Los Angeles, 1959.
29 *Ibid.*, p. 22.
30 *Ibid.*, pp. 26–31.
31 S. W. Taylor, "Freeways Shape the Modern City," in William Laas, ed., *Freedom of the American Road* (Detroit: Ford Motor Co., 1956), p. 70.

port late in 1939 proposing an initial 300 and eventually 600 miles of urban freeway. Under the stimulus of this and the earlier proposals Los Angeles, with state and PWA assistance, built the Pasadena Freeway (at first called Arroyo Seco) in 1940.[32]

The Second World War halted most major highway construction, but the critical steps had been taken. Connecticut and Pennsylvania had provided convincing demonstrations of what limited-access divided highways had to offer as trunk routes—saving of time, economy of operation, and greater safety. Los Angeles had introduced the urban freeway on a very limited scale, but it indicated a more efficient way to deal with metropolitan traffic.

32 A one-mile stretch of freeway through the Cahuenga Pass, between Hollywood and the San Fernando Valley, was also built at this time, later to be incorporated into the Hollywood Freeway.

II The Road Today

5 Economic Impact: Movement of People

The growth of the automobile industry and its place in the American economy have been thoroughly documented. It is an impressive record, but quite a straightforward one. Production and sales figures, earnings, employment and payroll data all constitute indexes by which automobile manufacturing can be rated among the nation's industries. What we are concerned with here is the economic effect of the combination of motor vehicle and highway as a completely novel method of transportation, and this is somewhat more difficult to measure accurately.

Transportation is a service, not a tangible commodity. The number of people or the volume of goods being moved can be counted, and the prices paid for these movements can be ascertained, but the results will at best give an approximation of the economic contribution of transportation. A study by the Port of New York Authority of future transportation needs for the New York metropolitan area points out that the values of transportation extend well beyond those directly enjoyed by the actual users of transportation.[1] Accessibility profoundly affects the value of property of any kind, and the economic well-being of a whole community will depend to a large extent on the adequacy of the transportation available to it. The cost of a specific transportation movement, or of a transportation facility, is therefore not necessarily the full measure of its economic value. A similar approach, this time dealing specifically with highway transportation, takes the position that highway transportation must be regarded as an intermediate rather than a final good, because most passenger and all truck trips are valued chiefly for what lies at the other end.[2]

1 Port of New York Authority, Comprehensive Planning Office, *Metropolitan Transportation—1980* (New York: Port of New York Authority, 1963), p. 4.
2 Herbert Mohring and Mitchell Harwitz, *Highway Benefits: An Analytical Framework* (Evanston, Ill.: Northwestern University, 1962), p. 26.

Is highway transportation then a special case with economic
effects that could not be equally well achieved by substituting
some other mode? When we combine the road with the mass-
produced motor vehicle, the answer is emphatically yes. Man
has always had transportation of some kind—his feet, if nothing
more. In the last hundred years or so, however, there has been
a drastic acceleration in the speed with which he can move, and
this has been a fundamental factor in economic and social
change.[3] Movement by road remained essentially at the slow pace
of previous millennia until the motor vehicle was introduced,
and this, as I have said before, transformed highway transportation into something entirely different. Speed, however, is not the
really distinctive feature of modern highway transportation. The
heart of the matter is neatly and succinctly presented by E. H.
Holmes, Director of the Office of Policy Planning in the Federal
Highway Administration, Department of Transportation: "But
highway transportation is different. It is a personalized form of
transportation primarily involving people moving themselves
and their goods in their own vehicles." [4]

Passenger Travel
This personalized transportation is the most striking consequence
of the automobile, and it is a direct creation of the combination
of mass-produced car and the hard-surfaced road. The combination first attained significant proportions in the 1920s when it
became evident that the motor vehicle was becoming a serious
threat to railborne passenger traffic, both intercity and intracity.
Since the subject of urban transportation will be considered sepa-

3 W. W. Carey, Jr., "Highway Research," *Transportation: A Service* (New
York: New York Academy of Science, 1968), p. 48, suggests that it has been
the most important single factor in social and economic change. The process
is certainly very recent. There was no significant change in the speed of
human travel until the steam railroad appeared about 1830.
4 Edward H. Holmes, "Highways in our Future," *Traffic Engineering* (May
1968), p. 34.

rately and in detail, we will be concerned here primarily with intercity passenger movement.

In 1920 railroad passenger travel in the United States reached the highest level it had ever attained, 47 billion passenger-miles, including commuting as well as long-distance trips.[5] It was the end of an era, although the fact went unrecognized at the time; never again would the railroad so thoroughly dominate domestic passenger transportation. The 1920 total was exceeded during the Second World War, but this was under abnormal conditions with very heavy troop movement and with other modes of travel severely curtailed. With this exception, the 1920 figure has not been equaled or exceeded.

The decline began almost immediately, as is shown in Table 5.1. In a period of prosperity noncommuting passenger mileage decreased. Commuter travel remained fairly steady; the slight increase that appears reflects longer trips rather than more passengers. Comparable figures for highway travel are fragmentary. During the 1920s the motor bus was a minor factor in intercity

Table 5.1 Railroad Passenger Traffic, 1922–1929 (in thousands of passenger-miles)

Year	Commutation	Other
1922	6,131,784	29,381,998
1923	6,400,779	31,607,400
1924	6,406,831	29,716,926
1925	6,592,186	29,367,767
1926	6,604,623	28,894,554
1927	6,649,871	27,006,452
1928	6,625,723	24,990,575
1929	6,898,473	24,180,151

These figures are for Class I steam railroads. Electric interurbans are excluded. Source: *Recent Social Trends in the United States*, Report of the President's Research Committee on Social Trends, p. 170. Copyright 1933 by the Research Committee on Social Trends, Inc. Used with the permission of McGraw-Hill Book Company.

5 Malcolm M. Willey and Stuart A. Rice, "The Agencies of Communication," *Recent Social Trends in the United States* (New York: McGraw-Hill Book Co.), p. 169.

passenger transportation, and the volume represented by private cars is guesswork. Nevertheless, there is no serious doubt that the decline in rail passenger traffic at this time was predominantly due to increasing use of private automobiles, encouraged by steady improvement of roads. As late as 1930 it was calculated that if all bus passengers had been carried by rail, the volume of rail passenger traffic would still have fallen well short of its high point of ten years before.[6]

More complete data became available when federal regulation was extended to interstate carriers other than rail, for highway traffic specifically through the Motor Carriers Act of 1935. Table 5.2 gives an adequate and revealing summary of what has happened since then. The figures deserve careful examination. They show a substantial increase in the total volume of intercity travel, which could be expected in view of the increase of population and the overall growth of the economy. The volume of travel, however, has increased much more rapidly than the population. Since 1920 the population of the United States has approximately doubled, while highway travel, measured in vehicle-miles, has multiplied ninefold.[7] Vehicle-miles have kept pace closely with the growth of the Gross National Product; they have, in fact, run slightly ahead for most of the years since 1930.[8] In recent years the public transportation agencies have been competing with each other rather than with the private automobile. As Table 5.2 indicates, passenger mileage totals for the public carriers remained reasonably constant for the years 1955 to 1960. In the same period, automobile travel also held steady at 88 to 90 percent of the total, and it has maintained this position since.

6 *Ibid.*, p. 178.
7 *Third Progress Report of the Highway Cost Allocation Study*, 86th Congress, 1st sess., House Document No. 91 (Washington, D.C.: Government Printing Office, 1959), p. 29.
8 *1968 National Highway Needs Report*, 90th Congress, 2nd sess., Committee Print (Washington, D.C.: Government Printing Office, 1968), p. 10.

The decline shown for bus and rail travel is manifestly accounted for by a shift to air transport rather than by automobile competition.

The only conclusion that can be drawn from the record of intercity passenger transportation is that the astonishing increase in automobile travel is predominantly self-generated. Practically all these billions of passenger-miles (vehicle-miles will give the same result) represent trips that were made because of the personal mobility conferred by the car-highway combination, and that would not have been made if only commercial transportation had been available. This element of automobile transportation was identified as long ago as 1931, in the *Recent Social Trends* study. One of these reports pointed out that the older travel media (rail and water) required the individual user to conform to schedules that he did not control, so that travel involved both physical and psychological impediments that did not exist with the private automobile.[9] For most people, therefore, rail or water travel over any distance was an event outside normal experience, whereas the motor vehicle offered "extensive and varied outlets" for travel of all kinds.

The phrase "extensive and varied outlets" is worth pondering because it pinpoints a feature of automobile travel that cannot be effectively demonstrated statistically. The private car is a multipurpose vehicle; this is an elementary fact that has to be periodically restated. It is impossible to separate intercity automobile trips by type; some are for business, some are for pleasure, but many, probably most, combine various purposes so that the participants themselves are not quite sure how to reply if they are questioned in a traffic survey.

Consider the professor at an eastern university who was invited to spend a summer at a California university. He and his

9 M. L. Willey and S. A. Rice, *Communication Agencies and Social Change* (New York: McGraw-Hill Book Co., 1933), pp. 47–48.

family made the trip by car. Westbound they visited friends in Pittsburgh and near St. Louis and swung off the main highway to see the Grand Canyon. In California they were able to use the car for weekend trips all the way from Yosemite to Tijuana.

Table 5.2   Intercity Travel by Mode, 1939–1967 (billions of passenger-miles)

Total			Private Carrier Auto		Air		Total	
Year	Amount	%	Amount	%	Amount	%	Amount	%
1939	311.0	100	275.4	88.6	0.1	—	275.5	88.6
1940	330.3	100	292.7	88.6	0.1	—	292.8	88.6
1941	371.7	100	324.0	87.2	0.1	—	324.1	87.2
1942	324.2	100	244.1	75.3	0.1	—	244.2	75.3
1943	295.7	100	176.0	59.5		—	176.0	59.5
1944	311.5	100	181.4	58.2		—	181.4	58.2
1945	347.6	100	220.3	63.4		—	220.3	63.4
1946	427.0	100	324.0	75.8	0.3	0.1	324.3	75.9
1947	428.9	100	347.8	81.1	0.6	0.1	348.4	81.2
1948	440.7	100	365.0	82.8	0.7	0.2	365.7	83.0
1949	479.4	100	409.4	85.4	0.8	0.2	410.2	85.6
1950	504.8	100	438.3	86.8	0.8	0.2	439.1	87.0
1951	571.2	100	498.1	87.2	0.9	0.2	499.0	87.4
1952	614.3	100	539.2	87.7	1.0	0.2	540.2	87.9
1953	651.4	100	575.8	88.4	1.2	0.2	577.0	88.6
1954	669.9	100	597.1	89.1	1.4	0.2	598.5	89.3
1955	712.5	100	637.4	89.5	1.5	0.2	638.9	89.7
1956	747.4	100	669.7	89.6	1.6	0.2	671.3	89.8
1957	748.3	100	670.5	89.6	1.8	0.2	672.3	89.8
1958	759.9	100	684.9	90.1	2.1	0.3	687.0	90.4
1959	764.8	100	687.4	89.9	2.1	0.3	689.5	90.2
1960	783.7	100	706.1	90.1	2.3	0.3	708.4	90.4
1961	791.3	100	713.6	90.2	2.3	0.3	715.9	90.5
1962	818.1	100	735.9	90.0	2.7	0.3	738.6	90.3
1963	852.6	100	765.9	89.8	3.4	0.4	769.3	90.2
1964	895.5	100	801.8	89.5	3.7	0.4	805.5	89.9
1965	920.3	100	817.7	88.8	4.4	0.5	822.1	89.3
1966	971.1	100	856.4	88.2	5.7	0.6	862.1	88.8
1967	1,020.6	100	889.8	87.2	7.0	0.7	896.8	87.9
1968	1,080.6	100	936.4	86.7	8.2	0.8	944.6	87.4
1969*	1,130.0	100	977.0	86.5	9.0	0.8	986.0	87.3

* TAA preliminary estimate.
Source: Transportation Association of America, *Transport Facts and Trends*, 6th ed., 1969.

They returned East by a route taking in the Grand Tetons and Yellowstone, plus a visit by one of the party to former Army buddies in Camp Carson, Colorado. This is an actual case; was it a business or pleasure trip?

Table 5.2 (*continued*)

Public Carrier Air		Bus		Rail		Water		Total	
Amount	%	Amount	%	Amount	%	Amount	%	Amount	%
0.8	0.3	9.5	3.0	23.7	7.6	1.5	0.5	35.5	11.4
1.2	0.4	10.2	3.1	24.8	7.5	1.3	0.4	37.5	11.4
1.7	0.5	13.5	3.6	30.6	8.2	1.8	0.5	47.6	12.8
1.7	0.5	21.3	6.6	55.1	17.0	1.9	0.6	80.0	24.7
2.0	0.7	25.9	8.8	89.9	30.4	1.9	0.6	119.7	40.5
2.9	0.9	27.3	8.8	97.7	31.4	2.2	0.7	130.1	41.8
4.3	1.2	27.4	7.9	93.5	26.9	2.1	0.6	127.3	36.6
7.2	1.7	26.9	6.3	66.3	15.5	2.3	0.6	102.7	24.1
7.1	1.7	24.8	5.8	46.8	10.9	1.8	0.4	80.5	18.8
6.8	1.5	24.6	5.6	41.9	9.5	1.7	0.4	75.0	17.0
7.8	1.6	24.0	5.0	36.0	7.5	1.4	0.3	69.2	14.4
9.3	1.8	22.7	4.5	32.5	6.5	1.2	0.2	65.7	13.0
12.0	2.1	23.6	4.1	35.3	6.2	1.3	0.2	72.2	12.6
13.3	2.2	24.7	4.0	34.7	5.7	1.4	0.2	74.1	12.1
16.2	2.5	24.4	3.7	32.3	5.0	1.5	0.2	74.4	11.4
18.2	2.7	22.0	3.3	29.5	4.4	1.7	0.3	71.4	10.7
21.3	3.0	21.9	3.1	28.7	4.0	1.7	0.2	73.6	10.3
23.9	3.2	21.7	2.9	28.6	3.8	1.9	0.3	76.1	10.2
26.3	3.5	21.5	2.9	26.3	3.5	1.9	0.3	76.0	10.2
26.4	3.5	20.8	2.7	23.6	3.1	2.1	0.3	72.9	9.6
30.5	3.9	20.4	2.7	22.4	2.9	2.0	0.3	75.3	9.8
31.7	4.0	19.3	2.5	21.6	2.8	2.7	0.3	75.3	9.6
32.3	4.0	20.3	2.6	20.5	2.6	2.3	0.3	75.4	9.5
34.8	4.2	21.8	2.7	20.2	2.5	2.7	0.3	79.5	9.7
39.4	4.7	22.5	2.6	18.6	2.2	2.8	0.3	83.3	9.8
45.5	5.1	23.3	2.6	18.4	2.1	2.8	0.3	90.0	10.1
53.7	5.9	23.8	2.6	17.6	1.9	3.1	0.3	98.2	10.7
63.7	6.5	24.6	2.5	17.3	1.8	3.4	0.4	109.0	11.2
80.2	7.9	24.9	2.4	15.3	1.5	3.4	0.3	123.8	12.1
93.0	8.6	26.2	2.4	13.3	1.2	3.5	0.3	136.0	12.5
102.0	9.0	26.0	2.3	12.0	1.0	4.0	0.4	144.0	12.7

The same thing could theoretically have been done by using one of the commercial transportation media, but only at greater cost and markedly less convenience. If it had not been possible to go by car, in all likelihood only the direct journey there and back would have been undertaken, and possibly it would not have been made at all.

This example can be multiplied many times. It may not be typical, since most intercity automobile mileage is composed of short rather than transcontinental trips, but it does illustrate that automobile travel is versatile in a way that no other mode can match. This helps to account for its fantastic growth.

Trailers and Mobile Homes

The type of personal mobility that the automobile brought with it has had a specialized extension in the passenger trailer, or, in its later and more elaborate form, the mobile home. The trailer has ancestors; in America the covered wagon of pioneer days was a mobile home, but definitely less mobile and far less habitable than its modern counterpart. In fact, the first mass-produced trailers were built by a Detroit firm called the Covered Wagon Company in 1933.[10] The trailers of those days were seldom more than twenty feet in length, compared with the fifty feet reached in the 1950s.

The production record is as follows: about 25,000 trailers were manufactured in 1937, the best year before the Second World War; in 1958 the output rose to 103,000 units; in 1968 it was 317,000 units.[11] Retail sales figures were[12]

10 Frank Fogarty, "Trailer Parks: The Wheeled Suburbs," *Architectural Forum*, vol. 111, no. 1 (July 1959), p. 127.

11 *The Automobile Between Wars* (Detroit: Automobile Manufacturers Association, 1944), Part 1, F. M. Reck, "How the Automobile Has Changed the Lives of People," p. 36; Fogarty, "Trailer Parks," p. 127; Harland Manchester, "Homes That Come Off the Assembly Line," *Readers Digest*, vol. 94, no. 564 (April 1969), p. 24.

12 Bureau of Public Roads, *Highways and Economic and Social Changes* (Washington, D.C.: Government Printing Office, 1964), p. 114.

1930	$ 1.3	million
1945	39	million
1954	324	million
1957	600	million

This is a striking record of growth. The rate of increase in dollar value of sales is considerably greater than is the number of units produced, signifying that, with due allowance for inflation, the trailer of the 1960s had become not only larger but also far more elaborate than its predecessor of the 1930s.

The change is symbolized in the term "mobile home," because what we are dealing with is not merely a towed vehicle. Trailers still come in a variety of sizes for a variety of uses. The most significant, economically and socially, is the use of the trailer as a movable residence. This function came into prominence during the Second World War when the government bought 38,000 twenty-five-foot trailers to house workers in war plants located where conventional housing was in short supply.[13] Thousands more were purchased privately for the same purpose, and the continuation of the housing shortage for some years after the war made for still greater acceptance of the mobile home.

The effect on the development of the trailer was that by the late 1950s the smaller units (up to twenty-five feet long) accounted for only a fifth of the total output.[14] The number of trailers used as housing rose from half a million in 1950 to 1.2 million in 1964, accommodating an estimated 3.5 million people.[15] This production of house trailers exceeded that of prefabricated houses and was a tenth of the total of new private housing started. The mobile home residents are a varied group, but about two-thirds are composed of skilled workers who move from job to job, some professional people in occupations that

13 Fogarty, "Trailer Parks," p. 127.
14 *Ibid.*
15 BPR, *Highways and Economic and Social Changes,* p. 114.

also call for a good deal of mobility (engineers, for example), and retired people. They are accommodated in 22,000 trailer parks, compared with 1,975 trailer "camps" in 1938, and they move on the average of about every twenty months. The large number of retired people living in house trailers accounts for a concentration of trailer parks in Arizona, California, and Florida.

Trailers have therefore become a substantial segment of the economy in their own right, and this segment has been brought into existence by the combination of motor vehicle and surfaced road. The ability to move house trailers economically about the country is a function of motorized highway transportation, even if the mobile home has now become so large that it has to be hauled by a truck tractor rather than by the family car. Without this particular form of mobility, most of these 3.5 million people would have to stay put. For many, this would mean lower earnings; for others, higher living costs. The development of the trailer, in short, is another illustration of the fact that freedom of movement is an economic asset.

The Growth of Bus Travel

The fact that intercity bus travel has leveled off since 1960 and has had a somewhat lesser proportion of the total volume of intercity traffic should not obscure the rise of the motor bus as a significant factor in long-distance transportation. Like the passenger automobile, the motor bus lends itself to a variety of uses. For intercity travel, the rise of the bus might be regarded as a revival of the stagecoach era, with a vehicle greatly superior in passenger capacity and speed. This is a romantic notion, but the differences between travel by stagecoach and travel by motor coach are so great as to make any attempt at comparison meaningless.

Intercity bus transportation began before the First World

War with short runs between communities where a need for public transportation was not met by rail or interurban service. One highly important start has been definitely pinpointed:

In 1912 an employee in an iron mine at Hibbing, Minnesota, became aware of a need for passenger transportation between Hibbing and South Hibbing. With a crudely fashioned passenger body on a truck chassis, he started the hauling of passengers. This was probably one of the first—if not the first—intercity common carrier bus lines in the United States. In 1916 the Missabe Transportation Company was formed and took over this route and established other lines in northern Minnesota. From this experiment in intercity bus transport, the Greyhound System has developed, and the employee who started the first route is now president of the Greyhound Corporation.[16]

The bus continued to be a truck chassis with a body mounted on it, usually with longitudinal (and uncomfortable) wooden seats, until the mid-1920s, when designed-for-the-purpose buses appeared, offering attractive appearance and comfortable riding. Between 1926, when accurate figures began to be available, and 1941 intercity bus travel grew from 4,375 million to 13,646 million passenger-miles, an increase of 211.9 percent.[17] There was also a marked increase in the length of bus runs. In the early 1920s thirty-five miles was regarded as a long haul, while in the late 1930s surveys in several states showed average runs ranging from 114 miles to 908.[18] The most rapid development of long-haul bus travel took place in the West, South, and Southwest, where there was rapid population growth in areas with limited rail facilities.

Since then, as Tables 5.2 and 5.3 show, the volume of intercity

16 *Highway Motor Transportation,* Report of Subcommittee on Motor Transport of the Railroad Committee for the Study of Transportation (Washington, D.C.: Association of American Railroads, 1945), p. 67. The founder of Greyhound was C. S. Wickman.
17 J. H. Parmelee and E. R. Feldman, "The Relation of Highway to Rail Transportation," in Jean Labatut and W. J. Lane, eds., *Highways in Our National Life: A Symposium* (Princeton, N.J.: Princeton University Press, 1950), p. 232.
18 *Highway Motor Transportation,* p. 152.

Table 5.3   Commercial Bus Travel, 1936–1968 (millions of vehicle-miles)

Year	Rural Roads	Urban Streets	Total
1936	733	1,031	1,764
1937	771	1,083	1,854
1938	771	1,083	1,854
1939	771	1,085	1,856
1940	808	1,136	1,944
1941	878	1,234	2,112
1942	1,036	1,456	2,492
1943	1,139	1,601	2,740
1944	1,327	1,866	3,740
1945	1,328	1,864	3,192
1946	1,414	1,987	3,401
1947	1,480	2,080	3,548
1948	1,474	2,074	3,548
1949	1,470	2,030	3,500
1950	1,394	1,877	3,271
1951	1,381	1,882	3,203
1952	1,444	1,750	3,194
1953	1,455	1,856	3,311
1954	1,372	1,657	3,026
1955	1,290	1,632	2,922
1956	1,175	1,595	2,922
1957	1,098	1,943	3,041
1958	1,060	1,854	2,914
1959	1,044	1,842	2,886
1960	1,023	1,849	2,886
1961	1,034	1,812	2,846
1962	1,030	1,826	2,856
1963	1,047	1,794	2,841
1964	1,089	1,803	2,892
1965	1,126	1,893	3,019
1966	1,137	1,871	3,008
1967	1,142	1,882	3,024
1968	1,152	1,879	3,031

Source: *Highway Statistics: Summary to 1965*, pp. 42–43; U.S. Department of Transportation, Bureau of Public Roads, *Highway Statistics: Summary to 1965, 1966, 1967, 1968.*

bus travel has approximately doubled. Some of this growth, but not all of it, represents traffic lost by the railroads. The statistics are based on real journeys by real people: to visit friends and relatives, to do business, to take vacations, and for multifarious other reasons. Since travel by bus has a strong appeal on grounds of low cost, it is certain that many of these journeys—an accurate estimate is impossible—were made because bus transportation was available and would not have been made otherwise. In addition, much of the traffic that shifted from rail to bus was traffic the railroads did not particularly want—that is, short-haul traffic requiring frequent stops, or low-density routes where rail service could not possibly be profitable.

The number of buses in service in the United States grew from 18,000 in 1925 to 314,000 in 1966.[19] Of those now in service three-fourths are school buses or in other nonrevenue uses, and three-fourths of the rest are employed in urban transit systems.[20] Thus only about one bus in sixteen operates on intercity routes, but these are the elite of the bus world in size and accommodations, and they log the largest total of passenger and vehicle miles.

A very important element in bus transportation is that, while it has to some extent been competitive with railroad passenger service, it has also been supplementary. The motor coach provided frequent and economical service on routes of low-density traffic, so that it became not only a substitute for but an improvement over passenger trains on lightly traveled branch lines. It also permitted discontinuance of lightly patronized main line stops. The railroads themselves were quick to realize these advantages. Substitution of motor coach for local passenger train service began in 1925, and in the same year the New Haven Railroad organized a bus subsidiary.[21] Within ten years some seventy railroads had followed this example. In addition, a number of the larger road companies acquired stock interests in national

19 *Highway Fact Book 1966* (Washington, D.C.: Transportation Association of America, 1967), p. 16.
20 *1968/Automobile Facts/Figures* (Detroit: Automobile Manufacturers Association, 1968), p. 21. The same proportions are shown in *Third Progress Report of the Highway Cost Allocation Study*, p. 11.
21 *Highway Motor Transportation*, p. 147.

bus systems such as Greyhound and Trailways, and this affiliation produced cooperation in scheduling and interchange of traffic.

The results were generally satisfactory, so that it seems regrettable that national transportation policy chose to treat the various carriers separately and to discourage rather than encourage the formation of coordinated transportation systems, providing traffic, in this case passenger travel, with a choice of services adapted to various conditions. Transportation is so vital an economic and social necessity that the overall welfare of the community sometimes requires an unprofitable system to be kept in operation because there is no satisfactory alternative. The canals built in the Middle West during the 1830s, for example, were financial failures, but they filled a need that could not be met otherwise at that time, and in so doing they contributed markedly to the economic growth of the regions they traversed.[22]

Today, however, with good roads and abundant motor vehicles, only very exceptional circumstances can justify maintaining an unprofitable operation for the transport of passengers. The exceptions occur in commuter railroad and rapid transit systems in large metropolitan areas. These are special situations that will be considered later in connection with the problems of urban transportation. In general, where other agencies are unable to provide for passenger transportation economically, the need can be met by highway vehicles, either buses or private automobiles. This is not to suggest that movement by road can or should replace other means of passenger transport, but merely to emphasize the fact that highway transportation by motor vehicle is readily adaptable to a variety of travel needs that cannot be as effectively met by other means.

22 See J. B. Rae, "Federal Land Grants in Aid of Canals," *Journal of Economic History,* vol. IV, no. 2 (November 1944), p. 167.

Highway Business

The record of passenger-miles and vehicle-miles accumulated in highway travel reveals a drama of mobility difficult to describe in its totality, but one fact that emerges with unmistakable clarity is that the impact on the American economy of these millions of people moving on the roads has been significant and stimulating. The growth of highway travel has a definite relationship to the increase in the Gross National Product, as Figure 5.1 shows. The chart itself does not tell what the cause-and-effect relationship is; that is, whether the increase in highway travel caused the GNP to rise, or whether greater productivity, and therefore affluence, made it possible for more people to travel. It appears to be essen-

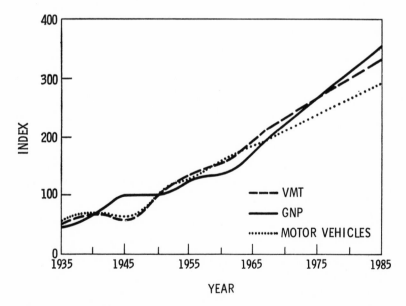

Figure 5.1 Gross National Product, motor vehicle registrations, and vehicle miles of travel (1950 = 100)
Source: U.S. Department of Transportation, *1968 National Highway Needs Report* (Washington, D.C.: Government Printing Office, 1968), p. 10.

tially a chicken-and-egg situation, except that where the influence of highway travel on the economy is concerned, there is no need to speculate; there is abundant evidence of how it has generated new economic activity.

First, of course, was the boom in road construction touched off by mass ownership and use of motor vehicles. This subject has been discussed in Chapter 4 and will be discussed again later. All that is necessary to mention here is that this enormous volume of road building (including the adjuncts such as bridges and tunnels) is economic activity on a massive scale that has been created directly by the automobile and that has been paid for largely by the automobile as well. Apart from the economic effects, the motor vehicle has also been responsible for some spectacular achievements in civil engineering that would not have been undertaken without the demand created by automobile travel. In the United States a very partial list would include the Golden Gate and Bay Bridges over San Francisco Bay, New York's Lincoln and Holland Tunnels, the bridges over the lower Hudson and the Verrazano Narrows, and the aerodynamically designed Mackinac Bridge.

The provision of highway facilities for the mobile millions was just the first step in meeting their needs. There had to be service for both cars and people. The servicing of cars has come a long way from the days when the motorist had to rely on the general store for his gasoline and the local blacksmith for emergency repairs. Parts and supply dealers and garages equipped for repairs to motor vehicles date back to 1899, and a station for storing and dispensing gasoline was opened in New York City in 1901.[23] From this start the business of keeping motor vehicles in operation has grown until in 1967 it included 211,473 gasoline service stations with 733,542 employees and 139,611 service and

23 Automobile Manufacturers Association, Inc., *Automobiles of America*, 2nd rev. ed. (Detroit: Wayne State University Press, 1968), pp. 21, 27.

Table 5.4   Highway Business, 1967

Type	Number of Establishments	Employees	Sales (thousands)
Motor vehicles, accessories, and parts: retail	87,232	834,815	$47,797,194
Motor vehicles, equipment: wholesale	28,895	307,732	36,583,709
Gasoline service stations	211,473	732,542	17,759,917
Petroleum bulk stations, terminals	30,873	151,613	21,485,414
Repair services, garages	139,611	425,340	5,443,938
Motels, tourist courts, trailer parks	51,353	242,821	2,153,201

Source: Automobile Manufacturers Association, Inc., *Automobiles of America*, 2nd rev. ed. (Detroit: Wayne State University Press, 1968), pp. 255–256.

repair establishments with 425,340 employees.[24] The number of jobs comes to 1,115,882, and it does not include 834,815 employees of the 87,232 dealers in motor vehicles, parts, and accessories, most of whom provide service facilities also. (See Table 5.4.)

The people had to be taken care of as well as their cars. Roadside tourist facilities scarcely existed in 1920. The earliest major development was the free camping ground, with running water and other elementary facilities. These were sometimes provided by communities, but more often by an owner who expected his profit in the sale of supplies and services to motorists. In time these facilities were superseded by tourist camps with cabins and cottages, and by 1930 many such camps in areas of heavy tourist travel offered services comparable to good hotels.[25]

However, the principal recourse of the traveling motorist of that era was most likely to be one of the thousands upon thousands of private homes that displayed signs reading "rooms for tourists" or "transients," and did an enormous but unmeasured

24 *Ibid.,* pp. 255–256.
25 Willey and Rice, *Communication Agencies and Social Change,* pp. 65–68.

volume of business. These tourist homes, in fact, were just as much ancestors of the motel as the tourist camps, because the successful owners were likely to expand their facilities. The term "motel" was not in common use before the Second World War. The more pretentious establishments of those days were likely to call themselves "tourist courts," and their services extended to serving some meals to their guests. They did not, as a rule, operate public restaurants. The roadside restaurant business was also booming in response to the accelerating volume of highway travel, and the wise restaurant proprietor sought to locate in the vicinity of tourist accommodations, but these were separate enterprises.

The growth of automobile-oriented tourist facilities was substantial enough in these early days to give some concern to operators of conventional hotels, although the data on the subject are uncertain. After 1920 the average daily number of hotel guests did not keep up with the growth of population,[26] a fact that may indicate a diversion of patronage to the tourist camps and homes. On the other hand, the new travel generated by the automobile—countless trips made by people who would have had to stay home if they had not had low-cost transportation and accommodation—accounts sufficiently for the rapid expansion of tourist accommodations; their business, that is, came predominantly from people who would not have been using hotels in any event.

The transformation of the tourist court or camp into the motel began in earnest after the Second World War and developed into really big business after 1950. The beginning stages have been described thus:

Highway or motor hotels, call them what you will, got their really big impetus from World War II. The same pent-up demand which created a boom in residential housing started over-

26 *Ibid.*, p. 69.

night housing on the highways. The construction boom in motels was phenomenal. In many cases overbuilding took place.

Almost all of the early motels were "Ma and Pa" establishments. Up to 1950 their average size was less than 25 units, most were 10 or 15. It was easy to become a motel keeper. Virtually all you needed was a few thousand dollars, a tract of farmland on the outskirts of town; and since operating overhead could be kept low by Pa acting as room clerk, cashier, and general handyman, while Ma was the maid of all work, in many respects running a motel was better than working at a job. Many couples who had reached retirement age chose to invest their savings in a motel and by-and-large they made out okay, too. At the height of the boom and with good business, you were able to pay off all indebtedness in three years. If you were not that lucky, it took no more than five years of just ordinary business to amortize your investment.[27]

After 1950 this situation changed rapidly. The burgeoning motel business attracted the attention of the major hotel chains; in 1950 the author of the passage just quoted made a survey of motel potentialities for the Hotel Statler Company. As it turned out, the hotel men moved slowly into this untested field, preferring to stay in operations where their experience counted most and appealing to the highway travelers by offering free parking and otherwise adapting their facilities to the tastes of the motoring public. More important was the growth of combination in the motel business. This took two forms: cooperating motels (Quality Courts, Best Western, and so on) with joint services for advertising and reservations, and a requirement of specified standards to be maintained in order to qualify for membership; and chains (Travelodge, Holiday Inns) operating predominantly on a franchise basis, with the central authority providing advice, architectural plans, and sometimes assistance with financing and management. By 1960 Travelodge had 110 motels; Howard Johnson, expanding from a highway restaurant chain into motels,

27 Edwin B. Dean, "Practicalities in Motel Development," *Urban Land*, vol. 19, no. 10 (November 1960), p. 3. Information is reprinted from Urban Land, Copyright, ULI—the Urban Land Institute, 1200 18th Street, N.W., Washington, D.C. 20036.

had 89; and Holiday Inns had 160, with 15,000 rooms, putting in next to the Hilton and Sheraton hotel chains in size.[28]

The next decade witnessed further significant growth. For one thing the motel, hitherto located in small towns or the outskirts of large ones, began to move into urban centers. The intown motel, to be economically viable, had to be bigger than its country cousins—at least 100 rooms, plus on-premises parking.[29] The trend helps to account for the fact that after 1965 the number of motels decreased but the number of rooms increased; in 1968 the average number of rooms per motel was 60, compared with 25 in the late 1950s.

From various sources it appears that in the five years from 1963 to 1968 the number of motels and motor courts grew by almost 50 percent, approximately 41,500 to 60,500, while their gross earnings trebled, from just over $2 billion to $6 billion.[30] The Bureau of Public Roads gives $11 billion as the annual earnings for hotels and motels in 1964.[31] By any standard the accommodation of travelers is a large-scale business operation, and most of it is highway-generated. Motels exist for highway travelers, except perhaps for a few located near major airports. For hotels the situation is not substantially different. Airport hotels and a few downtown hotels in large cities might just survive without the patronage brought by private automobile; the rest, the great majority, feel obligated to offer convenient parking and frequently to add motel-type annexes or special entrances for automobile travelers. Otherwise they lose business to the intown motel, or motor inn, including even types of business that have traditionally been

28 *Ibid.*
29 Stephen W. Brenner, "The New Motel from the Ground Up," *Urban Land,* vol. 29, no. 9 (October 1965), p. 3.
30 Automobile Club of Southern California, *Auto Club News Pictorial,* vol. 59, part 2, no. 6 (June 1968), p. 11; the 1963 earnings, taken from *AMA, Automobiles of America,* p. 256, are for trailer parks as well as motels and motor courts.
31 *Highways and Economic and Social Changes,* p. 155.

associated with hotels. As the 1960s began, for instance, an increasing proportion of motel patrons consisted of salesmen and businessmen, and facilities were being provided for group meetings, with the attraction of convenient access by car.[32]

Summary

There are other aspects of the economic effects of mass mobility, most of them important enough in themselves to be developed in detail later. The increased freedom of individual movement has permitted a wider range of opportunities for seeking jobs. This has been particularly important in the development of cities, but it has general implications also. About three-fourths of all trips by private automobile are made for economic reasons, 46 percent for travel to and from work or to make business calls, and 29.5 percent on family business, such as shopping.[33] Trips by public highway transportation—bus or taxi—are not included.

More could be added, but the evidence already appears to be conclusive that the freedom of personal movement conferred by the automobile and the surfaced road has been a major contributor to economic growth. Where the movement of people is concerned, the stimulus has been most pronounced in service enterprises—storage, maintenance, and repair of motor vehicles, gasoline stations, the provision of food and lodging for travelers, and public transportation by bus or taxi. There is also an intermediate stage between public and private transportation in car and truck rental agencies, over 7,000 in number. The most significant feature of this aspect of the impact of highway transportation on the economy is that the service enterprises offer the most promising prospect for maintaining a high level of employment, since they remain essentially dependent on human effort rather than on mechanization and automation. Highway-gener-

32 Dean, "Practicalities in Motel Development," p. 4.
33 AMA, *Automobiles of America*, p. 254.

ated and highway-oriented business constitutes an impressive segment of this vital area of economic activity; in wholesale, retail, and service operations it accounts for 18 percent of the number of establishments, 15 percent of the total employment, and 20 percent of the sales.[34]

34 *Ibid.,* p. 256, based on 1963 Census of Business.

6 Movement of Goods

More freight is carried in the United States today by motor truck than by any other agency. In ton-miles the truck is second to the railroad because most truck hauls are local rather than long-distance, in direct contrast to rail hauls, but in total tonnage the truck is well ahead. Approximately 75 percent of all freight goes by truck.[1] The movement of goods has in fact been transformed even more drastically than the movement of people by the development of motorized highway transportation. Truck registration in 1910 was 2 percent of motor vehicle registrations; in 1956 it was 16 percent and has remained at about this proportion since.[2]

This rise in the ratio of trucks among motor vehicles in service is eloquent testimony to the economic impact of this new technology for the carriage of freight. Until it was introduced, road transport was, as the earlier chapters have pointed out, a slow and expensive method of hauling goods. This fact can be emphasized for very recent times by the conclusions of an American engineer engaged in improving Turkey's road system just after the Second World War. He checked the cost of carriage by the oxcarts that were still in common use and reported:

The carts usually haul a quarter-ton of freight five miles a day, or a total of one and one-quarter ton miles.

The cart driver gets $1.25 for a long day's work. So wages alone make the cost $1 per ton-mile—not counting the cost of the ox and cart, profit for the owner, and other items.

This $1 per ton-mile cost applies roughly to all forms of primitive hauling—to men carrying loads on their backs, on donkeys, or on camels.

In contrast, the usual charge for truck hauls in the U.S. is less than 3 cents per ton-mile. This covers wages of all employees of

1 National Highway Users Conference, *The Highway Transportation Story* (Washington, D.C.: National Highway Users Conference, 1954), p. 12.
2 *Third Progress Report of the Highway Cost Allocation Study*, 86th Congress, 1st sess., House Document No. 91 (Washington, D.C.: Government Printing Office, 1959), p. 30.

the trucking firms, cost of the vehicle and its operation, and profit of the firm.

Where the ox-cart driver gets $1.25 for a long day's work, U.S. truck drivers get $16.

But a typical 10-hour truck haul carries 10 tons of freight 300 miles (or 3,000 ton-miles). So the driver earns just over half a penny a ton-mile, while the ox-cart driver is paid $1 per ton-mile.

To haul potatoes 20 miles in Turkey costs more than the price the farmer gets for them.[3]

This was primitive transportation, but a comparison of American conditions leads to the same conclusion. The Department of Agriculture found the ton-mile cost of wagon carriage in 1920 to be 33 cents, as against 15 cents for trucks[4]—this with roads and trucks both decidedly inferior to what they became later.

The Rise of Truck Transportation

The truck was a little slower than the passenger car to come into prominence, as is indicated by the minuscule proportion of trucks in the registration totals as late as 1910. They are not even listed separately in the production and registration statistics until 1904 and 1905. What there was of truck traffic at that time consisted of a handful of delivery vans on city streets and a very few bold souls attempting short hauls of farm products. Because they carried heavier loads, trucks were handicapped more than passenger cars by the poor quality of the roads. The trucks themselves were crude and clumsy, with the further disadvantage that they rode on solid tires, which had deleterious effects on both vehicles and loads—to say nothing of road surfaces. Yet despite these drawbacks, the promise of the future was there. In one midwestern city fourteen motor-driven vans replaced fifty horse teams for delivering newspapers,[5] and this experience was typical.

3 *Automobile Facts,* vol. 8, no. 5 (May 1949), p.4.
4 L. W. Moses and H. F. Williamson, Jr., "The Location of Economic Activity in Cities," *American Economic Review,* vol. 57, no. 2 (May 1967), p. 214.
5 Automobile Manufacturers Association, *Lifelines* (Detroit, 1966), p. 4.

Pneumatic truck tires were first experimented with in the United States in 1916 but did not receive general acceptance until the 1920s. Paul W. Litchfield, president of Goodyear Tire and Rubber and the man who persisted with pneumatic tires for trucks in the face of considerable discouragement, summed up the effect of this innovation thus:

It brought into existence the great trucking industry, rivaling the railroads (and buses, as well), and in so doing gave America the most effective transportation system of any nation, creating new values for every farmer and business house, and bringing the school bus to every door—and creating a million jobs which did not previously exist.[6]

The road-building program of the 1920s helped too. By the end of that decade truck transport was recognizably a feature of increasing importance in the American economy. *Recent Social Trends* noted the emergence of "economic regionalism"—that is, a grouping into trade areas, focused on a metropolitan center —and maintained that this was basically a product of motor transportation. As a more flexible carrier than the railroad, the truck stimulated more intensive exploitation of local resources and more direct relationships between the city and its surrounding settlements.[7]

The truck quickly established its ascendancy, which it has retained ever since, as the most economical short-haul freight carrier. On short hauls terminal costs become a disproportionately high part of the total cost, and trucks have the great advantage of having lower terminal costs than either rail or water transport. A survey by the Bureau of Public Roads in 1930 showed that this feature was well marked in areas other than intracity transportation:

Truck traffic on rural highways is predominately a short haul movement.—Only about 6 per cent of all trucks travel less than

6 P. W. Litchfield, *Industrial Voyage* (Garden City, N.Y.: Doubleday and Co., 1954), pp. 141–142.

7 *Recent Social Trends in the United States,* Report of the President's Research Committee on Social Trends, vol. 1 (New York: McGraw-Hill Book Co., 1933), p. 459.

20 miles per day; 15.5 per cent travel from 40 to 59 miles; and 13.8 per cent from 60 to 79 miles per day. Nearly 50 per cent of all trucks, therefore, travel less than 80 miles per day, while 58.3 travel less than 100. . . . While 80 miles is not usually considered a short distance, it must be remembered that this distance is the mileage per day on rural highways, and that it usually represents one or more round trips from origin to destination.[8]

This basic pattern has persisted through an exponential expansion of truck transportation, in numbers and sizes of trucks, volume of freight carried, and miles traveled. Twenty years later, the average rural truck load was about four tons, and the average rural truck trip was seventeen miles. At that time (1949) the average rail freight haul was 400 miles, and the average freight-car load was 40 tons; water hauls averaged 200 miles and air freight 500 miles. The vital service performed by the rural truck was that it carried these small loads for relatively short distances *to and from locations not served by other kinds of transport.*[9]

The impact of truck transportation on rural economy is a subject for further discussion, and it will be considered later. These short runs and light loads differ from the growth of long-distance heavy trucking, typified by the big tractor-trailer combinations that have become a familiar sight on American highways. Trailer trucks were almost unknown before the Second World War; by 1960 over a million were in operation. Even so, in the early 1960s three-fifths of the 12 million trucks in service were still small vehicles of less than four tons' capacity. Small and medium-sized single-unit trucks accounted for 60 percent of the total mileage of truck transport but only 25 percent of the ton-miles— clear evidence of small loads—whereas the long-distance trailer trucks logged 40 percent of the mileage but 75 percent of the ton-miles.[10]

Separating intercity truck traffic from strictly local, rural, or

8 *Ibid.*
9 *Automobile Facts,* vol. 8, no. 6 (June 1949), p. 6.
10 J. B. Rae, *The American Automobile* (Chicago: University of Chicago Press, 1965), p. 192.

urban hauls gives a somewhat different picture. To interpret the data properly it is necessary to understand that long-distance truck operations fall into three categories: the common carrier, normally operating on a fixed route and accepting whatever freight is offered; the contract carrier, operating under specific agreements or charters; and the private truck, carrying goods only for the business concern that owns it. The first two are subject to federal regulation under the Motor Carriers Act of 1935 if they are engaged in interstate commerce; the private trucks are not, except for regulations regarding safety and marking of vehicles. All truck transportation is of course subject to state regulation.

In the mid-1960s 42 percent of the intercity tonnage of manufactured products moved by truck, 32.6 percent by rail, and 25.4 percent by other means, principally pipeline and waterway.[11] If petroleum and coal products are excluded because they constitute a heavy volume moving in a very specialized pattern, the ratios become 51.7 percent for trucks, 42.7 percent for rail, and 5.6 percent for the others. The trucks have a lower proportion of the ton-mile totals. The average length of haul for the various media at the time when these percentages were calculated (1963) was[12]

Motor carrier (common and contract)	250 miles
Private truck	126 miles
Rail	494 miles
Air	878 miles
Water	773 miles
Other	642 miles

Truck and Train

Translating these figures into an overall estimate of impact on the nation's economy involves a good many complex factors. The

11 *Motor Truck Facts, 1966* (Detroit: Automobile Manufacturers Association, 1966), pp. 32–33.
12 *Ibid.,* p. 34, quoting 1963 Census of Transportation.

expansion of truck transportation is a demonstrable fact, but has this been a cause or an effect of economic growth, and have the trucks' gains been made merely at the expense of other carriers? Table 6.1 shows a steady increase in the total volume of intercity freight movement, which could be expected to accompany growth in population and the GNP. It also shows a general increase in the aggregate ton-miles carried by all the major transportation media but a shift in the proportion carried by each. The railroad share has declined, while trucking has gained appreciably since 1950 but not since 1960. The most marked recent advances have been registered by the airlines and pipelines.

Without a doubt truck competition did cut into railroad traffic, and it hurt because the highway carriers were most competitive in taking the high-value cargoes that traveled at classification rates, rather than the bulk freight that took the lower commodity rates. However, as with passenger transportation, the evidence is convincing that much of the traffic taken from the railroads by the highway carriers was traffic that could be handled more efficiently or more economically by truck—for the most part less-than-carload lots and relatively short hauls. The greatest advantage possessed by the truck is described thus:

The flexibility of the vehicle enables the motor carrier to adapt its service closely to the needs of its patrons. Private and contract carriers can accommodate their movements to any hours desired by the shipper, who, for example, often desires later closing hours for receiving freight than can be provided by rail. The possibility of routing a shipment by motor vehicle to its destination without delays in transit expedites delivery. A result of this flexibility displayed by motor transport has been the carrying of reduced inventories by retail merchants.[13]

The last sentence of this statement deserves special attention because it is such an excellent illustration of the effect of an im-

13 *Highway Motor Transportation,* Report of Subcommittee on Motor Transport of the Railroad Committee for the Study of Transportation, Association of American Railroads (Washington, D.C.: Association of American Railroads, 1945), p. 101.

provement in transportation technology. The kind of service described here can be offered only by a motorized highway carrier, and because it became available, merchants could reduce inventories—a clear economic benefit. A more efficient and economic method of moving goods means a more economic employment of resources and consequently a gain for the economy as a whole, even if one result is a loss of business for another means of transport. This is a general proposition; it is not intended to suggest that highway transport is in all respects superior to rail or other media. It is most certainly not. Each of the major transportation media has its advantages for certain purposes; the essential principle for maximizing the economic benefits of transportation is that the shipper, or the customer, should be able to choose the method best suited to his needs.

The railroads themselves early realized the value of the truck for providing door-to-door service. Several lines began to offer free pickup and delivery in the early 1920s, usually by contract with independent truck operators.[14] Shortly afterward several railroads incorporated truck subsidiaries, as they were doing with buses, to replace unprofitable branch line and local main-line services. Even at this time, therefore, the railroads had some gains from truck transportation to compensate for what they were losing.

The statistics of intercity freight movement suggest that since the late 1950s the decline in the railroads' share of the total ton-mileage has been due to competition from sources other than the highway carriers. During this period, in fact, the railroad gain in aggregate tonnage has been materially assisted by cooperation with truck transport in the form of "piggybacking," including both TOFC (trailer-on-flat-car) or COFC (container-on-flat-car) operations. The former refers to placing a truck trailer

14 *Ibid.*, p. 82. Shippers who chose to do their own trucking were compensated for it.

Table 6.1   Intercity Freight by Modes (including mail and express and in billions of ton-miles)*

	Rail		Truck		Oil Pipeline		Great Lakes		Rivers and Canals		Air		Total
	Amount	%	Amount	%	Amount	%	Amount	%	Amount	%	Amount	%	
1939	339	62.3	53	9.7	56	10.3	†76	14.0	†20	3.7	0.01	0.00	544
1940	379	61.3	62	10.0	59	9.5	96	15.5	22	3.6	0.02	0.00	618
1941	482	62.4	81	10.5	68	8.8	114	14.8	27	3.5	0.02	0.00	772
1942	645	69.5	60	6.5	75	8.1	122	13.1	26	2.8	0.04	0.00	928
1943	735	71.3	57	5.5	98	9.5	115	11.2	26	2.5	0.05	0.00	1,031
1944	747	68.7	58	5.3	133	12.2	119	10.9	31	2.8	0.07	0.01	1,088
1945	691	67.2	67	6.5	127	12.4	113	11.0	30	2.9	0.09	0.01	1,028
1946	602	66.6	82	9.1	96	10.6	96	10.6	28	3.1	0.08	0.01	904
1947	665	65.3	102	10.0	105	10.3	112	11.0	35	3.4	0.11	0.01	1,019
1948	647	61.9	116	11.1	120	11.5	119	11.4	43	4.1	0.15	0.01	1,045
1949	535	58.3	127	13.8	115	12.5	98	10.7	42	4.6	0.20	0.02	917
1950	597	56.2	173	16.3	129	12.1	112	10.5	52	4.9	0.30	0.03	1,063
1951	655	55.6	188	16.0	152	12.9	120	10.2	62	5.3	0.34	0.03	1,177
1952	623	54.4	195	17.0	158	13.8	105	9.2	64	5.6	0.34	0.03	1,145

1953	614	51.0	217	18.0	170	14.1	127	10.6	75	6.2	0.37	0.03	1,203
1954	557	49.6	213	19.0	179	15.9	91	8.1	83	7.4	0.38	0.03	1,123
1955	631	49.5	223	17.5	203	15.9	119 (105)	9.3	98 (64)	7.7	0.49	0.04	1,274
1956	656	48.4	249	18.4	230	17.0	111 (94)	8.2	109 (74)	8.0	0.58	0.04	1,356
1957	626	46.9	254	19.0	223	16.7	117 (101)	8.8	115 (79)	8.6	0.68	0.05	1,336
1958	559	46.0	256	21.1	211	17.4	80 (62)	6.6	109 (73)	9.0	0.70	0.05	1,216
1959	582	45.3	279	21.7	227	17.7	80 (68)	6.2	117 (79)	9.1	0.80	0.06	1,286
1960	579	44.1	285	21.8	229	17.4	99 (81)	7.5	121 (82)	9.2	0.89	0.07	1,314
1961	570	43.5	296	22.7	233	17.8	87 (67)	6.6	123 (84)	9.4	1.01	0.08	1,310
1962	600	43.8	309	22.5	238	17.3	90 (66)	6.6	133 (90)	9.7	1.30	0.09	1,371
1963	629	43.3	336	23.1	253	17.4	95 (68)	6.5	139 (94)	9.6	1.30	0.09	1,453
1964	666	43.2	356	23.1	269	17.4	106 (73)	6.9	144 (102)	9.3	1.50	0.10	1,543
1965	709	43.3	359	21.9	306	18.7	110 (76)	6.7	152 (110)	9.3	1.91	0.12	1,638
1966	751	43.0	381	21.8	333	19.1	116 (81)	6.6	164 (117)	9.4	2.25	0.13	1,747
1967	731	41.4‡	389	22.0‡	361	20.5	107 (75)‡	6.1‡	174 (128)‡	9.9‡	2.59	0.15	1,765‡
1968	757	41.2‡	396‡	21.5‡	391‡	21.3‡	112 (75)‡	6.1‡	179 (139)‡	9.7‡	2.90‡	0.16‡	1,838‡
1969‖	780	41.0	404	21.3	411	21.6	116 (79)§	6.1	186 (146)§	9.8	3.20	0.17	1,900

* Includes both for-hire and private carriers.

† See source data for figures in parenthesis, which are based on different reporting techniques.

‡ Revisions due to revisions published by the basic sources.

§ Breakdown estimated by TAA.

‖ Preliminary TAA estimate.

Source: Transportation Association of America, *Transport Facts and Trends*, 6th ed., 1969.

on a railroad flatcar for the line haul, with pickup and delivery handled as a road movement; the latter uses a container that is a trailer body demountable from its wheels.

Piggybacking has been especially useful for high-value goods and perishable commodities, where rapid, damage-free movement is necessary. It is most economical for hauls long enough to justify transferring the load, but not so long that the terminal costs become unimportant. For runs up to at least 200 miles it is more economical to make the entire trip by road; beyond 1,500 miles the greater efficiency of stowage in an ordinary boxcar (piggybacking unavoidably has more waste space and weight) will tend to offset the reduced terminal costs of piggybacking.[15] The optimum distance at present appears to be about 1,000 miles. In 1965 piggybacking (strictly TOFC or COFC and not such variants as automobile rack cars) was 3.5 percent of total railroad carloadings, but it was displaying an annual growth rate of 10 to 15 percent over a period when regular carloadings were declining.[16]

The great advantages of door-to-door containerized shipment without breaking bulk have led logically from piggybacking to "fishybacking"—that is, carrying truck trailers on ocean-going freighters. An account of an actual operation provides a lucid description of this new technique in transportation:

A New York manufacturer wants to send a shipment of goods to San Francisco. A particular "fishyback" company drives a semi-trailer to the manufacturer's shipping dock and leaves it there. The manufacturer loads the trailer and seals it, thus taking responsibility for the shipment. The trailer, 35 feet long, consists of a container, or box that can be lifted off the chassis underneath (as in railroad COFC). When the goods are loaded and sealed, the "fishyback" company hooks on a tractor and takes the semi-trailer to its fine new docks at Elizabeth, New Jersey. Here the container is lifted from the chassis by a traveling

15 P. J. Schwind, "The Geography of Railroad Piggyback Operations," *Traffic Quarterly*, vol. 21, no. 1 (January 1967), p. 243; *Metropolitan Transportation—1980*, p. 227; Edgar M. Hoover and Raymond Vernon, *Metropolis 1985* (Cambridge, Mass.: Harvard University Press, 1960), p. 66.
16 Schwind, "Railroad Piggyback Operations," p. 239.

gantry crane and deposited either on the deck or in the hold of the ship. If the ship happens to be one of the company's new Jumbos, 476 of these trailer-containers can be loaded and unloaded in 12 hours, an almost incredible performance.

At San Francisco, the container is lifted from the ship, loaded onto another chassis, and delivered to the customer in town.[17]

Over the years, in short, the motor truck has become an invaluable supplement to other agencies of transportation without ceasing to be a competitor in its own right. The shipper now not only has a choice among agencies but also has the option of sending his goods in a way that combines for the same shipment the advantages of several methods of transportation. The ability to optimize the movement of freight in this way is directly traceable to the motor truck, specifically the tractor-trailer combination, which alone makes possible this fusing of transport media. The economic benefits to be derived from this development are just beginning to be realized.

Flexible Mobility

Highway transportation by motor truck is more than a supplement to other transport agencies; it is a method of transportation with its own distinctive qualities and characteristics. It is even more than this; it is a medium which permits movements of goods that otherwise would not be economically possible, and therefore it is a creator of economic activity and opportunities. (See Table 6.2.)

In general, small business has been the principal beneficiary of truck transportation. For manufacturing, this claim is validated by two analyses of the 1963 Census of Transportation.[18] The first shows that there is an inverse ratio between the high-

17 AMA, *Lifelines,* pp. 24–25.
18 These studies are Donald E. Church, "Impact of Size and Distance on Intercity Highway Share of Transportation of Industrial Products," and Walter F. Buhl, "Intercity Highway Transport Share Tends to Vary Inversely with Size of Plant," *Highway Research Record,* no. 175 (Washington, D.C.: Highway Research Board, 1967), pp. 1–14.

Table 6.2   Relation of Motor Truck Use and Gross National Product, 1937–1958

Year	Gross National Product	Intercity Truck Ton-Miles	Ratio: Truck Ton-Miles per Dollar of Gross National Product
	Billions of 1954 dollars	*Billions*	
1937	183.5	32.3	0.18
1938	175.1	37.0	0.21
1939	189.3	52.8	0.28
1940	205.8	62.0	0.30
1941	238.1	81.4	0.34
1942	266.9	59.9	0.22
1943	296.7	56.8	0.19
1944	317.9	58.3	0.18
1945	314.0	66.9	0.21
1946	282.5	82.0	0.29
1947	282.3	102.1	0.36
1948	293.1	116.0	0.40
1949	292.7	126.6	0.43
1950	318.1	172.9	0.54
1951	341.8	188.0	0.55
1952	353.5	194.6	0.55
1953	369.0	217.2	0.59
1954	363.1	213.2	0.59
1955	392.7	223.3	0.57
1956	400.9	248.8	0.62
1957	408.6	254.2	0.62
1958	401.3	255.5	0.64

Source: Bureau of Public Roads, *Highways and Economic and Social Changes*, p. 53.

way share of the tonnage and the length of the haul, a conclusion that could have been expected from the data previously cited. There is a similar inverse relationship between the size of shipment and the highway share. Up to 50,000 pounds the road transport dominates; after that it falls off markedly. The second of these studies shows an equally definite inverse ratio between size of plant and reliance on highway transportation; that is, the smaller the plant, the greater the use of road transport. In the sampling that was employed, the median highway usage for small plants (under 20 employees) was 92 percent of the total tonnage shipped; for plants with 20 to 99 employees, the median was 84 percent; for plants with 100 to 499 employees it was 78 percent; and for plants beyond this size there was a marked drop to 48 percent.

There is also some differentiation according to commodities in the use of the various transportation media, as could be expected, but in general the factors of size of shipment and distance continue to apply with most commodities. Large firms may of course make small shipments, but the conclusion is inescapable that the smaller manufacturing concerns are the most acutely dependent on highway transportation—or, to turn the relationship around, the ability to use highway freight transportation in the form of the motor truck is essential to the existence of many of these industrial enterprises.

The effects of the truck on nonmanufacturing business have also been widespread and diversified. In distribution and marketing, for instance, especially in retailing, there is the fact previously stated that truck transport enables the retail merchant to operate with smaller inventories, with consequent greater economy of operation, and more rapid turnover of goods. To put it another way, "a retail store is no longer what it was originally—a store of goods patiently awaiting buyers. It is more like a pumping station speeding the steady flow of goods from factories through warehouses and distribution channels to consumers." [19]

Evaluating the influence of motorized highway transport on retailing requires that all highway vehicles—private automobile, bus, and truck—be considered together. The truck permits more flexible distribution of goods to retail outlets, but at the same time the greater freedom of passenger movement enables people to do their shopping over wider areas and therefore to exercise

[19] Bureau of Public Roads, *Highways and Economic and Social Changes*, (Washington, D.C.: Government Printing Office, 1964), p. 71.

more options over where to do their purchasing. The results differ somewhat between urban and rural communities. In the former, as will be described presently, highway transportation has produced a dispersal of major retail outlets from downtown business districts to suburban shopping centers; in country districts the tendency has been to promote concentration and specialization and reduce the importance of the local all-purpose general store. A study of secondary road improvement in rural Kentucky produces this conclusion:

> The evidence of the investigation reported in this paper appears to validate the premise that road improvements in rural areas lead to market adjustments, specialization of enterprise, and concentration of business. The market adjustments in the study areas are manifested in many ways. The number of stores in "open-country" locations has decreased, and in addition their dispersion geographically about the area—primarily county seat —trade centers has decreased secularly. Concurrently, the number of businesses in the trade centers has increased and many of the new businesses are specialized.[20]

Some sentimental regrets may be in order over the decline of the country general store, but the change has brought to country residents better stores and a more diversified selection of goods.

The great superiority of the truck as a carrier for comparatively light loads and short hauls should not be exaggerated into an assumption that its utility is limited to these functions. Long-distance trucking is an established fact, as anyone who travels American roads—or any other roads for that matter—can attest. The loads being carried have an endless variety—moving vans that may be taking a family's entire household effects door-to-door from one side of the country to the other; refrigerator trucks rushing perishable foods from producer to market; or, as has actually happened, a truck taking a complete automatic milk-bottling machine, 28 feet long and as wide as the truck, from

20 R. H. Stroup and L. V. Vargha, "Economic Impact of Secondary Road Improvements," *Highway Research Record,* no. 16 (Washington, D.C.: Highway Research Board, 1963), p. 12.

Detroit to the Atlantic coast for shipment abroad.[21] A vivid illustration of long-distance highway freight movement comes from abroad. On a visit to the Leyland plant of what is now the British Leyland Motor Corporation, the author was shown an enormous tandem-trailer "lorry" and was told that it left for Finland every week with a load of automotive parts. This trip meant traveling the length of England, crossing to the European continent by car ferry, and going all the way to Finland through Holland, Germany, Poland, and the Soviet Union, with all the inconvenience of frontier inspection—but it was cheaper and faster than sending the goods directly to Finland by sea.

To return to the United States, two specific examples demonstrate the striking change in economic operations that the motor truck was capable of bringing about. In 1950 only 17 percent of all Portland cement shipments moved by truck, because the difficulty of unloading bulk cement meant that cement was either bagged and carried in boxcars or loaded in bulk onto covered hopper cars if the destination was equipped for gravity discharge.[22] Then a truck was developed with an air pressure differential system that permitted bulk cement to be blown out into a temporary batching plant. The result was that by 1964 about 64 percent of Portland cement shipments went by truck. This was not just a gain for highway transportation, it was stimulus to more economical and efficient methods of handling cement. Barge lines designed hopper barges for safe handling of bulk cement, and the railroads came up with a pressure-differential rail car. The effect of these changes was that the proportion of cement shipped in bulk rose from 30 percent in 1946 to 87.6 percent in 1964.

The other example is in the lumber industry. Until about

21 AMA, *Lifelines*, p. 20.
22 W. B. Saunders, "The Role of Competition in Improving Transportation in Product Markets," *Transportation: A Service* (New York: New York Academy of Science, 1968), pp. 130–131.

1940 the hauling of heavy logs from forests to sawmills required water or rail transport, usually the latter. There were about 5,000 miles of private logging railroads in operation; these have virtually disappeared in favor of logging roads and trucks.[23] Roads are easier and cheaper to build in the rough terrain that comprises most forest areas. A truck can negotiate a 20 percent grade, while the maximum for a logging railroad is 5, and with present-day equipment a usable road can be built much faster than a railroad.

There are multiple consequences. Since road transportation makes it economically feasible to operate over more extensive areas, there is a stronger incentive for lumber companies to engage in sustained-yield forestry than when only the stands within immediate reach of a railroad could be cut profitably, because sustained-yield management requires enough acreage so that mature trees can be cut in one area while others are in various stages of growth in a planned cycle. There is also a change in the labor force. The company-operated logging camp was a picturesque institution, but it was a rootless and transient way of life. Access by road has permitted timber workers to travel daily from their homes to their jobs, so that farmers and others who are settled residents have come to make up a large segment of the logging force. The roads themselves have contributed to forest preservation by permitting easier and quicker access to forest fires and sometimes functioning as firebreaks.

Access to forest areas is just part of the story. The most recent figures on the movement of lumber show that in major timber-producing states (California, Washington, Oregon, Idaho) over 80 percent of all log production is carried by truck on public highways for at least part of its total haul, and that the average distance for the transportation of lumber is over 1,000 miles, com-

23 BPR, *Highways and Economic and Social Changes*, pp. 148–150, provides the data used here. See also AMA, *Lifelines*, pp. 32–33.

pared with 400 miles for other building materials from place of manufacture to use location.[24]

Highway Transportation and Economic Growth

It goes without saying that any society is better off for having good roads. The record of history is eloquent on this point, and to reiterate the feature of highway transportation that makes our era different, the addition of the motor vehicle has multiplied tremendously the economic impact of the road. For the American economy in particular, the impact has been so great and has been felt in such manifold ways that total measurement is probably impossible. There have been numerous studies of the effects of highway changes on specific communities or regions, and these have great value not only as sources of data but as indexes of what common factors emerge as significant.

To begin with, an enormous amount of data has been compiled regarding the effect of highway improvement on land values.[25] The findings are straightforward and obvious, and not really worth pursuing in detail. In general, highway improvement enhances the value of adjacent property, but this is true of practically any system of transportation, and these gains may be offset by losses for other property. The Bureau of Public Roads has a dispassionate appraisal of this problem:

Although many of the changes resulting from highway improvements are beneficial, some are not. Regardless of whether the gross benefits associated with a highway improvement equal or exceed disadvantages (and therefore whether there are any net benefits), it is indisputable that certain individuals benefit from some highway-inspired changes—for example, from increased land values.

In many cases, however, it is difficult to know just who benefits from highway changes and to determine the extent of these benefits. This is so because benefits accruing in the form of land value increases are ordinarily shared in varying degrees by in-

24 *Ibid.*, p. 148; *Third Report of the Highway Cost Allocation Study*, p. 54.
25 For a summary of such findings, see BPR, *Highways and Economic and Social Changes*, pp. 12–47, 135–145.

dividuals or groups whose activities are related to the land involved. In the conversion of land from rural agricultural to suburban residential, for example, beneficiaries often include such groups as farmers, land developers or subdividers, home builders, and suburban residents. Determining precisely who benefits from increased land values is possible only when no changes in land ownership occur during the period of land value changes.[26]

It is equally difficult to determine who does not benefit, or even loses. The research projects that have been conducted have used control areas considered to be outside the range of influence of the highway development. The control area usually shows a slighter accretion in value than the study area, or sometimes a decline, but there are enough exceptions to discourage generalization.

There are more satisfactory indexes of the overall economic effects of providing better road transportation in specific examples of growth stimulated by the availability of a good highway, even if we defer for the present any consideration of the remarkable influence of metropolitan freeways on industrial expansion. The Indiana Toll Road was opened to traffic for its entire length by the beginning of 1957; in the next three years, 150 of the 344 new industrial plants established in Indiana, or 45 percent, were located in a 45-mile band straddling the Toll Road.[27] This concentration is hardly coincidence. The New York Thruway (now the Thomas E. Dewey Thruway) was completed between New York City and Buffalo at the same time. By 1960 it was credited with attracting $150 million of new investment in industrial plant.[28] Among the companies to build or expand along the Thruway are General Electric, International Business Machines, General Motors, Chrysler, Bristol Laboratories, Westinghouse, Sears Roebuck, and American Machine & Foundry.

26 *Ibid.*, p. 47.
27 *Ibid.*, p. 53.
28 D. J. Bowersox, "Influence of Highways on Selection of Six Industrial Locations," *Highway Research Board Bulletin 268* (Washington, D.C.: Highway Research Board, 1960), p. 16.

One very useful sample of what good access by road can mean to communities of various kinds is offered in an analysis of highway transportation as a factor in rehabilitating depressed areas. The authors sensibly point out that highway transportation by itself is not a panacea for economic ills, but they nevertheless begin by saying:

High-quality highways are one of the most important elements in economic development in modern American communities. Although good highways alone are not sufficient to insure economic improvement in competition with other areas, they are a necessity to any area seeking to insure its attractiveness to new industry, its ability to retain existing industry, and its overall efficiency as a place to live and work.[29]

The article then proceeds to examine various kinds of depressed areas. For manufacturing communities, an interesting contrast is offered between two pairs of cities in Massachusetts that had formerly been one-industry textile centers: Lowell and Lawrence, on one hand, and Fall River and New Bedford, on the other. The first two are linked by express highways to Boston, some twenty-five miles away, and to Route 128, circling Boston at a radius of ten to fifteen miles. Again quoting directly:

This recent improvement in highway connections has had two effects. First, the radius of easy commuting by automobile for workers living in the distressed cities has been significantly increased, enabling them to find jobs in the burgeoning electronics and research operations along Mass. 128 and in other locations inside the circumferential. Secondly, the improved highway system has made industrial sites in the Merrimack Valley more attractive to manufacturers in the electronics and other advanced industries who want to tap the sizable labor pool in the Valley but who also wish to retain close physical proximity to the many assets of the Boston area. The Massachusetts Institute of Technology and a large supply of skilled scientists and engineers are among the more prominent of these assets. To a considerable extent, new sources of employment have offset the Merrimack Valley's heavy losses of textile jobs. Though the effects of highway transportation in this situation are difficult to isolate and

29 D. A. Grossman and M. R. Levin, "Area Development and Highway Transportation," *Highway Research Record*, no. 16 (Washington, D.C.: Highway Research Board, 1963), p. 24.

measure with precision, one major indication of the contribution of expressways to economic improvement can be seen in the fact that, during the hearings of the Senate and House committees on area redevelopment legislation in the 1950's, the Lawrence area was frequently cited as being typical of the kind of area the bill was designed to benefit. By the time the bill became law in 1961, however, the economy of the Lawrence area had improved to the point where it was no longer eligible for assistance as a "redevelopment area."

An interesting contrast to the the effect of new highways on the Merrimack Valley can be seen in the case of two other distressed Massachusetts cities: Fall River and New Bedford. These also were former textile centers, and have also been linked to the Boston area by radial expressways (Mass. 24 and 140). However, they lie 40 to 50 miles from the central city, roughly twice the distance that separates Lawrence and Lowell from Boston. This greater distance has diminished the spillover of industries and suburban residents, and other favorable impacts of the larger metropolitan area. Commuting is possible, but arduous, between the Fall River–New Bedford area and the Boston area. The distance between the growth areas along the western and northern segments of Mass. 128 and the Fall River–New Bedford area is an obstacle that good highways can only lessen, but not overcome. The situation is made more difficult for Fall River and New Bedford by the presence of a large number of potential industrial sites closer to Boston and Mass. 128. Another factor that might have benefited Fall River and New Bedford is their proximity to the larger Providence metropolitan area; however, the Providence area itself suffers from severe employment problems. To date, industrial development and other economic improvement efforts of the Fall River–New Bedford area have been noticeably less successful than those of the Lawrence–Lowell area.[30]

For depressed agricultural and mining areas the same general principles apply. The prospect of rehabilitation is greatly enhanced if road facilities permit ready access for new business or tourists to come in and allow the people whose jobs have disappeared to find employment in neighboring communities. Roads, like any other form of transportation, cannot replace the facts of geography, although good roads can help to reduce the handicaps of a poor location. And while highway improvement alone may not be a sufficient guarantee of economic progress, the

30 *Ibid.*, pp. 26–27.

inhibiting, in fact smothering, effects of an inadequate highway system are painfully obvious. West Virginia has not only been one of the chief sufferers from a secular decline in coal-mining employment but also lagged behind its neighbors in industrial growth. Its failure here has been attributed to "isolation imposed primarily by obsolete roads in a mountainous terrain." [31]

Finally, although the impact of automotive highway transportation on American rural life will be more fully treated in Chapter 8, something needs to be said here about the economic effect on agriculture of being able to move commodities by road freely and economically. The starting point can be conveniently set a hundred years ago, when groups of canny Scots were organizing companies to invest in the growing economy of the American West. In 1883 the directors of the Oregon Mortgage Company of Edinburgh instructed their American agent to loan no money on farms more than ten miles from a railroad station.[32]

Consider the implications of this instruction. If farmland was more than ten miles from a railroad—perhaps fifteen, which was regarded as the economical limit of wagon transportation—then it was undesirable, no matter how high its quality. To put it another way, poor land close to a railroad was worth more than good land farther away, and the community or farm that lacked immediate access to rail or water transport was effectively isolated. This situation is expressed in a different context: "During the water era New Orleans was literally closer to Memphis than it was to its own Louisiana hinterland. Likewise, during the railroad era, Cheyenne was nearer Chicago than it was to nearby rural hamlets which had been stranded by the railroads' passing a few miles away." [33]

31 BPR, *Highways and Economic and Social Changes*, pp. 56–57.
32 W. Turrentine Jackson, *The Enterprising Scot* (Edinburgh, Scotland: Edinburgh University Press, 1968), p. 40.
33 Walter Firey, C. F. Loomis, and J. A. Beetle, "The Fusion of Urban and Rural," in Jean Labatut and W. J. Lane, eds., *Highways in Our National Life: A Symposium* (Princeton, N.J.: Princeton University Press, 1950), p. 155.

Truck transportation has transformed this pattern. All that the "rural hamlet" or the individual farm needs is a reasonably good road connecting it to a highway network.

Two states, North Carolina and Wisconsin, offer specific examples of the stimulus given by road improvement to a rural economy. North Carolina is a unique case. The state undertook a modern highway program in 1921 at the urging of citizens who argued that both farming and industrial growth were being retarded by an obsolete road network, and in the next ten years constructed 6,128 miles of surfaced main highways.[34] When the depression came and local road maintenance was threatened by lack of funds, North Carolina took over the entire rural highway network, financing it by vehicle registrations, gasoline taxes, and federal aid. Even so, the secondary roads left much to be desired, and in the 1950s the state embarked on an ambitious program that built 21,365 miles of rural roads at a cost of $360 million and put 95 percent of the population within a mile of a paved road. The returns in terms of increased farm income, savings in transporting farm products, and establishment of new industries along the highway system have justified the investment.

The Wisconsin example is based on a study in depth of two counties in the northwestern part of the state, Dunn and St. Croix. Secondary roads were not a factor in this situation; responding to the conditions of its predominantly agricultural economy, Wisconsin had given priority to providing surfaced rural roads but had lagged in keeping its through highways up to date until construction of the interstate highways began.[35] The change in this situation was the completion in 1959 of I-94 across these two counties from Eau Claire on the east to Minneapolis–St.

34 Jay Dugan, "Every Farm Near a Paved Road," in William Laas, ed., *Freedom of the American Road* (Detroit: Ford Motor Co., 1956), p. 22.
35 W. H. Dodge, *Influence of a Major Highway Improvement on an Agriculturally Based Economy*, Wisconsin Commerce Papers, vol. III, no. 2 (Madison, Wis.: University of Wisconsin Press, August 1967), p. 24n.

Paul on the west. Previously the main east-west route through this territory was U.S. 12, which had become seriously congested by having to handle both through and local traffic.

Dunn and St. Croix counties are agricultural, principally dairying, with an average farm income below that of the rest of Wisconsin. The only city of more than 5,000 population, Menominee, is on the I-94–U.S. 12 corridor, in Dunn County. There has been a limited time for the impact of the new through highway to be felt, but some results have occurred that seem to be significant:[36]

1. I-94 has effectively separated through and local traffic in the corridor. Residents of the area no longer have to take circuitous routes to avoid congestion.

2. The two major trade centers on the highway corridor declined in ability to hold the trade of their own residents, but not in attracting out-of-town shoppers.

3. Trade patterns for the rural population of the two counties were changed in that more of them did business in Minneapolis–St. Paul and Eau Claire. This would appear to be a benefit, since farm residents had better access to superior shopping facilities.

4. There was little change attributable to highway improvement on the value of land used strictly for agriculture—a good example of the difficulty of using land values to measure economic impact. On the other hand, there was a reclassification of land for residential, commercial, and industrial use along both I-94 and U.S. 12, and this land did increase in value.

5. Reactions of local businessmen varied, but on balance the reduction of highway congestion was beneficial to business activity along the corridor. The gains came from the increased volume of through traffic on the Interstate and from better access for local traffic on both the old and the new roads.

36 *Ibid.*, pp. 17–20. This is a summary of the findings. The supporting data are in the main part of the monograph.

6. A comparison of broad economic trends with trends in similar nearby regions not experiencing highway improvement of this kind seemed to show that the influence of the improvement on the local economy was not substantial. The criteria employed were: population, effective buying income, and retail sales. It was conceded that all three were subject to influences other than transportation (population, for instance, was affected by farm mechanization), and there had been a very limited time for material economic changes to manifest themselves.

7. There was an observable trend toward conversion of farmland to other uses. In the period from 1960 to 1964 the amount of land so reclassified in a three-to-four-mile band along the highway corridor was fifty-eight times as great as in the period from 1954 to 1956. This marked increase indicates that the provision of better road facilities is introducing some diversity into the economy of the two counties, making them less exclusively agricultural. There is a regrettable lack of any reference to trucking, but the fact that the reclassified land is adjacent to the old and new roads makes it obvious that the new business enterprises are there because of the availability of highway transportation.

In any event, the case for the economic stimulus afforded by good roads is indisputable. Thomas McDonald can hardly be quoted as a disinterested witness on the subject of roads, but he has a fair amount of evidence in his favor when he says: "We were not a wealthy nation when we began improving our highways—but the roads themselves helped us create new wealth, in business and industry and land values. So it was not our wealth that made our highways possible. Rather it was our highways that made our wealth possible." [37]

37 BPR, *Highways and Economic and Social Changes*, p. 1.

7 The Social Impact: General Aspects

Trying to evaluate the impact of the automobile on American life seems like an exercise in measuring the unmeasurable. No other single innovation of the twentieth century, or possibly any century, has so profoundly influenced manners, customs, and living habits, but the nature and scope of the automobile's influence are far from clearly understood. Some of the preliminary effects arising from the introduction of the motor vehicle into American life have been described previously, and we have seen that soon after the mass production and use of automobiles was recognizably established, some efforts were made to evaluate the consequences. Although it was recognized that major social changes were in the making, there was insufficient evidence for judging precisely what directions these changes would take.

The Family Car

The transformation of the automobile from a luxury to a family necessity was noted in the 1920s as a direct consequence of the low-priced car. Not only did possession of an automobile generate new travel in extensive volume, but it also encouraged the evolution of habit patterns that gave the car an increasing role in the routines of everyday life.[1] In other words, the multipurpose character of the family car was becoming well established. The same vehicle could be used for travel to work, shopping, social visits, recreational travel, going to the doctor, or taking children to school.

The availability of low-priced automobiles was one factor, undoubtedly the major factor, in bringing this situation about, but it was not the only one. Apart from the essential matter of highway improvement, the ability of the average family to operate a car was materially aided by the discovery of extensive additional

[1] Malcolm M. Willey and Stuart A. Rice, *Communication Agencies and Social Life* (New York: McGraw-Hill Book Co., 1933), p. 48.

sources of petroleum and by the development of improved refining techniques, both serving to keep operating costs down. Another contribution to the overall utility of the family automobile was the rapid replacement of open cars by closed cars in the 1920s; between 1916 and 1926 closed cars grew from 2 to 72 percent of the total output of passenger cars in the United States. The closed car had a greater variety of potential uses than the open touring car because it was a "power-driven room on wheels —stormproof, lockable—you could close its windows against dust or rain." [2] For this reason it contributed significantly to the growth of the automobile-oriented society that emerged on the American scene between the First and Second World Wars.

The most illuminating case study on this subject is *Middletown*, a survey of Muncie, Indiana, during the 1920s.[3] Muncie was selected because it was considered to be a reasonably representative American city, and it was compact enough for a manageable survey to be practicable. Automobile ownership was just beginning to be general in Muncie at this time. There were 6,221 passenger cars in the city in 1923, about one for every six persons, which was approximately the national average for the period, or two for every three families. The breakthrough in automobile use at this time is reflected in the observation that, although for some people the use of an automobile was still a seasonal matter, *the increase in surfaced roads* [italics author's] and closed cars was rapidly making the car a year-round tool for leisure-time as well as earning-a-living activities; ownership of an automobile had reached the point of being an accepted essential of normal living.

This novel situation produced mixed reactions—as automotive highway travel has continued to do. Some businessmen complained that their sales were declining because people were

2 F. L. Allen, *The Big Change* (New York: Harper and Brothers, 1952), p. 123.
3 R. S. and H. M. Lynd, *Middletown* (New York: Harcourt, Brace and Co., 1929); the information that follows comes from pp. 253–263.

putting all their resources into buying cars, and there was a continuing attitude that an automobile was a luxury for which going into debt was unwarranted. On the opposite side, automobile ownership was promoted as a way to advancement. Similarly, there was complete disagreement on whether a car helped to keep a family together or to disperse it. Significantly, a number of lower-income families asserted that they would cut back on clothing or even food rather than give up their car, and what has been called "a fitting theme song for the automobile revolution" was a statement attributed to a Muncie housewife whose family owned a car but no bathtub: "Why, you can't go to town in a bathtub." [4] Actually no such statement appears in *Middletown*. The interviewers found twenty-one families in this situation when they inquired about several houses that looked particularly run-down, and the authors are very careful to state that this group was not typical.[5]

Some years later the authors returned to study the impact of the Great Depression on Muncie. They found that car ownership came astonishingly close to being depression-proof.[6] Registrations and gasoline sales declined imperceptibly. The most conspicuous indication of depression was a sharp decline in new car sales, from 2,401 in 1929 to 556 in 1932, but all this meant was that the population of Muncie rode in older cars, but just as much.

This statement indicates a significant feature of the place that the automobile has attained in American life. The demand for new cars is highly elastic—a fact that the automobile industry has been acutely aware of. The demand for automobile *use,* on the other hand, is definitely inelastic. As happened in Muncie in the 1930s, in times of depression or recession Americans defer the purchase of new cars, but they continue to operate the cars

4 Allen, *The Big Change,* p. 121.
5 Lynd and Lynd, *Middletown,* p. 256n.
6 R. S. and H. M. Lynd, *Middletown in Transition* (New York: Harcourt, Brace and Co., 1937), pp. 255–257.

that they have. This is precisely what happened in the early 1930s. It happened again during the Second World War, when the supply of new cars was cut off, and in the recessions of the late 1940s and 1950s. Two conclusions follow from this record. The first, and most obvious, is that for the great majority of American families possession of an automobile has become a feature of their life that they will give up with great reluctance and only under extreme pressure of adverse circumstances. Second, these stages in the history of the automobile throw some light on the overworked expression "planned obsolescence." An automobile may be designed for a limited life-span so that its cost can be kept within the reach of the buying public; yet when economic or war conditions have made it necessary to prolong this life-span, even the low-priced cars have displayed an astonishing ability to keep running. Like any other mechanism, a motor vehicle requires maintenance and repair, but most American cars will absorb a considerable amount of neglect and even abuse before they become unusable.

If we move on from the era described in *Middletown,* we find changes in scale but not in basic patterns. Today there are almost twice as many people, four times as many cars, and a little over twice as much mileage of surfaced road. The family car in Middletown averaged 5,000 miles a year; the national average has since risen to 9,500. But the car has continued to perform essentially the same functions in family life. It remains a vehicle adaptable to a variety of purposes, and this multiple utility is shown in the fact that no one use predominates. In view of our preoccupation with the automobile as a vehicle for commuting, it is worth looking carefully at the distribution shown in Table 7.1. Only a third of all trips by private cars are for travel to and from work, and less than half are related to earning a living. To these figures can be added two other points reflecting on the role of the family car: (1) housewives drive 10 percent of all reported

Table 7.1   Distribution of Passenger Car Trips, Travel, and Occupancy by Major Purpose of Travel

Purpose of Travel	Percentage Distribution		Average Trip Length One Way (miles)†	Occupants per Car*
	Trips*	Vehicle-Miles†		
Earning a living:				
To and from work	33.6%	26.8%	6.4	1.3
Related business	12.2	16.8	10.2	1.3
Total	45.8	43.6	—	1.3
Family business:				
Medical and dental	1.6	1.9	9.7	2.0
Shopping	15.8	7.2	3.8	1.9
Other	12.1	9.9	6.8	1.8
Total	29.5	19.0	—	1.9
Educational, civic, and religious:	7.6	3.7	4.1	2.4
Social and recreational:				
Vacations	0.1	4.9	296.0	2.7
Pleasure rides	7.2	12.7	14.2	2.5
Other	9.8	16.1	12.3	2.4
Total	17.1	33.7	—	2.4
All purposes	100.0%	100.0%	8.0	1.7

* From motor vehicle use studies in 16 states, 1951–1958.
† From motor vehicle use studies in 22 states, 1951–1958.
Source: U.S. Department of Commerce, Bureau of Public Roads, *Public Roads*, December 1963.

vehicle-miles for passenger cars; (2) almost half of all automobile trips are made on weekends, and three-fifths of these trips are classified as "social and recreational." [7]

Travel for Pleasure

The authors of *Middletown* found that in the 1920s regular vacations were still a novelty for most people, but they noted that

7 T. A. Bostick, "The Automobile in American Daily Life," *Public Roads*, vol. 32, no. 11 (December 1963), p. 243.

the family car made possible frequent short pleasure trips—a drive on a hot evening to cool off, or a longer outing on weekends. The compilers of *Recent Social Trends,* surveying the whole American scene, found the recreational use of the motor vehicle to be a factor of established and growing importance. They observed that pleasure travel had previously been a rarity for most people, represented if at all by a brief annual vacation, but that such travel had become frequent and normal, whether the trip was a journey of some length or a brief ride on impulse. They added that the major contrast between present and former habits was not just increased mobility as such; it was the ability of the individual to control the time and direction of his own travel.[8]

What is being described here is the beginning of a major transformation in recreational habits. Until the automobile age arrived, the wealthy escaped the hot summers of American cities by going to Nahant or Southhampton or Newport. Middle-income families might go to a summer cottage for a while, although the head of the family was likely to continue to work and join his family only on weekends. For the poor, there were Sunday afternoons at Coney Island, or, with good fortune, a weekend at Atlantic City. Almost exactly thirty years after the publication of *Recent Social Trends* a very different picture was presented:

Recreational travel has grown from an incidental type of endeavor into an activity generating many billions of dollars. A measure of the importance of the recreational travel business can be gained from the fact that the combined annual payrolls of 12 of the Nation's largest companies are equal to only about one-half of annual tourist expenditures.

The geographical influence of recreational travel is pervasive. Half of the States count travel among their three major sources of revenue, and altogether, 23 States and the District of Columbia consider travel among their three most important industries. Three States—Florida, Nevada, and New Jersey—and the Dis-

8 Willey and Rice, *Communication Agencies and Social Life,* p. 58.

trict of Columbia rate tourism as their most important industry. In New Hampshire, recreation accounts for about one-fifth of the State's annual income and in dollar volume is outranked only by the manufacturing industry. In Santa Fe, New Mexico, two out of every three residents depend directly or indirectly on tourist expenditures.

In New York State, also, the tourist, recreation, and resort business is a leading industry. Over a billion dollars was spent in the State on these items in 1948, with almost 90 per cent of the vacation travel being accomplished via private automobile or bus. . . .

Another measure of the importance of recreational travel to the economy can be obtained from a 1955 study which showed that about half of our people take a vacation trip every year and travel almost 12 million miles in the process. Although no consistent series of data are available on recreational travel, a study in 1941 estimated the annual recreational bill for travel in the United States at $6 billion. A survey 12 years later indicated that $8 billion were spent on long vacation trips and another $2 billion on weekend trips. Other estimates include $18 billion spent in 1953 and over $13 billion in 1956. Although these dollars are in current year values, they show that between 5 and 8 per cent of all family income is spent for recreation activities.[9]

As the statement suggests, most of this recreational travel was done by road and in private cars. Other modes of transportation share in this growing propensity to travel for pleasure, although in changing proportions. The once popular railroad excursion has virtually disappeared, but vacation trips by air or bus have more than compensated. (We are concerned with travel on the North American continent, not with journeys overseas.) Nevertheless, the vacation trip is still predominantly a highway phenomenon; most of this vast volume of recreational movement is a product of the convenience and low cost of highway travel by private automobile. A recent study on recreation concluded that nine out of ten families now take their vacations in the family car and offered specific illustrations of how highway improvement has been a direct stimulus of touring, as, for instance,

9 Bureau of Public Roads, *Highways and Economic and Social Changes* (Washington, D.C.: Government Printing Office, 1964), p. 154.

Between 1947 and 1954 the number of hotels operating in the three counties through which New Jersey's Garden State Parkway now passes suffered a sharp year-to-year decline despite a general boom in motel and tourist court construction. However, completion of the parkway in 1955 reversed this downward trend in the resort business and in retail sales. In 1956 sales for the three counties increased $92 million over 1954. Retail sales were about $118 million more than in 1954.[10]

The dependence on highway transportation is even more pronounced with long-distance travel for outdoor recreation. For instance, 95 percent of the visitors to national parks like Glacier, Great Smoky, Grand Canyon, and Yellowstone arrive by car.[11] These are remote from the major centers of population; if access were limited to those who could afford to go by public transportation, few Americans could become acquainted with their scenic grandeur at first hand. To take Yellowstone Park as a specific illustration, no automobiles were permitted inside the park from its opening in 1895 until 1917. During that time the largest number of visitors in any one year was 52,000. In 1917, 35,000 people visited the park; by 1929 the figure had risen to 228,000; now it exceeds 2 million every year.[12] State parks and other recreational areas show similar phenomenal increases.

As Table 7.1 shows, the long vacation trip is still a very small proportion of the total volume of recreational travel by automobile. Most pleasure trips are short, in both time and distance. They consist of a day or an afternoon at the nearest beach or a

10 Department of Commerce, *A Proposed Program for Scenic Roads and Parkways* (Washington, D.C.: Government Printing Office, 1966), p. 35.
11 BPR, *Highways and Economic and Social Changes*, p. 157.
12 Department of Commerce, *Scenic Roads and Parkways*, p. 36. The President's Council on Recreation and Natural Beauty has recommended two highway programs: a minimum of 54,411 miles of scenic roads and parkways, of which about 80 percent would be improvement of existing routes and the rest new construction, at an estimated cost of $4 billion; an extended program of close to 100,000 miles, at a cost of $8 billion, with 73 percent representing existing routes and the rest new construction. It estimates that a 63 percent increase in pleasure driving would yield enough in gasoline taxes to pay the cost of the full program.

weekend outing for camping or fishing or boating (sales of boat trailers exceed 150,000 a year, making the automobile an important adjunct to recreation by water). Use of the automobile has become so commonplace that the practice of taking a ride just for the sake of driving about has become less popular than it was a generation ago, but it is far from extinct. The "Sunday driver" is still with us—the driver who is wandering along the highway for no particular purpose and with no particular destination, and conspicuously with no concern about obstructing other traffic. The increasing mileage of multilane highway has helped to mitigate this nuisance, although the Sunday driver, and his weekday counterpart, the road hog, can be counted on to occupy the passing lane if it is at all possible to do so.

Subject to these minor annoyances, the highway and the car have opened to multitudes of people new opportunities to travel for recreation and pleasure, and the volume of such travel will expand. The growth of such driving for pleasure is certainly a social benefit in that it gives to an increasingly urbanized civilization a ready outlet for recreation, either in the form of travel for its own sake or in providing easy and economical access to recreational facilities. There have been problems as well. In an earlier book on the history of the American automobile I stated:

> Not all the consequences of this mass movement on the highways were desirable. It was very easy to get the impression that the American landscape was being overrun by a horde of ignorant and wantonly destructive savages, whose idea of enjoying the beauties of nature was to line the roads with empty beer cans, litter the beaches with refuse, throw rubbish into the geysers of Yellowstone, scrawl obscene remarks on imposing rock formations, and toss burning cigarettes into woodlands.[13]

This particular problem can be alleviated by education and energetic enforcement of antilitter laws, although no one has as yet been able to solve it completely. There is a much larger issue

13 J. B. Rae, *The American Automobile* (Chicago: University of Chicago Press, 1965), p. 94.

Table 7.2   Vacation Trips by Mode of Travel, 1953

Mode	Percent
Automobile	83.0
Railroad	14.3
Bus	11.4
Airline	4.8
Other	3.4

Source: Bureau of Public Roads, *Highways and Economic and Social Changes* (Washington, D.C.: Government Printing Office, 1964), p. 158. Total in the table comes to more than 100 percent because many trips involved more than one mode of travel.

to be faced, essentially a function of numbers. To cite the Yellowstone example, an area that is having 2 million visitors a year is bound to be different from what it was when the maximum was 50,000. The preservation of scenic and wilderness area has become a matter of acute and understandable concern. Unfortunately, however, this concern is frequently misdirected. It ignores the elementary point that the situation is an unavoidable consequence of a massive growth in population and puts the blame on the automobile, to the extent of demanding that access by road to scenic and wilderness areas should be virtually eliminated.

There is a fundamental social problem at stake here: Is the enjoyment of scenic beauties and outdoor recreation to be reserved for the elite few and denied to the great bulk of the people who live in our cities? This is what will happen if opportunities for highway travel are curtailed. Table 7.2 shows the commanding role of the automobile in the total volume of vacation travel. To elaborate, the automobile accounts for 93 percent of all trips for outdoor recreation, 83 percent of vacation trips, and 81 percent of the trips classified as "entertainment" and "other pleasure." The figures make it abundantly obvious that for most people recreational travel, especially if the journey is more than local, is not a choice between going by car or going by some other mode of transportation. For this kind of travel the automobile is far more convenient and flexible and as a rule definitely cheaper than any alternative now available or in prospect for the immediate future. Consequently, if the trip cannot be made by car, in all likelihood it will not be made at all. There would appear to be a heavy burden of proof on those who would restrict access by car to scenic or recreational attractions. These areas are the heritage of all the people; on what grounds are we to justify excluding the great majority of the people because the only way they can get there is by automobile?

The remedy is not to lock up recreational resources so that they can be enjoyed only by a minuscule (and largely self-selected) minority, but for public authorities at all levels to plan with foresight and intelligence for the preservation of these resources so that they will be of maximum benefit to our whole society. This is a task that will require careful study and full cooperation among governmental agencies and between them and private organizations, but there is nothing inherently impossible about it. (See Table 7.3.) Over many years the National Park Service has shown what can be done for the orderly recreational use of wilderness areas, while the United States Forest Service has dem-

Table 7.3   Visitors to National Parks, Selected Years

Year	Number of Visitors (thousands)
1941	21,150
1946	22,073
1950	33,782
1955	50,008
1960	72,254
1965	112,140
1968	143,985

Sources: *1970 Automobile Facts and Figures* (Detroit: Automobile Manufacturers Association, 1970), p. 50; BPR, *Highways and Economic and Social Changes*, p. 158.

onstrated with conspicuous success the feasibility of coordinated land management combining systematic commercial use, conservation, and recreation.

Population Mobility

Americans have always been a mobile people. The American continent was settled by what has been termed "one of the most impressive and sustained movements of population the world had ever seen." [14] It was the restless people who moved from the Old World to the New and then in successive waves across the North American continent. Some exception has to be made for the black people who were brought across the Atlantic without their consent, but since the abolition of slavery the American Negro has displayed the same migratory propensity as other groups in American life.

This American tendency to folk-wandering antedates the automobile, a factor easy to overlook. It has naturally been greatly facilitated by the mobility that the motor vehicle afforded and by the growth of a nationwide network of surfaced roads. In 1940, for the first time, an effort was made to measure accurately the proportions of this shifting of people. Census data revealed that 12 percent of the total population of the United States, almost 16 million people, lived in that year in a different county than in 1935 or had moved in or out of a city of over 100,000.[15] The majority, 56.5 percent, were urban residents, divided about equally between cities over 100,000 and smaller communities.

This movement of people climbed to a new peak during the Second World War. The proportion of civilians to move in the five years of war remained officially at about 12 percent, but this figure excludes an indeterminate number who moved during the

14 Francis E. Merrill, "The Highway and Social Problems," in Jean Labatut and W. J. Lane, eds., *Highways in Our National Life: A Symposium* (Princeton, N.J.: Princeton University Press, 1950), p. 135.
15 *Ibid.*, p. 136.

war and returned to their original homes before March 1, 1945.[16]
It also excludes the movement of military personnel within the
country. The return of peace brought no diminution of the
process. Twenty years afterward, indeed, the volume of movement was greater than ever. Census data for 1960 showed that
approximately one out of every five individuals moved to another
home in any one year, and that one-third of these people moved
to a different county in response to economic and social opportunities.[17]

The overall impact on American society of this almost limit-
less mobility is extraordinarily difficult to evaluate. There are
manifest advantages. On a broad scale, freedom of movement
provides greater opportunities for both work and play, as well as
a wider choice of places to live. It may at the same time create
an atmosphere of rootlessness—of people constantly on the move,
with no place they can consider to be "home," and unwilling or
unable to settle down. These are elements that do not lend themselves readily to quantification, and interpretation depends very
much on the point of view the observer brings to the problem.
A shrewd commentator has remarked of two conspicuous mass
movements of people, mainly by road, in modern American life:

> The importance of social definition of the same mass behavior
> was illustrated by the different public attitudes toward mobility
> during the depression and the war. Depression mobility was
> viewed by the general public and the authorities alike as an un-
> fortunate manifestation of an economically and socially stagnant
> society. The thousands of dilapidated automobiles clogging the
> western highways on the road to California were defined as an
> outward and visible sign of an inward decay of the social struc-
> ture. Similar movements, during the defense and war years, on
> the other hand, were considered an indication of a dynamic and
> virile social organization, which could assume the gigantic task
> of war production. . . . The fundamental social process was
> much the same in either case. The social definition was very
> different.[18]

16 *Ibid.*, p. 137.
17 BPR, *Highways and Economic and Social Changes*, p. 2.
18 Merrill, "Highways and Social Problems," pp. 138–139.

In short, it all depends on the point of view. One comment might be added. When *The Grapes of Wrath* was made into a moving picture, millions of people in other parts of the world did *not* see those "thousands of dilapidated automobiles" as a visible manifestation of a sick society. What they did see, greatly to the dismay of the promoters of the film, was a society in which even poor farmers owned cars. Their judgment was inherently sound. The plight of the Okies is a distressing episode in the American past, and it should not be underrated, but they did have the option of moving because they had transportation.

Services and Problems

Consideration of specific issues yields the same results—an assortment of pros and cons and few conclusions that can be agreed on as absolute. On the asset side rather definitely are services that can be rendered more effectively by automobile transportation. Access to medical care has been profoundly influenced. We have seen that physicians were prominent among the early purchasers of automobiles because they made it possible to visit more patients. But the vehicle that carries doctor to patient can also carry patient to doctor, and the present tendency is for most patients to go to the doctor's office or to a hospital for treatment, where more facilities and equipment are available than the physician can carry in his black bag on a house call. Automobile travel, moreover, permits medical services—hospitals, clinics, group practice—to be concentrated in units large enough to be well-equipped and effective.[19] The benefits, as we shall see in the next chapter, are more pronounced for rural than for urban areas, but they permeate the whole of American society. The average trip for medical care is almost ten miles (see Table 7.1),

19 There is a summary of the changes in medical services in BPR, *Highways and Economic and Social Changes*, pp. 86–87.

which means that people are not restricted to the nearest source of medical care but are able to choose and do so.

There is a comparable situation in education, based on a particular type of motor vehicle, the school bus. The benefit to education is that small schools can be consolidated into units large enough to afford diversified curricula. The National Education Association recommends that school districts have a minimum enrollment of 10,000 to 12,000 pupils in order to be able to provide instruction in specialized fields such as art, music, and vocational training.[20] As with medical services, the advantages derived from highway transportation have applied particularly to country districts, but not exclusively so. In large cities, bus transportation is now emerging as a means of removing inequalities in educational facilities. The extent to which the school bus has become an integral part of the American educational system is shown in Figure 7.1; in less than half a century the proportion of public school students carried by bus rose from 1.6 to 41 percent.

This growing trend toward transporting pupils by bus illustrates one of the complexities in the social impact of modern highway transportation: to wit, that in making it possible to provide better public services, improved communication by road also increases the demand for such services. It would still be possible for most city school systems to locate their schools so that pupils could walk or travel by public transportation, although it would be a more expensive and less satisfactory way to operate. The ease with which bus transportation can be supplied not only permits the benefits of consolidation but suggests other uses for this flexible and convenient form of mobility.

This factor appears more sharply in the matter of law enforcement and police protection. The motor vehicle has unques-

20 BPR, *Highways and Economic and Social Changes*, p. 174.

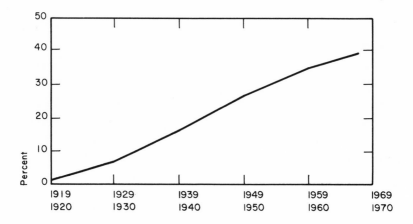

School Term	Number Students Enrolled	Number Transported at Public Expense	Percent Transported at Public Expense
1919–1920	21,578,000	350,000	1.6
1929–1930	25,678,000	1,903,000	7.4
1939–1940	25,434,000	4,144,000	16.3
1949–1950	25,111,000	6,947,000	27.7
1959–1960	32,477,440[1]	12,225,142[1]	37.6
1967–1968	43,891,449	17,275,318	39.4
1968–1969	44,961,662	18,467,944	41.1

Figure 7.1 School buses carry 41 percent of public school students
[1] Pupils in average daily attendance.
Source: Automobile Manufacturers Association.

tionably created new problems of law enforcement. The biggest is the consequence of the sheer volume of automobile traffic; a substantial proportion of the nation's police forces is engaged in controlling traffic and enforcing traffic laws and regulations. This is the primary concern of most state police organizations, and in large cities at peak traffic hours as many as one-fifth of the police officers may be directing traffic or protecting school crossings. Part of the difficulty here is that much of our traffic control in the past has been improvised; this point will be developed more fully later. With up-to-date methods of traffic control and properly designed road and street systems the same volume of traffic can be moved more efficiently with fewer people required to direct it.

In the broader area of law enforcement, the motor vehicle works two ways. It unquestionably gives the criminal greater mobility, but it does the same thing for the policeman. We are not, after all, living in a society where the criminal uses a fast car to escape from the sheriff's posse of the TV western. The motor vehicle can be used for the law as well as against it; in fact, it offers the advantage of permitting more effective deployment of police resources.

For example, in Kansas City, Missouri, the number of police officers increased by 21 percent between 1940 and 1960, while population was rising by 30 percent, motor vehicle registrations by 70 percent, and the municipal area by 90 percent.[21] The number of police cars tripled, and foot patrolmen were gradually eliminated. There was 1 policeman for 740 people in 1940, compared with 1 for 800 twenty years later. This trend is characteristic of American towns and cities. It may not be really desirable to have the ratio of policemen to population declining, and there are some community advantages to be realized by keeping some patrolmen walking beats in the old-fashioned way. But most of our police forces must continue to be motorized, not just because criminals use cars but predominantly because automotive transportation and electronic communications make possible maximum coverage of territory and at the same time concentration at points of need. The requirements of traffic regulation that have brought into being state police and highway patrol organizations have made for better law enforcement over widely scattered areas that previously lacked trained police protection. Other services can be listed that have either been made feasible or have been greatly improved by the advent of the motor vehicle

21 *Ibid.*, p. 176.

and the surfaced road. Fire protection, for example, is manifestly superior. The motorized fire engine not only can get to the scene faster than its horse-drawn predecessor but can also carry and provide power for a wealth of elaborate equipment for fire fighting and rescue.

However, we do not get an accurate picture of a highly mobile society if we merely itemize the conditions in which mobility is manifestly an asset. The liability side of the ledger has to be considered also. The automobile has been charged, for example, with breaking down social and moral standards by making it easier for people to engage in immoral conduct and with weakening the influence of religion by encouraging people to go on Sunday trips rather than attend church. It is an accepted fact, and has been since the 1920s, that dates between young people very often involve an automobile. Does this change in social custom result in greater immorality? Certainly the car makes it easier to get away from the supervision of parents or the observation of neighbors, and it also offers a place to engage in intimacies if the parties so desire. We are asked to assume that the incidence of immoral conduct has increased because the automobile has increased the opportunities for indulging in such conduct, yet neither part of the statement is supported by substantive evidence. Admittedly, this is a subject on which the collection of accurate data is difficult, but there is no convincing body of proof that immorality is significantly greater than it ever was, and measurement is complicated by the fact that standards vary from generation to generation. The automobile may provide a convenient means for evading moral codes or acceptable social behavior patterns, but whether the opportunities for such antisocial behavior are really greater or merely different is another matter. The expression "roll in the hay" suggests that earlier generations in a preurban, preautomobile society had their own ways of avoiding conventions.

The allegation that the automobile weakened the church-going habit carries a fair amount of weight, but at the same time it illustrates the difficulty of attempting to isolate one element in a complex social situation. That the automobile was a factor in encouraging people to spend Sundays elsewhere than in church is indisputable; it was, however, far from being the only factor, and it is questionable that it was even the most important. The general use of the automobile coincided with a period of critical change in many churches. Old standards and patterns of thought were breaking down, partly because of the impact of the long Darwinian controversy, which continued to reverberate well into the 1920s, and partly because of a general weakening of traditional dogma, especially among Protestant clergy and laymen.[22] As a result, the strict Sabbath observance of the past lost its hold, permitting a substantial expansion of commercial recreational facilities—moving picture theaters and commercial sports, for instance—available on Sundays, or allowing people to go without inhibitions to beaches and parks. However, these diversions acquired importance only because the hold of organized religion was visibly relaxing anyway, and if this was to be deplored, the alternatives were far from clear. The United States long ago consciously rejected the idea of compelling attendance at religious services, and there is little more attraction in suggesting that attendance should be stimulated by prohibiting counterattractions.

After all, the motor vehicle can carry people to church rather than from it, a fact that most churches were quick to discover. The automobile made it possible for people to travel greater distances to the church of their choice, and, as with the physician, it enables the clergyman to extend the area of his service. Many churches have bus and car operations organized to take children

22 *Recent Social Trends in the United States,* Report of the President's Research Committee on Social Trends (New York: McGraw-Hill Book Co., 1933), p. 1013.

to and from church schools, and frequently to transport those who want to attend services but because of age or infirmity would otherwise be unable to do so. There are even a number of drive-in churches.[23]

This change has required some adaptation. Schedules of services have been revised so that people who want to spend most of Sunday in recreation may do so. The Sunday evening service, once almost universal, is now a rarity. Early morning services and curtailed summer schedules are indexes of adaptation to a different order of things. Whether these changes are good or bad depends on the observer. There is, however, no evidence that American churches have been conspicuously weakened by the advent of the motor vehicle. If it has been a problem, it has, in view of the other critical issues faced by organized religion in the twentieth century, been a minor one. If the automobile were actually the principal culprit in drawing people away from church, then there should be a substantially smaller proportion of people attending church services regularly in the United States than in Europe; the actual situation is precisely the opposite.

Mobile Society

It is hardly necessary to keep compiling evidence of the extent to which American society has been permeated and influenced by motorized highway transportation. We have it thoroughly impressed on us in our day-to-day living. One additional illustration, however, may serve to hammer the point home: the variety of business and social functions that can be performed without leaving one's car, that is, by "drive-in" facilities, has become astonishingly large. A description published in 1969 gives an excellent summary, tracing drive-in restaurants back to the mid-1920s and drive-in theaters to 1933.[24] Since then it has become

23 Dorothy B. Warnick, "Drive-In America," *Ford Times* (May 1969), p. 49.
24 *Ibid.*, pp. 47–51.

possible to get laundry and cleaning done, make deposits and withdrawals in banks, borrow books, pay taxes, go to church, pay traffic fines, and even get married without leaving one's car. It is also possible to drive through some supermarkets and collect the family groceries, or to drive into a downtown hotel and park outside one's room.

It should be unnecessary to make the point that the American people freely chose the mobility represented by the motor vehicle, but much of the criticism directed at the automobile suggests otherwise, although none of the critics has ever explained the process by which cars were imposed on reluctant recipients. People have bought and used automobiles because they preferred this kind of mobility to alternative forms of ground transportation. The issue has been defined by Jerome B. Wiesner, formerly Science Adviser to the President of the United States and now president of the Massachusetts Institute of Technology: "The major exploitations of scientific ideas and inventions were done by individuals, and their ideas were accepted or not on the basis of a generalized vote by society. Society decided it wanted the automobile, and it bought the automobile." [25]

This phenomenon is becoming worldwide. Wherever people have the opportunity to acquire and use motor vehicles, they do so with the same zeal as Americans. Britain's Buchanan Report places the United Kingdom about a generation behind the United States and Canada on the way into the Motor Age but fully anticipates that the gap will close.[26] The same can be said of the whole of western Europe and of countries like Australia, New Zealand, Israel, and Japan; they are steadily approaching

25 Jerome B. Wiesner, "The Impact of Scientific Technology on Industry and Society," *Conference on Space, Science, and Urban Life*, (Washington, D.C.: National Aeronautics and Space Administration, 1963), p. 69.
26 *Traffic in Towns*, Report of the Steering Group and the Working Group appointed by the Minister of Transport (London: Her Majesty's Stationery Office, 1963), Introduction.

the North American pattern of automobile ownership and use because their people want it that way. The strength of this aspiration is such that it would be extraordinarily difficult for a free society to deny to its citizens the prospect of owning a motor vehicle.

8 Enrichment of Rural Life

Since man first began to live in cities, town and country have been at opposite poles of human society. City life could be unpleasant, but at the very least it offered vigor and bustle and companionship. The city was the locus of commerce and industry, learning and the arts; the very words "urbane" and "urbanity" show where the amenities of life were expected to be found. By contrast the country dweller throughout the ages has been characteristically "The Man with the Hoe," the peasant doomed to endless drudgery, isolated from his fellows or at best sharing the same drab existence with a few others in a small village, and cut off from the main current of progress. In the Western world the application of science and technology to agriculture and the improvement of transportation in the eighteenth century began to change this picture somewhat, but until the middle of the twentieth century it remained generally true that the townsman and the countryman were distinct and easily distinguishable types. To the American city dweller the farmer was an object of derision: "hayseed," "rube," "hick," awkward, badly dressed, uncultured, and ignorant. Like most categorizations, this one was unfair and inaccurate; but it does reveal a deep-seated cleavage between urban and rural life.

Rural life has its attractions, but until the advent of automotive highway transportation there was no escaping from the underlying factors of loneliness, lack of contact with other people, economic handicaps because of limited access to markets, and inferior public services. All these problems focus on transportation and communication, and the technological developments of the twentieth century in these fields have had a fantastic impact on rural society.

The Truck and the Farm

The twentieth century has seen remarkable changes in American agriculture. In 1930, 30.5 million people in the United States, roughly a quarter of the total population, lived on farms; in 1960 this number was reduced to 20.5 million, or about one-ninth.[1] During the same time the yield of wheat per acre increased from thirteen to twenty-seven bushels and the yield of corn from twenty-three to seventy-three bushels per acre.[2] Where a century ago one farm worker was needed to produce the food for five other people, now one worker can supply thirty nonfarm persons.

The role of motor vehicle transportation in this process has been vitally important. Admittedly, it is one of many factors contributing to the striking increase in farm productivity (100 percent from 1947 to 1958). There have also been marked advances in agronomy, in the utilization of chemical fertilizers and pesticides, and in farm technology—but it is fair to ask how much value these would have had without low-cost transportation. The potential for increasing yields would have had limited practical application if it had not been possible to move the crops to market easily and economically. Table 8.1 shows in some detail the movement of farm products by highway. The percentages are impressive, the more so if the trend they represent is appreciated. For Florida fruits and vegetables, the two-thirds now hauled by road is an increase from one-half in 1954 and one-eighth in 1945.[3] Bulk shipments of milk to the New York metropolitan area now arrive almost entirely by truck, where 80 percent was hauled by rail in 1939.

1 Bureau of Public Roads, *Highways and Economic and Social Changes* (Washington, D.C.: Government Printing Office, 1964), p. 124.
2 Homer Hoyt, "The Changing Principles of Land Economics," *Technical Bulletin 60*, (Washington, D.C.: Urban Land Institute, 1967), p. 8.
3 BPR, *Highways and Economic and Social Changes*, p. 139.

Manifestly there has been a considerable substitution of highway transport for other methods, chiefly rail. The change is readily understandable. Shipping products from most farms requires a road haul of some kind, either directly to market or to reach rail or water transport, and with good roads and motor trucks it is frequently easier and more economical to make the entire trip by road. More important, the farmer now has an option that he previously lacked. He may use highway transportation exclusively, or rail, or water, or a combination, whichever is most to his advantage. In the past, shipping to distant markets could be done only by rail or water; the farmer who lacked convenient access to either was limited to markets in the immediate vicinity. In terms of economic benefits, providing this option has been the most pronounced impact of the motor truck and the surfaced road on rural life. A community or individual farm with ready access to a good road is automatically in the mainstream of economic activity. The importance of transportation to agriculture is summed up in this way: "Increased production alone does not determine the importance of any area involved in supply. Without adequate means of distribution, especially in the field of perishable supply, production borders on the secondary." [4]

This statement is illustrated by specific examples:

A study in California notes the tendency for decreased transportation costs to encourage agricultural specialization and efficiency, especially farming operations (e.g., dairying) requiring frequent deliveries. In Texas, observers report that watermelons are grown primarily on farms located near roads that have smooth surfaces and strong bridges. . . . A University of Minnesota study reports that the easy access to markets by way of a hard-surfaced road has brought land into production that was once considered too far from market. The direct relationship between highway transportation and agricultural production has also been noted by the Maryland Agricultural Experiment Sta-

4 *Ibid.*, p. 128.

Table 8.1   Motor Truck Hauls of Farm Products

Truck Hauls of Fruits and Vegetables to Leading Markets

Fruits and Vegetables (carlots)	Hauled by Truck				Percent of All Shipments			
	1967	1966	1965	1964	1967	1966	1965	1964
Albany, N.Y.	4,105	3,851	4,001	3,783	70.3	66.7	65.2	61.4
Atlanta, Ga.	20,139	19,747	22,447	22,095	88.2	87.8	91.0	89.6
Baltimore, Md.	12,617	12,058	14,234	13,954	58.9	55.7	60.9	60.1
Birmingham, Ala.	9,252	9,084	11,711	11,398	83.7	82.5	89.8	89.2
Boston, Mass.	17,165	17,866	20,289	20,237	48.4	48.2	50.3	48.9
Buffalo, N.Y.	6,497	6,290	6,768	6,841	58.6	54.4	57.4	57.3
Chicago, Ill.	21,045	21,463	24,870	26,356	38.0	36.5	40.9	43.2
Cincinnati, Ohio	9,497	8,728	9,555	8,662	56.6	51.9	53.6	50.8
Cleveland, Ohio	17,283	15,408	15,096	16,623	63.8	59.3	59.5	61.6
Columbia, S.C.	13,828	13,628	13,969	13,251	93.2	93.2	93.8	92.4
Dallas, Texas	17,854	16,846	19,441	19,267	89.3	87.1	89.0	86.7
Denver, Colo.	16,909	17,274	17,822	20,715	93.4	91.4	94.9	95.1
Detroit, Mich.	17,422	15,213	15,772	14,623	50.2	45.9	47.8	45.7
Fort Worth, Texas	3,806	3,670	3,986	4,943	89.1	87.9	88.2	88.3
Houston, Texas	8,502	5,942	7,406	6,794	73.0	62.2	71.8	66.7
Indianapolis, Ind.	10,436	10,893	9,507	8,043	79.9	77.9	74.2	67.4
Kansas City, Mo.	9,059	8,697	9,338	9,436	77.4	74.3	79.4	77.3
Los Angeles, Calif.	80,304	80,906	93,005	93,375	83.6	84.2	86.9	86.4
Louisville, Ky.	7,277	6,906	6,579	6,520	70.4	67.0	66.7	65.0
Memphis, Tenn.	4,728	4,755	6,393	6,583	71.3	67.1	74.9	74.5
Miami, Fla.	8,933	7,462	8,439	8,762	77.4	71.1	75.3	74.0
Milwaukee, Wis.	3,458	3,654	5,087	6,219	54.0	52.6	56.1	55.7
Minneapolis/St. Paul, Minn.	6,251	6,187	7,753	8,026	49.1	46.1	53.0	54.8
Nashville, Tenn.	3,051	2,585	2,700	2,839	62.9	58.7	63.1	63.4
New Orleans, La.	13,479	10,261	10,785	9,423	85.8	70.3	75.2	64.2
New York, N.Y./Newark, N.J.	52,260	52,413	64,076	62,886	38.5	38.8	43.8	42.6
Philadelphia, Pa.	27,444	26,300	28,270	30,104	57.6	55.9	57.0	56.8
Pittsburgh, Pa.	13,558	11,087	16,064	15,582	59.1	53.0	61.4	59.2
Portland, Ore.	9,842	10,101	11,647	10,781	81.3	85.9	86.1	84.7
Providence, R.I.	3,713	3,925	3,871	3,795	74.1	76.4	75.6	68.1
St. Louis, Mo.	9,540	9,252	11,270	12,401	50.4	48.2	57.5	57.1
Salt Lake City, Utah	5,738	6,160	6,451	6,610	96.4	94.8	93.8	93.8
San Antonio, Texas	10,819	11,110	11,821	11,554	86.9	86.3	88.2	86.2
San Francisco/Oakland, Calif.	39,926	35,922	40,194	41,708	94.2	89.1	89.6	88.8
Seattle/Tacoma, Wash.	12,986	12,868	14,072	13,605	75.3	75.5	76.9	74.7
Washington, D.C.	11,116	11,737	12,079	11,899	67.2	67.6	68.9	67.0
Wichita, Kansas	2,510	2,405	2,579	2,660	84.1	78.7	82.0	80.9
Total	542,349	522,654	589,347	592,353	64.6	62.5	65.9	64.9

Source: U.S. Department of Agriculture, Consumer and Marketing Service, *Fresh Fruit and Vegetable Unload Totals.*

Truck Deliveries of Livestock at Major Markets (thousand heads)

	Cattle	Calves	Hogs	Sheep, Lambs		Cattle	Calves	Hogs	Sheep, Lambs
1951	12,828	3,735	30,977	6,171	1960	17,346	2,729	28,300	8,389
1953	17,837	4,636	25,258	8,308	1961	16,704	2,448	26,878	8,877
1955	18,573	4,269	29,758	8,287	1962*	13,576	1,601	23,622	5,828
1956	19,591	4,389	31,680	8,416	1963	13,127	1,505	23,725	5,208
1957	18,155	3,775	28,529	7,949	1964	13,204	1,542	21,355	4,003
1958	17,056	3,040	27,389	7,622	1965	13,007	1,519	18,277	3,373
1959	17,064	2,827	31,518	8,654	1966	12,158	1,336	17,823	3,310

* Trend affected in 1962 by the reduction in the number of stockyard reports. The results for 1962 and 1963 reflect the data received directly by A.T.A., from 27 of the larger public stockyards; while 1964 data are from 24 markets and 1965 from 25 markets. Prior to 1962, the number of stockyards that reported varied from 54 to 68, including many of the smaller markets. However, beginning January, 1962, the Department of Agriculture discontinued publishing data on truck deliveries of livestock at public markets.
Source: U.S. Department of Agriculture, 1951 through 1961; American Trucking Associations, Inc., 1962 and later years.

Table 8.1 (*continued*)

Six Major Farm Product Unloads in 41 Cities, 1967

Apple Unloads		Cabbage Unloads		Green Corn Unloads		Orange Unloads		Potato Unloads		Tomato Unloads	
By Truck	% of Total	By Truck	% of Total	By Truck	% of Total	By Truck	% of Total	By Truck	% of Total	By Truck	% of Total
143	87	234	83	115	81	172	51	618	66	170	73
618	62	1,545	100	804	99	884	99	3,478	76	1,243	94
585	70	1,323	99	580	79	421	33	3,167	78	686	72
376	61	780	100	367	100	568	99	1,194	65	655	94
970	77	1,117	83	484	63	498	17	4,090	53	560	39
520	91	281	76	152	74	236	38	1,307	70	255	54
1,413	56	1,778	73	837	67	829	23	1,586	14	1,561	64
805	74	647	72	248	53	294	46	1,487	51	693	91
792	63	777	81	356	65	618	47	2,551	55	1,257	96
397	76	925	100	524	99	622	97	1,062	84	1,435	97
686	81	757	100	369	100	674	99	3,339	67	1,060	99
767	93	480	100	270	99	715	100	4,388	88	627	87
997	70	524	49	264	43	447	21	4,726	75	1,004	66
210	93	115	98	61	100	119	100	668	65	178	96
680	81	288	100	256	98	662	100	991	34	439	69
343	77	776	94	128	77	478	87	2,462	70	459	96
519	94	440	97	346	94	531	88	1,223	44	442	90
4,873	91	2,266	100	1,829	97	4,247	100	11,726	73	4,842	94
428	68	414	86	215	69	349	86	2,120	64	407	87
375	85	398	99	167	92	445	95	781	45	116	94
535	78	350	100	414	100	782	100	916	69	394	94
256	67	109	64	65	76	143	44	613	40	182	100
555	75	181	62	115	75	301	42	2,111	59	203	49
139	45	241	90	113	70	144	96	543	42	413	93
251	41	491	97	422	99	633	99	1,726	66	409	76
4,724	65	3,840	88	1,983	73	1,858	20	6,549	38	2,891	59
1,333	64	2,325	95	877	67	1,240	33	4,348	60	1,137	59
891	69	1,271	87	538	82	345	25	1,666	48	997	94
397	100	298	83	170	85	549	76	2,019	73	417	87
151	85	207	97	196	87	67	30	528	64	157	79
578	62	641	83	335	67	408	41	447	11	599	90
157	100	121	98	52	75	385	100	992	88	285	100
414	71	997	100	355	99	454	100	1,051	54	649	87
2,070	99	887	100	672	100	2,306	100	5,964	87	1,843	99
798	100	438	95	260	88	600	70	1,813	58	548	72
488	55	726	97	358	78	532	68	1,953	68	570	80
96	79	70	100	38	93	79	89	1,046	73	31	100
30,330	74	29,058	89	15,335	81	24,635	52	87,249	57	29,814	79

Note: "Number of Unloads" expressed as carlot equivalents.
Source: U.S. Department of Agriculture, Consumer and Marketing Service, *Fresh Fruit and Vegetable Unload Totals.*

Truck Deliveries of Livestock at Major Markets (percent of total receipts)

	Cattle	Calves	Hogs	Sheep, Lambs		Cattle	Calves	Hogs	Sheep, Lambs
1947	66.5	69.5	69.9	38.4	1957	86.1	84.2	89.4	62.5
1948	68.7	72.6	73.9	41.8	1958	88.3	83.7	90.5	64.9
1949	71.7	74.7	76.7	44.2	1959	89.5	86.6	90.7	66.7
1950	75.8	77.8	79.2	44.2	1960	91.2	87.0	91.5	67.0
1951	75.4	79.1	80.0	45.0	1961	92.0	86.7	91.7	70.7
1952	75.7	80.4	81.3	48.8	1962	93.0	84.8	99.1	77.6
1953	79.7	82.3	85.2	52.1	1963	94.5	89.7	99.0	81.1
1954	80.9	82.0	86.8	52.7	1964	94.9	88.3	99.6	82.1
1955	82.5	84.8	87.0	54.1	1965	96.1	90.0	99.8	85.5
1956	83.2	82.1	87.2	56.1	1966	95.9	91.8	99.9	87.1

Source: U.S. Department of Agriculture, 1947 through 1961; American Trucking Associations, Inc., 1962 and later years.

Table 8.2   Motor Vehicles on Farms in the United States, 1930–1965
(in thousands)

Year	Farm Population	Trucks	Automobiles
1930	30,529	900	4,135
1935	32,161	890	3,642
1940	30,547	1,047	4,144
1945	24,420	1,490	4,148
1950	23,048	2,207	4,100
1955	19,078	2,675	4,140
1960	15,635	2,825	3,629
1965	12,363	3,023	3,587

Sources: U.S. Department of Commerce, *Statistical Abstract of the United States,* 89th ed. (Washington D.C.: Government Printing Office, 1968), p. 594; U.S. Department of Agriculture, *Changes in Farm Production and Efficiency* (Washington D.C.: Government Printing Office, 1969), p. 11.

tion, which reports that farms on hard-surfaced roads market about 20 per cent more tonnage than otherwise comparable farms on dirt or gravel roads.[5]

Supplementary evidence of the significance of automotive transportation in the economic expansion of American agriculture appears in the ownership of motor vehicles by farm families (see Table 8.2). Since 1930 the number of passenger cars has remained fairly stable, a proportional increase because the farm population has declined by one-third. The number of trucks in use on American farms has risen impressively; while only about one-tenth of the American people live on farms, they own one-fifth of the trucks.[6] There is a correlation between greater agricultural productivity and the rise in vehicle use. Since 1940 the area of cultivated cropland in the United States has remained essentially unchanged. The doubling of food production in this time has involved, among other things, a threefold increase in

5 *Ibid.,* p. 129.
6 *Motor Truck Facts 1968* (Detroit: Automobile Manufacturers Association, 1968), p. 29.

trucks and a fourfold increase in tractors.[7] The role of the truck
in the new economy of the farm extends well beyond its function
as a carrier of farm products to market or of supplies to the farm.
As long ago as the 1940s it was estimated that for every ton of
goods hauled to or from American farms, four tons were hauled
about the farm; one interesting consequence has been that between 1920 and 1960 the number of horses and mules on American farms dropped from 25 million to 3 million while the number of trucks rose from 139,000 to 3 million.[8]

The motor vehicle has also affected the labor situation in
agriculture. Modern farm methods are capital intensive rather
than labor intensive, but they have seasonal needs for additional
labor that must be met promptly if ruinous loss is to be avoided.
The result is that while farm population—people living on farms
—has declined, the number of people with some farm employment has risen from about 3 million in 1945 to over 4.3 million,
and the proportion of these with less than twenty-five days of
farm work a year has had the fastest rate of increase.[9]

About one-tenth of these farm workers can be classified as
migratory. The problems of migratory farm labor are a familiar
part of the American scene, but they are problems of wage standards and living and working conditions rather than of transportation. Migrant labor existed before the automobile; one of
the prominent founders of the American automobile industry,
Charles W. Nash, started as an itinerant farm worker. The effect
of the motor vehicle has been twofold: it gives the migrant a

7 I am indebted to Dr. J. Arthur Campbell, Chairman of the Chemistry Department at Harvey Mudd College, for calling this relationship to my attention.
8 Harold Barger, *The Transportation Industries, 1889–1946* (New York: National Bureau of Economic Research, 1951), p. 222; *Automotive Information*,
vol. 1, no. 6 (February–March 1964), p. 5.
9 BPR, *Highways and Economic and Social Changes*, pp. 129–130.

wider range and therefore more job opportunities; more important, it encourages the use of "day-haul" labor, drawn from distances up to fifty miles from the job.

Automotive transportation also stimulates a reverse movement by making it easier for farm residents to find off-farm employment. Since 1930 the number of farm operators working 100 or more days off the farm per year has more than doubled, to include about a third of all farm operators.[10] Part of this trend is due to the increased dispersal of industry into rural areas, which is in turn a consequence of improved highway transportation.

Health and Education
Rural life has undergone economic changes, most of them for the better, as a result of improved highway transportation. It has also undergone social changes that may be even more far-reaching and significant in that they have introduced to country areas some of the amenities and advantages that had previously been available only to the townsmen.

The most conspicuous gain is in the field of medical care. The classic picture of the dedicated country doctor, going out in horse and buggy at all times and in all weathers to serve his patients, is a perfectly accurate one. What is omitted is that the factors of time and distance meant that very few patients could be so served. Most rural residents had to get along with home remedies and amateur treatment. Getting the services of a trained physician was difficult at best, impossible at worst, and for the remote farm or village there could be no such thing as a prompt response to an emergency, even with the best intentions in the world. For most country people, access to a hospital was just out of the question.

The attraction of the horseless carriage for the physician has

10 *Ibid.*, p. 132.

already been noted. For the country doctor in particular, it offered an opportunity for greater service, even when motor vehicles were crude and unreliable and rural roads were notoriously deficient. As vehicles and roads improved, so did the scope of rural medical service. Consider the case of Dr. P. S. Scheurer, who began practice in Manchester, Michigan, in 1909.[11] At that time Manchester was a town of 1,000 people, with six doctors and fifteen practical nurses to serve it and the surrounding countryside. To make his calls in winter Dr. Scheurer had to keep six horses. In 1919 he bought a Model T Ford, and six years later he got rid of his horses. Dr. Scheurer was still in practice in 1942, serving patients in a radius of 50 miles from Manchester and driving 35,000 miles a year in the process. In addition, if his patients needed hospitalization, there was now a modern hospital that they could reach quickly by car or ambulance. This individual example is corroborated by a survey of a rural county in Illinois, made under the auspices of the American Medical Association. It found that

Sixteen physicians in 1950 provided more service for more people than 42 physicians had provided in 1920. In the 1920's roads were so poor that physicians spent an hour or two making a call five miles from town and a 40 mile hospital trip took about six hours. Now patients in this rural county can reach town in twenty minutes, and a hospital in an hour or less.[12]

A similar study of western Pennsylvania found that many patients traveled to physicians in Pittsburgh from counties beyond the Pittsburgh metropolitan area, and this movement was especially pronounced along the Pennsylvania Turnpike east of Pittsburgh. This is a mountainous, essentially rural area where convenient access to a large city undoubtedly makes a higher quality of medical care available than would otherwise be possible.

11 This account appears in *The Automobile Between Wars* (Detroit: Automobile Manufacturers Association, 1944), p. 12.
12 BPR, *Highways and Economic and Social Changes*, p. 86.

While the trend of travel for medical care is mainly in the direction of having the patient go where there are facilities for treatment—hospital or doctor's office—motor vehicle transportation also permits moving the facilities if the situation requires. This is most common with public health activities, where mobile units have proved extremely valuable. They can be sent to the spot to do such things as sample water, make immediate tests if contagious disease is suspected, or administer treatment. As an example, a mobile x-ray unit in South Carolina served about 3,500 people in 1940 and 99,000 in 1957.[13]

Highway transportation has also made possible significant changes in educational opportunities for rural areas. The one-room schoolhouse is a fond memory in American folklore, and in favorable circumstances it provided pupils with a solid educational foundation. But there was never a time when the one-room rural school could offer as much as the city school systems, and it could not possibly have kept up with the educational developments of the twentieth century. Keeping the one-room school must inevitably have resulted in a constantly widening gap between the quality of education available in rural areas and that available in cities. The remedy for this situation has been the consolidated school, which is possible in country districts only because pupils can be carried over substantial distances by bus. The advantages of consolidation have been described in Chapter 7.

The number of one-teacher schools in the United States declined from 190,000 in 1920 to 25,000 in 1958,[14] and this type of school is definitely on the way to oblivion. The same trend has also produced a reduction in the number of school districts, with consequent gains in efficiency and economy of operation. Some of this consolidation, both of schools and of districts, has taken place in urban areas, but it is predominantly a rural phenomenon. The

13 *Ibid.*, p. 177.
14 *Ibid.*, p. 174.

contribution of the highway to the process is reflected in the fact that since 1930 the average daily travel for a school bus has increased from 22 to 40 miles.[15] An average this high can be achieved only by accumulating mileage on long hauls over country roads. Forty-one percent of public school pupils are transported to and from school by bus, but in rural areas the proportion is higher. Idaho, for instance, had 47 percent of its pupils using school buses in 1958, when the national proportion was 36.5 percent.[16] The aggregate numbers do not distinguish between city and country, and it is probable that the majority of the students using school buses are in cities. However the pupils who benefit most are those who are able to travel long distances to consolidated rural schools and would otherwise have to accept inferior educational facilities.

The motor vehicle has made other educational and cultural opportunities more accessible to the county resident. It is easier to get to a library than it was in the horse-and-buggy era; beyond that, the library can be taken to the user. "Bookmobiles" carry books, records, and films to places too remote or too small to have adequate library resources of their own. One county in South Carolina had the circulation of books via bookmobile increase from 34,000 to 116,000 in twenty years.[17]

Various other items can be added whereby highway transportation has made country living more comparable to city living. Cultural and recreational facilities that would formerly have been inaccessible can now be reached by car. (I still have vivid recollections of a one-time student casually explaining that his family thought nothing of driving ninety miles from their South Dakota farm home to the movies.) In most country districts there is daily delivery of mail. The growth of rural free delivery routes appears

15 *Ibid.*, p. 173.
16 *Ibid.*, p. 175.
17 *Ibid.*, p. 180.

Table 8.3   Rural Free Delivery Routes, Selected Years

Year	Number of Routes	Length of Routes (thousands of miles)	Average Length	Annual Travel (thousands of miles)
1900	1,259	29	23	—
1919	41,079	993	24	303,007
1920	43,445	1,152	27	348,627
1930	43,278	1,335	31	404,738
1940	32,646	1,402	43	424,704
1950	36,619	1,493	46	453,260
1959	31,377	1,733	56	532,677

Source: Bureau of Public Roads, *Highways and Economic and Social Changes* (Washington, D.C.: Government Printing Office, 1964), p. 179. Adapted from *Statistical Abstract of the United States*, 1960.

in Table 8.3—this is a service begun in a very tentative way in 1896. Besides the factor of growth, the table indicates the effect of improved highways. The number of RFD routes reached its maximum back in 1920. Since then there has been a quite consistent trend to covering more mileage with fewer routes. In other words, rural mail delivery can cover greater distances in the same amount of time; specifically, in 1959 it was 2.5 times as fast as it was in 1900 and twice as fast as in 1920.

"Rurban" Society

The term "rurban" appears in an article written in 1950 dealing with the fusion of rural and urban elements in American society.[18] The authors identify the highway as the predominant factor in the process of blending urban and rural society, and they attempt to evaluate the gains and losses that this process entails. The salient points in their views are these:

1. Before the highway era, the city was sharply separated from

18 Walter Firey, C. P. Loomis, and J. Allan Beegle, "The Fusion of Urban and Rural," in Jean Labatut and W. J. Lane, eds., *Highways in Our National Life: A Symposium* (Princeton, N.J.: Princeton University Press, 1950), pp. 154–163.

its own rural hinterland. There was an abrupt physical transition from built-up areas to open countryside; the social and cultural gap was equally pronounced.

2. The advantage of the motor vehicle as a flexible short-distance, small-load carrier brought the first really intimate contact between the city and its hinterland.

3. Motorized highway transportation has broken down the seclusion and provincialism that formerly characterized rural life. In the process some local institutions of considerable value have been unavoidably weakened, because the predominant pattern has been for urban standards to spread outward; rural areas are becoming culturally urbanized.

4. The loss of "quaint, rustic ruralism" is offset by the acceptance of a "homogeneous, internally consistent, and universally accepted value system."

The authors manifestly believe that the influence of the highway in fusing urban and rural life has yielded more gains than losses, and this judgment is still valid. In any social change something will be lost, and the loss simply has to be accepted if it is outweighed by the gains. Since we are dealing with social and cultural values that do not lend themselves to quantification, it is out of the question to draw up a balance sheet that will itemize the gains and losses to everyone's satisfaction; there will not even be general agreement on what are gains and what are losses.

One fact, however, seems to be indisputable. If we want rural life to be "quaint" and "rustic," then it must be isolated from urban society, and it must therefore accept inferiority in such fields as medical care, education, and cultural opportunities, and almost certainly in economic status as well. There may be advocates of this option; it is doubtful that any of them live on a farm, or rather, to be more accurate, have to make a living on a farm.

Highway transportation is not the only contributor to the

creation of a "rurban" society. The telephone, radio, and television have also played a major part in bridging the age-old gap between town and country. So has the widespread distribution of printed matter made possible by power presses and modern transportation. Nevertheless, the primary factor is facility of movement for people and goods. This, of course, is not exclusively a highway function. Railroads and to a lesser extent waterways have had a share in breaking down rural isolation.

The critical importance of good transportation for the farmer lay at the heart of the long controversy over railroad regulation in the latter part of the nineteenth century. The first farm organization to take up the issue was the Patrons of Husbandry (the Grange), which was founded initially as a social organization to help alleviate the loneliness of farm life. That the Grange should have turned its attention to railroad rates demonstrated convincingly that the social and economic problems of the farmer were both intimately tied to transportation. Actually railroad rates were only one of a complex of causes responsible for the "farm problem" of this period, and not necessarily the most important. Other major factors were overproduction for the existing market demand and the long deflationary cycle that followed the Civil War. The overproduction was in part a function of transportation, in that economical long-distance transportation by rail and steamship brought new producing areas (for example, the American and Canadian West, Australia, Argentina) into the world market that formerly would have been too remote to be competitive. The level of railroad rates in fact declined, but to the extent that there was discrimination among shippers the farmer was in a weak bargaining position, because traffic on and off the individual farm is most likely to be small-scale, low-density, and seasonal.

This is the type of traffic that is least economical for railroads to handle but which is admirably suited to movement by motorized road transportation. For this reason the railroads by themselves could not have effected the transformation of rural life that has occurred in our time. There had to be a method of transportation that could furnish fast and economic access to every farm and hamlet, and this method, as we know, was the combination of improved road and motor vehicle. It has made the country dweller for the first time really free to come and go, and it has given him far wider options than he possessed in the past for marketing his products. Homogeneity and even a universally accepted value system may not necessarily be goals in themselves, especially if other socially desirable customs and institutions have to be sacrificed to attain them. Equality of opportunity—economic, social, educational, cultural—is something else again. For the country family to be on the same level as the city family in this respect it is worth giving up some local peculiarities and some traditional institutions. It is a novel situation in history, and it is attributable entirely to motorized highway transportation.

9 Realistic Highway Policies

In Chapter 4 the evolution of highway policies adapted to automotive transportation was traced to the end of the 1930s. At that point sufficient knowledge existed to make clear the qualities that a good highway system should have, that is, that arterial routes should be dual highways with controlled access and grade separation and that with other roads, including city streets, there should be a differentiation according to function. By 1940 some stretches of freeway-type road had been constructed in the United States, not enough to have any material effect on the flow of traffic but sufficient to demonstrate effectively the potential of properly designed express highways.

By this time also it was evident that, despite the massive achievements in highway improvement since 1920, much of the road mileage was already obsolescent and could not be brought up to the standards necessary for large-scale motor vehicle traffic because too little consideration had been given to future requirements: "Failure to buy up the necessary land to ensure economy in any future expansion of the facilities, and failure to protect the right of way by controlling access, had in effect frozen much of the highway system to the designs hastily adopted from the original horse and carriage roads." [1] Another major defect was the exclusion of urban areas from federal and state highway programs, a defect just beginning to be recognized in the 1930s.

The fundamentals of a national highway program—what was needed and what should be done—were therefore well understood before the Second World War came along, and some were embodied in two reports compiled by the Bureau of Public Roads, "Toll Roads and Free Roads" (76th Congress, 1st sess., House Document 272, 1939); and "Interregional Highways" (78th

1 Wilfred Owen and Charles L. Dearing, *Toll Roads and the Problem of Highway Modernization* (Washington, D.C.: The Brookings Institution, 1951), p. 33.

Congress, 2nd sess., House Document 379, 1944). The first was a response to a request for a feasibility study of a plan for three east-west and three north-south superhighways, to be financed through tolls. The conclusion was that tolls would produce less than half the annual costs of these roads, but it did not exclude the possibility of limited stretches of highway being supported by tolls. "Interregional Highways" was the preliminary blueprint for the Interstate system. This report recommended improvement of 34,000 miles of primary road to express highway standards.

The war itself stopped further development of the highway network and in fact caused some deterioration because shortages of labor and materials made adequate maintenance difficult. Yet the effect of the war was to emphasize the need for more and better rather than fewer and poorer roads. For one thing, thousands of communities and millions of people were now wholly dependent on highway transportation. A survey undertaken to determine the possible extent to which the use of motor vehicles might be curtailed in view of the shortages of gasoline and rubber found that some 57 million people in rural areas, constituting 43.5 percent of the total population, depended on some 10 million cars for their normal mobility: for marketing farm products, purchasing supplies, recreation, and access to governmental facilities. This situation was not a creation of the automobile; it derived from the elementary fact that rural mobility has always depended predominantly on public roads. The urban situation was startling: about 13 million people, 17 percent of the urban population, lived in 2,320 towns and cities that had no system of mass transportation, and they therefore depended on approximately 3 million automobiles for normal local mobility.[2]

Beyond this the war demonstrated convincingly the impor-

2 Charles L. Dearing, *Automobile Transportation in the War Effort* (Washington, D.C.: The Brookings Institution, 1942), pp. 7–8. Most of these communities were small, with less than 10,000 population, but many were suburbs of large cities.

tance of a first-class highway system for national defense. The performance of the railroads was magnificent. They handled the heavy extra burdens of wartime traffic without the confusion and snarls of the First World War, but in this effort they were materially aided by the fact that the highways could carry a much greater share of the total load than had been possible in 1918. The road system, with its admitted inadequacies, emerged as both an adjunct and an alternative to the railroads. The second function, the alternative, had a significance of its own. When war erupted in the Pacific, the rapid movement of military forces and materials from the East and Middle West to the Pacific Coast became a matter of vital concern, and the number of rail lines available for this purpose was limited—nine, counting the Canadian systems. Most have long stretches of single track through mountainous territory, so that the possibility had to be faced that some might be cut by enemy action or other causes or even that military forces might have to be deployed in areas where rail facilities were sketchy or nonexistent.

In addition, when the time came to plan for the return of peace, it was quite evident that the country should have a long-range, coordinated highway program. The outcome of these various pressures was the Federal-Aid Highway Act of 1944, which authorized

a national system of Interstate Highways, not exceeding 40,000 miles in total extent, so located as to connect by routes as direct as practicable, the principal metropolitan areas, cities, and industrial centers, to serve the national defense, and to connect at suitable border points with routes of continental importance in the Dominion of Canada and the Republic of Mexico.[3]

The act also made provision for aid on a systematic basis for the urban portions of the primary road network and for the secondary roads to which federal support had been extended in the 1930s. Since 1944 this part of the highway program has been

3 *U.S. Statutes at Large,* vol. 58, pt. 1 (1944), pp. 838–843.

termed the A-B-C program, and funds have been allocated on a 50-50 matching basis in a ratio of 45 percent for the regular primary routes, 30 percent for the secondary system, and 25 percent for urban projects.

Congress authorized an expenditure of $1.5 billion for this total program in the three years after the war, with the unforeseen consequence that the projected Interstate network lagged. The need for rehabilitation of existing roads was urgent, and with some 600,000 miles of both primary and secondary roads eligible for federal aid, the available funds were absorbed rapidly. In addition, states were hesitant to embark on expensive superhighway construction when they had to bear half the cost. Yet in regions of high population density and heavy traffic volume, specifically the Northeast and California, something had to be done beyond patching up existing roads, so that alternative solutions to the problem of financing had to be found.

The Toll Roads

One such solution was already functioning in the form of the toll highways built in Connecticut and Pennsylvania, particularly the latter because the pressure was for trunk routes to carry all kinds of traffic, not just passenger cars.[4] In its few years of operation the Pennsylvania Turnpike had falsified the gloomy predictions that motorists would not pay to use a superhighway if alternative free routes were available. In 1939 "Toll Roads and Free Roads" estimated the daily traffic for the Pennsylvania Turnpike at 715 vehicles;[5] the actual figure two weeks after the Turnpike opened was 26,000. By 1946 the Turnpike was clearly a success both financially and in moving traffic and was accordingly an example of keen interest to neighboring states.

4 Most of the information in this section has been provided by the toll road and turnpike authorities of the various states. To avoid elaborate annotation, only data from other sources will be identified by footnote.
5 Owen and Dearing, *Toll Roads*, p. 141.

The next state to adopt the toll road as a remedy for traffic problems was Maine. It all started because a prominent Maine political figure, George D. Varney, wanted a stretch of state highway for his district and was told that he could not have it because the federal highway authorities insisted on action being taken first to relieve the terrible bottleneck where U.S. Route 1 passed through Ogunquit.[6] Actually the Ogunquit situation merely repeated the experience of every town on the Maine coast during the summer months when masses of tourists following Route 1 had to make their way through the middle of every town they came to.

Varney was a man of enterprise and imagination. If a bypass had to be built around Ogunquit, why not go the whole way and build a complete express highway, toll-financed, as an alternative to Route 1? The Maine Turnpike Authority was created by act of the state legislature of 1941 to construct and operate a controlled-access highway, financed through bonds issued by the Authority and supported by tolls without tax or other assistance from the state. The money was raised after a traffic survey indicated that the project was feasible. Construction began after the war, and the first section, forty-seven miles from Kittery to Portland, was opened at the end of 1947. The Turnpike was extended to Augusta in 1953, for a total length of 106 miles. Initially the Turnpike was intended to go all the way across Maine to the Canadian border, but the adoption of the Interstate highway program changed this plan, as it did others. North of Augusta the express highway now continues as Interstate 95. Traffic volume on the Maine Turnpike exceeds 7 million vehicles and 300 million miles annually, this in a sparsely populated state. Much of this travel is recreational. Out-of-state cars make up 60 percent of all trips, 80 percent in summer. The total of Turnpike

6 Charles Rawlings, "Maine's 'Big Rud,'" William Laas, ed., *Freedom of the American Road* (Detroit: Ford Motor Co., 1956), pp. 34–35.

bonds issued was $78,600,000. Redemption began in 1964, and the entire issue is expected to be retired before 1989. In 1948, the first year of the Turnpike's operation, revenues were $670,000; twenty years later they exceeded $8 million.

This new turnpike era reached its peak in the 1950s. Of 3,557.6 miles of toll road in operation in 1963, only 313 had been built since 1959 (see Table 9.1). For the states of the Northeast

Table 9.1   Miles of Toll Highways in Operation in 1963

State	Mileage in Use	Cost (thousands)	Period Built
Colorado	17.3	$ 6,237	1952
Connecticut	193.9	502,092	1940–59
Delaware*	11.2	30,000	1963
Florida*	206.6	171,783	1950–64
Georgia	11.1	3,150	1924
Illinois	185.3	445,623	1958–59
Indiana	156.9	280,000	1956
Kansas	240.9	179,500	1956–59
Kentucky*	204.7	185,500	1956–64
Maine	112.2	79,406	1955–57
Maryland*	42.3	74,000	1963
Massachusetts	124.4	239,000	1957
New Hampshire	77.2	43,524	1950–57
New Jersey	309.2	821,200	1952–57
New York*	628.8	1,130,951	1926–60
Ohio	241.0	326,000	1955
Oklahoma	174.3	106,714	1953–57
Pennsylvania	469.3	539,664	1940–57
Texas	30.1	58,500	1957
Virginia	34.6	75,150	1958
West Virginia	86.3	133,000	1954
Totals	3,557.6	$5,430,994	

* Denotes mileage added since 1959 as follows: All mileage in Delaware, 79.1 miles in Florida at a cost of $93,183,000, 164.7 miles in Kentucky at a cost of $147,000,000, all mileage in Maryland, 5.7 miles in New York at a cost of $34,200,000. In addition toll road projects underway in 1964 will account for 182.3 miles of toll highways when completed. Projects that are proposed for financing would add approximately 120 miles.
Source: Data provided by Bureau of Public Roads.

in particular the toll road appeared as the solution to handling heavy volumes of through traffic without increasing local tax burdens. A superhighway was a special service for which a user charge in the form of tolls could properly be imposed, whereby out-of-state vehicles would carry their share of the costs. In the absence of more substantial federal aid, the alternative to tolls was higher gasoline taxes, which would have borne most heavily on local traffic, much of which would make little or no use of the express highway. Tolls, on the other hand, meant that every user of the highway, local or long-distance, in-state or out-of-state, was sharing the cost on equal terms.

The heart of the toll road network was on the heavily traveled routes between New York and Chicago. The Pennsylvania Turnpike reached the Ohio state line in 1951 and the Delaware River in 1954, although it had to have a temporary connection to New Jersey until the Delaware River Bridge was opened in 1956. Meanwhile the neighboring states were working on connecting routes. The Ohio Turnpike was authorized in 1949, work began in 1952, and the entire 241-mile route across the state was opened in 1955. Indiana continued this route with the 157-mile Indiana Toll Road, completed to the Illinois border in 1956. On the other side, the New Jersey Turnpike was authorized in 1948. It had its own independent origin in the overloading of New Jersey's highways, burdened with a heavy volume of through traffic between New York and Philadelphia, along with the local traffic generated by both metropolitan areas. After the Second World War, New Jersey's state highway system had a traffic density seven times the national average, and main routes approaching New York City were carrying twice their planned capacity.[7] A survey in 1946 estimated that the state's highway needs would cost $600 million. This figure appeared prohibitive if it had to be raised

7 The origin of the New Jersey Turnpike is described in H. J. Cranmer, *New Jersey in the Automobile Age: A History of Transportation* (Princeton, N.J.: Princeton University Press, 1964), pp. 62–63.

by taxation, and the toll road emerged as the most practical alternative. Construction of the 117.5-mile main stem began in 1950, and it was finished in 1952. Extensions to connect with the Lincoln Tunnel to New York and with the Pennsylvania Turnpike, both opened in 1956, brought the total length to 131 miles. In its first complete year of operation, 18 million vehicles used the New Jersey Turnpike.

This group of toll roads provided a continuous 840-mile express highway between New York and Chicago. Its immediate effect on the movement of traffic was measured by the Indiana Toll Road Commission in April 1957 in a series of test runs conducted in cooperation with a major truck concern and the Indiana Motor Truck Association. Table 9.2 shows the results, an impressive record of savings in time, fuel consumption, and wear and tear on the vehicle. Financially these toll roads were successful also. Pennsylvania paid off its original Trust Indenture in 1965, twenty-three years ahead of schedule; the Ohio Turnpike Commission expected to retire its entire bond issue of $362 million in 1979 instead of 1992 as originally contemplated; and the New Jersey Turnpike Authority had retired about a fourth of the bonds issued up to 1955. All these roads are in a constant state of renewal and improvement, conspicuously the two with the heaviest traffic volume. The Pennsylvania Turnpike added the Northeast Extension, 120 miles to Scranton, in 1957, and the

Table 9.2   Indiana Toll Road Truck Tests, Chicago-Jersey City, April 1957

Factor	Turnpikes	Routes 30 and 22	Turnpike Savings
Elapsed time	64 hrs. 49 min.	94 hrs. 43 min.	29 hrs. 54 min.
Travel time	41 hrs. 5 min.	52 hrs. 22 min.	11 hrs. 17 min.
Gasoline consumption	363.9 gals.	394.4 gals.	30.5 gals.
Speed per hour	40.93 miles	32.73 miles	8.20 miles
Gear shifts	777	3,116	2,339
Brake applications	194	890	696
Full stops	58	243	185

Source: Courtesy of Indiana Toll Road Commission.

original road has been extensively rebuilt in the light of experience. The most substantial operations have been bypasses eliminating three of the tunnels and the doubling of the other tunnels so that traffic does not have to be compressed into two lanes. The New Jersey Turnpike not only is part of the New York-Chicago route but is also the main road from New York to Philadelphia and Washington, and it carries a very heavy volume of local traffic in northern New Jersey. It therefore became necessary to adopt an extensive widening program for the northern thirty miles.

The largest single toll road is the New York State Thruway, since 1964 the Governor Thomas E. Dewey Thruway. Its total length is 559 miles, and it cost over a billion dollars to build. The "main line" runs for 496 miles from New York City through Buffalo to the Pennsylvania border; the rest of the mileage consists of connections to the Connecticut and Massachusetts Turnpikes, New Jersey's Garden State Parkway, and Ontario's Queen Elizabeth Way. The highway was projected in 1942, and construction began in 1946. The route from New York to Buffalo was finished in 1956, and to the Pennsylvania line in 1957. The Thruway did not connect directly with the Pennsylvania or Ohio Turnpikes. Express highway conection to the west had to wait for the Interstate system, but this has not in the least diminished the value of the Thruway for the state of New York. The General Electric Company offers an illustration:

The huge General Electric Electronics Park adjacent to the New York Thruway at Syracuse is the headquarters, with the Thruway providing the necessary accessibility, for GE plants at Buffalo, Auburn, Utica, and Schenectady, N.Y. In a study of operating economies for GE trucks using the Thruway between the Buffalo and Schenectady plants, trucks traveled at a rate over 10 miles per hour faster than on parallel routes, saved 14 gallons of fuel, had to make 298 fewer gear shifts, and 69 fewer full stops. The trucks saved 38 miles on round trips and 4 hours 29 minutes in transit time. Use of the Thruway also resulted in a rebate on their truck insurance because of the lower accident rate. This is typical of the advantages accruing to other firms establishing themselves along the Thruway.[8]

New England has, besides the Maine Turnpike, two important toll roads in Massachusetts and Connecticut, plus several short stretches in New Hampshire. The main part of the Massachusetts Turnpike, 123 miles from a junction with Route 128 outside Boston to a connection with the Berkshire Section of the New York Thruway, was built between 1954 and 1957; subsequently an 11-mile section into downtown Boston was added. The Connecticut Turnpike was authorized in 1953 and completed, 129 miles, to Killingly on the Rhode Island border in 1958. It was intended to do what the Merritt and Wilbur Cross Parkways had done twenty years earlier—relieve congestion on the Boston Post Road, U.S. 1. The parkways actually reduced Post Road traffic by 25 percent when they were first opened, but growth over twenty years had brought the problem back. The Connecticut Turnpike claims to have the world's longest section of urban freeway, 49 miles from the New York border at Greenwich through New Haven. To this should be added the 15-mile New England section of the New York Thruway which continues the route from Greenwich into the Bronx. However, the most interesting part of the Connecticut Turnpike is the one that traverses eastern Connecticut, a partly rural, partly small manufacturing town area, suffering in the 1950s from the prolonged decline of the New England textile industry. The impact of the Turnpike on this region has been studied in detail, comparing a group of towns within five miles of the Turnpike with a control group beyond this limit. The results are summarized as follows:

1. Manufacturing employment in the area served by the Turnpike increased by 27 percent between 1956 and 1962, compared with no change for the state as a whole and a slight decline

8 *Third Progress Report of the Highway Cost Allocation Study,* 86th Congress, 1st sess., House Document No. 91 (Washington, D.C.: Government Printing Office, 1959), p. 37.

in the control area. Favorable transportation facilities, and especially the Turnpike, were cited as a major contributing factor, both by permitting rapid and economical movement of materials and by enabling labor to be drawn from a wide area.

2. Tourist trade increased in the area served by the Turnpike. Motel capacity grew by 64 percent between 1957 and 1962, and new motels and summer homes added $4 million to assessment lists.

3. Between 1958 and 1964 population in the Turnpike area increased 15.9 percent, compared with 13 percent for Connecticut as a whole and 10.7 in the control area.

4. Retail sales grew 56 percent in the Turnpike area, again higher than the state generally and the control area.

5. Real estate values appreciated more rapidly in the Turnpike area. New construction also took place at a higher rate in the Turnpike area. In the vicinity of the interchanges land values more than doubled.[9]

The toll road enthusiasm produced several other major projects. The Illinois Tollway provided a bypass around Chicago from the Indiana border to the Wisconsin border, with branches to Aurora and Rockford. Besides its Turnpike, New Jersey built the 173-mile Garden State Parkway from the state's northern border to Cape May. It was planned in 1945 and finished ten years later. Virginia built a short stretch of toll road (34 miles) between Richmond and Petersburg, which has become a useful link on a main north-south trunk route and also carries a heavy volume of local traffic. Neighboring West Virginia had the least happy experience with a toll road. The 88-mile West Virginia Turnpike has sometimes been called "the Road to Nowhere." It was built between 1952 and 1954 through a region of low-density traffic, and did not earn its annual interest charges until

9 Walter C. McKain, *The Connecticut Turnpike—A Ribbon of Hope* (Storrs, Conn.: University of Connecticut, 1965), pp. 5–6.

1969. Yet it cannot be written off as a blunder. The road was expected to be a link in a north-south chain of toll roads, but the others were never built. In view of West Virginia's urgent need for high-quality roads, the Turnpike may be a valuable contribution to the economy of the state as a whole, even if it operates at a loss. It becomes a link in a through highway as part of Interstate 77.

Two major toll road systems were built west of the Mississippi. Oklahoma authorized the Turner Turnpike in 1947 and constructed it between 1950 and 1953, followed by the Will Rogers Turnpike, 1955 to 1957, the two forming a continuous express highway from Oklahoma City to Tulsa and the northeast corner of the state near Joplin, Missouri. Two others, the Bailey Turnpike and the Indian Nation Turnpike, were projected at this time but not built until ten years later. The Kansas Turnpike, from Kansas City to Lawrence, Topeka, Wichita, and the southern border of the state, was begun in 1954 and opened in 1956. Elsewhere, Colorado built a short toll road (17 miles) from Denver to Boulder; Texas one of 30 miles between Dallas and Fort Worth; and Florida began its toll parkway running north from Miami. Kentucky constructed the 40-mile Kentucky Turnpike from Louisville to Elizabethtown and in the 1960s added some 150 miles of parkway on a generally east-west line through the middle of the state.

When the enthusiasm for toll roads reached its apex in the middle 1950s, some 12,000 miles were built, started, authorized, or projected. The boom came to an abrupt halt in 1956 when the Interstate Highway Act offered federal financing for express highways. Since then the only major additions to the toll road network have been the Florida and Kentucky parkways and a little over 50 miles of what is now I-95 in Delaware and Maryland, built to relieve the heavy traffic on U.S. 40 between Wilmington, Delaware, and Baltimore.

Table 9.3   Toll Road Travel

	Vehicles		
	Passenger	Commercial	Total
Pennsylvania Turnpike (1968)	43,632,416	6,160,110	49,792,526
Maine Turnpike (1968)	not given	—	7,556,764
Ohio Turnpike (1967)	14,261,453	3,492,170	17,753,623
New Jersey Turnpike (1967)	59,143,528	11,105,373	70,248,901
New York Thruway (1967)	110,572,974	15,941,057	—
Connecticut Turnpike (1968)	5,995,289	1,220,066	7,215,355
Kansas Turnpike (1967)	6,857,917	991,046	7,848,963
Richmond-Petersburg Turnpike (1969)	43,582,165	7,135,558	50,717,723
West Virginia Turnpike (1968)	1,625,234	755,220	2,380,454

Source: Turnpike and Highway Authorities of the states listed.

The toll roads filled a gap in the development of American highways at a time when express highways were urgently needed to handle the growing volume of traffic in heavily traveled regions and the federal government was not yet ready to make a long-range commitment to a nationwide network of such roads (see Table 9.3). The critical problem for state authorities was finance, and the toll system provided a solution. The toll roads made other contributions. They demonstrated that express highways were well worth their cost as a means of moving large quantities of vehicles quickly and safely. The safety record has been impressive, to some extent because toll road authorities as a rule maintain their own detachments of state police, and so the highways are well patrolled. With national averages for highway fatalities on the order of 5.6 per 100 million vehicle-miles, the New York Thruway had a cumulative average of 2.42 and a record for 1967 of 1.92. The New Jersey Turnpike had a fatality rate of 2.17 per 100 million vehicle-miles in 1962, and the Garden State Parkway an incredible 0.66 in 1961.[10]

The toll roads also provided useful experience in design that would later be applied to the Interstates. On the earlier turn-

10 Cranmer, *New Jersey in the Automobile Age,* pp. 64, 66.

pikes median dividers were usually too narrow; the Pennsylvania Turnpike eventually had to install a steel median guardrail. Later practice kept the roadways well apart and encouraged plantings in the median. It was also found that long straight stretches caused "highway hypnosis." Curves and landscaping were used to break monotony. In addition much was learned about the design of on and off ramps to promote greater smoothness and safety.

California's Freeways

During the period of the toll road boom California was a conspicuous exception in that it undertook an ambitious program of express highway construction but chose to finance it from tax revenues. For a state whose economy and social structure have been strongly automobile-oriented, California started from a very inadequate highway base. An informed account states:

Since the turn of the century California had a history of almost perpetual crisis over the highways. The state, which is over 1,000 miles long, grew up after the era of railroad building. One-third of its towns have no railroad facilities. Trucks carried 85 per cent of the farm products to the Los Angeles market and 50 per cent of the state's heavy tonnage. During World War II it was found that 65 per cent of all passenger car traffic had to be classified as essential.

In 1938, California's future depended on a highway system that was falling apart at the seams. The state had been paying less and less for more and more, as the expenditure for highways dropped from 2.4¢ per vehicle mile in 1921 to less than 1¢. The 3¢ gasoline tax had been put into effect in 1927, when there were 7,000 miles of state highway. Since then, the state highway system had doubled—but ½¢ of the tax revenue had been spread to include improving city streets and connecting state highways through towns, while 1¢ had always gone to the state's 58 counties. This left only 1½¢ for a 14,000-mile system being pounded to pieces by 831,592 more vehicles traveling 8,785 million more miles than in 1927.

During the war the rickety highway structure really went to pieces. In 1944, the State Division of Highways listed critical deficiencies that would cost $629 million to patch up.[11]

11 Samuel W. Taylor, "How California Got Fine Roads," *Freedom of the American Road*, p. 11.

A salient feature of the California situation, which has general relevance in any consideration of highway financing, is that it was not just a question of inadequate funds; how the available funds were spent was also a critical factor. California had a confused conglomeration of local authorities spending half the state's road funds, and even the state highways were subject to political log-rolling in determining what was built and where.

The man principally responsible for reorganizing California's highway policy was Randolph Collier, elected to the state senate from the northern California city of Yreka in 1938. After the war he became interested in the state's highway problem and after an intensive campaign sponsored a landmark piece of legislation, the Collier-Burns Act of 1947. It laid down a ten-year master plan for a 14,000-mile state highway system at an estimated cost of $2.4 billion, approximately twice what California had spent on roads from 1912 to 1945.[12] The needed funds were to be provided by increasing the tax on motor fuels and by other user taxes. Local roads were turned back to the counties; the vehicle taxes were to be applied to state highways and approved primary roads and city streets. Freeways and expressways were to be built where conditions called for them.

When this program was adopted there were 19 miles of freeway in California. In the next ten years about 300 more were added, principally in and about Los Angeles and San Francisco, where the need was most urgent. The urban freeway systems will be discussed in connection with the overall problem of urban transportation; the important feature here is that California chose to regard urban freeways as an integral part of its state highway system. Some local pressure continued to function. In the early 1950s the citizens of the communities south of San Francisco decided that the state was not moving fast enough to deal with the appalling traffic conditions on Bayshore Highway, which

12 *Ibid.*, p. 12.

was then carrying 50,000 vehicles a day between San Francisco and San Jose and was referred to locally as "Bloody Bayshore." [13] A few miles consisted of six-lane freeway, and this section had an accident rate one-tenth of the rest of the highway. A concerted drive led by the editor of the Palo Alto *Times* resulted in the budget provision for the Bayshore Freeway in 1953.

After ten years of the Collier-Burns programs it was evident that they were not proving adequate for the needs of a fast-growing state. With Senator Collier again taking the lead and on the basis of elaborate studies of California's current and prospective highway requirements, the legislature in 1959 created the California Freeway and Expressway System, to comprise 12,500 miles of road and to be completed in 1980.[14] The roads designated for this purpose constituted 10 percent of the state's highways, roads, and streets and carried 40 percent of its traffic in 1958. The completed system would be 8 percent of California's road mileage and is expected to carry 60 percent of the traffic. Financing, as before, was through gasoline and various user taxes, registration fees, plus (since the Interstate Highway program was now in operation) substantial federal aid. In 1957 the sources of revenue for all California highways broke down as follows:[15]

Gasoline tax	54%
Motor vehicle fees	12%
User taxes	5%
Federal aid	29%

13 S. W. Taylor, "Bayshore Campaign Aimed High," *ibid.*, pp. 51–54.
14 The information on the California Freeway and Expressway System is taken from State of California, Department of Public Works, *The California Freeway and Expressway System. 1968 Progress and Problems. Summary Report* (Sacramento, 1969); J. Allen Davis, "Raids on the Gas Tax" (Los Angeles: Automobile Club of Southern California Manuscript, 1960), p. 1; presentation by Herbert Hoover, Jr., to officials of the city of Los Angeles, May 15, 1967.
15 *California Highways and Public Works*, vol. 37, nos. 1, 2 (January, February 1958), p. 27.

For California this method of financing was well suited to the conditions. Where express highways in the East were intended to carry a large proportion of vehicles passing through the state —as a rule, half the traffic on the major toll roads consisted of out-of-state vehicles—California was dealing with predominantly intrastate movement. It has over 10 percent of all the registered motor vehicles in the country, and because of its size—the third largest state in the Union in area—most motor vehicle trips are entirely within the state. Consequently, California could justifiably employ gasoline and other motor vehicle taxes instead of tolls to support its express highways, because although such taxes fall most heavily on the local population, in California the local population is the principal user of and beneficiary from the freeways and expressways.

The major drawback has been that mounting costs in the 1960s resulted in revenues being insufficient to maintain the contemplated schedule of construction. As of 1968, some 2,800 miles of the system had been constructed, about half as much as had been contemplated in 1959. (See Figure 9.1.) This is an unfortunate situation because it leads to assumptions and accusations that new freeway construction cannot handle the state's transportation needs, whereas if the program had been able to keep to its planned schedule, jammed freeways would be far less common than they are now. Even with its limitations, the California system was proving reasonably effective both in expediting traffic in urban areas and in increasing highway safety. In 1966, for example, California's freeways had a fatality rate of 2.78 per 100 million vehicle-miles compared with 6.97 for the rest of the roads in the state, even though the freeways, with one-sixtieth of California's highway mileage, carried one-fourth of its traffic.[16] (See Table 9.4.)

16 Davis Dutton, "Traffic Fatality Rates—A Downtrend for California," *Westways*, vol. 59, no. 10 (October 1967), p. 35.

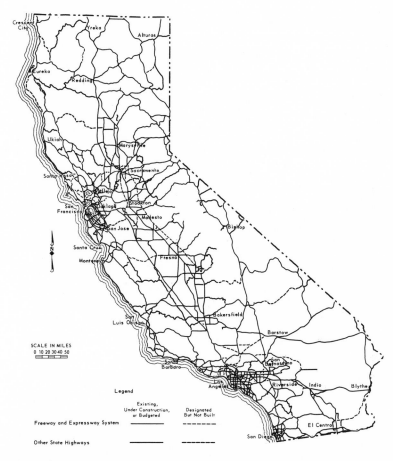

Figure 9.1   The California State Highway System
Source: State of California, *The California Freeway and Expressway System,*
March 1969.

The Interstate Highway System

The culmination of American highway policy as the nation
entered the decade of the 1970s has been the Federal-Aid Highway Act of 1956 [17] and its subsequent amendments. The highway
program restated the fundamental principles of the 1944 act re-

17 *U.S. Statutes at Large,* vol. 70 (1956), p. 374.

Table 9.4   California Highway Safety Data, 1966

	Vehicle-Miles (billions)	Total Accidents	Traffic Fatalities
Urban freeways	21.4 (21%)	34,446 (11%)	423 (9%)
Rural freeways	6.3 (6%)	6,313 (2%)	300 (6%)
Other roads	73.3 (73%)	284,249 (87%)	4,107 (85%)
Totals	101.0 (100%)	325,008 (100%)	4,830 (100%)

Source: California State Chamber of Commerce.

garding a system of Interstate and Defense Highways, this time authorizing 41,000 miles of express highways, of which 5,000 would be urban freeways. The Interstates were toll-free, but provision was made for incorporating existing toll roads into through routes, and about 2,300 miles of toll roads were made part of the Interstate network. No federal aid, however, is given for construction or upkeep of the toll sections of Interstate routes.

The key feature of the 1956 law was the arrangement for financing the program. It established a Highway Trust Fund composed of receipts from federal taxes on motor fuels, tires and tubes, new buses, trucks, and trailers, and a use tax on heavy trucks. Road construction would be based on the money available in the trust fund. This fund pays for 90 percent of the construction cost of the Interstate highways. The states pay the rest, except that allowances are made for states with a large acreage of tax-free public domain and for such special features as highway beautification projects. It is possible for the federal aid to go as high as 95 percent.

The original cost estimate for the entire system was $27 billion. This was raised to $39.5 billion in 1958, then to $46.8 billion in 1965, and the final figure will undoubtedly be well over $50 billion. The discrepancies reflect neither incompetence nor misconduct in the planning or execution of the program. They were due in the first place to the persistent inflationary pressures of the period, which pushed construction costs to unforeseen levels, and beyond that to accretions to the initial program, such as a stipulation that special local conditions should be provided for if they did not conflict with the requirements of the system as a whole. An analysis made for the banking community attributes a fourth of the increase in cost to inflationary price rises. The rest has been due to improvements not originally provided for: additional interchanges in urban areas, more lanes to accommodate heavier volumes of traffic, changes in bridge design for greater safety, and sturdier pavements.[18] Even the development of long-range ballistic missiles was a factor, because transporting them demanded higher bridge and tunnel clearances than the initial estimates called for.

Consequently, in spite of periodic tax increases, the income of the Highway Trust Fund has not been enough to keep construction of the Interstates on its projected schedule. As of 1969 approximately 30,000 miles were open to traffic, and it was evident that completion of the total system would be deferred from its target date of 1972 until 1975 at least. (See Figure 9.2.) When it is finished, the Interstate network will contain 1.2 percent of all road and street mileage in the United States, but estimates are that it will handle 24 percent of the traffic.[19]

The projected gains to be realized from the Interstate system are staggering in their immensity. The Bureau of Public Roads estimates the equivalent of $11 billion annually in reduced vehicle operating costs, savings of time, a lower accident rate, and other factors, to say nothing of a substantial saving of lives.[20] The experience of the toll roads and other freeways has been repeated on the Interstates, to drive home the point that greater

18 "Modernizing U.S. Highways," *The Morgan Guaranty Survey* (June 1967), pp. 4–5.
19 Wilbur Smith and Associates, *Future Highways and Urban Growth* (New Haven, Conn.: Wilbur Smith and Associates, 1961), p. viii.
20 "Modernizing U.S. Highways," p. 3.

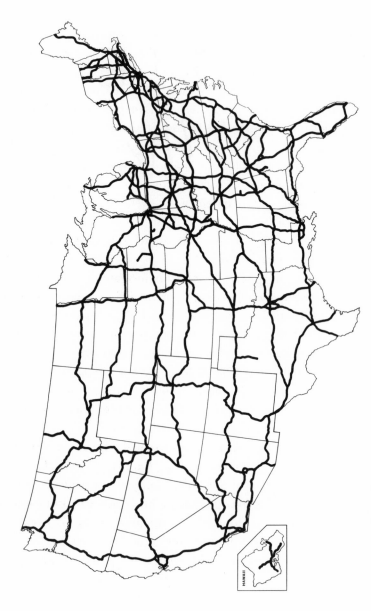

Figure 9.2 The national system of interstate and defense highways

safety is achieved by controlled-access, grade-separated, divided highways. On the Interstate mileage open in 1967 the fatality rate was 2.89 per 100 million vehicle-miles, closely comparable with the toll roads and the California freeways and contrasting with a 5.66 fatality rate for all roads and 6.9 for the other trunk roads carrying long-distance traffic.[21] Wilbur Smith and Associates computed the accumulated gains from the Interstates in 1980 as $9 billion and 75,000 lives saved, on the assumption that the system was completed on schedule.[22]

The impact of the Interstates can be judged on a more tangible basis than projections for the future. An evaluation of the program as an investment of public funds made fairly early in the growth of the system questioned whether rural Interstates were economically justified in terms of the volume of traffic on them, but said of the urban segments: "Of the possible alternative highway investments, the urban Interstate system appears to be the one that maximizes the stream of future income to society." [23]

This is a reasonable evaluation, subject to two qualifications: the level of traffic on the rural sections of the Interstate network has increased steadily since this study was made, and the national defense factor in the program justifies a considerable mileage of rural freeway even if normal traffic density is light. This work also questions whether the Interstate system will create new investment opportunities, on the ground that the ratio between ton-miles of transported commodities and the GNP has remained stable for some twenty years. This position is valid only if a one-

21 Robert P. Jordan, "Our Growing Interstate Highway System," *National Geographic,* vol. 133, no. 2 (February 1968), p. 198; Joseph C. Ingraham "Progress Report on the Interstate Road System," *New York Times,* June 8, 1969.

22 Wilbur Smith and Associates, *Future Highways,* p. vii.

23 Ann F. Friedlander, *The Interstate Highway System. A Study in Public Investment* (Amsterdam, Holland: North Holland Publishing Co., 1965), p. 3.

way causal relationship is assumed, that is, that changes in the GNP determine the volume of goods transported. It ignores the converse possibility—more than a possibility, a fact with over-whelming historical evidence to support it—that ability to move goods and people more economically and efficiently will cause the Gross National Product to rise. This latter premise gains support if total vehicle-miles of highway travel is used instead of ton-miles of freight, since during this same twenty years the rise in vehicle-miles has been somewhat ahead of the rise in the GNP (Figure 5.1). The vehicle-mile figure is more valid, because it includes movement of people, which is definitely part of the national economic picture.

With the system still unfinished, the impact of the Interstates cannot now be accurately appraised, but some information does exist as a basis for judgment. A survey of twenty-one manufacturing firms in Kentucky with one hundred or more employees revealed several distinct advantages to location near an Interstate highway: labor can be drawn from distances ten or fifteen miles greater than would otherwise be feasible; skilled labor and management personnel can be attracted from large cities because the city remains readily accessible; commercial carrier rates do not increase; and some of the advantages of highway improvement generally, such as ability to reduce inventories, are realized more intensively.[24] In one specific situation, the building of I-75 extended the Cincinnati commercial zone thirteen miles outward to Florence, Kentucky, where a 930-acre industrial park was built adjacent to an interchange. Since a number of highway common carriers can operate in Kentucky only within the area defined as the "Cincinnati commercial zone," the construction of the Interstate was directly responsible for this industrial development.

24 C. P. Care, "The Interstate Builds Business," *Highway User* (February 1968), pp. 28–30.

A broader picture appears in an unpublished study prepared in the Economic Development Administration of the United States Department of Commerce.[25] It compared 106 pairs of cities, each pair as much alike as possible, except that one was a "freeway" city, within seven miles of an Interstate, and the other was a "non-freeway" city, at least sixteen miles from the nearest Interstate exit. The conclusion was that superior highway facilities are an important stimulus to industrial growth in certain regions and under certain conditions. Nationally, the freeway cities grew slightly faster in terms of new manufacturing jobs per thousand capita than the nonfreeway cities, but the difference was not statistically significant. The freeways had the greatest effect in fast-growing regions (Southeast, East Midwest, and Pacific Northwest) where dense population and uneven terrain created a substantial difference in time and cost between freeways and ordinary roads. The slow growth rate of the Northeast made comparisons difficult, but as far as there was a measurable difference the freeway cities had the advantage. The Rocky Mountain states and central and southern California were omitted because of a lack of suitable pairs. In the California case, the lack existed because there are practically no nonfreeway cities in the southern two-thirds of the state.

The Interstate system cannot be judged by economic factors alone. The ease and greater celerity of both long-distance and local travel must of necessity have a major social impact. There are some qualifications to be made. The Interstates do not have special police detachments like the toll roads, so they are as a rule less intensively patrolled, and as a result the motorist who has car trouble some distance from an interchange may have a long wait for help to arrive. In addition, because of an occasional

25. Leonard F. Wheat, "The Effect of Modern Highways on Urban Manufacturing Growth," paper presented at 48th Annual Meeting, Highway Research Board, Washington, D.C., January 13–17, 1969.

excessive zeal for "beautification," the traveler seeking fuel, food, or lodging must frequently go off at an interchange without any idea of what he is going to find. Some states (in the author's experience, Minnesota and Virginia) have found a remedy by putting up signs with the same design as their regular highway signs giving information about the specific services and accommodations available at each interchange. This is a quite satisfactory solution and shows a sensible appreciation of the traveler's need to know what his options are: a gourmet restaurant or a one-arm greasy spoon, one motel or several, or a gas station where his credit card will be accepted. But there are also long stretches of Interstate highways where an occasional advertising sign affords, or would afford, a welcome relief without in any way impairing the scenery. The Interstates might have had service areas, like the toll roads, but in view of what has happened on the toll roads, this would have been a dubious benefit. During the summer months when tourist travel is at its heaviest, the service areas on the major toll roads are chronically overcrowded so that service is frequently slow and poor.

The flaws in the Interstates are minor when they are set against the advantages. The motorist who goes through Providence and Pawtucket, Rhode Island, on I-95 and remembers what it was like to try to follow U.S. 1 through them, or who crosses Wyoming on I-80 and has had experience of doing the same thing on two-lane stretches of U.S. 30, with unending lines of heavy trucks in each direction, will unhesitatingly agree that the change has definitely been for the better. Since the Roman Empire built its 50,000 miles of main highway, there has been no road system in the world to compare with the 41,000 miles of U.S. Interstate. Germany's network of *autobahnen* is considerably smaller. If we put the motor vehicle into the picture, as we must, then there has never been anything to compare with the Interstates.

III   The Road and the City

10   Urban Transportation: The Background

Transportation and the life of the city are inseparable. The earliest known cities were centers of trade, and therefore of transportation; they grew up on harbors, at fords of rivers, or at junctions of trade routes. The exceptions were cities built at readily defensible points (like Athens and Edinburgh, both with nearby seaports), or at seats of government. Transportation also to a large extent determined the shape that cities would take. Until fairly modern times, specifically until gunpowder and cannon made city walls useless, cities were compact in order to be more easily defensible. They were also compact because the residents were limited in their mobility. There could be no lengthy travel between home and work. The merchant's house was his place of business, or adjoined it closely; the craftsman's house was his shop. This condition, in fact, persisted into the twentieth century. One can still see in the older industrial towns and cities of Europe and America the rows of workers' houses clustered about the factories because the work force had to walk to and from the job.

Cities were therefore characteristically centralized and crowded. Urban life in the past evidently had a number of the problems that we are prone to think of as peculiar to contemporary metropolitan society, including traffic congestion. Ancient Rome prohibited wheeled vehicles from using the city streets during the daytime, and women were not allowed to drive chariots in the city at all. Descriptions of London traffic in bygone days read very much like descriptions of twentieth-century traffic except that the vehicles were horsedrawn rather than self-propelled. A British student of traffic problems summarizes the situation thus: "We are apt nowadays to think of street congestion as entirely a product of the motor age. This is not at all the case, for there are numerous references for centuries back to the streets, particularly of London, being choked with people, horses, dogs, carts, carriages, and even sledges." [1]

Few cities were planned; most just grew along lines of least resistance and certainly with little consideration for the smooth flow of vehicular traffic. Comprehensive urban planning is largely a phenomenon of modern times. The reconstruction of Paris under both Napoleons was intended partly for beautification, partly for prestige, and quite largely to facilitate the suppression of revolts by replacing narrow, crooked streets with broad, straight boulevards. Major Pierre L'Enfant, the French engineer, and Benjamin Banneker, the American Negro astronomer, designed Washington, D.C. for the same purpose. The circles were intended to be capable of conversion into fortified points commanding the streets and avenues radiating from them; certainly no one can claim that they do anything to facilitate the movement of traffic. Among other American cities, Philadelphia was a pioneer example of the rectangular grid street pattern, which makes for orderly property lines but is poorly adapted to the control of traffic, because it not only takes no account of the direction of traffic flow but also forces streams of traffic to cross each other at frequent intervals. New York, or more accurately the Borough of Manhattan, had its streets laid out in the early nineteenth century with some consideration for the movement of people and goods. As the city expanded northward, it had only a few (twelve in all) north-south avenues but many east-west streets, because, Manhattan Island being long and narrow, it was taken for granted that the long-distance traffic, moving on the north-south axis, would go by water.[2] But travel over any appreciable distance between home and work, or for family

1 C. D. Buchanan, *Mixed Blessing: The Motor in Britain* (London: Leonard Hill (Books) Ltd., 1958), p. 112.
2 E. M. Hoover and Raymond Vernon, *Anatomy of a Metropolis* (Cambridge, Mass.: Harvard University Press, 1959), p. 216. This estimate of Manhattan's traffic needs was made in 1811.

business or recreation, was a rarity. Most cities still have the relics of wealthy homes in their downtown areas, mementos of an era when proximity to one's place of business was an asset.

The Growth of Metropolis

The twentieth century has witnessed a far-reaching change in the growth pattern of cities and their relationship to their total environment. Industrialization inevitably promotes urbanization both by requiring large concentrations of people in factory areas and by advancing farm technology so that a progressively smaller proportion of the population is needed to remain on the land and produce food. Beyond this, the process of urbanization has taken a new direction. The most significant growth has been occurring in metropolitan areas—areas, that is, consisting of a central city core with suburbs clustered around it. The British call them "conurbations"; the United States, at least the Bureau of the Census, terms them Standard Metropolitan Statistical Areas (SMSAs). According to the Bureau,

except in New England, an SMSA is a county or group of contiguous counties which contains at least one city of 50,000 inhabitants or more, or "twin cities" with a combined population of at least 50,000. In addition to the county, or counties, containing such a city, or cities, contiguous counties are included in an SMSA if, according to certain criteria, they are essentially metropolitan in character and are socially and economically integrated with the central city. In New England, SMSA's consists of towns and cities rather than counties.

As of 1967 there were 228 SMSAs (see Table 10.1).

These are the focal areas of population growth in the United States. The rural population is declining, and the smaller cities and towns about hold their own. The increase has been concentrated in the metropolitan areas, and in recent years the suburbs have outrun the central cities. This process has been going on at an accelerating rate since the beginning of the century. The census of 1920 for the first time showed more than half the

Table 10.1   Growth of Central Cities and Rings of Standard Metropolitan Areas (SMAs), 1900–1956*

Census Year	No. of SMAs	Percent of U.S. Population			Percent Increase during Preceding Decade			Percent of Total U.S. Population Growth Claimed by SMAs during Preceding Decade		Total U.S. Population
		Total Metropolitan Areas	Central Cities	Rings	Total Metropolitan Areas	Central Cities	Rings	Central Cities	Rings	
All SMAs										
1956	168	58.6	31.3	27.3	14.8	4.7	29.3	15.6	69.1	164,308,000
All SMAs										
1950†	162	56.8	32.8	24.0	21.8	13.9	34.7	31.6	49.0	150,697,361
Principal SMAs										
1950	147	56.1	32.3	23.8	21.8	13.7	34.8	30.7	48.6	150,697,361
1940	125	51.4	31.6	19.5	8.3	5.1	13.8	22.8	34.9	131,669,275
1930	115	49.8	31.8	18.0	27.0	23.3	34.2	43.3	32.9	122,775,046
1920	94	43.7	28.9	14.8	25.2	26.7	22.4	46.8	20.8	105,710,620
1910	71	37.7	25.0	12.7	32.6	35.3	27.6	37.4	15.7	91,972,266
1900	52	31.9	21.2	10.7	—	—	—	—	—	75,994,575

* Sources: Donald J. Bogue, *The Growth of Standard Metropolitan Areas: 1900–50*, December, 1953; U.S. Department of Commerce Bureau of the Census, *Statistical Abstract of the United States, 1958.*
† 168 areas have been combined into 162.
From: Wilbur Smith and Associates, *Future Highways and Urban Growth* (New Haven, Conn.: Wilbur Smith and Associates, 1961), p. 333.

Table 10.2   Rural and Urban Population in the United States, 1900–1960*

Year	Urban	Rural	Percent Urban	Percent Rural	Total
1900	30,159,921	45,834,654	39.7	60.3	75,994,575
1910	41,998,932	49,973,334	45.7	54.3	91,972,266
1920	54,157,973	51,552,647	51.2	48.8	105,710,620
1930	68,954,823	53,820,223	56.2	43.8	122,775,046
1940	74,423,702	57,245,573	56.5	43.5	131,669,275
1950†	88,927,464	61,769,897	59.0	41.0	150,697,361
1950‡	96,467,686	54,229,675	64.0	36.0	150,697,361
1956	103,631,000	60,677,000	63.1	36.9	164,308,000
1959§	118,352,000	60,428,000	66.2	33.8	178,780,000
1960‖	120,000,000	59,500,000	67.1	32.9	179,500,000

* Source: U.S. Department of Commerce, Bureau of the Census.
† Old census definition of rural and urban is used for consistency.
‡ New census definition.
§ Total population estimated by Bureau of the Census as of November 1959.
Percent urban and rural estimated by *Sales Management* as of January 1, 1959.
‖ Total population from preliminary census.
From: Wilbur Smith and Associates, *Future Highways and Urban Growth*, p. 332.

American people living in urban communities (defined as having 2,500 or more population). (See Table 10.2.) By midcentury more than half of all Americans lived in metropolitan areas, and by 1975 more than half will be living in suburbs. To be more specific, the urban population of the United States rose from 6 percent of the total in 1800 to 70 percent in 1960. During the last ten years of this 160-year span, 84 percent of the nation's population growth occurred in the areas classified as SMSAs. These had an overall increase of 26 percent, but suburban growth was 49 percent compared with 11 percent for central cities,[3] and these trends are continuing. In short, what has made the problems of the city loom so large in our society is that urbanization has attained an unprecedented scale of magnitude and is expanding at an accelerating rate. In 1910 the United States had just three cities (New York, Philadelphia, Chicago) with a million or more

3 Wilfred Owen, *The Metropolitan Transportation Problem,* rev. ed. (Washington, D.C.: The Brookings Institution, 1966), p. 8.

inhabitants, and no other total metropolitan area was this large. Fifty years later there were still only five cities containing a million or more people within their limits (Los Angeles and Detroit were the newcomers), but there were now 24 SMSAs with over a million population. In the same half-century the number of urban areas with populations between 250,000 and a million rose from 16 to 46, and the number between 50,000 and 250,000 from 90 to 282.[4]

This transformation of the city has been largely a consequence of developments in transportation and would have been impossible without them. Most cities of the past were kept small by limitations on internal mobility and by dependence on wagon transportation to bring food supplies from the surrounding countryside. The few metropolises that did emerge (Alexandria, Rome, Constantinople, Paris, London) all had water transportation to serve their needs.

The beginning of the current urban revolution was the appearance of the railway, which for the first time permitted people to live at a substantial distance from their work—those at least who could afford the service. By the end of the nineteenth century every major city in the Western world had its network of commuter rail lines. Rail transport also provided for local travel within cities in the form of street railways, operating horse cars and cable cars at first but going over completely in the early years of the twentieth century to the electric-powered trolley car. The trolley lines frequently expanded into interurban service, competing with the railroads for commuter traffic.[5] Finally, in very large cities there were rapid transit systems, underground or elevated. In view of much of the contemporary discussion of

4 Jean Gottmann, "Mankind Is Reshaping its Habitat," in C. E. Elias, Jr., J. Gilles, and S. Riemer, *Metropolis: Values in Conflict* (Belmont, Calif.: Wadsworth Publishing Co., 1967), p. 5.
5 See G. W. Hilton and J. F. Due, *The Electric Interurban Railways in America* (Stanford, Calif.: Stanford University Press, 1960).

urban transportation, it is worth noting that these rapid transit systems were undertaken more than seventy years ago, when the horseless carriage was still a novelty, in order to relieve congestion on surface streets.[6] There were even those who suggested that it would be advisable to resolve the problems of the cities of that day by "starting on a bold plan on comparatively virgin soil rather than by attempting to adapt our old cities to our newer and higher needs."[7] This was proposed in 1902.

Railborne transport initiated the great outward movement of city dwellers to Suburbia. Communities grew along the commuter and interurban lines like beads on a string. The analogy is quite exact because in the absence of good highway transportation these communities had to be attached to a rail line. As late as 1925 only 2 percent of the closely developed residential land in the New York metropolitan region was more than a mile from a station, while in the next fifteen years 10 percent of the new development was outside this distance.[8]

Within the central city limits the same pattern developed. People could live farther from the central business district, or from factories, as long as they were within reasonable walking distance of a streetcar line. But one overmastering fact persisted. Paradoxically, the transportation system that permitted people to live farther away from the center of the city also intensified concentration on the central business district (CBD), because rail transportation, to be economically viable, must operate on corridors of high-density traffic. The effect on urban growth is lucidly described by Dr. George W. Hilton, who is both a transportation economist and a historian of transportation.

In the nineteenth century a variety of forces combined to create a fairly standard pattern, among cities, of a central business district surrounded by a periphery of residential areas. It is uni-

6 Owen, *Metropolitan Transportation Problem,* p. 6.
7 *Ibid.*
8 Hoover and Vernon, *Anatomy of a Metropolis,* p. 221.

versally recognized that rail passenger transport was a major contributing influence to this pattern. Whether the service was provided by the horsecar, the cable car, or the electric streetcar, the inflexibility of transportation on steel rails was an incentive to centralize economic activity of a wide variety. It was attractive to be able to make a single rail trip to an area where one could work, shop, dine, and amuse oneself with only foot passage between points, and then to make another single trip home. Rail passenger transportation was so inflexible that it could provide little but the trip to and from the central business district. Cities as large as New Orleans and Washington, D.C. had but one crosstown car line each; every other line served the central business district. Only Chicago and Brooklyn developed comprehensive grids of streetcar lines.

The electric streetcar was, for all its inflexibility, a highly successful innovation. By 1906 it was providing some 90 percent of trips by urban passengers, most of whom—as usual—anticipated no change in their habits.

Rapid transit and suburban railroad service were adaptations of the same technology to longer, more heavily traveled, or more severely rush-hour-peaked routes. What the technology of rapid transit and suburban main-line railroading gained in speed, peakload capacity, and freedom from street traffic, relative to the streetcar, it won only at the cost of increased inflexibility. It was unthinkable to use the capital-intensive technology of rapid transit or main-line railroading for anything but service to and from a major central business district. Any trips such forms of transportation could provide other than the trips in and out of the central business district were incidental, depending on what secondary focal points lay along the line. Accordingly, rail rapid transit was restricted to the largest metropolitan areas: New York, Chicago, Philadelphia, and Boston. . . . Large-scale railroad commutation services were characteristic of the same cities, with the addition of San Francisco. Smaller-scale commutation operations served most other large cities. Los Angeles had a vast network of suburban, interurban, and street railway trackage in the form of the Southern Pacific Lines' Pacific Electric system.[9]

Dependence on rail transport for moving freight had a similar centralizing effect. The railroad still has no equal as a means of carrying large quantities of freight overland expeditiously and

9 G. W. Hilton, "Rail Transport and the Pattern of Modern Cities: The California Case," *Traffic Quarterly*, vol. XXI, no. 3 (July 1967), pp. 379–380. Reprinted by permission of the author, *Traffic Quarterly*, and the Eno Foundation for Highway Traffic Control, Inc.

economically. Water transport is cheaper but slower and limited in its availability; pipelines are also cheaper but usable only for a few commodities. For small loads (less-than-carload) and short hauls the railroad is less effective. The full potential of rail transport is best realized by utilizing to the utmost the economies of scale, and the high fixed costs of railroad operation press in the same direction. Among other things, it is desirable that freight yards and terminals should be as highly centralized as possible.

In an era when the railroad dominated land transport, this meant that industry had an incentive, in fact a compulsion, to cluster as closely as possible about the main freight yards.[10] At the very least a factory had to have a railroad siding. The result was the grubby industrial districts common to nineteenth-century cities. Substituting water for rail transportation made no difference, because water transport likewise is most economical for bulk shipments, and factories simply concentrated around the dock area instead of the railroad yards. Even a light industry, using materials in small quantities, could hardly locate at any distance from rail or water transport unless its products were intended purely for local consumption. In any event, a factory in an outlying district would have to be very small because it would have great difficulty finding labor.

Highway transportation, while not exactly unimportant, had a limited role in urban life before the motor vehicle appeared on the scene. It was used for local cartage of freight and to a limited extent (cabs, for instance) for local movement of passengers. Insofar as there was any distinction between main and secondary streets, the main arteries, like the rest of the city's transportation, converged on the central business district.

At the beginning of the twentieth century, therefore, there was a prevalent, almost universal, urban pattern, consisting of a cen-

10 On this subject see L. N. Moses and H. F. Williamson, Jr., "The Location of Economic Activity in Cities," *American Economic Review,* vol. 57, no. 2 (May 1967), p. 213.

tral core in which business, industry, and most of the recreational activities were concentrated, surrounded by residential districts extending outward in an ascending scale of affluence. There were of course infinite local variations because geography, topography, climate, and other factors (including history) make it impossible for two cities to be exactly alike. The basic pattern was there nonetheless, but it should be evident that there was no divine or natural law requiring cities to develop according to this pattern. The governing factor determining how cities grew was transportation, and the core-plus-suburb pattern was, if not a historical accident, certainly an unplanned consequence of the introduction of specific transportation technologies. Railroads, for instance, were originally planned for intercity traffic. Commuter service was an afterthought, adopted as a method of securing additional revenue and fuller utilization of existing track.[11] If good highway transportation in the form of an effective combination of a self-propelled vehicle and a surfaced road had been developed before rather than after the railway, present-day cities would have a very different character.

The Motor Vehicle Arrives

This was the urban environment in which the automobile made its appearance, and the first clumsy horseless carriages to bounce along cobbled city streets did not look like the harbingers of an urban revolution. There was little appreciation of the fact that this was a new transportation technology that permitted people to control their own movements rather than depend on the schedules of railroad or traction companies, although there had to be some realization that the automobile was not only a more individual but also a more flexible mode of transport. If a family wished to visit friends in a different section of the city, it could

11 As an example, see Charles J. Kennedy, "Commuter Service in the Boston Area, 1835–1860," *Business History Review*, vol. 36, no. 2 (Summer 1962), pp. 153–170.

go directly by car, as far as the street layout permitted, while using public transportation almost invariably required a trip downtown, a time-consuming change, and a trip out again.

Essentially, however, the automobile had to function on street systems that had never been designed for it and were about as poorly adapted to it as it was possible to be. Some optimists in the early days hoped that fast-moving vehicles would relieve traffic congestion. They should have been right, and they might have been if the nature of automotive transportation had been recognized sooner and if prompter measures had been taken to adapt to it. Instead motor vehicles were expected to merge into existing traffic and transportation patterns and to share the same streets with trolley cars, carriages, wagons, bicycles, and pedestrians, with no discrimination between local and through traffic or between fast and slow vehicles. The automobile, moreover, quickly emerged as an attractive way of traveling to work, but since the predominant urban pattern had business and industry concentrated at the center, commuting by car resulted in increasing masses of vehicles converging on the central city area and inevitably in the massive rush-hour traffic congestion that plagues cities everywhere.

The response for the most part was—and regrettably too frequently still is—to improvise. If conditions at an intersection became sufficiently intolerable, a traffic light would be installed. Crowded narrow streets were made one-way, and parking in congested sections was restricted. An occasional bypass or circumferential route was marked through side streets, frequently over the opposition of retail merchants who were afraid of losing business if traffic was diverted from their doors—until they discovered that traffic jams and inadequate parking were far worse for business.

In time these techniques became more sophisticated. Traffic lights could be synchronized or activated by the flow of vehicles

Plate 1   Poor roads and frightened horses were among the hazards faced by pioneer motorists. Courtesy Automobile Manufacturers Association, Inc.

instead of having to change at arbitrary intervals. They even became a status symbol and were installed at points where they served nothing but civic pride, unless it was to trap out-of-town motorists for the benefit of local revenues. But while there were improvements, none were a satisfactory substitute for systematic street design and location. These were expensive measures, and most municipalities felt unable to accept the cost, even though the alternative was to accept the higher but indirect costs of congestion.

In spite of the handicaps under which it had to function, the motor vehicle in a surprisingly short time became the dominant element in urban transportation and therefore in urban development. Its first conspicuous effect was on existing transit systems. Two forces were at work here. First, as automobile ownership increased, people used their own cars for trips that they would formerly have made on public transportation. Second, railborne transit, especially streetcar and interurban lines, found itself in a losing contest with the motor bus, which was cheaper to operate and also enjoyed a flexibility that no railborne system could have.

The interurbans went first, leaving behind nostalgic and generally inaccurate memories about the quality of their service. Central city streetcar lines followed; most were gone by the Second World War. A few survived in large cities into the 1960s, but for the United States as a whole the trolley car is now a museum piece. Rapid transit continued to function where it was already established, subject to chronic financial difficulties for which automobile competition was only partly responsible. Commuter rail service stood up well during the 1920s because the increase in suburban population was great enough to offset a steady decline in the proportion of suburbanites commuting by

Plate 2 A variety of vehicles contributed to early road congestion. Courtesy Automobile Manufacturers Association, Inc.

rail.[12] The depression years, however, brought a sharp drop in patronage, which has continued, except for the temporary stimulus given by the Second World War, to the point where rail commuter service has disappeared from all but a few major metropolitan areas. Even in those it has to be subsidized by public funds to keep it in existence.

The specific shifts in emphasis among transport media depended on the characteristics of each city. In the article previously cited, Professor Hilton identifies two broad metropolitan patterns. One, with New York as the outstanding example, has a large financial community or some other business structure whose tendency is for firms to concentrate in the central business district, and natural barriers that inhibit dispersal and define travel corridors rather rigorously. Boston, Philadelphia, Chicago, and San Francisco share some of these characteristics with New York, and all have retained railborne transportation. San Francisco's initial network of commuter and interurban lines shriveled, but the city is now in the forefront of "the second generation of rapid transit projects—built, not in the expectation of profitability, but in the hope that their incidental consequences of reduction of traffic and stimulation of central business districts will provide substantial social benefits.[13] At the opposite end of the spectrum is Los Angeles, with no major financial community, few industries congregating about the central business district, and ample room to spread out. It became so diffused that only highway transportation could serve its needs. Its extensive interurban electric system was not suited to a dispersed metropolis and disappeared; 95 percent of all trips between all points in greater Los Angeles came to be made by automobile. Similar conditions existed in large cities like Houston and Indianapolis, and in most small and

12 G. W. Hilton, "The Decline of Railroad Commutation," *Business History Review*, vol. 36, no. 2 (Summer 1962), p. 172.
13 Hilton, "Rail Transport and the Pattern of Modern Cities," pp. 381–384.

medium-sized American cities, and these likewise became dependent on buses and automobiles.

Detroit is not a financial center, and neither its automobile
factories nor their executive offices congregate in the downtown
area. It does have both a water barrier and an international
boundary on its east side, but neither has noticeably constrained
Detroit's expansion, and Detroit relies entirely on the highway
for urban transportation. Cleveland, where rapid transit has
survived, is a special case. It has a sizable financial community and
some channeling of growth by Lake Erie and the gorges of the
Cuyahoga and Rocky rivers. However, its rapid transit began
as a synthetic product stemming from a real estate operation in
the 1920s and entering the downtown area on the right-of-way
of the Nickel Plate Railroad, so it was poorly located to serve the
shopping district. The subsequent development of the system is in
San Francisco's "second generation" category.

For those who see only the streets and freeways choked with
cars at the rush hours and who assume that getting rid of the cars
would get rid of congestion, the shift from mass to individual
transportation is to be deplored. Historically, this position con-
fuses cause and effect. The automobile intensified urban congestion, but the congestion was there first, and it will remain as
long as economic and other activities are concentrated in a
limited central city area. There is also the undoubted fact that
these masses of motor vehicles contribute to pollution of the atmosphere. This is a serious problem, and it will be discussed in
more detail later. In our present context the essential point is
that automobile-generated pollution stems fundamentally from
having too many cars in too small an area, so measures taken to
reduce congestion will automatically reduce pollution also.

The second conspicuous impact of the automobile on urban
development relates directly to the problem of congestion,
namely, the decentralizing effect of automotive transportation.

Figure 10.1   Changing patterns in urban traffic flow

Washington, D.C.'s growth has been governed by traffic and living patterns as shown by these area maps developed by the National Capital Planning Commission. In the 1930s, downtown Washington drew heavy traffic, but by the mid-1950s cross-movement of traffic began to develop and the urban area had enlarged as a result. By 1980, traffic will still be heavy to the center of the city but cross-traffic will increase greatly, demanding a transportation system that serves both types of movements.

(See Figure 10.1.) The rail transit systems began the dispersal of urban residential areas; the automobile permitted the process to be carried much further because it greatly enlarged the area of choice. The expansion of cities followed the rail and transit lines until about 1935, when it began noticeably to spread to other areas.[14] The nature of the change is shown in the fact that urban residential building in the 1920s emphasized apartments and two-family houses just outside the central city and near mass transportation, while after the Second World War the bulk of residential construction was single-family homes farther out from the center, with availability of public transportation a secondary consideration.[15] Thus, like its predecessors, automobile transportation promoted both concentration and dispersal. By providing a cheap and flexible means of transportation, it enabled people to live a greater distance from work than had previously been fea-

14 Homer Hoyt, "The Influence of Highways and Transportation on the Structure and Growth of Cities and Urban Land Values," in Jean Labatut and W. J. Lane, eds., *Highways in Our National Life: A Symposium* (Princeton, N.J.: Princeton University Press, 1950), p. 203.
15 Raymond Vernon, *Metropolis—1985* (Cambridge, Mass.: Harvard University Press, 1960), pp. 137–138.

sible, but it also enabled them to pour into central business districts in unmanageable numbers. What was not understood was that the centralizing aspect was an unnecessary consequence of restricting the potentialities of highway transportation by confining them within an urban structure designed for past conditions.

We have developed a society in which four-fifths of all families own an automobile and use it by preference for their ordinary day-to-day journeying—and all over the world other people are doing exactly the same thing as fast as they are given the opportunity. It is also a society whose inhabitants have made it clear that for the most part they prefer single-family dwellings with at least a suggestion of open space to central city apartments (or tenements). This proposition may seem self-evident, but it need not be accepted on faith. It has been elaborately investigated, with results that show a definite linkage between housing preference and the availability of automotive transportation. The following are some of the conclusions that have been reached.

1. A large proportion of the people studied wanted to move away from the city center and were not deterred by considerations of distance or inconvenience.

2. More people wanted to move from apartments to single-family dwellings than vice versa.

3. The choice of mode for the journey to work was not especially sensitive to cost considerations. Many people do not attempt to estimate the cost of traveling to work by car, and those who do have widely differing results.

4. People overwhelmingly preferred to go to work by car if the factors of cost and time were no greater than what was offered by public transportation.[16]

16 J. B. Lansing and Eva Mueller, *Residential Location and Urban Mobility* (Ann Arbor, Mich.: University of Michigan, 1964), pp. iv–v; and J. B. Lansing, *Residential Location and Urban Mobility: The Second Wave of Interviews* (Ann Arbor, Mich.: University of Michigan, 1966), pp. 1–3.

Urban Trends

The decentralizing tendencies of motor vehicle transportation and the outward thrust of residential preferences created powerful counter forces to the centripetal pull of the central business district. They have been, indeed, so powerful that the crux of our urban problem has been the decay of central cities because of the migration of both population and business to the suburbs. Since the advent of the automobile the forces of urban decentralization seem to have been in the ascendant. Perhaps they should be, but in the meantime the central cities are here, representing an enormous investment in human and material resources.

The decline of central cities can be and frequently is attributed to the rise of the motor vehicle, but this is at best only part of the story. Blighted areas, slums, and ghettos are not an invention of the twentieth century; they have been inherent in urban life since cities began. What the twentieth century really has to offer is the technological and economic capability of doing something about them, and modern highway transportation is an inherent part of this capability. Automobile transportation is not by any means incompatible with the existence of healthy urban core areas. It is unlikely that central business districts will recover the dominant position they once possessed, but it is equally unlikely in the foreseeable future that all the activities that make up the life of a city can be so completely decentralized as to make the CBD unnecessary.

The reason for whatever adverse effects the motor vehicle has had on the central city has been explained: a new transportation technology was forced into an old transportation network. It can be restated in the words of the great architect and city planner Constantine Doxiadis:

In the growth trend we demolish, we choke the center of our cities. Why? Because we allow a city which was prepared to stand up to the pressures of half-a-million people to get 5 million people and later 20, and then 50 million. If I asked any business man here who has a generator of 50,000 kilowatts to enlarge this generator so that it will be a generator of 100,000 kilowatts, he would laugh at me. But this is what we try to do with our cities. We bring all of our machines, all of our pressures, all of our cars downtown, and we choke downtown to death.[17]

Recognizing the problem is one thing; finding remedies is another. The improvisations of the past have manifestly not worked, and there is nothing to suggest that they will do any better in the future. Among possible long-range solutions, the revival of public transportation systems, and especially of rapid transit, attracts a good deal of support, and deservedly so. Good public transportation is an absolute necessity for any city, large or small, because many people must make trips who cannot drive a car or do not have one available. A survey made in Pittsburgh showed that 85 percent of the transit system's patrons either had no driver's license or no car, and a survey in Chicago showed that half the users of rapid transit and 65 percent of all public transportation patrons were in the same category.[18]

The largest share of attention is going to rapid transit systems, railborne on their own rights-of-way, as the most promising method of carrying large numbers of people without overloading the streets. Technical improvements, as demonstrated in Toronto and Montreal, can provide rapid transit that is smoother and faster than the subway and elevated lines built early in the century. The technical problems involved in building rapid transit systems are in fact the easiest to solve. The real difficulties are social and economic. Rail transit may be greatly improved qualitatively, but it remains subject to the limitations described by Professor Hilton; to be economically feasible it requires

17 Constantine Doxiadis, "Toward the Ecumenopolis," *Rotarian*, vol. 112, no. 2 (March 1968), p. 20. He proposes "cells" of 50,000 people within each metropolitan complex.

18 A. S. Lang and R. H. Soberman, *Urban Rail Transit: Its Economics and Technology* (Cambridge, Mass.: The M.I.T. Press, 1964), p. 88. These surveys were made in 1959 (Chicago) and 1961 (Pittsburgh).

high-density traffic along fixed corridors, and only a few American cities can meet this condition. For most cities, public transportation needs can be adequately met by bus service. Besides, as the experience of Chicago and Pittsburgh testifies, people who are accustomed to driving their own cars are poor prospects as patrons of mass transit, and it will take a good deal of persuasion, perhaps even compulsion, to make them change their habits.

There are advocates of compulsion—not in the physical sense, but in terms of proposing in all seriousness that automobiles be excluded from "downtown." (Presumably the ban would not extend to trucks, since this would stop the movement of essential commodities in and out of every central business district in the country.) Such a policy might just work if only those people who had jobs in the CBD needed to be considered. They could come and go by public transportation, although for most cities a substantial expansion of public transportation facilities would be necessary—and expensive, since these facilities would be used only for two hours inbound in the morning and two hours outbound in the afternoon. But if the revival of the central city is what is desired, there also has to be an influx of people to do business there—to shop, dine out, seek entertainment—and few such people will take a long bus or rail trip downtown when they can do the same things elsewhere by car. The issue was expressed pungently by the Cleveland *Plain Dealer* when the mayor of that city was quoted as saying that cars would have to be kept out of the central city:

> While no one would deny that the mayor of Cleveland has a great many problems, he really ought to be told that keeping cars out of downtown is NOT one of them. Suburban shopping centers, with their department and discount stores, theaters, restaurants, health spas and recreation centers, along with free parking and other blandishments, are doing quite a job of keeping cars [people] out of the central city, and this is what ails downtown. . . . Take cars out of downtowns and you really have ghost cities.[19]

19 Quoted from *The Ohio Motorist* (March 1969).

While the central city has nothing to gain by excluding cars indiscriminately, it can definitely be helped by keeping out of the downtown area the cars that do not belong there and do not even want to be there. Traffic surveys have repeatedly demonstrated that at least two-thirds of the cars in city centers are simply passing through. There is no need for them to be where they are, but the configuration of city street systems is such that they are forced to pass through the center, thereby adding quite unnecessarily to downtown congestion.

Thus the adjustment of the metropolitan core to the situation created by automotive transportation seems to fall into two broad categories. First, an adequate public transportation system is called for, capable of providing ready access between center and outskirts. The character of this system, whether railborne or highwayborne or a combination of the two, has to be determined by the nature and needs of the urban area to be served. Second, the central city needs a street network designed and located so that traffic in and out of the CBD can move with reasonable facility and a minimum of congestion and also so that traffic that is merely passing through is routed around the CBD, preferably outside the central city area altogether.

There have been two major inhibiting factors to taking steps of this kind. One is cost. Construction of both urban highways and rapid transit facilities in built-up areas is expensive, and cities lack the resources to undertake such work on their own on the scale that is really necessary, particularly in an era when demands for other municipal services have been mounting rapidly. Yet failure to act has put central cities in a damaging downward spiral. As inadequate transport facilities produce greater congestion, more people and more business concerns move out, leaving the central city with diminished resources and therefore less able to provide adequate services. Not until the passage of the Interstate Highways Act was really effective federal aid made available for urban highway development. Since that time additional federal programs have opened the possibility of a thorough approach to urban transportation and traffic problems.

The second handicap is more difficult to deal with. It is the chaotic and largely archaic structure of municipal government. Without exception, the American metropolis is a conglomeration of conflicting and overlapping political jurisdictions. This situation seriously obstructs coherent and coordinated planning for present-day urban needs, including highway and transportation systems. There has of course been a fair amount of success in dealing with specific mutual interests through metropolitan commissions and authorities, established to administer joint functions such as public transportation, water supply, or parks. These bodies, however, have limited powers; they do not deal with the problems of the metropolitan complex as a whole. Yet a comprehensive view and some overall authority are desirable, indeed necessary, if the transportation facilities of Metropolis are really to serve the total community. Decisions have to be made regarding such matters as the design and location of freeways, the relationship between core area and suburbs, the integration of highway improvement with plans for urban renewal, and the type of mass transit to be adopted. The issues are complicated and frequently controversial.

Dealing with them intelligently requires keeping facts straight. There is a vociferous body of opinion which asserts that American cities have been detrimentally given over to the automobile and which supports its claim by citing figures on the amount of ground space allocated to freeways, streets, and parking facilities. Los Angeles, the most completely dependent on motor vehicle transportation of major metropolitan complexes in the United States, probably in the world for that matter, is usually cited as the prime example, with the assertion that two-thirds, or three-fifths, or more than half of the area of downtown Los Angeles (depending on how the calculation is made) is devoted to the automobile. The actual figures appear in Table 10.3, with comparative figures (street area only) for other cities in Table 10.4.

The Los Angeles CBD gives 59 percent of its ground area to

Table 10.3   Los Angeles Central Business District Area Ground and Floor Uses

The following figures, based upon the Los Angeles Central Business District (CBD) Parking Study of 1967, indicate the area taken by the various ground and floor uses in Los Angeles. The ground area for roadways and sidewalks (35%) compares favorably with that found for CBD land uses in other major cities, such as Chicago (31%), Detroit (38%), Pittsburgh (38%), and Minneapolis (35%). Ground area used for surface parking lots and single-use (freestanding) parking garages total 24%. This percentage is above that utilized in the cities previously noted, which range from 10% to 14%. The trend toward increasing the number of parking spaces in structures which is taking place in Los Angeles would tend to reduce this variance in the future.

Comparison of Study Area Ground and Floor Uses

Type Area	Square Feet (1,000)	% of Total
Ground area		
Ground area occupied by buildings and grounds*	22,825.8	41.0
Ground area occupied by sidewalks (10.5%), roadways, and alleys†	19,542.0	35.2
Ground area occupied by single-use parking garages	359.3	0.6
Ground area occupied by parking lots	12,920.3	23.2
Total study ground area	55,647.4	100.0
Floor space and ground area§		
Building gross floor area‡	57,694.7	60.0
Ground area occupied by roadways, alleys, sidewalks, malls, plazas, etc.†	19,542.0	20.4
Parking garage floor area	5,829.6	6.1
Ground area occupied by parking lots	12,920.3	13.5
Total area inventory	95,986.6	100.0

* Includes internal parking, but excludes freestanding garages.
† Includes sidewalk area in street right-of-way, which is 10.5% of the land area.
‡ Excludes parking facilities.
§ Total area in use.
Source: Compiled by Vince Desimone, Transportation Planning Engineer, Automobile Club of Southern California, 1968.

Table 10.4   Proportion of CBD Land Devoted to Streets and Parking

Central Business District	Year	Total Acres	Percent of CBD Land Devoted to		
			Streets	Parking	Streets and Parking
Los Angeles	1960	400.7	35.0	24.0	59.0
Chicago	1956	677.6*	31.0	9.7	40.7
Detroit	1953	690.0	38.5	11.0	49.5
Pittsburgh	1958	321.3*	38.2	†	†
Minneapolis	1958	580.2	34.6	13.7	48.3
St. Paul	1958	482.0	33.2	11.4	44.6
Cincinnati	1955	330.0	†	†	40.0
Dallas	1961				
Core area		344.3	34.5	18.1	52.6
Central district		1,362.0	28.5	12.9	41.4
Sacramento	1960	350.0	34.9	6.6	41.5
Columbus	1955	502.6	40.0	7.9	47.9
Nashville	1959	370.5	30.8	8.2‡	39.0
Tucson	1960	128.9	35.2	†	†
Charlotte	1958	473.0	28.7	9.7	38.4
Chattanooga	1960	246.0	21.8	13.2	35.0
Winston-Salem	1961	334.0	25.1	15.0	40.1

* Excludes undevelopable land.
† Not itemized.
Source: Transportation and land-use studies in each urban area.
From: Wilbur Smith and Associates, *Transportation and Parking for Tomorrow's Cities*, p. 59.

streets and parking: 35.2 percent to roads, streets, alleys, and sidewalks, and 23.8 percent to parking lots and garages not incorporated in buildings with other functions. One important qualification is that sidewalks are included in the street area, and they constitute 10.5 percent of the total acreage. Since the sidewalks are for pedestrians, the area allegedly devoted to the motor vehicle has to be reduced by this amount, which makes the street area actually used for vehicular movement about a quarter of the whole CBD. And is this space really "devoted to the motor vehicle?" True, it is *used* by motor vehicles, but cities had streets for several millennia before the automobile was born, and they would continue to need streets even if the automobile had never existed. The purpose of streets is to permit movement about the city and to give access to property; the method of movement is secondary.

Analysis of the data reveals that motor vehicle transportation actually requires less street space than most cities had in the pre-automobile era, even including the substantial area taken by freeways. The reason is that when the fast-moving through traffic is put on built-for-the-purpose arterial roads, then the amount of ordinary street space needed for strictly local movement and for access to property drops sharply. Even the amount of land taken for urban freeways turns out to be surprisingly small in terms either of total urban acreage or of the volume of traffic they carry. No existing or contemplated urban freeway system requires as much as 3 percent of the land in the areas it serves, and this would be exceptionally high. The Los Angeles freeway system, *when complete,* will occupy only 2 percent of the available land; the same is true of the District of Columbia, where only 0.75 percent will be pavement, with the remaining 1.25 percent as open space.[20] California studies estimate that in a typical California urban community 1.6 to 2 percent of the area should be devoted to freeways, which will handle 50 to 60 percent of all traffic needs, and about ten times as much land to the ordinary roads and streets that carry the rest of the traffic. By comparison, when John A. Sutter laid out Sacramento in 1850, he provided 38 percent of the area for streets and sidewalks. L'Enfant proposed 59 percent of the area of the District of Columbia for roads and streets; urban renewal in Southwest Washington, incorporating a modern street network, reduced the acreage of street space in the renewal area from 48.2 to 41.5 percent of the total. If we are to have a reasoned consideration of the impact of highway

20 The data that follow come from F. C. Turner, "The Highway Program Faces New Challenges," address to the Illinois Editors' Highway Safety Seminar, Rockton, Ill., May 3, 1968.

transportation on contemporary urban development, it would be well to approach the subject in the spirit of this statement by the Executive Director of New York's Citizens' Housing and Planning Council:

Many components of a city are highly desirable, but only two are absolutely essential. One is people, and the other is transportation. Sometimes the critics need to be reminded that without transportation the people would be unable to build shelter, or feed themselves, or have water to drink, or power to light their homes. Without transportation, urban men would choke on some of their own waste products and find themselves buried in others. Transportation makes cities possible.

The assumption by critics that cities necessarily deteriorate has led them to write about technology, which grows constantly more vital to the cities, as though it were a distressing law that could be repealed, like Prohibition, or a state of affairs to be overcome with prayer and protest, like segregation in public accommodations. They refuse to understand that the problem is not how to ban technology and its products, such as the automobile, but how to use them to widen human chances in the city as a whole.[21]

21 Roger Starr, *The Living End: The City and Its Critics* (New York: Coward-McCann, 1968), pp. 185–186.

11 The Suburban Explosion

The most conspicuous and unquestionably the most important change in the structure of modern urban communities is the accelerating expansion of suburbs. Just to say that the United States is becoming a society in which a majority of the people live in suburbs conveys little of what this fact implies for change in all aspects of American life—economic, social, cultural, political. In fact, the suburban explosion is so recent that the full implications of its effects cannot be completely identified and will not be for some time to come. However, it is possible to examine what has happened and arrive at some reasonable judgments regarding the nature and direction of change, and in particular to appreciate the role of transportation.

Like most other features of cities suburbs go far back into history, but they have drastically changed their character. The early suburbs were slums. They were inhabited by the people unable to live near the center of activity because of poverty or because they were newcomers and not accepted as full-fledged residents. These people huddled outside the walls, a district called by the Romans *sub urbe*. It is only in modern times that living outside rather than inside a city has come to be considered a privilege.

As described in Chapter 10, the residential suburb as we know it today was a product of rail transportation, which made it possible for the first time for considerable numbers of people to live in the country and work every day in the city. By the 1890s commuter railroads were carrying 400,000 passengers a day into London,[1] at that time the world's largest metropolis. New Yorkers are credited with having begun to move outward as early as the 1850s, and by the turn of the century the same trend was discern-

1 Wilfred Owen, *The Metropolitan Transportation Problem*, rev. ed. (Washington, D.C.: The Brookings Institution, 1966), p. 6.

ible in other large American cities—Baltimore, Boston, Cincinnati, San Francisco, and St. Louis.[2] This was railborne expansion, but the contribution the motor vehicle might make toward realizing the attractions of suburban living was well recognized in the United States by 1908, according to this advertisement: "The Sears is the car for the business man who has tired of home life in a congested neighborhood and yearns for a cottage in the suburb for his family." [3]

The outward trend of population in American cities was clearly visible in the 1920s. Figures for eighty-five metropolitan districts (which would now be termed SMSAs) show a growth pattern in which the rate of increase for outlying territory was twice as great as in the central cities.[4] At that time the suburban population was 30.9 percent of the metropolitan total, although in eleven of these districts the population outside the central cities was already greater than that inside. In addition, there was evidence of a tendency for large cities to lose population in their inner zones.

This movement of people within cities must not be overlooked as part of the suburban migration, because the vagaries of city boundaries can easily create distorted impressions. Data for Chicago and Philadelphia illustrate the extent of population shift from inner to outlying sections of the central city itself.[5] In 1900, 43.2 percent of Chicago's inhabitants lived within 4 miles of the CBD and 94.2 percent within 8 miles; in 1950 these proportions were down to 24.6 and 75.7 percent, respectively. The median distance of the population from the CBD increased in

2 Wilbur Smith and Associates, *Future Highways and Urban Growth* (New Haven, Conn.: Wilbur Smith and Associates, 1961), p. 10.
3 B. F. Karolevitz, *This Was Pioneer Motoring* (Seattle, Wash.: Superior Publishing Co., 1968), p. 53.
4 *Recent Social Trends in the United States,* Report of the President's Research Committee on Social Trends, vol. 1 (New York: McGraw-Hill Book Co., 1933), pp. 462–463.
5 Wilbur Smith and Associates, *Future Highways and Urban Growth,* p. 15.

this time from 3.4 to 5.9 miles. In Philadelphia 24 percent of the population lived within 2 miles of the CBD and 72.6 percent within 5 miles in 1900; for 1950 the comparable figures were 3.1 and 14.1 percent. Median distance from downtown grew from 3.6 to 5 miles. Since 1950 central cities that have noticeably increased in population have either extended their boundaries or had large quantities of undeveloped land within their 1950 limits.

The Car and Suburban Growth

The investigators who observed the acceleration of suburban growth in the 1920s had no hesitation in attributing this phenomenon to motor transportation; they also found aspects of Suburbia that have remained constant:

> The motor car, bringing the country nearer in time, has caused an unprecedented development of outlying and suburban residential subdivisions. While this development pertains to families of a wide range of income, special attention has been given in the past decade to the promotion of exclusive residential districts designed for occupancy by the higher income classes. The lure of rural scenery is indicated by the extremely high rates of increase of suburbs bearing names denoting attractive physical features, such as heights, vistas, parks, and water frontage. Here are some well-known suburbs with their percentage increase from 1920 to 1930: Beverly Hills, 2,485.9; Glendale, 363.5; Inglewood, 492.8; Huntington Park, 444.9 (suburbs of Los Angeles); Cleveland Heights, 234.4; Shaker Heights, 1,000.4; Garfield Heights, 511.3 (suburbs of Cleveland); Grosse Pointe Park, 724.6; Ferndale, 689.9 (suburbs of Detroit); Webster Groves, 74.0; Maplewood, 70.3; Richmond Heights, 328.3 (suburbs of St. Louis); Elmwood Park, 716.7; Oak Park, 60.5; Park Ridge, 207.9 (suburbs of Chicago).[6]

There was a slight deceleration of suburban growth during the depression years as many people were impelled to seek cheaper housing and lower commuting costs, but this was temporary. The revival was delayed by the Second World War, when both nonmilitary housing and highway construction were suspended, but the effect of the delay was merely to give the expan-

6 *Recent Social Trends,* pp. 464–465.

Table 11.1   Population Changes 1950–1960 for the 27 Largest Metropolitan Areas in the United States,* 1950–1960

Place	Metropolitan Area			Central City		
	1950	1960	Percent Increase (1950–1960)	1950	1960	Percent Change (1950–1960)
New York	9,555,943	10,545,300	10.4	7,891,957	7,660,000	− 2.94
Los Angeles–Long Beach	4,367,911	6,690,069	53.2	1,970,605	2,448,018	+24.24
Chicago	5,177,868	6,150,532	18.8	3,620,962	3,492,945	− 3.54
Philadelphia	3,671,048	4,081,827	11.2	2,071,605	1,959,966	− 5.39
Detroit	3,016,197	3,761,220	24.7	1,849,568	1,672,574	− 9.57
San Francisco–Oakland	2,240,767	2,721,045	21.4	775,357	715,609	− 7.71
Boston	2,410,372	2,561,450	6.3	801,444	677,626	−15.45
Pittsburgh	2,213,236	2,394,623	8.2	676,806	600,684	−11.25
St. Louis	1,719,288	2,040,188	18.7	856,796	740,424	−13.58
Washington, D.C.	1,464,089	1,968,562	34.5	802,178	746,986	− 6.88
Cleveland	1,456,511	1,780,263	21.5	914,808	869,867	− 4.91
Newark	1,468,458	1,726,862	17.6	438,776	396,252	− 9.69
Baltimore	1,405,399	1,706,076	21.4	949,708	921,363	− 2.98
Minneapolis–St. Paul	1,151,053	1,477,080	28.3	521,718	481,026	− 7.80
Buffalo	1,089,230	1,304,581	19.8	580,132	528,387	− 8.92
Houston	806,701	1,234,864	53.1	596,163	932,680	+56.45
Milwaukee	956,948	1,186,875	24.0	637,392	734,788	+15.28
Seattle	844,572	1,096,778	29.9	467,591	550,525	+17.74
Dallas	743,501†	1,074,756	44.6	434,462	672,117	+54.70
Cincinnati	904,402	1,059,026	17.1	503,998	487,462	− 3.28
Kansas City	814,357	1,027,562	26.2	456,662	468,325	+ 2.55
Atlanta	726,989	1,014,349	39.5	331,314	485,425	+45.52
San Diego	556,808	1,003,522	80.2	334,387	547,294	+63.87
Denver	612,128†	923,161	50.8	415,786	489,217	+17.66
Miami	495,084	917,851	85.4	249,276	282,600	+13.37
New Orleans	685,405	860,205	25.5	570,445	620,979	+ 8.86
Portland	704,829	815,745	15.7	373,628	370,339	− 0.88
Total	51,259,094	63,124,372	23.1	30,093,524	30,553,478	+ 1.53

* Source: U.S. Census of Population, 1950 and 1960 (Preliminary Reports).
† 1950 figures for Dallas and Denver include all counties embraced by the currently defined "metropolitan area."
From: Wilbur Smith and Associates, *Future Highways and Urban Growth* (New Haven, Conn.: Wilbur Smith and Associates, 1961), p. 13.

sion greater force when it came, accentuated by the sharp increase in population that followed the war also. Table 11.1 confirms the character of the change: central cities static or declining, suburbs expanding rapidly. To view the process from another aspect, between 1950 and 1960 urban population grew by about 45 percent, but it occupied about twice as much land: 12,804 square miles in 1950 compared with 25,554 square miles in 1960.[7] The reason,

7 Robinson Newcomb, "Urban Land Use Shifts to Low Gear," *Appraisal Journal,* vol. 32, no. 3 (July 1964), p. 376.

quite simply, is that the outward shift of urban population is also predominantly a shift from multiple- to single-family dwellings.

This expansion is automobile-based; without the motor vehicle it simply could not have taken place. Because highway transportation was readily available in a convenient and economic form, suburban development, as has been noted, began in the 1920s to break away from dependence on commuter or rapid transit rail lines. Public transportation for such communities could be and usually was provided by bus, but, as we have seen, by 1940 over 2,000 urban communities had no public transportation whatsoever (see Chapter 9). This situation has since accentuated. In thirteen SMSAs with central city populations of over 250,000, the fastest growth rates after 1940 were in satellite communities with highway but no rail transportation, and an estimate of 1968 concluded that there were about 50 million commuters in the United States, of whom some 82 percent traveled by private automobile, and that half of these did not have access to public transportation.[8]

The metropolitan pattern that has developed consequently relies principally on the highway for its transportation needs. Travel to and from work is an important part of all metropolitan passenger travel, but it accounts for less than half of all trips by car, even though it attracts more attention than all the rest. The other trips are less and less likely to be made between suburb and central city. The evidence is overwhelming that the journey to work is the longest trip (other than vacation travel) that people are normally willing to take. For shopping and other services, and for entertainment, they are most likely to prefer neighborhood facilities, easy to reach by car and with ample parking.[9]

8 Gene Wunderlich, "Costs of Communicating by Transportation," *Journal of Economic Issues,* vol. 1, no. 3 (September 1967), p. 203n.
9 T. A. Bostick, "The Automobile in American Daily Life," *Public Roads,* vol. 32, no. 11 (December 1963), p. 241; Port of New York Authority, Comprehensive Planning Office, *Metropolitan Transportation—1980* (New York: Port of New York Authority, 1963), p. 284.

In fact, half of all the residents of metropolitan areas go downtown less than once a month, other than to work, and these trips are mainly for shopping.[10]

This is simply a matter of convenience, but it has deep-seated implications for the structure of Metropolis. A study in depth of the New York metropolitan region makes the specific point that low-density residential development implies a high rate of automobile ownership and requires the provision of the necessary travel facilities.[11] For an urban travel corridor to require a passenger-carrying capacity as large as 25,000 persons per hour, by rail or road or combination thereof, calls for a densely populated area at the residential end and a compact CBD at the other.[12] Only a few such corridors exist, and these are in only the very largest cities. Moreover, while this preference for low-density housing continues, all indexes are that the number of such corridors and the density of their use will remain static or possibly decline; any increase is unlikely.

Service Enterprises

This outward migration from city centers has had economic as well as social effects. People require retail services to provide food, clothing, and the other necessities of day-to-day living; the converse of this proposition is that if retail enterprises are to prosper, they must be located where they can be conveniently reached by their customers. When urban transportation systems produced concentration at the center, the CBD was preeminently the shopping district. It contained the department stores and the principal specialty shops. The suburbs were limited to corner grocery

10 John B. Lansing and Eva Mueller, *Residential Location and Urban Mobility* (Ann Arbor, Mich.: University of Michigan, 1964), pp. 38–39.
11 Port of New York Authority, *Metropolitan Transportation—1980*, p. 284.
12 Nathan Cherniak, "A Statement of the Urban Passenger Transportation Problem," *Transportation*, United Nations Conference on the Application of Science and Technology for the Benefit of the Less Developed Areas, vol. V (Washington, D.C.: 1963), p. 34.

stores and other minor operations. In 1920, before the influence of the automobile was really felt, 90 percent of the sales of general merchandise in metropolitan areas were made in the central business districts, whereas forty years later in all SMSAs of over 100,000 population retail sales outside the CBDs were twice those within.[13]

Like the suburban expansion itself, this shift of retail enterprise has accelerated since the middle of the century. The Highway Cost Allocation Study found a decline of retail sales in the CBDs of sixty-nine cities between 1948 and 1954 but offered the caution that for this purpose the CBD should not be considered synonymous with the central city as a whole.[14] For 168 central city areas studied in this period the total number of retail establishments grew by 4 percent and retail sales by 22 percent. The dispersion of retail and service business is a decentralizing move out of the CBD, and not necessarily from central city to suburbs. These businesses follow their customers, and whether this takes them to the outskirts of the city proper or into separate suburban jurisdictions is a haphazard consequence of where local political boundaries happen to be drawn—haphazard but nonetheless important, because it makes a great deal of difference to a central city whether this decentralization is done in such a way that it retains or loses taxable property. The small cities, whose population remains largely within city limits, retain most of their retail business. In the metropolitan area, however, where suburban population is of significant magnitude, the larger the metropolis, the smaller the proportion of retail business done in the central city and the higher the proportion of retail sales credited to suburbs.

13 Homer Hoyt, "The Changing Principles of Land Economics," Urban Land Institute, *Technical Bulletin 60* (1967), p. 16.
14 *Third Progress Report of the Highway Cost Allocation Study,* 86th Congress, 1st sess., House Document No. 91 (Washington, D.C.: Government Printing Office, 1959), p. 37.

Table 11.2   Number and Size of Shopping Centers in the United States, October 1960

Size of Center (square feet of floor area)	Number	Total Floor Area (square feet)	Average Size (square feet)
1,000,000 and over	19	21,565,000	1,135,000
700,000–999,000	17	12,876,000	757,000
600,000–699,000	10	6,315,000	632,000
500,000–599,000	12	6,330,000	528,000
400,000–499,000	37	16,650,000	450,000
350,000–399,000	35	12,250,000	350,000
300,000–349,000	61	19,825,000	325,000
250,000–299,000	67	18,425,000	275,000
200,000–249,000	145	32,625,000	225,000
100,000–199,000	503	75,450,000	150,000
50,000–99,000	415	31,050,000	75,000
Under 50,000	477	16,695,000	35,000
Total reporting	1,798	270,056,000	150,197
Estimate for shopping centers not reporting store area	2,043	153,225,000	75,000
Total	3,841	423,281,000	110,200

Source: Compiled by Homer Hoyt in "The Status of Shopping Centers in the United States," *Urban Land*, Vol. 19, No. 5, Urban Land Institute, October 1960. Tabulations based in part on information in *Directory of Shopping Centers in the United States and Canada*, 1961 Edition, National Research Bureau, Inc., Chicago, Illinois.
From: Wilbur Smith and Associates, *Future Highways and Urban Growth*, p. 21.

This development shows up strikingly in the growth of shopping centers, located outside central business districts, with ample parking space and easy access by automobile. The pioneers began operation in the early 1920s, and in 1946 there were 8 in the entire United States.[15] Since then the original 8 have grown to some 4,000 (see Table 11.2), with new ones being added continuously. Their recorded effect on retail sales reinforces what

15 Homer Hoyt, "The Status of Shopping Centers in the United States, October, 1960," *Urban Land*, vol. 19, no. 9 (October 1960), p. 5. These were: Country Club Plaza, Kansas City (1922); Upper Darby Center, West Philadelphia (1927); Ardmore, Pa. (1928); Highland Park Shopping Village, Dallas (1931); River Oaks, Houston (1937); Hampton Village, St. Louis (1941); Colony, Toledo (1944); Shirlington, Arlington, Va. (1944); Belleview Square, Seattle (1946).

has been said about the migration of retail business from the CBD. As early as 1950, in ninety-four SMSAs with an aggregate population of 92 million, sales of general merchandise outside the CBD were 19 percent higher than inside, and in 1954 retail sales outside the downtown area in the cities (not the SMSAs) of over a million population exceeded those in the CBDs for the first time.[16] The new centers built between 1946 and 1960 had the capacity to sell $35 billion in goods annually, or 23 percent of all retail sales in the United States, exclusive of motor vehicles, lumber, and building materials, which were not usually sold in shopping centers, and gasoline service station sales.[17]

Shopping centers come in a variety of sizes and styles. The largest, those with store areas over 400,000 square feet, require at least forty acres of land. They normally have a large department store as a nucleus, with adjoining specialty shops whose business depends heavily on the pull of the major store. The smaller centers, running as a rule from five to twenty-five acres, are favored by supermarkets and by outlets of national chains such as Sears Roebuck, Montgomery Ward, and J. C. Penney. They all have one feature in common: they are based on the existence of highway transportation. The whole rationale of the shopping center is that it attracts customers because it offers convenient access by car and adequate parking. No large shopping center, and very few small ones, could live on the business it would get from the number of shoppers who could reach it on foot. Patronage for a major center may on occasion come from a radius of ten or twenty miles; there is evidence of residents of East St. Louis, Illinois, driving across the Mississippi and through St. Louis to park and shop in modern shopping centers on the western side of the city.[18]

16 Hoyt, "Sales in Shopping Centers," *Urban Land,* vol. 15, no. 8 (September 1966), p. 3.
17 Hoyt, "Status of Shopping Centers," p. 4.
18 Bureau of Public Roads, *Highways and Economic and Social Changes* (Washington, D.C.: Government Printing Office, 1964), p. 82.

Table 11.3   Distribution of Retail Sales by Size of City, 1954

Size of City	Percentage of Retail Sales	
	Center	Suburbs
Below 200,000	60	40
200,000–400,000	30	70
400,000–1 million	26	74
Over 1 million	22	78

Source: Bureau of Public Roads, speech by David R. Levin, "The Impact of Highway Improvement on Urban Areas," 15th Annual Ohio Highway Engineering Conference, April 5, 1961.

This is automobileborne business. The availability of public transportation has been a minor factor in determining location; most shopping centers, indeed, have no access to mass transit.[19] The customer drives to the center in his or more often her car and has the vehicle to take the purchases home. The location of the center outside the congested CBD has an additional advantage in that the merchandise can be transported to the stores by truck with far less risk of delay.

The rise of the shopping center is a logical response to the outward trend of urban population and to the flexibility of movement afforded by the automobile. It also illustrates how a response can become a stimulus. Dispersal made the shopping center possible; the shopping center in turn encourages further dispersal because it diminishes the need to have access to a downtown shopping district. The figures cited on the distribution of retail sales in metropolitan areas are a clear indication of what has been happening (see Table 11.3). In the middle 1950s department stores in suburban shopping centers were predominantly branches of the main store downtown, with a smaller selection and variety of merchandise; this situation has markedly changed. Certainly in the larger shopping centers the nucleus department store will have as much to offer as its downtown

19 Hoyt, "The Changing Principles of Land Economies," p. 9.

affiliate, and occasionally the downtown store has vanished altogether. This is why nonwork travel between suburb and city centers has become less frequent.

Whether this trend should be approved or deplored is a matter on which opinions are bound to differ, depending on whether we want a centralized or decentralized city, but there can be no question that the trend exists on a massive scale. The suburbanite may still make his living in the central city, although this too is changing, but for other functions the suburban family can satisfy most of its wants within its own community, or at least within a suburban cluster so that travel downtown becomes less and less essential. The word "essential" must be noted in this context. The spreading out of retail enterprises has admittedly had an adverse effect on central business districts, and it is highly unlikely that the CBD will regain its once dominant position in retailing. But it does not follow that the CBD must wither away. It retains some advantages as the area in most cities that is accessible to the largest number of people, and it has a substantial daytime commuter population for whom it remains the most convenient place to trade. The governing factor is transportation. If the suburban shopper can get downtown conveniently, then she can choose between the shopping center or the CBD. But the downtown establishments must be comparable in ease of access to the suburban shopping center—not necessarily equal, which would be difficult to achieve in most existing CBDs, but at least not so disparate as to discourage the prospective customer from even considering the trip into town.

New York and Los Angeles

A clearer picture of suburban growth can be gained by looking at the two metropolitan areas that appear to represent the extremes of concentration and dispersal, New York and Los Angeles.

The area defined as the New York Metropolitan Region covers 6,914 square miles, has 16 million inhabitants, and includes 22 counties in three states.[20] It extends north to Dutchess County in New York, south to Monmouth County, New Jersey, east to Suffolk County on Long Island, and Fairfield County, Connecticut, and west to Morris County, New Jersey (see Figure 11.1). New York City itself comprises about 320 square miles of this total and has 8 million of the population. This is the core of the region, with Manhattan Island south of Sixty-first Street classified as the central business district. Outside the city are an inner ring and outer ring, as shown on the figure. Population density in the core is 77,195 persons per square mile in Manhattan and 24,000 for the city as a whole. The Manhattan density is one of the highest in the world (see Table 11.4), but it declined by a fourth between 1920 and 1960 in a trend that sent New York City's population outward from the crowded island. The region includes other large cities (Newark and Jersey City, for instance). In general, the same forces operate on them as on New York City.

Some of the characteristics of this expansion have been described. It began along the railway and transit lines, but in the 1930s it rather markedly diffused as reliance on the highway grew. Thirty years later car ownership was so widespread outside the largest cities that people could consider various places to live without taking access to public transportation into account. For this type of residential development it made no difference whether the commuter drove his car all the way to work or just to the railroad station. The key factor in his choice was the ability to leave and return to his home by automobile.[21]

One indication of change in the composition of the New York Region has been a shift in the mode of travel used to reach the Manhattan CBD. Table 11.5 gives a survey over a thirty-year

20 Edgar M. Hoover and Raymond Vernon, *Anatomy of a Metropolis* (Cambridge, Mass.: Harvard University Press, 1959), p. 3.
21 *Ibid.*, pp. 318, 220.

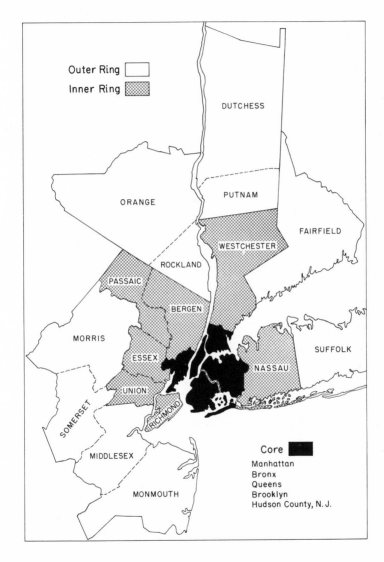

Figure 11.1 The three main zones of the New York Region
Source: Edgar M. Hoover and Raymond Vernon, *Anatomy of a Metropolis* Cambridge, Mass.: Harvard University Press, 1959), p. 10. Reprinted by permission from: Edgar M. Hoover and Raymond Vernon, *Anatomy of a Metropolis*, Cambridge, Mass.: Harvard University Press, Copyright, 1959, by Regional Plan Association, Inc.

Table 11.4   Population and Density of Selected Major Cities

United States and Canada

Central City	Year	Population	Area (sq. mi.)	Density (persons per sq. mi.)
New York (Manhattan)	1920	2,284,000	22	103,818
New York City	1923	5,927,625	299	19,825
Chicago	1923	2,886,971	195	14,805
Philadelphia	1923	1,922,788	127	15,141
Average*		3,579,120	207	17,262
New York (Manhattan)	1960	1,698,281	22	77,195
New York City	1960	7,781,984	315	24,697
Chicago	1960	3,550,404	224	15,836
Los Angeles	1960	2,479,015	455	5,451
Philadelphia	1960	2,002,512	127	15,743
Detroit	1960	1,670,144	140	11,964
Montreal	1956	1,109,439	47	23,525
Average*		3,098,916	218	14,215
Average excluding Los Angeles*		3,222,966	181	18,891

Rest of World

Central City	Year	Population	Area (sq. mi.)	Density (persons per sq. mi.)
London (excluding outer ring)	1921	4,484,523	117	38,329
Paris	1921	2,856,986	30	95,233
Berlin	1905	2,033,900	29	70,134
Tokyo	1905	1,969,833	30	65,661
Moscow	1902	1,092,360	32	34,136
Glasgow	1921	1,034,174	30	34,472
Average		2,245,290	45	50,268
Tokyo	1960	9,124,217	207	44,078
Greater London	1960	8,210,000	722	11,377
Shanghai†	1953	6,204,000	345	17,982
Osaka	1960	5,158,010	123	41,935
Berlin	1960	4,244,600	344	12,339
Buenos Aires†	1955	3,575,000	74	48,310
London	1948	3,339,000	117	28,538
Bombay†	1960	3,000,000	30	100,000
Rio de Janeiro†	1955	2,900,000	60	48,333
Calcutta	1961	2,926,498	39	74,200
Paris	1960	2,800,000	34	83,580
Average		4,680,120	190	24,573
Average excluding Greater London Conurbation		4,327,132	137	31,516

* Excludes Manhattan.
† Denotes that some estimates were made to obtain consistent population and area values.
Source: Compiled from U.S. and world census data from John C. Weaver and Fred E. Lukermann, *World Resource Statistics* (Minneapolis: Briggs Publishing Co., 1953); University of California, International Urban Research, Institute of International Studies, *The World's Metropolitan Areas* (Berkeley: University of California Press, 1959); and 1920–1930 data from Herbert B. Dorau and Albert G. Hinman, *Urban Land Economics* (New York: Macmillan Co., 1928). Data shown only for cities where available.
From: Wilbur Smith and Associates, *Transportation and Parking for Tomorrow's Cities*, p. 16.

Table 11.5 Number of Persons Entering Manhattan Central Business District* in Vehicles on a Typical Business Day, by Mode of Travel, Selected Years, 1924–1956

	Thousands of Persons					Percentage of Total Number				
	1924	1932	1940	1948	1956	1924	1932	1940	1948	1956
Total	2,343	2,697	3,271	3,691	3,316	100.0	100.0	100.0	100.0	100.0
Auto and taxi	249	430	503	577	736	10.6	15.9	15.4	15.7	22.2
Bus	—	40	150	290	246	—	1.5	4.6	7.8	7.4
Truck	82	86	116	80	92	3.5	3.2	3.5	2.2	2.8
Trolley	161	88	59	24	3	6.9	3.2	1.8	0.6	0.1
Rapid transit	1,531	1,752	2,169	2,389	1,970	65.3	65.0	66.3	64.8	59.4
Railroad (commuter)	217	216	206	283	233	9.3	8.0	6.3	7.6	7.0
Ferry (pedestrians)†	103	85	68	48	36	4.4	3.2	2.1	1.3	1.1

* Here defined for convenience as Manhattan south of 61st Street.

† Pedestrians are not counted unless they entered by ferry.

Source: Regional Plan Association, Bulletin 91, *Hub-Bound Travel in the Tri-State Metropolitan Region: Persons and Vehicles Entering Manhattan South of 61st St., 1924–1956* (New York, 1959).

Reprinted by permission of the publishers from p. 217 of: Edgar M. Hoover and Raymond Vernon, *Anatomy of a Metropolis*, Cambridge, Mass.: Harvard University Press, Copyright, 1959, by Regional Plan Association, Inc.

period. Railborne transit remains the principal means of access, and must continue to be, given the geographical situation and the immense numbers involved, but both the percentage and total numbers using commuter and rapid transit lines show a decline, while the use of the highway has increased. By 1960 automobile usage on weekdays had risen to 25.9 percent of the total, except that between 7 and 10 A.M. it was only 12.5 percent.[22] In other words, people going to work in lower Manhattan preponderantly rely on public transportation; those coming in for shopping or recreation make somewhat greater use of the private automobile.

A more important feature of this pattern is a declining dependence of the outlying areas on the center. Over 80 percent of the Region's inhabitants work in the zone where they live, which of course places the vast majority in the core area, 15 percent commute to a more central zone, and the rest are reverse commuters.[23] Reverse commuting is a new and growing urban phenomenon stemming from the outward movement of business and industry, which will be the subject of the next chapter. In New York reverse commuting from upper Manhattan to jobs in New Jersey has become heavy enough to balance the normal rush-hour flow of traffic on the George Washington Bridge. Figure 11.2 shows the proportional volumes of work travel between and within the zones of the Region. The heaviest flow is within the core area, as could be expected. What is more noteworthy is that the volume of work travel within both inner and outer rings either matches or exceeds the flow out of each.

As with other metropolitan areas, retail business in the New York Region has tended to follow its customers (see Figure 11.3). Fifth Avenue undoubtedly still has far more to offer than the shopping centers of New York's suburban area; in retail merchandising Manhattan has a greater advantage over its suburbs

22 Port of New York Authority, *Metropolitan Transportation—1980*, p. 295.
23 Hoover and Vernon, *Anatomy of a Metropolis*, pp. 145, 212.

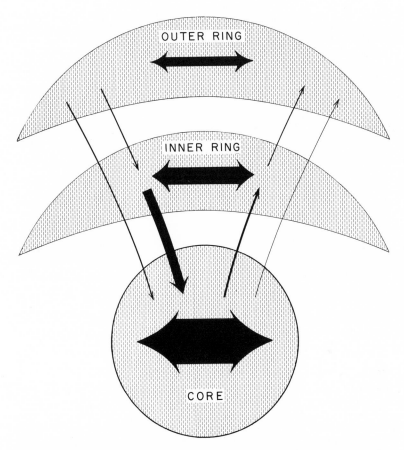

Figure 11.2 Commuter flow within and between zones of New York Metropolitan Region, 1956
Thickness of arrows is proportional to number of commuters. Horizontal arrows show commuting from one place to another in the same zone.
Source: Hoover and Vernon, *Anatomy of a Metropolis*, p. 146. Reprinted by permission of the publishers from: Edgar M. Hoover and Raymond Vernon, *Anatomy of a Metropolis*, Cambridge, Mass.: Harvard University Press, Copyright, 1959, by Regional Plan Association, Inc.

than the CBDs of other major cities. Nevertheless, the trend is there. For most purposes the suburban shopper has little need to make the long trip to Manhattan's retail establishments—or Newark's or Jersey City's either. She certainly does not have to

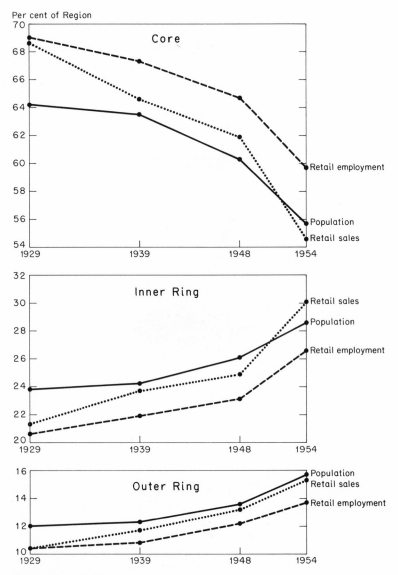

Figure 11.3 Trends in retail employment, retail sales, and population in main zones of New York Metropolitan Region, 1929, 1939, 1948, 1954 (region = 100 percent)

Source: Hoover and Vernon, *Anatomy of a Metropolis,* p. 117. Reprinted by permission of the publishers from: Edgar M. Hoover and Raymond Vernon, *Anatomy of a Metropolis,* Cambridge, Mass.: Harvard University Press, Copyright, 1959, by Regional Plan Association, Inc.

go downtown to do business with Macy's or Gimbel's or Bloomingdale's; they have come to her.

Fundamentally, therefore, the New York situation is just the same as other metropolitan areas. There is a much higher degree of concentration in the core, and this will continue, but growth now and in the foreseeable future will be more rapid in the outlying districts than in the core. What this means for transportation in the Region is summed up by the Port of New York Authority:

There is a vital certainty that in the decades ahead there will be an even greater dependence than there is today on the automobile for regional transport, as intersuburban, reverse-direction, and leisure-time travel continue to grow. Unless there is a drastic change in the metropolitan growth pattern, a multitude of travel paths, widely scattered throughout the region, will come to be employed as increasing numbers of workers travel from their quarter-acre home sites in an outlying county to campus-type factories, laboratories, or office establishments in other suburbs. There will be limited opportunities for channelization of this travel into a few high-volume routes, and it will have to rely primarily on private transportation. Technical gadgetry will not yield a painless solution to the passenger transport problem. The evolving pattern of metropolitan travel is a response to deep-seated forces and in itself is neither irrational nor perverse. Wise and skillful statesmanship by civic leaders and public officials in the fields of finance, law and management, is the requirement.[24]

For transportation purposes the Los Angeles metropolitan region can best be considered as the area covered by the Los Angeles Regional Transportation Study (LARTS) in 1960. In size it is astonishingly close to the New York Metropolitan Region, 9,025 square miles in three counties—Los Angeles, Orange, and Ventura—and part of two others, Riverside and San Bernardino.[25] It contains almost 10 million people, of whom over

24 Reprinted by permission from *Metropolitan Transportation—1980*, p. 305. Published by the Comprehensive Planning Office, The Port of New York Authority.

25 LARTS is not the same thing as the Southern California Rapid Transit District (SCRTD), which is restricted to Los Angeles County, although it

7 million are in Los Angeles County and about 3 million in the city of Los Angeles itself. The city covers 452 square miles, approximately 50 percent more than the city of New York.

Railborne transit had an important part in Los Angeles metropolitan growth early in the century through the interurban lines that were consolidated in 1911 into the Pacific Electric system, at its peak the largest interurban electric operation in the United States.[26] The Pacific Electric survived the 1920s successfully while other interurbans were vanishing, but it became unprofitable in the 1930s and gradually declined. Its last passenger run, from downtown Los Angeles to Long Beach, was made in April 1961. By then such track as the system retained was used exclusively for freight service. Local streetcar service in Los Angeles ended two years later. Since there was no rail commuter service by then either, the metropolitan area depended exclusively on highway transportation for local passenger movement.

Although some of the metropolitan expansion followed the interurban routes, the bulk of it has been highway based. The rapid growth period began in 1920 and accelerated with the industrial boom of the Second World War, after the rail system had passed its peak. Within the Greater Los Angeles region there are few natural barriers to channel the direction of suburban expansion or to create well-defined travel corridors. Added to these conditions is a central business district that has never had the dominating position of CBDs elsewhere; only 5 percent of the jobs in the Los Angeles area are in the downtown district.[27] Table

participated in this survey. The LARTS material was made available through the courtesy of the Automobile Club of Southern California. I am especially indebted to Mr. J. Allen Davis.

26 G. W. Hilton and J. F. Due, *The Electric Interurban Railways in America* (Stanford, Calif.: Stanford University Press, 1960), pp. 406, 409, gives a good description of the rise and decline of the Pacific Electric.

27 P. G. Koltnow, "The Los Angeles Commuter," *Westways*, vol. 59, no. 9 (September 1967), p. 18. The Los Angeles CBD is the area enclosed by Temple Street, Figueroa Street, Pico Boulevard, Maple Avenue, and Los Angeles Street.

Table 11.6   Persons Entering Downtown Los Angeles, 1924–1953

Year	Automobile	Public Transportation	Total
1924	239,855	383,145	623,000
1931	434,986	262,256	697,242
1938	384,788	239,512	624,290
1941	396,493	246,440	642,933
1947	455,000	240,500	695,500
1950	446,000	247,450	693,450
1953	470,000	211,300	681,300

Source: P. T. McElhiney, "The Freeways of Los Angeles," p. 52, Ph.D. thesis, School of Business, University of California at Los Angeles, 1959.

11.6, giving the numbers of people entering downtown Los Angeles in a period comparable with what was used for New York, is revealing. In over thirty years in which the population of Los Angeles rose from 576,000 to about 2 million, the number of persons entering the CBD remained almost constant; thus the CBD has remained static while the rest of the metropolitan area was growing.

The travel pattern for the Los Angeles metropolis is fundamentally multidirectional and low density. The backbone of the transportation system is the network of freeways, of which about 450 miles have been completed out of an ultimately planned total of 800 miles. The existing freeways represent about 4 percent of the total street mileage but carry 44 percent of the traffic.[28] They have not eliminated congestion; any motorist in the Los Angeles area can testify to that. It does not follow that the concept of the freeway system is faulty, although in some respects the execution can be criticized. The first Los Angeles freeways converged on a single point at the civic center, so that at rush hours an enormous mass of vehicles inevitably converged on this single point also, including large numbers that were going across the

28 State of California, Department of Public Works, *The California Freeway and Expressway System. 1968. Progress and Problems, Summary Report* (Sacramento, California: March 1969), p. 2.

city rather than to or from the CBD. Not until the middle 1960s was it possible to bypass the "stack," the four-level interchange in the middle of Los Angeles. Two other factors caused trouble for the freeway planners. One is that the Los Angeles area has the heaviest concentration of motor vehicles in the world, and the number of people and cars continues to grow rapidly. The other is that spiraling costs and other factors have put the building of the freeway network behind schedule. If the contemplated mileage had been built on schedule, some of the severe traffic pressures would have been alleviated.

At any rate, Los Angeles stands as the symbol of metropolitan dispersal (its critics would probably call it "sprawl") and decentralization. Despite some energetic steps toward renewal and stimulation of the core area, there is no serious indication that this decentralizing process can or will be reversed. There is nothing in the geography of the area to encourage centralization rather than dispersal—quite the contrary. Nor does downtown Los Angeles have anything approaching the concentration of business and financial establishments that is found in downtown New York, or the Chicago Loop. Its retail outlets have to compete not only with suburban shopping centers but with high-quality retail centers in adjoining communities like Pasadena, Beverly Hills, Westwood, and Long Beach.

To return to the fundamental point, New York and Los Angeles appear to be at opposite poles of metropolitan structure, one intensely concentrated at the core, the other highly dispersed. Yet their current growth patterns are similar—the most rapid expansion now and in the predictable future is occurring in the suburbs. What is true of the extremes is equally valid for the metropolitan areas that come somewhere in between. For this kind of metropolitan expansion, and it must be emphasized that this is the kind that is taking place with no sign of any probable reversal, the basic reliance for transportation must be the highway. The need and desirability for some mass transportation system to link core with periphery is not excluded, nor is the possibility of further development of air travel within metropolitan regions, but for practical purposes we must accept the road as the best medium now at hand for the multidirectional, highly individualized movement of metropolitan structures where population is becoming preponderantly suburban.

Conclusions

The growth of Suburbia has not occurred without objections. The critics are numerous, articulate, and frequently distinguished. The objections to suburban expansion are familiar: defacing the countryside with suburban sprawl, "ribbon" development along main highways, denuding the central city of taxable property and taxable people, lack of a sense of community involvement because the head of the family works in one town and lives in another (those who believe this have never attended a suburban PTA meeting when a controversial matter was up for discussion), and so on. By contrast the defense of Suburbia is likely to be apologetic at best.

Some of the criticisms are valid enough. The rows of identical dwellings in suburban tract developments have little scenic value, nor do endless strings of gas stations, motels, hamburger stands, new and used car lots, and other commercial establishments lining suburban highways. Community relationships and the matter of shifting tax resources are genuine problems, and not readily soluble because of the tangle of local government in American metropolitan areas.

None of this can alter the plain fact that American suburban life is here, that it is a major and integral part of American society, that this is so because a sufficient number of people prefer suburban existence as a way of life, and that it is a way of life with positive qualities. The defects were preventable and are remediable. Sprawl can be corrected by foresight and planning, and ribbon development is simply a product of the failure to differentiate among highway functions that has characterized our traffic policy in the past. The major difficulty, as summed up by a distinguished authority on highways, is that main highways too often are expected both to move traffic and to provide local access to land, and these two functions cannot be performed efficiently by the same road.[29] Unrestricted entrance and exit to commercial or residential establishments along the roadside unavoidably reduces the capacity of the highway, as well as impairing safety. Service roads or controlled access offer a remedy that is less expensive in financial and social costs.

The freeway, in fact, is an antidote to ribbon development, because commercial establishments will congregate about the interchanges. It would be pointless for them to string along a highway to which they had no access.

This is by no means exclusively an American problem. Britain made the same mistakes. A British commentator's description of his country's suburban expansion shows duplication of the American experience, but he observes that ribbon development could have been beneficial if the architecture had been good and the structures well set back on service roads separated by glades of trees from the main highway.[30]

Curiously, the critics of our highway-oriented Suburbia seldom refer to these comparable experiences elsewhere. They seem to prefer to cite situations that have a negligible relevance to American conditions, such as the intemperately antihighway work that rhapsodizes the citizens of Moscow (Russia, not Idaho) "enjoying the beauty and efficiency of their world-famous subway system, with its spacious, well-lit, well-ventilated stations, some ornately decorated and hung with chandeliers between marble

29 Owen, *The Metropolitan Transportation Problem*, p. 39.
30 C. D. Buchanan, *Mixed Blessing: The Motor in Britain* (London: Leonard Hill (Books) Ltd., 1958), p. 60.

columns." [31] The excellence of the Moscow subway can be conceded, but it is odd that the writer of this passage has nothing to say about the trains. It is less odd, considering his predilections, that he should not raise the question of what the citizens of Moscow would do if automobile ownership in the USSR were as widely distributed as in the United States.

Americans who wish to live in apartment clusters close to public transportation should certainly have the option of doing so. This is quite different from insisting that all urban complexes should be so designed and all urban residents should live in this manner. Lenin is quoted as having said during the Russian Revolution that the Russian soldiers voted for peace with their feet —by going home. In similar fashion American urbanites who are in a position to do so vote decisively for suburbs with their cars.

It is a justifiable and well-founded preference. There is no real body of evidence to prove that urban residential dispersal is bad for either society or the individual, and there is much to be said in its favor. Granted that many suburban tract areas are monotonous and uninspiring, they are still an improvement over the city tenement and may even compare favorably with the apartment block. Architectural choices come down in the end to individual taste, and the millions who are making their homes in the suburbs are seeking more than architecture. They are looking for open space and a sense of community that the impersonality of the great city does not provide.

There is a respectable body of scientific opinion suggesting that they are right. In 1966 an anthropologist, E. T. Hall, published *The Hidden Dimension,* in which he argued that people need, beside food, water, and shelter, a certain amount of space in which to conduct their daily lives. This thesis is based on a very substantial volume of research on territoriality among ani-

31 A. Q. Mowbray, *The Road to Ruin* (Philadelphia: J. B. Lippincott Co., 1968), p. 207.

mals, conclusively demonstrating a fundamental need for minimum space requirements among living organisms. The application to humanity has not been definitely established, but Hall's own studies find that the disappointing outcome of many low-cost housing projects is due to failure to find out how the residents really want to live and may be related to ignorance of what people's requirements for space are.

There is, in short, still a case for the democratic principle that if people are allowed to choose freely, and are informed on the options, they will make the right choices more often than the wrong ones. Metropolitan living is just such a case. There are people who want to live in the central city, and there are obviously many more who would rather live in suburbs. Some of the people who would like to live in suburbs are locked into the central city by discrimination or poverty, and this condition needs to be remedied. We are concerned here primarily with transportation, and in this field the maximum opportunity for freedom of residential choice requires adequate facilities for movement by road, by both private car and bus.

12 The Dispersal of Business and Industry

There are two major centrifugal forces operating on American cities. One is the migration of population to the suburbs. The other is a growing tendency for industrial and other business establishments to locate on the outskirts of metropolitan areas. This is not the shift of retail and service enterprises to follow their customers that was described in the previous chapter. It is a separate phenomenon essentially independent of the outward movement of people for residential purposes. This industrial decentralization is more dependent on highway transportation than the growth of residential suburbs. The latter began with rail transport and could have continued to expand on that basis, although probably not on the same scale and certainly on a very different pattern.

Relocation of Industry

The changes in industrial location have their own distinct origins and motivations. First is the rapid development of industrial technologies stressing continuous flow of materials and automatic controls, which may require production processes involving straight-line movements of considerable length. In addition, modern methods of handling materials with mechanized equipment, such as conveyors and fork-lift trucks, work best in one-story structures. These factors in combination demand space and therefore encourage location where the cost of land is comparatively low, a condition more likely to be met in outlying than in central city areas.

This incentive to disperse must be balanced against other considerations. The factory has to have a site permitting ready movement of goods in and out and accessible to the work force. In the past these factors limited locational choices, since the places where land was plentiful and cheap were likely to have inadequate transportation and to have too few people within practical traveling distance. The motor vehicle and the highway greatly expanded the options. The passenger car solves much of the problem of personnel and is a major locational factor in its own right, allowing a plant to be in open country and draw its labor supply from as far as thirty to forty miles.[1] Parking facilities, in fact, may require more land than the plant itself, another incentive to seek open space.

Important as the passenger automobile has been, the motor truck has been a still more powerful influence on industrial dispersal, a position convincingly presented in this passage:

Within cities vehicular movement of *people* was largely carried out by a mode that was closely related to that employed for the inter-city movement of goods and people, the street railway and trolley. Intra-city movement of *goods*, however, involved a technology that had remained essentially unchanged for centuries, the horse and wagon. The cost of moving goods within the nineteenth century city was high relative to the cost of moving people. This relative cost situation played a crucial role in the emergence of the core-dominated city. Given the structure of transport costs it was, in general, more economical to move people to areas in which jobs were concentrated and to concentrate jobs near the central freight terminal. Such an arrangement tended to reduce total transport cost by reducing intra-city movement of goods. . . .

The decline of the core, on the other hand, is often attributed to the automobile. Such a view is not in conflict with the *theoretical* argument of the present paper if it is also stated that the introduction of the automobile increased the cost—time, disutility and/or money—of intra-urban person travel relative to goods travel. The present authors do not happen to share this view, feeling that the cost of personal travel by auto for those who choose this mode is less than the cost by the alternatives available to them. Their view is that the introduction of the truck in the early 1900's reduced the cost of goods relative to person's movement within cities. It allowed firms to locate in the satellite area and take advantage of the more favorable factor supply conditions available there.

The influence of the truck on the location of economic activity in large urbanized areas was felt in two stages. The first, roughly

1 Victor R. Fuchs, *Changes in the Location of Manufacturing in the United States Since 1929* (New Haven, Conn.: Yale University Press, 1962), p. 93.

from the turn of the century to World War II, was marked by improvement in city streets and increases in the efficiency of the small, predominantly intra-urban truck. In this state, the core retained a dominant position in the receiving, shipping, and other aspects of goods handling for export and import. In the second, post World War II stage, immense additions to the interstate highway system were made. Much larger and more efficient trucks were also developed. Motor carriage came to replace rail for many long distance shipments. Firms in the satellite area of one city could, for example, buy from or sell directly to firms in the satellite area of another city, the central area of both being bypassed. This increased the rate of suburbanization of economic activity and caused a decline in the core's goods handling and related service industries.

Motor carriage not only encouraged suburbanization but also influenced the form that it took. An important characteristic of the new distribution of economic activity in metropolitan areas is that it is highly dispersed rather than concentrated in a few, new, large centers. In part this pattern of development reflects the fact that economies of scale in trucking are much more limited than in rail transportation so that typically there are many firms operating in major metropolitan areas. Because of limited scale economies, each trucking firm tends to have its own terminal. To avoid congestion costs, firms do not tend to locate their terminals close to one another when they shift to satellite areas. Thus, goods handling in satellite areas has not become concentrated. Neither is there a strong tendency for manufacturing and other firms to concentrate in a few areas, either around truck terminals or elsewhere. Such concentration would reduce some of the advantages, such as low land costs, of locations in the satellite area. Firms can select sites quite distant from truck terminals because suburban distribution costs are relatively low.[2]

In addition, as business came to rely increasingly on truck transportation, it had an additional incentive to leave the old city centers where obsolescent and crowded streets imposed needless handicaps and delays on truck movement. This feature of the urban economic structure is spelled out more elaborately:

The economy of the American city is largely imprisoned in multistory factory buildings with painfully slow elevators. Commerce, in the nation's older ports, is trapped on piers clustered too close to permit the use of modern barges; the other piers face

2 L. N. Moses and H. F. Williamson, Jr., "The Location of Economic Activity in Cities," Ms., Transportation Center, Northwestern University, 1966. Reprinted by permission.

marginal streets along the river's edge. They lack storage and freight assembly areas, a deficiency which produces a nightmare of tangled trucks when cargoes arrive. Truck highways are essential to bring freight access to factories, new and old, within the cities, if their raw materials and produce are to move, their workers are to be kept employed.[3]

Port areas cannot be moved, but factories can move, and where it is practical, they are doing so as a remedy for congested and uneconomical locations. In an eight-year period (1947 to 1954) the number of industrial plants in Chicago's suburbs doubled; during the same eight years Detroit had a 47 percent increase in central city manufacturing establishments but a 220 percent rise in the suburbs.[4] At longer range and on a broader scale, before the Second World War nine out of ten new factories were built in metropolitan areas; by the mid-1950s new construction was about evenly divided between urban and country districts; subsequently the proportion of new factories located outside metropolitan regions has risen to 80 percent[5]—a striking measure of the extent of industrial dispersal. (See Table 12.1.)

As with the development of residential suburbs, the railroads contributed to this outward movement of industry. The first organized industrial districts, offering planned sites for industrial development, were promoted principally by railroads.[6] Since 1950, however, the railroad share has declined, and private developers have largely taken the lead (see Table 12.2). This change in sponsorship is probably reflected in the fact that most industrial parks are fairly small—75 percent less than 400 acres and

3 Roger Starr, *The Living End: The City and Its Critics* (New York: Coward-McCann, 1968), p. 36.
4 Bureau of Public Roads, *Highways and Economic and Social Changes* (Washington, D.C.: Government Printing Office, 1964), p. 58.
5 B. A. Shriever and W. W. Seifert, *Air Transportation 1975 and Beyond: A Systems Approach* (Cambridge, Mass.: The M.I.T. Press, 1968), p. 157.
6 J. R. Lee and G. K. H. Wong, *An Analysis of Organized Industrial Districts* (Menlo Park, Calif.: Stanford Research Institute, 1958), p. 8. There is no clear distinction between industrial districts and industrial parks. The latter term is generally applied to highway-oriented developments.

Table 12.1   Growth of Organized Industrial Districts

Year Development Began	Number of Districts	Percent of Total Reporting
Before 1900	3	1.0
1900–1909	5	1.7
1910–1919	5	1.7
1920–1929	8	2.8
1930–1939	12	4.2
1940–1949	74	25.6
1950–1954	84	29.1
Since 1955	98	33.9
Total	289	100.0

Sources: *Organized Industrial Districts*, U.S. Department of Commerce, 1954; *Industrial Development, 1957 Site Selection Handbook Edition*, Conway Publications, October 1956; Stanford Research Institute.
Reprinted by permission from Stanford Research Institute.

40 percent less than 100 acres. The smaller parks are more likely to depend on highway than on rail transportation, since a large volume of freight is needed to justify rail service.

There are limitations to the dispersal of industry. Heavy industries, especially those which depend on bulk shipments of raw materials or finished products, must perforce locate where rail or water transport is accessible. Such sites may not and need not be

Table 12.2   Sponsors or Owners of Industrial Districts

	Number	Percent
Private developers	124	41.1
Railroads	88	29.1
Community organizations	52	17.2
Governmental agencies	17	5.6
Community organizations in cooperation with others	21	7.0
Total	302	100.0

Source: R. E. Boley, "Effects of Industrial Parks on the Community," *Urban Land*, vol. 17, no. 10 (November 1958), p. 4.
This information is reprinted from *Urban Land*, Copyright, ULI—the Urban Land Institute, 1200 18th Street, N.W., Washington, D.C. 20036.

in central city locations. One authoritative work on urban transportation suggests that the most advantageous sites would be at the intersections of rail lines with circumferential highways or urban freeways, far enough out from built-up areas to have vacant land available.[7] Other conditions may also affect the choices. During the period just referred to when suburban industry was growing in Chicago and Detroit, Milwaukee's industries remained centralized. The reasons were the following:

1. The city's heavy capital goods industries required rail and water transportation.

2. There was excess plant capacity in the central city.

3. Land in outlying districts was not zoned for industrial use.

4. Failure to control access reduced the utility of highways on the outskirts of the city.

As a general rule, large industrial firms relocate more readily than small ones. Data collected for eight metropolitan regions (Baltimore, Denver, New Orleans, northeastern New Jersey, Philadelphia, St. Louis, San Francisco–Oakland, and Washington, D.C.) showed that 69 percent of the small plants but only 45 percent of the large ones were in the central cities.[8] The reason for this difference is that small establishments may not need or be able to afford their own buildings and so seek locations where space can be shared with others. This is especially likely to apply to a concern that is new or marginal. Such space can be found in the structures vacated by larger firms that have moved out. In addition, small companies will try to locate where they can take advantage of "external economies"—that is, where specialists and subcontractors are available to whom work can be farmed out, thereby eliminating the necessity of installing expensive specialized equipment and incurring burdensome fixed charges. These and other pressures tend to attract the smaller plants to the core

7 J. R. Meyer, J. M. Kain, and H. Wohl, *The Urban Transportation Problem* (Cambridge, Mass.: Harvard University Press, 1965), p. 19.
8 BPR, *Highways and Economic and Social Changes*, p. 59.

areas, where, besides the specialized services, labor and materials are easier to get on short notice, and rented loft space can be had without a long-term commitment.[9]

Nonmanufacturing Enterprise

The forces that stimulated industrial dispersal worked with even greater effect on warehousing and distribution activities. As with factories, developments in materials handling have made single-story structures desirable for warehouse operations. Studies by the Department of Agriculture indicate that unit handling costs are 30 to 40 percent lower in single-story than in multistory warehouses.[10] Since the cost of rebuilding in the older warehouse districts of most cities would be prohibitively high, warehouse operators, including wholesalers and distributors, prefer to relocate where they have space to take advantage of up-to-date materials-handling techniques. The study that cites this Department of Agriculture finding also points out that warehouse operation has changed drastically. The modern warehouse is no longer a storehouse but a "transit shed" for continuous inventory replenishment. More space is devoted to processing orders, docks, and aisles for self-propelled vehicles than to actual storage.

Truck transportation is fundamental to these changes in warehouse location and practice. The modern warehouse can be a transit shed primarily because trucks make possible a continuous flow of goods in and out, and it can be located in an outlying district because distribution by truck can be made conveniently from any part of a metropolitan area to any other. The paramount role of the truck in intraurban freight movement needs no elaboration; practically all hauling of goods within urban areas

9 For a discussion of the locational requirements of small plants, see Edgar M. Hoover and Raymond Vernon, *Anatomy of a Metropolis* (Cambridge, Mass.: Harvard University Press, 1959), pp. 49–53.
10 Port of New York Authority, Comprehensive Planning Office, *Metropolitan Transportation—1980* (New York: Port of New York Authority, 1963), p. 89.

is done by truck, and this has had a definite locational effect because there is no particular advantage to having a truck terminal or distributing center located in a downtown area, and there are some rather obvious disadvantages. Apart from the higher cost of space, an intown location means that the trucks have to travel on the most congested streets to reach the terminal. Companies that relocated along the Santa Ana Freeway in Southern California found that the travel time to central Los Angeles was less than from their former intown sites.[11]

The critical importance of motor freight transportation as a decentralizing influence is reflected in the fact that businesses like banking and insurance, where movement of goods is not a factor, show a less obvious tendency to disperse. There is some evidence that as the retailing function of the CBD declines, it is being offset by an increase in activities using office space. To the extent that this may be a continuing trend, it has important implications for planning the rehabilitation of central business districts. This expansion appears to be in main offices of large companies, because the increases in CBD office space have been greater in large than in small cities.[12]

The picture, however, is mixed. There has been a definite shift of insurance company offices to suburban locations. Such moves have been desirable in order to reduce rental costs and provide adequate parking for employees.[13] Banking has had a dual development. The great bulk of deposits, 75 to 80 percent, remain in the central business district banks.[14] On the other hand, the majority of new banking establishments are in outlying or suburban areas. These are small banks, or branches of the big institutions, and this trend was to be expected, since banks, like other businesses, want to be convenient to their customers.

11 BPR, *Highways and Economic and Social Changes,* p. 62.
12 *Ibid.,* p. 76.
13 *Ibid.,* p. 77.
14 *Ibid.,* p. 79.

The New York Region

As was true with the suburban expansion of population, the New York Metropolitan Region affords a fascinating case study of industrial and business dispersal. Figure 12.1 shows the same trend as exists in the other metropolitan regions: manufacturing employment declining at the core, increasing on the periphery.

The geographical configuration of the New York area provides an unusually striking illustration of the effect of transportation technology. New York gained its primacy among American cities because of its unique advantage in water transportation—an excellent harbor and access to the interior by the Hudson River and the Erie Canal—when water transportation was the most economical, indeed the only economical way to move heavy freight. The city became not only a major commercial and financial center but a major manufacturing center also. When the railroad era arrived, New York City, especially Manhattan Island, was at some disadvantage, because all but two of the lines coming from the west terminated on the New Jersey side of the Hudson, and only one of the two gave direct freight service to Manhattan. Consequently, industries with substantial transportation requirements tended to favor New Jersey locations, while Manhattan specialized in products such as clothing, in which shipping costs were small.[15]

Truck transportation began to modify this metropolitan pattern in the 1920s. The advantages of a New Jersey location for reaching national markets became somewhat less; so also did the advantage of a New York City location for distributing to the local market. In effect, the truck "homogenized the Region's land area, making one place less unlike another." [16] More important, industry could spread out more freely to the locations where there

15 For an analysis of this situation see Edgar M. Hoover and Raymond Vernon, *Metropolis 1985* (Cambridge, Mass.: Harvard University Press, 1960), pp. 14ff.
16 *Ibid.,* p. 24.

Thousands of workers
(ratio scale)

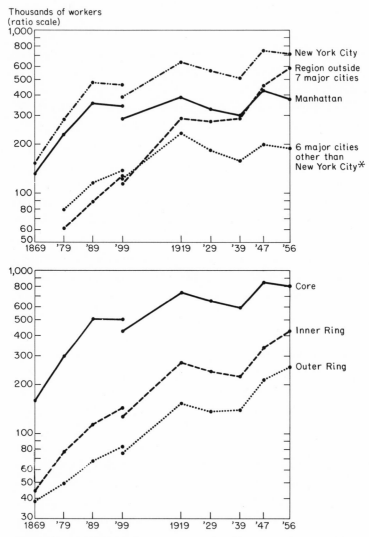

Figure 12.1 Manufacturing production workers by parts of New York Metropolitan Region, 1869–1956
Source: Edgar M. Hoover and Raymond Vernon, *Anatomy of a Metropolis*
(Cambridge, Mass.: Harvard University Press, 1959), p. 26. Reprinted by permission of the publishers from: Edgar M. Hoover and Raymond Vernon,
Anatomy of a Metropolis, Cambridge, Mass.: Harvard University Press, Copyright, 1959, by Regional Plan Associates, Inc.

Table 12.3   Plant Sites with Railroad Sidings, New York Region, 1956

Year Site Acquired	Entire Region	New Jersey Counties	Rest of Region
Prior to 1920	63	71	50
1920–1945	50	59	39
1946–1956	40	42	36

Source: Questionnaire replies from 476 manufacturing plants, practically all of them outside of New York City. Of the 476, those which acquired their present sites prior to 1920 numbered 120 (76 in New Jersey and 44 elsewhere in region); those which acquired them between 1920 and 1945 numbered 160 (90 in New Jersey and 70 elsewhere); and those which acquired them after 1945 numbered 196 (123 in New Jersey and 73 elsewhere).
Reprinted by permission of the publishers from p. 37 of: Edgar M. Hoover and Raymond Vernon, *Anatomy of a Metropolis*, Cambridge, Mass.: Harvard University Press, Copyright, 1959, by Regional Plan Association, Inc.

was room for efficient plant layout. For the New York Region there were some special factors, none seriously affecting the basic tendency to industrial dispersal. The communications-oriented industries (advertising, publishing, radio-television) had special locational forces that kept them concentrated. Industries with growing employment showed a faster outward shift from New York City than those whose employment had remained the same or decreased, and large plants moved out faster than small. In New York as elsewhere the small firms tended to stay where they could take advantage of external economies, but they were still involved in the outward thrust. To an increasing degree they were renting space on Long Island or in New Jersey that had been vacated by larger concerns that moved there from Manhattan and have now gone to modern suburban locations.[17]

Attributing the relocation of industry in the New York Region entirely to highway influence would be an exaggeration. Some of it was due to expansion of rail services, and some of it to sheer lack of space in the core area, which would have forced some industries to move out and utilize whatever transportation

17 *Ibid.*, p. 117.

facilities—rail, water, or highway—were available. But the highway impact should not be underrated either. Table 12.3 is illuminating. Before 1920, 63 percent of the plant sites in the Region had railroad sidings; in the decade 1946 to 1956 only 40 percent of the new plants felt railroad sidings to be necessary. Furthermore, the New Jersey segment of the Region, which is most readily accessible by rail, has the highest proportion of rail sidings, but it is still a declining percentage.

Changes in the distribution of truck terminals tell an equally, perhaps more significant story. Before 1940 most of New York's motor freight terminals were concentrated on Manhattan's lower West Side, along with Brooklyn, Jersey City, Newark, and Paterson-Passaic.[18] Since then, while a substantial concentration remains in Manhattan close to the waterfront and the Hudson River tunnels, the center of motor freight handling in the New York area has moved to the Hackensack Meadows in New Jersey, convenient to U.S. 1 and the New Jersey Turnpike (see Figure 12.2). The Hackensack Meadows district has 27 percent of the truck terminals and 43 percent of the truck bays in the Greater New York area.

A detailed analysis of the industrial prospects of the New York Region sees continuing conditions favorable to growth in the outer portions, including the expansion of air freight and of piggyback rail freight, which will extend the advantages of rail service to *any point that a truck can reach* [author's italics], and the construction of circumferential high-speed highways.[19] The search for added space and the desire to avoid the congestion at the center will stimulate industry to take advantage of the locational opportunities offered by these methods of transportation.

In the nonmanufacturing enterprises, New York has a unique

18 This description of truck terminals is from Port of New York Authority. *Metropolitan Transportation—1980*, p. 217.
19 Hoover and Vernon, *Anatomy of a Metropolis*, pp. 43–44.

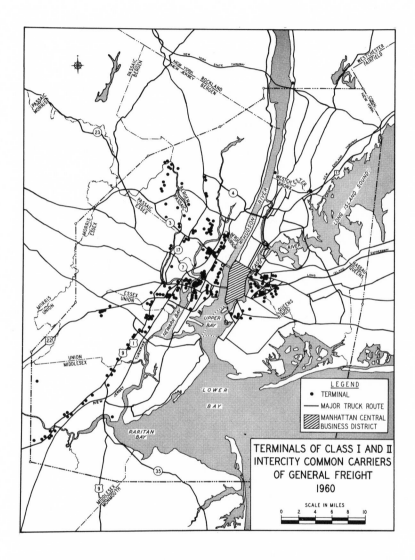

Figure 12.2 Truck terminals, New York Region
Source: Comprehensive Planning Office, Port of New York Authority, *Metropolitan Transportation—1980* (New York: Port of New York Authority, 1963), p. 216. Reproduced by permission from the Comprehensive Planning Office, Port of New York Authority.

position as the world's major financial center, and this has a gravitational effect in keeping a tremendous mass of office activities in the core area of Manhattan. Yet some of the forces common to other metropolitan complexes can be discerned in New York also. Between 1929 and 1954 Manhattan's proportion of wholesale jobs in the Region declined from 76 to 59 percent.[20] Banking shared the general pattern. From 1947 to 1956 commercial bank employment grew by 19 percent in New York City, 9 percent in Essex and Hudson counties (Newark and Jersey City), 132 percent in Nassau and Suffolk counties (Long Island), and 53 percent elsewhere in the Region.[21] The reason is that an increasing share of the business of commercial banks is with individuals, and as people and jobs move outward, banking facilities have to follow. Insurance offices show a generally similar trend. For these activities the transportation impact is indirect but none the less important; they are pulled outward from the core because changes in transportation, predominantly highway-based, have moved their customers out.

Route 128

An outstanding example of the impact of a single highway on both industrial dispersal and growth is Massachusetts Route 128, a circumferential freeway swinging in a vast area around Boston from Nantasket on the south to Cape Ann on the north (see Figure 12.3). The idea of such a circumferential route originated with a Massachusetts highway engineer, Franklin C. Pillsbury, as far back as 1930.[22] All that existed then, and for some years to come, was a typical bypass of the period, a collection of local roads winding through the centers of Boston's suburbs and marked 128. Some sections of the new freeway were built in the

20 *Ibid.*, p. 84.
21 *Ibid.*, p. 94.
22 Frank Fogarty, "Boston's Magic Semicircle," in William Laas, ed., *Freedom of the American Road* (Detroit: Ford Motor Co., 1956), p. 42.

1930s, but the main part had to wait until after the Second World War, and the bulk of the construction was done between 1951 and 1957.

The total length from Braintree to Gloucester is about seventy miles, and most of the route is about ten miles from Bos-

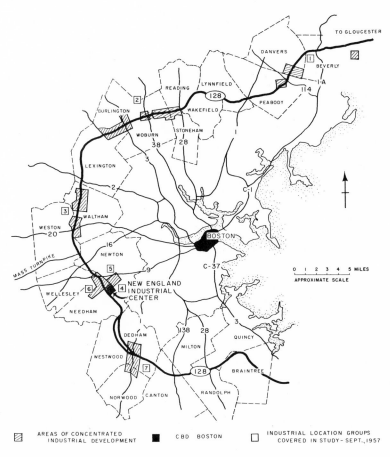

Figure 12.3 Layout of Route 128 showing areas of industrial development
Source: A. J. Bone and Martin Wohl, "Massachusetts Route 128 Impact Study," *Highway Research Board Bulletin 227* (1959), p. 22.

Table 12.4   Origins of Plants on Massachusetts Route 128, January 1958

Origin of Plant	Total	Percent of Total
New industry	6	6.1
Relocated industry	59	59.6
New branch plant	13	13.1
Relocated branch plant	21	21.2
Total	99	100.0

Source: A. J. Bone, "Economic Impact Study of Massachusetts Route 128," presented at Annual Meeting, Highway Research Board, Washington, D.C., January 8, 1958, p. 12.

ton's CBD. Traffic on the most heavily traveled part, the central segment from the intersection with U.S. Route 1 north of Boston to the intersection with the same route on the south, was 40,000 to 50,000 vehicles daily in 1960. The road was located in vacant land just outside existing developed areas so that:

The highway gave access to low priced land in areas on the edge of the metropolitan labor market, not too far from the core of the city and yet close to attractive suburbs. At the same time many in-town businesses were expanding to the point where they could no longer operate efficiently in obsolete buildings on cramped sites. Developers took advantage of this situation and promoted the development of Route 128 industrial sites.[23]

At the end of 1957 there were 99 industrial plants adjacent to Route 128, employing 17,000 persons and representing a total investment of $94 million (see Tables 12.4 and 12.5). New plants then under construction added another $40 million. One-fifth were new main or branch plants; the rest had moved, principally from sites in central Boston. For the relocated companies the move was an expansion not only in space occupied but in scale of operation as measured by employment (see Table 12.6).

There is a definite growth along Route 128, and it has continued since these surveys were made. One question that must

23 A. J. Bone and Martin Wohl, "Massachusetts Route 128 Impact Study," *Highway Research Board Bulletin* 227 (Washington, D.C.: 1959), pp. 21–22.

Table 12.5   Type of Industry on Massachusetts Route 128, January 1958

Type of Plant	Type of Industry			
	Production	Research and Development	Service	Distribution
New industry	4	1	0	1
Relocated industry	23	8	5	23
New branch plant	5	2	1	5
Relocated branch plant	1	1	—	19
Total	33	12	6	48

Source: A. J. Bone, "Economic Impact Study of Massachusetts Route 128," p. 12.

be asked is whether, and to what extent, this growth has been at the expense of the older industrial sections of Boston. The available evidence indicates that the New York pattern is repeated in Boston: as established companies move to outlying districts, smaller firms move into the vacated space. In the spring of 1958 much of the floor space occupied by twenty-five firms that had moved from in-town Boston to Route 128 sites was partially occupied by sixty-one companies (64 percent; 4 percent had been

Table 12.6   Employment in Companies Relocating on Massachusetts Route 128, January 1959

Type of Industry	Employment		Change	
	Before Move	After Move	Total	Percent
Distribution	1699	1866	+ 167	+ 9.8
Production	6664	8528	+1864	+28.0
Research and development	1097	1546	+ 449	+40.9
Service	382	358	− 24	− 6.3
Total	9842	12,298	+2456	+25.0

Source: A. J. Bone and Martin Wohl, "Route 128 Impact Study," Highway Research Board Bulletin 227, Washington, D.C., 1959.

demolished and the rest was vacant) with about $2 million less assessed valuation and 1,673 fewer jobs.[24] For the metropolitan area as a whole there was a positive gain in property valuations and employment, but the central city had at least a temporary loss. The majority of these sixty-one companies gave a need for expansion and greater efficiency as their principal reason for taking over the space vacated by their predecessors, so that in their way they were responding to the same kind of pressures as the companies moving out to Route 128.

Because there has been detailed examination of the impact of Route 128, we have a clear picture of the motives for business enterprise to locate on or near a major freeway on the outskirts of a metropolitan area. It also affords an insight into some of the advantages and drawbacks encountered by some of the firms making such a choice. All companies wanted better access; the research and development firms sought convenient employee access, and the manufacturing and distributing concerns wanted this plus commercial accessibility and room for expansion. This locational advantage was secured by being near the highway, not directly on it—unattainable with controlled access in any case. The benefits of easy accessibility to the entire metropolitan region were considered to outweigh the inconvenience of limiting access to the highway itself.[25]

The principal handicap of a Route 128 location was that occasional difficulty was experienced in getting unskilled labor. Lack of public transportation was given as a drawback to recruitment of labor; yet when some companies provided bus service, it was so little used that it was discontinued.[26] A minor lack was frontage roads; some companies had to build their own.

24 *Ibid.*, p. 27.
25 *Ibid.*, p. 35.
26 A. J. Bone, "Route 128 Study. Survey of Industrial Development," presented at Annual Meeting of Highway Research Board, Washington, D.C., January 8, 1958, pp. 25–28.

It also happened that employees in Route 128 plants used the highway in preference to more direct routes in their journeys to and from work. Workers living in the central Boston area, where there seemed to be the least to be gained by using Route 128, were found to go considerable distances out of their way in order to travel on the express highway. The author of this particular study concluded: "Distance need no longer be measured by miles but by minutes and convenience. By increasing the distance which a worker can travel in a given period of time, Route 128 is effectively increasing the size of the labor market. . . ." [27]

An analysis of peripheral commuting in Chicago, based on business and industrial firms in the West Suburban area, found somewhat similar results. Employees tended to cluster near the plants or in adjacent suburbs, and managerial and professional personnel lived closer to their place of business than their counterparts who worked in the CBD.[28] Peripheral commuters averaged 5.23 miles compared with 6.72 for CBD commuters. The two situations are not completely parallel, because the Chicago firms studied were not adjacent to a freeway; in fact, they were some distance east—toward the central city—of the Illinois Tollway.

This clustering is understandable because it is easier to live close to a suburban business establishment than one in the CBD, and it by no means excludes the opportunity, given good highway access, of drawing some of the work force from considerable distances. The chief implications for metropolitan development are twofold: first, continued growth of suburban business and industry will inevitably intensify the forces drawing population

27 J. P. Fehan, "The Influence of Massachusetts Route 128 on the Travel Patterns of Workers at the New England Industrial Center, Needham, Mass." Bachelor's Thesis, M.I.T., May 1959, pp. 42–44.
28 E. J. Taaffe, B. J. Garner, and M. H. Yeates, *The Peripheral Journey to Work. A Geographic Consideration* (Evanston, Ill.: Northwestern University, 1963), pp. 70, 82–83, 88.

outward from the central city; second, the structure of urban transportation must increasingly be geared both to intersuburban commuting and to facilitating travel for central city residents to employment opportunities on the periphery. The Chicago study is quite explicit on the kind of transportation called for:

The high-capacity, off-street modes, such as the commuter railroads and the elevated-subway, are of negligible significance in commutation to the West Suburban district. Together they account for only 2 per cent of the peripheral commuters, as opposed to 40 per cent of the CBD commuters. The bus is the only form of mass transportation of any significance to the peripheral commuter, and it accounts for 7 per cent, approximately as many as walk to work.[29]

Freeway Industry

The impact of the highway has understandably been most pronounced on the so-called "freeway industries." They are the light industries—the electronic companies, the "think tanks"—in which the volume and type of materials flowing in and out of the plant can be handled by truck and are secondary in importance to technical skill and "know-how." Indeed, location near an educational center may be regarded as more important than access to materials or markets. The proximity of Harvard and M.I.T. is one of the major attractions of Route 128. Other examples can be found throughout the United States. Freeway industry is only partially an outcome of migration from central city locations; much of it consists of new enterprises that have consciously chosen their locations for the advantages offered by ample space and convenient highway access both for materials and for skilled managerial and technical personnel.

Needless to say, California's elaborate freeway network has had its impact on industrial growth. South of San Francisco there is a cluster of freeway industries in the vicinity of Palo Alto (Stanford University). Across the Bay, a study in 1954 of a 7.5-

29 *Ibid.*, p. 9.

mile section along the East Shore Freeway in Alameda County, which includes Oakland and Berkeley, revealed that although the study area contained only 9 percent of the industrial acreage in the county, it had 43 percent of the expenditure for new industrial construction.[30] For the Los Angeles area, a 1962 report on freeway development observes:

We note along the Santa Ana Freeway the expansion of the Los Angeles Central Manufacturing District, the industrial development westerly of Buena Park and in the Anaheim area. In the Woodland Hills–Canoga Park area and at Newberry Park along the Ventura Freeway we see new manufacturing centers being established.

In its brochure to industry the Pomona Chamber of Commerce stresses the availability of the existing San Bernardino (Interstate Route 10) and Corona Freeways as well as the proposed Foothill and Pomona Freeways. In the northeastern section of Anaheim adjacent to the Riverside Freeway a rapid expansion of industrial and manufacturing plants is taking place. In southern Santa Ana near the proposed intersection of the Newport Freeway, the proposed San Diego Freeway and MacArthur Freeway [this intersection has since been completed], a high concentration of new industrial plants is occurring.[31]

The development described here has continued unabated as the freeway system has expanded. Other examples can be added: Atlanta, for instance, where the land adjacent to the North and Northeast Expressways has changed from residential to commercial and industrial use with a consequent appreciation in value.[32] There is no need to pad the record; there is something to be said for balancing it. Not all highway site choices are definitely formulated. An analysis of six industrial concerns in Michigan, two small-sized (one to three plants), two medium (four to six plants), and two large (seven or more plants), concluded: "The influence

30 D. J. Bowersox, "Influence of Highways on Six Industrial Locations," *Highway Research Board Bulletin* 268 (Washington, D.C., 1960), p. 17.

31 E. T. Telford, "Los Angeles Area Freeways," *California Highways and Public Works* (March–April 1962), p. 12.

32 J. H. Lemly, "Changes in Land Use and Values along Atlanta's Expressways," *Highway Research Board Bulletin* 227 (Washington, D.C., 1959), pp. 19–20.

of highway facilities on the selection of these six plant sites was considered as important but not critical. If the road was paved and in good condition, it was judged adequate." [33]

The writer goes on to speculate on the meaning of this six-company survey in the light of extensive nationwide industrial development adjacent to major roads. Is one type of highway just as good as another for industrial location, or have some firms failed to understand the effect that an up-to-date highway can have on their business activities? The weight of the evidence is heavily in favor of the second alternative.

Freeway industry has another consequence. No one can drive along Route 128 in Massachusetts or the Ventura Freeway in California, or others, without becoming aware that this is a new style in industrial architecture. The factory buildings are modern in design, attractive in appearance, and set in neatly landscaped surroundings. They do not, for the most part, belch smoke and fumes, and they are seldom noisy. This is the predominant pattern of suburban industry; it is something to be put to the credit of the highway and the motor vehicle.

Access to Airports
The airport has become an increasingly important feature of the economic structure of Metropolis. Air passenger travel more than doubled between 1957 and 1967; air freight, including mail and express, more than quadrupled; and general aviation has been keeping pace with them.[34] With larger aircraft coming into use, the volume of traffic handled at airports is bound to grow at an

---

33 Bowersox, "Influence of Highways," pp. 21–22.
34 David K. Witheford, "Airports and Accessibility," *Traffic Quarterly,* vol. 23, no. 2 (April 1969), p. 275. I am also indebted to three unpublished papers for information on airport access: S. M. Silence, "A Preliminary Look at Ground Access to Airports," 47th Annual Meeting, Highway Research Board, Washington, D.C., January 1968; E. M. Whitlock and E. L. Cleary, "Planning Ground Transportation Facilities for Airports"; S. G. Lardiers, "Impact of Projected Air Travel Demand on Airport Access," both 48th Annual Meeting, Highway Research Board, Washington, D.C., January 1969.

accelerating rate. But this is not all. Airports attract other business —hotels, restaurants, and recreational facilities to supply the wants of travelers and visitors; industrial complexes composed of firms related to aviation or simply companies that find immediate access to air transport desirable. In short, the airport has come to have the role in the life of the city that the railroad station had in the past, with the vital difference that the main railroad station was in the center of the city—frequently it *was* the center of the city—while the airport of necessity has to be far enough out to have plenty of open space.

The airport is therefore an additional factor, and one that is bound to become more and more influential, in encouraging the outward movement of metropolitan business and industry. Unfortunately, few existing airports were planned with adequate consideration for ground access. Apparently if a major highway was somewhere close by, this was considered sufficient, with the result that ground access has become as critical a problem for airports as the control of their air traffic.

Efforts to solve this problem have concentrated heavily on improving connections between the airport and the central business district, and this is unquestionably the most urgent need. Cleveland extended its rapid transit system to the Cleveland-Hopkins Airport, and Boston's Logan Airport has bus connection to a nearby transit station. Other cities have contemplated similar systems, but these, even if adopted, will be quite rare.

Ground access to airports has to be principally by road, for reasons that have nothing to do with any preference for one type of transportation over another. The airport is not just an outlying appendage of the CBD. Even for strictly travel purposes, it handles more people from outside than inside CBDs (see Table 12.7). At least a third of the passengers at major airports originate in or are destined for suburban communities.[35] Beyond this, an

35 *Ibid.,* p. 278.

Table 12.7   Percent of Air Traveler Origins in Central Business Districts

Airports	Percent of Air Travel Trips Originating in CBD
Chicago	33
Kennedy, N.Y.	47
San Francisco	20
Washington (National)	42
Newark	38
La Guardia, N.Y.	55
Philadelphia	15
Cleveland	28
Pittsburgh	25

Source: D. K. Witheford, "Airports and Accessibility," *Traffic Quarterly*, vol. 23, no. 2 (April 1969), p. 277.
Reproduced by permission of the author, *Traffic Quarterly*, and the Eno Foundation for Transportation, Inc.

airport becomes a business and industrial center in its own right. Air passengers actually account for a minority of all person trips to and from airports, between 14 and 43 percent. Airport employee trips range from 23 to 70 percent, and the rest are social-recreational—people seeing passengers off or meeting them, or just visiting the airport.[36] These figures do not include people traveling to and from business and industrial establishments in the vicinity of the airport.

Only a small part of this nonpassenger travel is CBD-related. Most of it is multidirectional and low-density, like suburban travel generally. For air freight the same consideration applies; the freeway industries are far more likely to use it than the heavy industries concentrated in older urban areas. Consequently, planning for airport access must take into account what is expressed here:

Planning travel facilities in the sixties only to meet air passenger needs is like planning downtown transportation facilities forty years ago with only railroad users in mind.

Airports, like most CBDs, distribute travel in all directions, since most trip ends are related to the distribution of population

36 *Ibid.*, p. 280.

in the urban area. The single most important corridor will continue to be that connecting with the CBD. But circumferential routes, in the context of the urban area transport system, also serve as principal means of access to airports. Because growing traffic generators within and around airports exhibit traditionally peaked time characteristics, the principal airport transportation need may be for adequate highway capacity in all directions within a mile or two of the site. Beyond such a distance, travel will be dispersed, some to offices and industries but most to residences. To meet such conditions, many urban areas may need improved circumferential facilities more than an improved connector to the CBD.[37]

A searching investigation into the future of air transportation arrives at the same conclusion: namely, that the principal means of ground access to airports must continue to be the highway.[38] Other modes, whether on the ground by railborne transit or in the air by helicopter, V/STOL aircraft, or prospective new technologies, may relieve some of the load on the roads; but for the predictable future there is complete agreement that local travel to and from airports will be primarily by private car, bus, limousine, or taxi.

Summation

The dispersal of business and industry carries with it a fundamental change in the structure of the city. It means that, on the basis of established trends, not only will a higher proportion of the populations of urban areas be living in outlying districts, but more of them will be working in these districts also. There are some finite limits to the process. The central city is not going to vanish; people will continue to live and work there because some of them prefer it and some things can be done better there. Nor can all industry decentralize; some by its nature has to concentrate.

Nevertheless, the economic importance of the center relative

37 *Ibid.,* p. 284.
38 Shriever and Seifert, *Air Transportation,* p. 31.

to the outskirts has been declining, and there is no indication that this pattern will be altered for a long time. With the progress of electronic communications and data processing, there may be less need in many business operations for person-to-person contact and therefore for bringing large numbers of people together. If so, this will be another force for decentralization.

The implications for urban planning go deep. Central city renewal must take into consideration the economics of industrial location. The firms that are moving out of city centers do so to find lower-cost operation; trying to put them back into high-cost areas seems an unpromising method of promoting economic growth. More might be gained by enabling the people to go where the growth is actually occurring.

Transportation, principally by road, made the dispersal of business and industry possible, the governing factor being the flexibility and economy of freight movement provided by the motor truck. In turn, this dispersal reacts on urban transportation systems. The flow of commuters from suburb to center and back remains a major problem for all cities, but it should not become the sole focus of attention. At least equal weight has to be given to the other transportation requirements of the emerging pattern of metropolitan organization—suburb to suburb and reverse commuting where the movement of people is concerned and the indispensable function of the truck for the movement of intraurban freight.

13 Urban Transportation: The Options

The urban situation presents, if not the most important, certainly the most acute transportation problem facing the United States, and practically everyone else for that matter. The only societies that do not have an urban transportation problem are those that do not have cities. Traffic congestion is a hard fact, impairing the economic and social well-being of many urban areas with the most serious impact falling on the central cities where the congestion is worst. The problem is obvious; the solution is not. Cities have to find methods of enabling people and goods to move expeditiously and economically; these have to be practical methods, technically and financially feasible, and they have to provide the desired mobility in such a way as to promote the maximum well-being of the whole community.

If this subject is to be discussed intelligently, qualifications and definitions are essential. To begin with, we have to reject the oversimplification that "cars cause congestion," with the corollary that getting rid of the cars would get rid of the congestion. There is ample proof that city streets have been congested ever since there were cities. The cause is not a specific type of vehicle; it is a concentration of people and vehicles in too limited a space. The cure for congestion begins with identifying the reasons for this excessive concentration and trying to determine if and how it can be eliminated.

Second, no two cities are alike, and therefore no single formula for urban transportation exists which can be applied universally. At the same time there are some general issues that most cities share. They are all concerned with keeping unnecessary traffic out of their downtown areas, but they also want to maintain the convenience of access that downtown business must have if it is to stay in existence, or at any rate stay downtown. Likewise, public transportation is a necessity; almost all urban authorities have to wrestle with the question of what kind of public transportation will best serve their particular conditions, and usually with the still more vexing question of how it is to be supported.

Finally, in a free society, public acceptance of a policy is a vital element. A transportation system can be designed to maximize technical efficiency or minimize cost, but "the ultimate test of a transportation system lies not in any technoeconomic indices of efficiency but in the extent to which it finds acceptance within the total value scheme of the community it serves." [1]

The value scheme can vary between communities, and it can change over time. There are, moreover, conditions that require some limitation on individual choices in transportation (to give a very simple illustration, a traffic light restricts the freedom of the individual, but no one seriously questions that such a restriction is a proper one for the good of the community as a whole). But, broadly speaking, the transportation planner who disregards the preferences of the community is headed for disaster.

Urban transportation planning would be difficult enough under contemporary conditions, in view of the rapid expansion of urban population and the growing complexity of metropolitan structures and problems. Unfortunately, urban transportation has also become an emotionally charged issue. Discussions of projected programs, of choices to be made, generate heated reactions from individuals and groups whose good intentions often outrun their information. The options are seldom clear-cut and in a large city can practically never be "either-or" as between, let us say, railborne transit or highways.

The ideal solution is to find "balanced transportation," but defining balance has its own difficulty. To quote the executive director of Washington's National Capital Downtown Committee:

1 A. S. Lang and R. M. Soberman, *Urban Rail Transit: Its Economics and Technology* (Cambridge, Mass.: The M.I.T. Press, 1964), p. 90.

What may be a proper balance for one city would be an obvious imbalance for another. . . . It might be helpful if we could arbitrarily say that equal utilization of each available mode of transportation—measured in terms of persons carried, or passenger miles, or any other comparable yardstick—constituted a proper balance. Unfortunately, however, few, if any, of our cities could survive, as we now know them, if this formula were arbitrarily applied. We must, then, each of us, recognize what kind of city we are working with, consider our existing and potential transportation elements, decide how we want these elements to help shape our future city, and then determine the proper balance to do the job.[2]

This book is concerned with highway influence and not with making a case for or against other forms of transportation, but it may help to clarify the urban picture to examine the advantages and disadvantages of these "existing and potential transportation elements."

Commuter Railroads

In the context of this discussion urban rail transit means a rail-borne system using its own right-of-way for the carriage of passengers on trips within metropolitan areas. This definition includes conventional railroads operating commuter service and the subway and elevated lines classified as "rapid transit." It excludes streetcar systems, because one certainty in American urban transportation is that the trolley car is too cumbersome and unmaneuverable to survive in our changing urban environment.

The basic characteristics of urban rail transport have been described in Chapter 10. It has a high passenger-carrying capacity in relation to the space occupied, and it is fast and ordinarily free from traffic congestion. On the other hand, because it has heavy fixed costs, a high level of utilization is necessary to justify the investment, and once built it cannot be moved to adapt to changes in the urban structure.

2 Knox Banner, "Balanced Transportation Service Downtown," *The Dynamics of Urban Transportation*, Symposium Paper 6, Detroit, October 1962, p. 1.

Commuter rail lines and rapid transit systems share these characteristics, but they also have their differences. The commuter train normally operates on the same tracks as intercity rail traffic, and its principal function is to carry passengers between the CBD and the metropolitan region outside the central city. It is the fastest method of urban transportation, and it has by far the greatest passenger-carrying capacity.[3] The high speeds are possible because stations are widely spaced, so passengers as a rule must use other forms of transportation at each end of the rail trip. Moreover, in common with other public transportation systems, commuter railroads carry most of their traffic at peak hours, which means a substantial investment in equipment that has to stand idle most of the day. High fixed costs and declining revenues have eliminated rail commuter service from all but a very few American cities. Of the SMSAs with populations of over half a million in 1960, forty-one had rail commuter service in 1935 on 240 separate routes. In 1961 the number of such areas had shrunk to twenty, and the commuter routes in operation to eighty-three.[4]

Even to maintain rail commutation where it still exists demands substantial support from public funds. Expansion of rail commuter services, whether additions to present lines or construction of new ones, would require not only operating subsidies but heavy capital outlays for rebuilding track, eliminating grade crossings, and doing the other things necessary for frequent operation of high-speed trains. The expenditure might be justified as socially beneficial if the result was a substantial decline in traffic congestion, but past experience offers little encouragement on this score. The city of Philadelphia began a program of subsidizing commuter service on the Pennsylvania and Reading

3 For a comparison of peak-hour travel times, see Editors of Fortune, *The Exploding Metropolis* (Garden City, N.Y.: Doubleday and Co., 1958), p. 38.
4 U.S. Department of Housing and Urban Development, *Tomorrow's Transportation* (Washington, D.C.: Government Printing Office, 1968), p. 11.

Railroads in 1958 and 1959. Patronage increased by 30 percent in the first year, but operating deficits rose sharply also, because under the subsidy agreement the companies were running more trains and charging lower fares. A decline of 10 percent in rush-hour traffic on the most heavily traveled highways in the area was claimed for the first year, but this gain has diminished. An investigation of patronage late in 1959 showed an increase of 1,371 riders a day, of whom 734 rode in rush hours and 444 were former automobile commuters. It was estimated that 370 cars were kept off the city streets at a cost in subsidy of $3.32 per car per day. It is very much open to question, however, whether this gain was actually realized and still more whether it has been retained, because traffic on the Schuylkill Expressway has not been noticeably affected. On the contrary, it has increased at a uniform rate each year.[5]

In New York, where rail commuting is indispensable to the functioning of the city, a survey by the Institute of Public Administration showed that 14,800 residents of Westchester County in New York and Fairfield County in Connecticut drove regularly to work in Manhattan. Only 3,900, 26 percent, worked within a twenty-minute trip by car or subway from the Grand Central Terminal.[6] Of these, 2,000 might have been potential railroad patrons, since the others used their cars for business (they might, of course, have rented cars in New York, but that would merely increase their own costs and contribute nothing to relieve congestion in the city's streets). If these 2,000 persons had actually shifted to trains, traffic on each of the twenty-four highway lanes

5 On governmental programs for the support of rail commuter services, see G. W. Smerk, *Urban Transportation. The Federal Role* (Bloomington, Ind.: Indiana University Press, 1966), pp. 140–151, and G. W. Hilton, "The Decline of Railroad Commutation," *Business History Review,* vol. 36, no. 2 (Summer 1962), pp. 176–186.
6 Sumner Myers, "The Technology of Evolutionary Transit," paper presented at Transportation Research Forum, Montreal, Canada, September 1967, p. 7.

into New York from Westchester and Fairfield counties would have been reduced by one-third of a car per minute for two peak hours.

Improvement of railroad commuter service is a desirable objective in its own right; it might well attract more patronage. However, the only function the commuter train performs is to carry passengers from suburbs to CBD and back, and while this function should be continued, the prospect that it can be measurably expanded, at least on an economically viable basis, is remote. Metropolitan growth patterns are quite consistent in showing CBD employment as static or even declining, which necessarily affects commuter travel. Work trips into Philadelphia's CBD declined from 260,000 to 220,000 between 1947 and 1960, and outbound commuter travel in Chicago dropped from 225,000 to 223,000 between 1950 and 1961.[7] Caution therefore needs to be exercised about regarding the commuter railroad as a remedy for traffic problems. It could be an expensive investment for an uncertain gain.

Rapid Transit

Rapid transit systems as a rule operate within central city areas, although there is no reason why they should not extend to the suburbs. In the Boston metropolitan complex, what is now the Massachusetts Bay Transit Authority took over the Newton Highlands branch of the Boston and Albany Railroad, a straightforward commuter line, and incorporated it into the rapid transit system. San Francisco's Bay Area Rapid Transit project (BART) reaches out to the suburbs of the San Francisco–Oakland metropolitan region. If there is to be a renewal and expansion of intraurban, or intrametropolitan, rail transportation it is much more likely to take the form of rapid transit systems than of railroad commuter service.

7 *Ibid.*, p. 9.

It would therefore be helpful to have wider public understanding of the advantages and limitations of rapid transit than now exists, if only to reduce the volume of uninformed "transit versus freeway" argument that too often obstructs rational evaluation of urban transportation problems. There are some situations in which a rapid transit system would be the best answer to an urban transportation problem; there are others in which it would be better to build freeways; there are even some in which it would be desirable to do both.

The question of capacity is as good a place to start as any. In the transit versus freeway arguments it is usually said that a single rail transit track can carry 60,000 passengers an hour, the equivalent of twenty lanes of freeway. There is nothing wrong with the figures themselves. A rapid transit line *can* carry that many passengers an hour, and a freeway lane has an approximate capacity of 2,000 vehicles an hour. If these are all passenger cars and have the normal average occupancy of 1.5 persons, then the lane carries 3,000 persons an hour. There is, of course, some inequity in comparing the total capacity of a transit track with actual rather than potential freeway performance. If those 2,000 passenger cars were fully loaded, as transit cars must be to reach the 60,000 figure, the freeway would look better, and if we put fully loaded buses on the freeway as well, it would look better still.

The only city in North America where rapid transit passenger volume exceeds 40,000 per track per hour is New York. (New York City, in fact, accounts for 80 percent of all rail transit passengers in the United States.) There the most heavily traveled express tracks reach and occasionally exceed the 60,000 figure. To do so requires running at least 30 ten-car trains (the longest the station platforms will accommodate) an hour, each car fully loaded with 200 persons of whom 40 are seated. (See Tables 13.1 and 13.2.) No rail transit system currently existing or planned can carry even 40,000 passengers per track per hour at normal operat-

Table 13.1   Capacity of Rapid Transit Cars

	New York					
	IND	IRT	Toronto	Cleveland	Chicago	Philadelphia
Seats	50	44	62	54	51	56
Maximum passengers	250	200	220	196	181	190
Maximum speed (mph)	45	45	47	55	50	55

Source: Lang and Soberman, *Urban Rail Transit* (Cambridge, Mass.: The M.I.T. Press, 1964), p. 60.

Table 13.2   Peak-Hour Passenger Volumes on Urban Transit Routes
Rail Rapid Transit

				Passenger Movement	
	City	Facility	Trains per Hr.	Actual Peak Hr.	15–20 Min. Rate per Hr.
Rail rapid transit installations	New York	IND 6th & 8th Ave. express	32	61,400	71,790
	New York	IND 8th Ave. express	30	62,030	69,570
	New York	IRT Lex. Ave. express	31	44,510	50,700
	Toronto	Yonge St. Subway	28	35,166	39,850
	New York	IRT 7th Ave. express	24	36,770	38,520
	Chicago	Congress St. expressway*	25	10,376	14,542
	Cleveland	Private R/W and Subway	20	6,211	8,349

* Stretch represents densest "transit" mile of rail rapid transit operation on the expressway, where two routes converge; consists of track and four auto lanes in each direction. (Transit passenger flow shown is for the prevailing direction only.)
Source: *Dynamics of Urban Transportation* (Detroit: Automobile Manufacturers Association, 1962).

ing speeds without half of them being standees.[8] The cars for San Francisco's BART have seventy-five seats; with ten-car trains, ninety-second headways, all passengers seated, this comes to 30,000 passengers per track per hour. Shorter headways are possible, but only at the cost of reduced speeds. The Toronto subway approaches the 40,000 mark, but then the volume drops sharply even for as large a metropolitan region as Chicago.

The New York system is admittedly old; transit systems built today could be much more attractive, as the Toronto and Montreal systems are. Bigger stations can be built, as well as larger cars, but this means greater cost, and there are limits to the useful length of transit cars. Longer cars, for example, require wider curves. Technical improvements do not present a serious problem, but no technical improvement by itself will overcome crowding at rush hours. If every transit passenger had a seat during rush hours, the system would have to be either grossly underused or grossly overbuilt.

The speed of transit trains is also subject to misunderstanding. Top speeds of 70 to 80 mph are easily attainable, more if the costs in track and signaling are accepted. In New York such speeds would be impractical during the periods when there is a two-minute headway or less between trains, but fully automatic controls might resolve this difficulty. However, for the transit patron the speed that counts is the actual rate of progress toward his destination, and in determining this maximum, potential speeds are of less importance than the frequency and length of stops and the rate of acceleration and deceleration.

These are straightforward calculations. If passengers are not to be tossed about, acceleration and deceleration should be held

8 J. W. Stover, "Some Nonuser Implications of Urban Transportation," *Defining Transportation Requirements* (New York: American Society of Mechanical Engineers, 1969), p. 299.

to three to four miles per hour per second, with three as the figure generally accepted.[9]

If stations are one mile apart and stops are twenty seconds long, the highest average speed attainable is 35 mph; with two-mile spacing it is 45 mph. Longer stops of course reduce the average. Not until stations are five miles apart does a vehicle with a maximum speed of 100 mph have an advantage over one with a 55 mph maximum. Five-mile spacing, however, is much too far for adequate service intown and excessive even for suburban runs. Some speed can be gained by having trains make alternate stops, as is done in Chicago. Separate express tracks, such as the New York subway has, are justified only where the volume of traffic is exceptionally high.

There is no single prescription for the conditions that justify rail rapid transit. Costs of construction and operation vary from city to city, and much depends on whether the system is expected to be self-supporting or is to be subsidized. The pattern of travel corridors for the area in question has to be taken into account also. If a new installation is contemplated, estimates of patronage will depend very much on whether the estimator is trying to promote or oppose a rapid transit system. It is not even possible to find agreement on the minimum volume of traffic required for economical operation; the figure ranges from 10,000 to 25,000 passengers per hour at peak hours. The most accurate calculation comes from Atlanta, Georgia, where a detailed study of the city's traffic problems concluded that peak-hour loads in excess of 12,000 passengers per hour could be more effectively and economically handled by rail.[10] Below that level, the economic advantage for public transportation is with the bus on the highway, and what was proposed for Atlanta was a ten-mile rail transit

9 See Lang and Soberman, *Urban Rail Transit,* pp. 42–44.
10 William P. Maynard, "The Busway to Make Rapid Transit Work—Now," *Traffic Quarterly,* vol. 23, no. 3 (July 1969), p. 354; *Atlanta Constitution,* April 12, 1969.

line supplemented by fifty-four miles of exclusive "busways," which could later be converted to rail if the need arose, plus additional freeways and improved streets.

With a peak level of 10,000 passengers an hour, rail transit costs about 10¢ a passenger-mile (in 1969 prices). These same 10,000 persons can be moved by 250 buses on a freeway for about 2¢ a passenger-mile. At lower levels the disparity in favor of the bus increases sharply. For a peak demand of 4,000 passengers per hour, still high for most American cities, the cost is 23¢ a passenger-mile by rail and 3¢ by freeway bus.[11] The question of economical operation is independent of the price charged for the service—that is, the fare structure. If the transit system is to relieve traffic congestion, fares have to be low enough to persuade people to use it instead of driving their own cars, but even if public transportation should be offered free, the cost factor remains. It is merely transferred from the users to the community. If a community has a choice of modes of public transportation and selects a high-cost method when a lower-cost one would serve the purpose equally well, it is misusing its resources.

The experience of existing transit systems affords some evidence as a possible basis for judgment. The financial record of even the up-to-date rapid transit systems is discouraging. The Montreal subway produced a 10 percent increase in patronage for the city's total transit system but lost $2 million in 1967, the year of the Expo. Toronto's subway attracted more passengers than were anticipated in the planning and proved so popular that it was extended from four to twenty-one miles, but it has to be supported by taxation to the tune of $10 million a year.[12]

Profitability cannot be made the sole test of a public transportation system. The serving of community needs may be a legitimate charge on public funds. With rail transit in particular,

11 Stover, "Nonuser Implications," p. 300.
12 St. Louis Post-Dispatch, July 20, 1969.

subsidization can be justified—and usually is—on the ground that it relieves traffic congestion. Unfortunately, proof that such relief is actually obtained is nonexistent, except perhaps for a highly specialized combination of geography and population density like New York City—which is certainly not free of congestion. For other cities the pattern described in this statement is reasonably general:

The Eisenhower Expressway in Chicago, which has a rapid transit line in its median strip, bears over 150,000 vehicles per day, and the Long Island Expressway, which serves an area honeycombed with electric railway facilities, carries a similar volume of traffic. The superficially anomalous fact that electric railway facilities have a minor effect on traffic congestion is easily explicable; the great majority of passengers on electric trains would be on buses if the railway did not exist. On the Congress Street rapid transit line in Chicago about 88 per cent of passengers respond to inquiry that they would ride a bus in the absence of the train. On the Yonge Street line in Toronto the percentage is 90. Since a bus handles about forty people in the space of two and a half automobiles, the existence or nonexistence of rival rail facilities is not a major consideration in traffic congestion.[13]

Americans are frequently enjoined to observe the excellent railborne mass transportation systems of European cities. They are, without question, excellent. But when they are offered as examples of alternatives to motor vehicle transportation, then, as one prescient observer remarks, "it is most helpful to the force with which this argument is put forward not to have visited Europe for the past several years." [14] Among the major metropolitan areas of the world Paris and London rate very high, along with New York, in line miles of rail transit per million population.[15] Anyone who has driven in these cities will agree

13 G. W. Hilton, "Rail Transit and the Pattern of Modern Cities: The California Case," *Traffic Quarterly* (July 1967), p. 389.
14 Roger Starr, *The Living End: The City and Its Critics* (New York: Coward-McCann, Inc., 1968), p. 196.
15 Wilbur Smith and Associates, *Transportation and Parking for Tomorrow's Cities* (New Haven, Conn.: Wilbur Smith and Associates, 1966), p. 93.

that rail transit facilities are no panacea for congestion. To use another well-worn example, critics of dependence on the motor vehicle like to cite the monumental traffic jam that occurred in Boston on December 30, 1963, when 100,000 vehicles were trapped in a downtown snarl that lasted for about five hours. The critics admit some exceptional conditions: street capacity limited by snow and a deadline date both for renewing automobile registrations and exchanging or returning Christmas presents. But if this incident is evidence of the need for rail transit to cure traffic congestion, Boston was the wrong place for it to happen—Boston has an extensive rail rapid transit system, second only to New York among American cities in proportion of line miles to population.

Rail transit, like the commuter railroad, carries most of its passenger load during four peak hours (Figure 13.1). The proportion of peak-hour traffic to the total is in fact increasing, which accentuates the economic difficulties of rail transit systems because it means more idle equipment in off-peak periods. The peak-hour business itself has been reduced by the general adoption of the five-day week. There is no promising remedy for this situation. If access by road to central business districts were made more difficult or expensive, the most probable consequence would not be a shift of off-peak travelers from automobiles to transit; there would simply be less travel to the CBD.

Thus, where an urban area has at least one high-density travel corridor, with a minimum peak-period volume of 12,000 passengers an hour, a railborne transit system can be an asset and may be a necessity. Experience with existing systems indicates that even with an exceptionally high volume of travel, as in New York, subsidization is needed, but where conditions require mass movement on a sufficient scale, public support can be considered a legitimate social cost. The appropriate com-

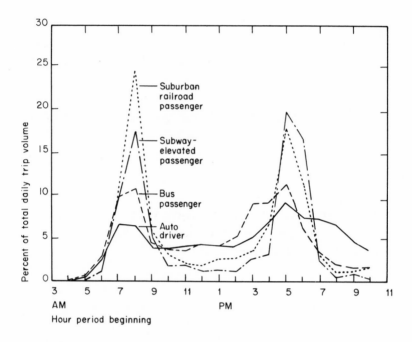

Figure 13.1 Hourly percentages of total daily trip volume of each mode of travel

Source: Chicago Area Transportation Study, *Final Report,* Vol. 1 (Chicago, 1959), p. 48.

bination of conditions is quite rare; probably not more than ten metropolitan areas in North America really need or could economically use rail transit. It is not an automatic remedy for traffic congestion, nor is it a cure for air pollution.[16] Given the variety and complexity of the urban problems that are pressing for solutions, a metropolitan area would be unwise to devote resources to a rail transit system if its needs for mass transportation can be met in some other way.

16 The point on pollution was made by John W. McMahan, Director, Development Research Associates, at meeting of the Town Hall of California, January 4, 1968, on the subject of a rapid transit system for Los Angeles. What may be gained by reduction in motor vehicle traffic is partially offset by the need to generate more electric power.

Bus Transportation

The public transportation requirements of most cities are met by bus service and will continue to be until a major new development occurs in the technology of mass transportation. Since 1919 the motor bus has climbed from a negligible place as a transit vehicle to being the carrier of about 70 percent of all public transportation passengers. The shifts in transit patronage appear in Table 13.3. Some of the advantages of the bus are self-evident. It does not require its own right-of-way but can share roads and streets with other vehicles; it can maneuver in traffic; it is free to change routes if conditions require it, although little has actually been done with flexible routing. Against these advantages is the fact that a bus is subject to the hazards of traffic congestion; at rush hours in particular it can be seriously delayed on crowded streets.

The bus is not only a medium of mass transportation but of rapid transit also (see Table 13.4). The capacity of bus systems, actual and potential, varies considerably. On ordinary streets a single lane would accommodate 150 to 175 buses an hour, or 7,500 to 9,000 passengers. On high-speed highways an exclusive lane would take 500 to 600 buses an hour operating nonstop; if

Table 13.3   Trends in Methods of Transit, 1919–1968
(in billions of total passengers)

Year	Street Car Passengers	Per-cent	Rapid Transit Passengers	Per-cent	Trolley Coach Passengers	Per-cent	Motor Bus Passengers	Per-cent	Total Passengers
1919	13.4	90	1.5	10	—	—	—	—	14.9
1924	13.1	80	2.2	13	—	—	1.0	6	16.3
1929	11.8	70	2.6	15	0.005	—	2.6	15	17.0
1934	7.4	61	2.2	18	0.07	0.6	2.4	20	12.0
1939	6.2	48	2.4	19	0.4	3.0	3.9	30	12.8
1944	9.5	41	2.6	11	1.2	5.0	9.6	42	23.0
1949	4.9	26	2.3	12	1.7	9.0	10.2	53	19.0
1954	1.5	12	1.9	15	1.4	11.0	7.6	61	12.4
1959	0.5	5.3	1.8	18.9	0.7	7.4	6.5	68.4	9.5
1964	0.3	3.6	1.9	22.9	0.3	3.6	5.8	69.9	8.3
1968	0.3	3.8	1.9	23.7	0.2	2.5	5.6	70.0	8.0

Source: Data supplied by the American Transit Association.

Table 13.4   Peak-Hour Passenger Volumes on Urban Bus Routes

Buses on City Streets

	City	Facility	Buses per Hr.	Passenger Movement	
				Actual Peak Hr.	15–20 Min. Rate per Hr.
Local buses, city streets, parking prohibited:	New York	Hillside Ave.	150	10,251	10,824
	San Francisco	Market St.	130	7,553	8,500
	Cleveland	Euclid Ave.	90	4,316	5,600
	Chicago	Michigan Ave.	75	4,240	4,770
	Baltimore	Baltimore St.	76	4,387	4,758
Local buses, city streets, reserved transit lane:	Rochester	Main St.	93	4,982	—
	Chicago	Washington Bl.	66	3,235	3,600
	Atlanta	Peachtree St.	67	2,807	3,504
	Dallas	Commerce St.	67	3,069	3,444
	Birmingham	2nd Ave., N.	44	2,301	2,712
Express buses, city streets, parking prohibited:	St. Louis	Gravois St.	66	2,918	4,185
	Cleveland	Clifton Bl.	32	1,872	2,700
	Chicago	Archer Ave.	29	1,896	2,500
	San Francisco	Van Ness Ave.	17	1,234	1,784
	New Orleans	Earhart Bl.	25	1,267	1,620

Buses on Expressways

	City	Facility	Buses per Hour	Passenger Movement	
				Actual Peak Hr.	15–20 Min. Rate per Hr.
Express buses, on expressways	Chicago	Lake Shore Dr.	99	5,595	6,350
	Cleveland	Shoreway West	32	1,872	2,700
	San Francisco	Bayshore Expy.	35	2,270	2,700
	Los Angeles	Hollywood Fwy.	41	2,268	2,640
	St. Louis	Mark Twain Hwy.	52	1,767	2,295
	Atlanta	North Expy.	19	803	1,892
Express buses, on terminal ramps, tunnel approaches, tunnels and bridges:	New York	P.A. Bus Term.	511	23,187	28,556
	Union City, N.J.	Route 3	397	17,800	23,000
	New York	Lincoln Tunnel	480	21,600	22,860
	San Francisco	Oakland Bay Br.	216	7,812	10,945
	New York	Geo. Wash. Br.	136	6,936	9,468

Source: *Dynamics of Urban Transportation*, pp. 7–14.

the conditions of rail rapid transit were matched—that is, stops at one-mile intervals—the capacity is 120 buses an hour with a speed of 45 mph and a 30-second headway.[17] All these calculations assume fifty seated passengers in each bus.

17 These calculations of bus system capacities come from Port of New York Authority, Comprehensive Planning Office, *Metropolitan Transportation—1980* (New York: Port of New York Authority, 1963), pp. 298–299; W. R.

These are not just theoretical calculations. In December 1965, the New Jersey Turnpike Authority conducted tests on the feasibility of a reserved bus lane, using the link between the freeway and the Lincoln Tunnel for the purpose.[18] This experiment readily accommodated the volume of over 500 buses an hour inbound to New York in the morning commuter rush; in fact, the Tunnel approaches handle 400 buses an hour under ordinary conditions.

Finally, tests made by General Motors in 1963 indicate that a single lane of buses, operated under complete manual control by the drivers, form a stable stream of traffic and have an optimal flow of about 1,450 buses/hour for a speed of 33 miles per hour for an exclusive roadway type facility. This is equivalent to over 70,000 seats per hour for 50-passenger vehicles.[19]

It is therefore possible for bus transportation to offer as much carrying capacity and speed as rail transit, but it does not necessarily follow that the bus is the preferred alternative. An exclusive bus lane on freeways or other roads is justifiable only if bus traffic is heavy enough to utilize the lane's full capacity, and if a travel corridor has 25,000 people per hour using public transportation (500 fifty-seat buses), there is a strong case for rail transit. Local conditions will determine the choice. If a rail transit system is already operating, it would probably be unnecessary to reserve a freeway lane for buses and certainly uneconomic to construct additional freeway capacity exclusively

---

McConochie, "Exclusive Lanes for Express Bus Operation in Cities of One to Three Million," *Urban Land*, vol. 22, no. 11 (December 1963), p. 5. Nathan Cherniak, "Urban Passenger Transportation," p. 33, asserts that a reserved freeway lane would accommodate 720 buses an hour at 40–60 mph.

18 W. J. Flanagan, "The Necessity of Separating Commercial and Passenger Traffic," paper delivered at World Meeting, International Road Federation, London, September 22, 1966, pp. 11–13.

19 J. W. Scheel and J. E. Foote, *Bus Operation in Single Lane Platoons and Their Ventilation Needs for Operation in Tunnels*, Research Publication GMP-808 (Warren, Mich.: General Motors Corporation, 1968).

for buses. Where there is a freeway network and no rail transit, the express bus and the reserved freeway lane may serve the community's needs for rapid transit adequately, and this is the most common situation in American cities. (See Table 13.5.) There is the additional consideration that at off-peak hours a bus system has idle vehicles but no idle track. The freeways and streets can be and are used by other traffic; even the reserved bus lane is strictly a rush-hour arrangement.

St. Louis, Missouri, has developed a regional transportation plan with express bus service providing rapid transit. When the twenty-four-mile Mark Twain Expressway was opened in 1961, the St. Louis Public Service Company was ready with a plan to operate a "rapid" bus service using the freeway. Its record has been:

The eight rush-hour lines make a total of from 75 to 80 daily trips in each direction involving over 1,000 miles per day on the expressway. The shopper lines make about 20 daily trips in each direction involving some 200 daily miles on the expressway. The direction that each route operates on the expressway varies from 3.8 to 11.9 miles, with an average of 7.4 miles.

The overall terminal-to-terminal speeds of the rapid lines range

Table 13.5 Travel Corridor Volumes, Selected Cities

		Cumulative Trips at Distance from CBD (24 hours)					
		2 Miles		4 Miles		8 Miles	
City	Route	Total	Work	Total	Work	Total	Work
Atlanta	I-85 (Northeast Fwy.)	16,000	—	5,000	—	4,000	—
Cincinnati	I-75	15,000	—	14,000	—	6,000	—
Detroit	Lodge Fwy.	68,000	—	46,000	—	14,000	—
Houston	I-45 (Gulf Fwy.)	23,000	11,000	17,000	8,000	5,000	2,500
Minneapolis	I-35W	50,000	—	22,000	—	3,000	—
Pittsburgh	I-76 East (Penn-Lincoln)	25,000	13,000	19,000	8,000	8,000	3,500
St. Louis	Daniel Boone	14,000	7,000	10,000	5,000	4,000	1,700
	Mark Twain	14,000	7,000	9,000	4,000	3,000	1,500

Source: V. G. Stover, "Nonuser Implications of Urban Transportation," *Defining Transportation Requirements* (New York: American Society of Mechanical Engineers, 1969), p. 314.
Reprinted by permission of the American Society of Mechanical Engineers.

from 15.6 to 20.8 m.p.h. On the expressway itself, the buses travel with the general traffic at speeds of from 40 to 50 m.p.h.[20]

New Technologies

For a gadget-minded people the idea of some "instant technology" to solve urban transportation problems has a strong attraction. Someone, we are confident, will invent a device or a system that will permit us to travel where we want, when we want, how we want, without delay, congestion, smog, or accident. Perhaps some such miracle will happen; responsible urban transportation planners have to have something more tangible to go on. However, the crisis of mobility in cities has generated enough effort and attention so that some major technical developments in urban transportation are a reasonable prospect.

The feasible possibilities for mass transit have been compiled by the Department of Housing and Urban Development. Interestingly, the Department's survey begins with urban bus systems because

buses represent a promising subject for new technology because they can go anywhere on present rights-of-way. This ubiquity is significant. Because buses can go wherever streets go, they have the potential for door-to-door service—and that may be essential if public transit is to attract patronage in the future. It also means that bus systems can involve relatively low initial investments because they avoid the tremendous cost burden of building and maintaining their own rights-of-way or guideways.[21]

For improvement of conventional bus operations the HUD study suggests these innovations, all feasible with existing technology:

1. Traffic control systems giving priority to buses, including

20 G. W. Anderson, "Rail and Bus Rapid Transit for Downtown Access," *Dynamics of Urban Transportation* (Detroit: Automobile Manufacturers Association, photocopied, 1962), pp. 10–11.

21 Department of Housing and Urban Development, *Tomorrow's Transportation. New Systems for the Urban Future* (Washington, D.C.: Government Printing Office, 1968), p. 32.

unrestricted bus access to freeways where on-ramps are metered for other traffic.

2. Computer-assisted scheduling: test projects indicate that service can be made more flexible and demand-responsive.

3. Improved bus design, including dual-mode buses, capable of operating on either tracks or streets; articulated buses, not suited for ordinary streets but promising for express service on freeways; and double-decking, common in other countries, but with new techniques for steering and better methods of loading and collecting fares.

4. Dial-a-bus, also termed Demand Activated Road Transit (DART). This is a system combining the economy of the bus with the flexibility of the taxi.

It would pick up passengers at their doors or at a nearby bus stop shortly after they have telephoned for service. The computer would know the location of its vehicles, how many passengers were on them, and where they were heading. It would select the right vehicle and dispatch it on some optimal routing which had been devised for the system. Thus, the system could readily link many origins to many destinations.[22]

Since DART could respond to door-to-door travel demands at the time they were made, it might attract off-peak business to an extent that existing mass transit media cannot do; if so, it would be less subject to the financial difficulties caused by having equipment idle for all but three or four hours a day.

This report also discusses some prospects for new technologies of urban transportation, including various forms of controlled guideway, automated capsule systems, and moving belts (like Disneyland's "people-mover"). None has progressed beyond preliminary experimentation. There is also monorail, with samples in Wuppertal, Germany, or again in Disneyland, but so far the technical complexities of monorail operation have prevented it from living up to the claims of its enthusiasts. Other prospects for future urban transportation are air cushion vehicles, gravity

22 *Ibid.*, p. 58.

tubes, rail systems that pick up and discharge passengers without stopping, and short-range aircraft, although V/STOL aircraft are not now economical for trips of less than ten miles.[23] Appraising or even itemizing the various possibilities is a futile exercise; any or all of them might emerge in a future urban transportation system. We do not lack technology. The basic and still unsolved issue was stated at a forum on transportation engineering in 1968: the problem of urban transportation, specifically public transportation, is not one of technology but of economics.[24] To put it another way, the new transit technologies will be subject to much the same economic considerations as the old. Any system requiring a fixed guideway—rail, electronic, or anything else—makes economic sense only in high-volume, high-density travel corridors, and these are limited to a few very large metropolitan areas.

Summary

A consideration of urban or metropolitan transportation should perhaps include reference to the emerging problem of Megalopolis, the prospective merging of metropolitan areas into a vast urban complex. One such complex is coming into existence along the Atlantic seaboard, from Boston, Massachusetts, to Washington, D.C., including New York, Philadelphia, and Baltimore. Other potential megalopolitan regions are the California coast from Santa Barbara through Los Angeles to San Diego, the corridor from Milwaukee through Chicago to St. Louis, the Chicago-Pittsburgh corridor, and the shore of Lake Erie from Buffalo through Cleveland to Toledo and Detroit. Only the Boston–New York–Washington megalopolis is sufficiently far advanced to

23 B. A. Shriever and W. W. Seifert, *Air Transportation 1975 and Beyond: A Systems Approach* (Cambridge, Mass.: The M.I.T. Press, 1968), p. 32.
24 Walter S. Douglas, "Present State and Technical Position of Urban Transportation," *Transportation: A Service* (New York: New York Academy of Science, 1968), p. 302.

pose a special transportation problem. In effect, Megalopolis has to combine the features of inter- and intraurban transportation.

The heavy volume of passenger travel along the Northeast Corridor has focused attention on the development of a high-speed ground transportation system based on the main line of the Penn Central Railroad (incorporating the former Pennsylvania line between New York and Washington and the New Haven between New York and Boston). The purpose of this project is as much to relieve air traffic congestion as highway congestion, and if it should be successfully developed, its principal impact will probably be on air travel along the corridor. It will certainly not reduce the need for highway facilities. Truck traffic will not be affected at all, nor will the local movement (less than ten miles) that constitutes 80 percent of all automobile travel. The high-speed ground transportation project aims at speeds of 100 mph or more; it would be a wasteful employment of resources to use such a system for local travel.

Megalopolis, indeed, is likely to have much the same transportation needs as Metropolis. The greater area will offer more scope for air transport, and the longer distances make really high-speed ground transportation at least a technical possibility. But barring an improbable change in social habits and patterns and in economic realities, Megalopolis too will be characterized by dispersal of population as well as of business and industry.

Urban mobility is now and will remain for a long time to come overwhelmingly a function of transportation by road, whether the movement occurs in mass transit vehicles or private cars. It is also worth emphasizing that any issue of road versus rail or other alternative in urban transportation involves exclusively the movement of people. No one has ever found a satisfactory way to distribute intraurban freight other than by road.

Consequently, the first requisite for securing adequate mobility in urban areas is the optimizing of the road and street network in order to enable it to meet the demands made on it. One of these demands is public transportation, to serve those who for one reason or another cannot travel by car—defined by the Department of Housing and Urban Development as "the poor, the handicapped, the secondary workers (the family car used by another member), the elderly and the young." [25] For most cities this service can be provided by bus, with a combination of adequate capacity for the needed volume of movement, minimum cost, and flexibility. HUD, indeed, makes it clear that the greatest need is for more flexible systems of mass transit:

As more central business district jobs become white-collar, and an ever larger proportion of unskilled and semiskilled jobs move to outlying sections, poor people are more disadvantaged than ever by public transportation systems which focus on central business districts and also stop at city limits. . . .

To serve the nondriver, it is not enough to provide more of the existing transportation facilities. Although new bus routes and more buses in poverty areas significantly increase the mobility of the residents, most trips are still unnecessarily long, tiresome, and expensive. Buses limited to fixed routes, and stalled by traffic congestion, and rapid transit systems crowded and noisy, will not meet the minimal transportation needs of urban areas.[26]

The Department's observations are a useful reminder that our thinking about urban transportation can easily become focused excessively on the commuter flow in and out of the CBD to the neglect of other important elements. If a technological miracle can produce a transit system that will eliminate downtown congestion without imposing an undue economic burden in the process, let us by all means work the miracle—as long as we remain aware that the commuter rush is only part of urban transportation. The need for an up-to-date, efficient road and street network will continue unchanged. It is needed for the truck movement that keeps cities alive. It is also needed for types of

25 HUD, *Tomorrow's Transportation*, p. 15.
26 *Ibid.*, pp. 16–18.

personal mobility made possible by the automobile which are growing in importance and for which mass transportation cannot be substituted. Some of these have been discussed in earlier chapters. New York, densely populated and transit-oriented, offers an example worth adding here. Between 1950 and 1960 the number of person trips across the Hudson River by all modes of transportation grew by 24.9 million, from 255.7 million annually to 291.6 million, and of this increase 17 million occurred on Saturdays, Sundays, and holidays. The source that cites these figures observed that much of this weekend and holiday travel is family travel to widely scattered destinations by widely dispersed travel paths.[27] For this purpose the automobile is distinctly more convenient and economical than any mode of public transportation.

In our preoccupation with the conditions produced by using the automobile to get *into* town, we may well overlook the value of the automobile for getting *out* of town. On this score alone a good highway system will remain a prime essential for urban areas regardless of what other forms of transport may be introduced.

27 Port of New York Authority, *Metropolitan Transportation—1980,* p. 277.

14 City Streets and Urban Freeways

In 1965 there were 507,000 miles of urban highway in the United States, of which 7,135 miles were classified as Interstates, 27,690 were part of the federal-aid primary system, and 20,544 were part of the federal-aid secondary system.[1] The rest consists of city and suburban roads, streets, and alleys. These half-million miles, now and for many years to come, are the foundation on which all urban transportation must be built. Whatever other systems may be employed—railborne, electronic guideways, air-cushions, or anything else—are supplemental to the roads and streets, sometimes necessary but still supplemental.

At the risk of being repetitious, streets are vital to the life, to the very existence, of the city, regardless of what type of vehicle uses them. The motor vehicle has a considerable edge in convenience, economy, and speed over any other mode of movement by road, but even if it were to be eliminated, the need for streets would not diminish in the least. The only difference would be that the traffic would be slower, more cumbersome, less efficient, and more expensive.

About the only thing that city street systems have in common is that few of them were designed for automobile traffic. As a matter of fact, few city street systems were designed for traffic at all. Some grew accidentally from footpaths or cowpaths or other trails that just followed the easiest routes. Those that were planned were laid out in neat geometrical patterns that looked good on blueprints and, in the specific case of the gridiron pattern, made for simpler identification of property lines but bore little or no relationship to a rational flow of traffic. The deficiencies of city street systems have already been discussed. William L. Pereira sums it up by saying that we have not built a single city

1 U.S. Department of Transportation, *Highway Statistics. Summary to 1965*, p. 119.

as the result of the automobile, because it came on us too fast.[2]
He might have added that we have not been catching up very
well either. The older central city areas are difficult and expensive to change, but even in new developments there has been
insufficient attention to highway design and traffic engineering
in the layout of roads and streets.

If we could tear down our cities and rebuild them from
scratch, we could undoubtedly equip them with a road network
that would handle their traffic smoothly, but this is hardly a practical remedy. At the same time most cities face massive reconstruction in the process of urban renewal and outward expansion
as suburban growth continues. These processes can give opportunities for careful examination of urban road networks and
techniques of traffic control. Each urban area needs to determine
for its own needs the proper combination of freeways and conventional roads and streets plus the optimization of traffic flow
on them.

Optimizing Street Systems
For all cities, large and small alike, the basic transportation resource is the network of ordinary roads and streets. New construction will be required to meet current needs and to provide
for change and growth, but it will represent a small proportion
of total urban highway mileage and will not in the least diminish
the desirability of making the best possible use of existing roads
and streets. Furthermore, the proportion of express highways in
urban road mileage is small and will remain so. The best available estimates of traffic needs (see Table 14.1) give 6 percent as
the maximum suggested share of freeways in urban road mileage,
and no freeway system as yet has approached this proportion.

2 Interview in William L. Pereira, "Transportation: What's Ahead for
Southern California," *Westways*, vol. 59, no. 11 (November 1967), p. 5.

Table 14.1   Division of Street Mileage

Population of Metropolitan Areas	Percentage in Each System		
	Expressways (Freeways)	Major and Collector	Local
Under 25,000	—	25 to 35	65 to 75
25,000 to 150,000	—	20 to 30	70 to 80
150,000 to 500,000	2 to 4	20 to 25	75 to 80
Over 500,000	4 to 6	15 to 20	75 to 80

Source: Gordon Sessions, *Getting the Most from City Streets* (Washington, D.C.: Highway Research Board, 1967), p. 3.

One of the great assets of the controlled-access type of road is that a limited mileage can carry a very large volume of traffic.

Urban street systems can be classified functionally as follows:
1. *Freeways:* These are intended for high-speed through traffic.
2. *Major streets* (may be called "arterials" or "main thoroughfares"): These carry the bulk of the city's total traffic they connect through highways or major sources of traffic.
3. *Collector streets:* These are links between major and local streets; they carry much of the through traffic within neighborhoods and connect adjacent neighborhoods.
4. *Local streets:* As the name indicates, they are (or ought to be) intended for access to residential or business property and not to carry through traffic.[3]

The major streets yield the greatest returns from well-planned measures of traffic control. They are seldom more than a quarter of total urban street mileage, but studies have demonstrated that they account for at least three-fifths of urban traffic accidents and are the principal sources of congestion. The need to put effort on major street systems applies regardless of present or prospective

3 Gordon Sessions, *Getting the Most from City Streets* (Washington, D.C.: Highway Research Board, 1967), p. 3.

freeway development, because express highways are and will remain a very limited segment of all urban roads and streets. The major streets must continue to carry a substantial share of the traffic load, and it is desirable that they should be able to do it smoothly and efficiently, not only on the negative ground of reducing accidents and congestion but on the positive basis that free-flowing traffic is essential to healthy urban life, both social and economic.

Some of the steps that may be taken can be itemized, with the caution that no single formula for traffic control is applicable to all cities, or even to all major streets in the same city. Each situation requires individual expert study and solution.

1. *Signals and signs:* These are the most familiar of all devices for controlling traffic, but unnecessary or poorly planned installation can make conditions worse instead of better. "To be effective, signals must be modern. They must be located so that they are clearly and continuously visible: in the driver's line of vision. . . . And, they must be justified, by the character of the intersection and the traffic." [4]

Electronic controls offer the possibility of having coordinated signal networks for entire urban areas. Toronto installed such a computer-controlled system in 1963, initially on nine routes with 159 signals. The results showed distinct advantages, along with a need for careful design and planning. New York undertook a more elaborate system, initially with ten digital computers controlling 2,700 intersections. Eventually 9,000 intersections will be so controlled. [5]

Electronically controlled signal systems can also be developed to give preference to large vehicles such as buses. Such a system would alleviate the delays in traffic that are perhaps the worst

4 *Ibid.*, p. 25.
5 Paper delivered by Henry A. Barnes, Commissioner of Traffic, New York City, to International Road Federation, Mideast Regional Meeting, Beirut, Lebanon, May 9, 1967.

handicap in bus operation. Preferential treatment for buses not only would speed up schedules but would probably also encourage bus patronage in the congested central city areas.

2. *Controlling turns:* As with signals and signs, this procedure calls for expert study of each specific situation. It does no good to prohibit a left turn at one intersection if the effect is merely to create difficulties at the next. But where prohibition is justified, it is worthwhile. Stopping left turns at Broadway and Columbus Avenues in San Francisco reduced accidents by 52 percent and travel time by 11 percent for former left turners on their new route and 35 percent for other traffic. Where left turns have to be made, special lanes or bays are extremely helpful; in California they have reduced accidents by half.

3. *Median strips:* On arterial routes a raised median, preferably landscaped if the width of the road permits, is invaluable in separating opposing streams of traffic. Painted medians are less satisfactory but better than none at all. Where there is ample width, the boulevard arrangement with the traffic roadway in the center and service roads on each side can be useful. Even so, median strips should be employed.

4. *Reversible lanes:* This method is one of the most efficient ways of increasing rush-hour capacity. It requires streets with three or more traffic lanes, so that one lane is available in the low-volume direction. This technique has been used very effectively in Chicago and a number of smaller cities. It has a hazard if drivers become confused about lane directions; clear and positive identification is an absolute necessity. Some cities (Washington, D.C., for instance) have experimented successfully with making entire streets reversible.

5. *One-way streets:* These are a very effective way of increasing capacity. There are some disadvantages: they may necessitate additional travel, and strangers may become confused if signs are inadequate or poorly placed. (This could be an argument for

adopting the uniform traffic signs used in most of the rest of the world; there is far less likelihood of confusion if the sign is familiar.) Against these drawbacks are much greater advantages. Turning problems are reduced, signal timing is simplified, and accidents decline. Here are some examples:[6]

In New York City after conversion of Third, Lexington, Seventh, and Eighth Avenues and the Avenue of the Americas to one-way movement, surveys obtained these minimal results:

Pedestrian accidents reduced	20%
Total trip time reduced	22%
Stopped time reduced	60%
Number of stops reduced	65%
Bus running time reduced	17%

Syracuse, New York: On main streets, average speed increased 13 mph and street capacity 20 and 40 percent; Sacramento, California: Speed increased 25 to 40 percent, and accidents were cut 14 to 30 percent on a twenty-six-mile conversion. The cost of the conversion was $90,000. Street widening to achieve the same capacity would have cost $4 million.

6. *Parking:* It is needless to state that parking is a major and so far unsolved problem for all cities. In the early days of the automobile it simply pulled up at the curb along with the buggies and bicycles, and unfortunately no provision was made for anything else long after conditions changed. The automobile at rest became a much more acute problem than the automobile in motion—including finding a place for the automobile to rest.

In downtown sections where traffic is heavy, curb parking is an obstructive nuisance. A single car can close an entire street lane. Moreover, cars maneuvering in or out of parking spaces are a prolific source of accidents. Car storage can and should be integrated with other land uses; that is, incorporated into office

6 Sessions, *Getting the Most from City Streets*, p. 21.

buildings, theaters, and department stores. Underground garages have been very successful in many cities.

When Washington, D.C. stopped curb parking on Pennsylvania Avenue, S.E., on the inbound side during the morning rush and the outbound side in the evening, the results were that travel time for automobiles was reduced 23 percent, for buses 10 percent, travel speed increased to 25.7 mph, and delays due to stopping were reduced 34 percent. Savings in vehicle operating costs were calculated at $54,000 a year. In New York, Traffic Commissioner Henry A. Barnes reported in 1967 that strict enforcement of parking regulations had reduced the time needed to drive across midtown Manhattan from thirty or forty-five minutes to ten, and summed up the essentials of the parking problem very neatly: parking regulations will work only if they are rigorously enforced and also supported by the public; cars must be given a place to stop in downtown districts, and for this purpose off-street parking is the only remedy. The Commissioner was no advocate of excluding automobiles from CBDs:

Those who advocate the banning of motor vehicles from cities are advocating a measure which would destroy the essential nature of the city. Throughout the world, cities are the outgrowth of the market place. They are the result of man's natural urge to meet and trade with his fellow man. They sprang up wherever the caravans of commerce crossed. Today's caravans are composed to a large extent of motor vehicles. If they are banned from our present cities, the natural flow of goods to market, and the natural movement of people toward each other for social, cultural and educational contact will be forced into new channels. New cities will spring up to the detriment of the businesses and the institutions which have grown and thrived in the other cities. We will not have solved our old problems. We will have created new ones.[7]

Parking facilities not only can pay their own way but can also be a powerful force in maintaining healthy activity downtown. Prime examples of what can be done are Detroit's Cobo Hall, Baltimore's Sports Coliseum, and the Music Center in Los An-

7 Barnes, paper to International Road Federation.

geles. All attract business to their CBDs because people can drive to them with confidence that they will find convenient parking. In Baltimore the presence of the Coliseum generated the building of a hotel nearby, then a theater, followed by two new office buildings—all tied to underground parking for 4,000 cars.[8]

The considerations that apply to major streets apply also to collector streets, except that the latter will not ordinarily extend for long distances. In addition, since they provide access to abutting property, they need to allow for turning movements, parking, and loading and unloading people and goods.

With local streets the basic objective is to keep them local. Where streets are laid out in the gridiron arrangement, through traffic will use the side streets to avoid congestion on the arterial or bypass a stop sign. This practice can be discouraged by installing barriers or making segments of local streets one-way, but these remedies have their own defects—blocking access for emergency vehicles, for instance. In new or redevelopment areas, local streets can be laid out to deter through traffic; some can be dead ends, others routed so that they offer no advantage for anything but local access. In every case where new streets are planned, intersections should be of the T design. The T intersection is at least five times as safe as the conventional four-way crossing.

Urban Freeways

Although some urban freeway construction, as we have seen, was begun as far back as the 1930s, its large-scale development came as a result of the federal aid provided by the Interstate Highway Act. The urban freeway serves two major functions. It is the best method of providing circumferential routes so that traffic passing through an urban region or intraurban traffic not destined for or

8 G. W. Anderson, "Rail and Bus Rapid Transit for Downtown Access," *Dynamics of Urban Transportation* (Detroit: Automobile Manufacturers Association, photocopied, 1962), pp. 28–29.

originating in the CBD can avoid the crowded core area. The Interstate bypass routes circling Baltimore and Washington are conspicuous examples. Before the freeways were built, Baltimore was a nightmare for the motorist passing through, and Washington was little better; now the traveler can pass by without getting involved in city traffic at all. The second major function of the urban freeway is to carry motor vehicles in and out of central business districts, but since this function involves building freeways through central cities, it frequently becomes an acutely controversial matter.

There is another very important element in urban transportation as it affects the CBD, namely, the movement of goods. It has been discussed in previous chapters, but it merits repetition because it is so likely to be obscured by the problems of the movement of people, and yet it is just as fundamental to CBD prosperity. The essence of this question is summed up thus:

Many central business districts are declining in importance partly because they are difficult to support logistically. They must be supplied with enormous quantities of goods, both for consumption and resale. Thus there is a continuous flow of goods, into and out of the central area, accomplished almost entirely with trucks. Yet the demands generally have grown without a corresponding increase or improvement in goods-handling facilities, so that travel and terminal activities become increasingly intolerable.[9]

The terminal facilities, like the parking of passenger cars, are a matter of providing off-street loading and unloading and do not relate directly to freeway decisions. On the broader scale, it is worth reiterating that there is no possible substitute for road transport to handle the vast complex of intraurban freight movements. For example, a medium-sized SMSA like Baton Rouge, Louisiana, with a population of 245,000, generates 81,500 truck trips a day, for 318,000 vehicle-miles with 148,000 ton-miles of

9 Wilbur Smith and Associates, *Motor Trucks in the Metropolis* (New Haven, Conn.: Wilbur Smith and Associates, 1969), pp. 4–5.

Table 14.2   Vehicle Speeds in Relation to Road Design (average mph)

Road Design	Road Location		
	Urban	Suburban	Rural
Full access control	47.3	49.2	47.4
Partial access control	—	42.3	49.5
No access control	26.4	38.9	44.9

Source: Wilfred Owen, *The Metropolitan Transportation Problem* (Washington, D.C.: The Brookings Institution, 1966), p. 41. Reprinted with permission of the publisher.

cargo.[10] To put it bluntly, without motor truck transportation American cities would literally starve.

Consequently, steps to improve the economy and efficiency of truck operation will contribute to healthy urban life, and these steps happen to be the same as those which will facilitate the movement of passenger cars. As a main arterial route for carrying large volumes of traffic, the freeway has no rival. A major city street with traffic signals can accommodate 750 cars per lane per hour at speeds not greater than 30 mph. Progressive signal control increases this capacity somewhat. Grade separation at intersections raises capacity to 1,500 vehicles an hour, and full control of access to approximately 2,000.[11] Control of access also permits higher speeds (see Table 14.2). In general, a freeway will carry two and one-half to three times as many vehicles per lane as a conventional street and at approximately twice the speed. We know also that freeways have a substantially lower accident rate than other streets.

On the other side of the picture is the argument that freeway

10 *Ibid.*, p. 34.
11 Paul T. McElhiney, "The Freeways of Metropolitan Los Angeles. An Evaluation in Terms of Their Objectives," Ph.D. Thesis, School of Business Administration, University of California at Los Angeles, 1959. California freeway capacities are somewhat higher than elsewhere—about 2,200 vehicles per lane per hour. Evidently California drivers leave less space between vehicles.

construction in densely populated central cities is extremely expensive, requires unduly large amounts of land where space is at a premium, and leads to destruction of neighborhoods and dislocation and hardship for the people who have to be moved away. These claims have some validity, and they need to be examined carefully.

The cost element is obvious; the construction of urban freeways may run from $1 million a mile to the estimated $100 million per mile for the proposed Lower Manhattan Expressway. Specific figures (see Table 14.3) are interesting but may be misleading because of widespread variations in land and construction costs, as well as of changes in the price structure which have to be allowed for in comparing dollar figures for different periods. We are aware that very large amounts of money are spent on freeways; unfortunately, few of us are equally aware that very large amounts of money are saved by freeways, because the savings are an accumulation of individual small items, for the most part unknown to the beneficiaries themselves. A condensation of studies of freeway savings over operating costs on ordinary city streets concludes that they average 4.35¢ per vehicle-mile, allocating 97¢ to operating costs, 72¢ to reduced accidents, and 2.66¢ to savings in time for both passenger and commercial vehicles.[12] With vehicle-miles on urban highways at about 500 billion annually and increasing, and with freeway use ranging from a fourth of the total vehicle-miles in small cities to almost half in major metropolises, the aggregate savings are impressive.

The space question is equally open to misunderstanding. An urban freeway may take up to forty acres of land per route mile, depending on the width of the roadway and the frequency of interchanges. This is a substantial amount of land, but it is not as frightening a figure as it first appears—and as opponents of

12 Wilbur Smith and Associates, *Future Highways and Urban Growth* (New Haven, Conn., Wilbur Smith and Associates, 1961), p. 294.

Table 14.3   Urban Highway Costs

I. Examples of Expressway Costs*

Expressway	Total Cost (in thousands)	Miles	Cost per Mile (in thousands)
Hollywood Freeway	$ 55,000	10	$ 5,500
Arroyo Seco Freeway	11,000	8	1,375
John Lodge and Edsel Ford Expressway	207,000	24	8,625
Major Deegan Expressway	63,600	7.5	8,480
Cross-Bronx Expressway	112,000	5	22,450
Penn Lincoln Parkways	150,000	20	7,500
Boston Central Artery	125,000	3	41,667
Congress Street Expressway	50,000	8	6,250
Schuylkill Expressway	80,000	17	4,705

II. Average Cost per Mile†
(in thousands)

Road System	Average Cost Right-of-Way	Average Cost Total	Range of Cost Low 10 Percent	Range of Cost High 10 Percent
Interstate, urban:				
4-lane	$ 359	$1,414	$ 845	$ 2,250
6-lane	1,208	3,896	2,300	6,200
Over 6-lane	2,453	7,819	4,600	12,500
Federal-aid primary urban:				
4-lane	211	789	410	1,450
6-lane	810	2,312	1,425	3,760
Over 6-lane	1,000	2,819	1,600	4,960
Other city streets	35	140	57	300

* *Engineering News-Record* (February 17, 1955), pp. 124–30; Paul O. Harding, "Southern Freeways," *California Highways and Public Works* (January–February 1954), p. 13.
† U.S. Bureau of Public Roads, *Highway Needs 1955 to 1964. All Roads and Streets* (October 1954), Sec. D, pp. 4–5.
Source: Wilfred Owen, *The Metropolitan Transportation Problem* (Washington, D.C.: The Brookings Institution, 1966), p. 44. Reprinted with permission of the publisher.

freeway construction like to make it appear. We have already seen that 2 to 3 percent of the land area is the maximum that any urban freeway system, present or prospective, requires, and that less than half of this proportion is pavement (see Chapter 10).

In fact, if urban freeways could be built on vacant land, preferably undesirable for other purposes, opposition to them would be considerably muted, including the complaint about removing valuable land from the tax rolls. This contention may well be the least valid of all the objections to urban freeways, inasmuch as survey after survey has demonstrated that increases in the value of land adjacent to freeways more than offset for tax purposes the loss of the freeway acreage. The taxable value of property abutting the Central Expressway in Dallas, Texas, rose by 544 percent from 1941 to 1955.[13] However, urban freeways serving the central city must go through densely populated sections and so do displace people and business, and may threaten historic or architecturally significant structures and impinge on scenic or aesthetic values. Frequently, too, urban freeway routes have to go through slum or ghetto neighborhoods, imposing the hardships of relocation on the people least able to accept them.

We can concede that some freeways have been unintelligently planned and located, and that highway authorities have on occasion been arbitrary. Recognition of these grievances led Congress to amend the Interstate Highway Act in 1962 to approve assistance for relocation and to stipulate that highway projects in urban areas of over 50,000 population must be based on a "continuing, comprehensive transportation planning process," and again in 1968 to require highway departments to consider not only economic factors but "the social effects of such a location, its impact on the environment, and its consistency with the goals

13 American Automobile Association, *Transportation and Tomorrow's Cities* (Washington, D.C., n.d.), p. 8.

and objectives of such urban planning as has been promulgated by community." [14]

This legislation is essentially a statement of good intentions, whose implementation requires a considerably greater degree of cooperation among municipal and highway authorities than has usually existed. Freeway construction can be an integral part of planning for urban renewal and in fact can contribute significantly to it. Freeways can be designed to fit aesthetically into their environment and may even enhance the attractiveness of central cities. California, for example, raised its expenditure for landscaping and planting on freeways from $1 million to $10 million in the decade from 1958 to 1968. People will still have to be moved and buildings torn down, but this is inherent in any conceivable scheme for urban renewal, regardless of highway considerations. If slums are to be eliminated, dilapidated structures must be destroyed and the residents housed decently elsewhere. The kind of coordination that is needed has been proposed for the Century Freeway in Los Angeles, which is planned to pass through the predominantly low-income Watts district. What is contemplated is a large-scale project shared by the Division of Highways and the Watts community whereby new houses and apartments, emphasizing neighborhoods, would be built for the people dislodged by the freeway.[15]

There are other methods of fitting freeways into land-scarce central cities. Where freeways are elevated, the space under them can be used for parking or other purposes. New York City has apartment and office buildings over the Cross-Bronx Expressway near the approaches to the George Washington Bridge, Cobo Hall in Detroit straddles the John Lodge Expressway, and the extension of the Massachusetts Turnpike into downtown Boston

14 *U.S. Statutes at Large,* vol. 76 (1962), pp. 1146, 1148. 1968 Act quoted in *Transportation and Tomorrow's Cities.*
15 *Los Angeles Times,* January 22, 1968.

Plate 3 Downtown areas expand vertically to overcome space shortages with a trend toward use of airspace above freeways, as in this view of high-rise apartments spanning New York's Cross-Bronx Expressway. Courtesy Port of New York Authority.

Plate 4 Night view of the George Washington Bridge Bus Station as seen from the east tower. The three-level terminal spans expressway approach to the bridge. High-rise apartments are in background. Courtesy Port of New York Authority.

passes under the Prudential Center. This extension uses a part of the former New York Central right-of-way that was built for heavy rail commuter traffic and is no longer needed for that purpose. In view of the general decline in rail passenger travel, more consideration could be given to putting freeways on or over the railroad rights-of-way that lead into the heart of central cities.

One contention sometimes advanced is that freeways should not be built into downtown areas because they simply generate more traffic and increase congestion. If the claim is valid, presumably so is the converse: that not building freeways will cause traffic to decline. Which is better for central business districts? Traffic means people—customers—and to discourage it is hardly the way to promote the CBD. Actually the contention is unfounded. Freeways get congested at peak hours, but there is ample evidence that even then they move the traffic faster than an ordinary street network can do. Congestion itself can be alleviated but not eliminated without a major change in American customs. To quote an eminent authority on transportation:

It is simply quite unrealistic to speak about the elimination of congestion as a major goal for urban transportation planning, at

Plate 5   Detroit's huge exhibition center, Cobo Hall, bridges the city's Lodge Freeway. Courtesy Automobile Manufacturers Association, Inc.

Plate 6 Chicago's post office spans the Eisenhower Expressway. Courtesy Automobile Manufacturers Association, Inc.

least so long as most businesses choose to close shop at approximately the same hour of the day. To speak of eliminating most congestion in or around major central business districts during the evening rush hour under such circumstances is very much like speaking of eliminating congestion in or around a major football stadium just after the final whistle. To do so would require an inordinately large transport capacity—inordinately large in the sense that the cost of completely eliminating congestion under such circumstances would probably be considered outrageous by most consumers.[16]

Traffic control techniques can expedite movement on freeways as well as on ordinary streets. Lane signals, diverting traffic from freeway lanes blocked by congestion or accident, are used in some cities, notably Chicago and Detroit. Their utility, how-

16 John R. Meyer, "Urban Transportation," in J. Q. Wilson, ed., *The Metropolitan Enigma* (Washington, D. C.: Chamber of Commerce of the United States, 1967), pp. 40–41.

ever, lies in diverting traffic after an emergency has developed, not in preventing congestion from occurring. For this purpose ramp metering, that is, controlling the flow of vehicles onto freeways at on-ramps, has greater promise. Metering compels some traffic to seek alternative routes, but where the technique has been tried, this has not caused serious difficulty. Motorists will seek a freeway if one is reasonably accessible, even though it may mean a longer journey. The result is that adjacent arterial streets are likely to have unused capacity, even in central business districts at rush hours. Ramp metering can be controlled so as to give priority to buses, another method of speeding up bus movement and encouraging greater use of bus transportation during peak traffic periods.

A detailed analysis of on-ramp metering was made in Seattle in 1966, when a 2.4-mile section of the Seattle Freeway (Interstate 5) was obstructed by construction work. The report gives a clear illustration of how metering, to be effective, demands careful study of the specific freeway being metered to determine the conditions for optimum traffic flow. In addition, constant surveillance should be maintained during the period of ramp control (usually confined to rush hours) to adjust the input of vehicles in order to maintain optimum flow.[17] It was found that uncontrolled on-ramps often developed queues at the point of merge which resulting in breakdowns of the merging operation, with the effect of lowering operating speeds and creating greater accident exposure on the freeway itself. Metering produced a marked improvement in this situation. An unexpected consequence was that it actually was faster before and during metering to travel around the construction or congested area on a parallel arterial. Average speeds on these routes decreased less than two miles an

17 R. E. Dunn, C. E. Dunn, and C. L. Kurtzweg, "Practical Application of Freeway On-ramp Metering for Reconstruction Area Traffic Control," State of Washington Department of Highways, July 1967. I am indebted for this report to my former student, Jerome W. Hall.

hour during the metering operation. When the construction project was finished, travel speed via the freeway materially increased while speed on the arterials resumed its previous level.

Urban Highways in Operation

Discussion of theories and principles of urban highway planning are sterile in themselves; the decisive question is, do they work? We cannot analyze the function of street systems in every city in the United States, and in fact we do not need to. The critical problems occur in the major metropolitan areas, and there are enough samples of these to be reasonably representative and informative.

Los Angeles: Los Angeles is an appropriate place to begin: the second largest metropolitan area in the country in population, with the heaviest concentration of motor vehicles, complete dependence on the highway for public as well as private transportation, and the world's most elaborate network of metropolitan freeways. Tables 14.4 and 14.5, based on the situation at the end of 1958, deserve careful study. This was about twenty years after serious work on the Los Angeles freeways began, and the figures make it quite clear that the freeways were doing just what was expected of them. They had relieved congestion on badly overloaded arterial streets and in spite of becoming overloaded themselves had significantly reduced driving times. The observations for Table 14.5 were made between 6 and 9 A.M. and 3 and 7 P.M.; thus they include the peak traffic hours.[18]

The overloading of the freeways was, and is, partly due to underestimating the rate of growth of both population and automobile ownership in Southern California but rather more to the fact that these freeways were limited segments of the total projected system and were therefore carrying loads that would even-

18 P. T. McElhiney, "Evaluating Freeway Performance in Los Angeles," *Traffic Quarterly*, vol. 14 (July 1960), pp. 304–305.

Table 14.4 Comparison of Average Daily Traffic Carried by Surface Routes and Major Los Angeles Freeways before and after Freeway Openings (thousands of vehicles per twenty-four-hour-period)

Facilities		Before Freeway	After Freeway	Now
South Figueroa Street	(1955)	45,713		
A.D.T. Capacity 39,000	(1956)		15,634	
Comparable route to	(1958)			13,542
The Harbor Freeway				
A.D.T. Capacity 126,000	(1956)		93,480	
	(1958)			160,522
Sunset Boulevard	(1950)	35,016		
A.D.T. Capacity 26,000	(1952)		18,512	
Comparable route to	(1958)			20,856
The Hollywood Freeway				
A.D.T. Capacity 126,000	(1953)		76,764	
	(1958)			144,020
North Figueroa Street	(1940)	24,298		
A.D.T. Capacity 26,000	(1941)		18,849	
Comparable route to	(1958)			25,637
The Pasadena Freeway				
A.D.T. Capacity 93,900	(1941)		33,622	
	(1958)			82,097
Valley Boulevard	(1953)	23,540		
A.D.T. Capacity 26,000	(1954)		16,898	
Comparable route to	(1958)			20,346
San Bernardino Freeway				
A.D.T. Capacity 93,900	(1954)		49,432	
	(1958)			105,971
Telegraph Road	(1953)	38,126		
A.D.T. Capacity 26,000	(1955)		17,770	
Comparable route to	(1957)			19,720
The Santa Ana Freeway				
A.D.T. Capacity 93,900	(1954)		65,414	
	(1958)			92,319

Sources: California, State Highway Engineer, *Annual Traffic Counts*, Sacramento: published annually. Los Angeles, City Traffic Department, data abstracted from original worksheets of traffic counts by the author. Los Angeles, County Road Department, *Traffic Counts*, Los Angeles: 1958.
Reproduced from P. T. McElhiney, "Evaluating Freeway Performance in Los Angeles," *Traffic Quarterly*, vol. 14 (July 1960), p. 303, by permission of the author, *Traffic Quarterly*, and the Eno Foundation for Highway Traffic Control, Inc.

Table 14.5   Comparison of Elapsed Driving Times on Surface Routes and Major Los Angeles Freeways before and after Freeway Openings (time shown in minutes and seconds)

Route	Street		Freeway
	1936–1937 Studies	1956–1958 Studies	1956–1958 Studies
South Figueroa Street vs. The Harbor Freeway From Civic Center to Santa Barbara Avenue	17:	12:41	5:50
Sunset Boulevard vs. The Hollywood Freeway From Civic Center to Hollywood and Vine Streets	20:	N.A.	7:35
Figueroa St.–York–Fair Oaks Boulēvards vs. The Pasadena Freeway From Civic Center to Glenarm Street	31:	21:48	10:30
Valley Boulevard vs. San Bernardino Freeway From Civic Center to Rosemead Boulevard	31:	21:41	12:51
Olympic Boulevard–Telegraph Road vs. The Santa Ana Freeway From Civic Center to Norwalk Boulevard	37:	35:13	16:40

Sources: Automobile Club of Southern California, *Traffic Survey Los Angeles Metropolitan Area, 1937*. Los Angeles, County Regional Planning Commission, *Highway Traffic Survey in the County of Los Angeles, 1937*. California, Division of Highways, *Reports of Speed and Delay Studies*, (various freeways, 1956–1958, unpublished).
Source: McElhiney, "Evaluating Freeway Performance in Los Angeles," *Traffic Quarterly*, vol. 14 (July 1960), p. 305. Reproduced by permission of the author, *Traffic Quarterly*, and the Eno Foundation for Highway Traffic Control, Inc.

tually be distributed over other parts of the system. The most astonishing, and perhaps the most significant, feature of the Los Angeles experience is the ability of its freeways to carry substantial overloads and still expedite the movement of traffic. The Hollywood Freeway was operating at 50 percent over its planned capacity a year after it opened in 1954, and the Harbor Freeway was believed to be the most heavily traveled highway in the world; it may have lost this distinction to the Santa Monica Freeway, which in 1967 carried 210,000 vehicles daily past the Western Avenue overcrossing.[19]

Nevertheless, between 1957 and 1965 commuting speed on the freeways rose by 30 percent, partly because of additions to the system, even though the population increased from 6 to 8 million and motor vehicles from 3.3 to 4.2 million, and a citizens' committee interested in promoting public transportation acknowledged in 1967 that the freeway network was adequate for off-peak traffic but needed to be supplemented at rush hours.[20] During this same period the Los Angeles Department of Traffic found that the number of vehicles using streets in the CBD (excluding freeways) had decreased from 626,152 daily in 1955 to 579,099 in 1966. The Department attributed the decline to the completion of a freeway loop around the downtown area. The existence of intown freeways has been a stimulus to redevelopment in the Los Angeles CBD. When the building of the new Occidental Center was announced, for example, accessibility to freeways was specifically stated as a reason for choosing the site, and the design included parking for over 3,000 cars.

No one who has driven on the Los Angeles freeways will deny

19 Citizens Advisory Council on Public Transportation, *Improving Public Transportation in Los Angeles* (1967), p. 31; McElhiney, "Freeways of Los Angeles," p. 83.
20 Peter S. Koltnow, "The Los Angeles Commuter," *Westways*, vol. 59, no. 9, p. 17; *Public Transportation in Los Angeles*, p. 6. The population figure is an approximation for the metropolitan area.

that they become congested at peak hours and because of accidents. The peak hours have to include not only the commuter rush periods but also Friday evenings and late Sunday afternoons and evenings, when recreational travel reaches heights matching, and even exceeding, weekday work travel. But occasional congestion is not a valid argument against urban freeways unless it can be demonstrated that congestion would be less without them —and all the evidence points in exactly the opposite direction. We may refer again to William L. Pereira:

We talk about the fellow on the freeway struggling along at 10 to 20 miles per hour as he goes to work or returns home. But you don't see him gnashing his teeth or shaking his fist because of it. The point is that he has a vehicle that will also enable him to go fishing this weekend or to a movie tonight. He can move wherever he wants and whenever he wants. . . .

One of the problems of the city today is that we refuse to take public responsibility for the automobile. It is as if the automobile propagated itself, as if it polluted the air by itself. The man who screams the loudest about air pollution does not stop driving his car. The man who screams the loudest about congested freeways wants to have other means to get about the city. But he probably would not be able to use them because his travel needs differ from other men who regularly commute at the time he does.[21]

Chicago: Chicago has a population approximating that of Los Angeles, but it is concentrated in a smaller area. The Chicago Area Transportation Study, published in 1959, covered an area of 1,236 square miles, inhabited by 5.2 million people.[22] The city had then 66 miles of freeways (called expressways in Chicago) and 2,796 miles of arterial streets. The expressways, with 2.3 percent of the mileage, carried 15 percent of the traffic and moved 3.5 times as many vehicles an hour as the arterials. Streets of all kinds took 40 percent of the land within two miles of the Loop; after that the figure dropped to 32 percent; for the downtown area this is surprisingly close to the Los Angeles figure.

21 *Westways* interview, p. 4.
22 *Chicago Area Transportation Study*, vol. 1, *Survey Findings.* Unless specifically cited, data on Chicago are from this volume.

Since 1959 the Chicago expressways have been extended. If the Illinois Tollway is included, as it should be because it gives Chicago a circumferential metropolitan freeway, the mileage is now more than 200 out of 520 contemplated. The completion of the Dan Ryan Expressway in 1962 yielded time savings of as much as fifteen minutes on a seven-mile trip, and a check on the effect of the Kennedy Expressway on streets that offered alternative routing showed a marked improvement on them.[23] On Elston Avenue it took thirty-six minutes to travel 6.9 miles, an average of 11.3 mph before the Expressway was opened. Afterward, the same distance took sixteen minutes for an average of 24.7 mph.

Chicago also has rail rapid transit. In recent years the system has been extensively modernized, including putting the CBD section underground and demolishing the historic but unsightly elevated structure that formed the "Loop." There have also been efforts at the rehabilitation of rail commuter service. One innovation has been to use freeway medians for rapid transit lines, beginning with the Eisenhower (Congress Street) Expressway. This arrangement has permitted a direct comparison of freeway and transit use:

Transit riding peaks on the immediate approaches to downtown while highway traffic peaks several miles to the west. This is because more than three fourths of all downtown travelers in the corridor use rapid transit, while the expressway to a large extent serves trips between nondowntown areas. The expressway operates at capacity during peak hours, the rapid transit route at about half capacity.[24]

The pattern of travel in Chicago has not changed radically since the Transportation Study. At that time in the twelve-square-mile region surrounding the Loop, 14.2 percent of the person trips were made by rapid transit and 44.5 percent by transit and

23 Wilbur Smith and Associates, *Transportation and Parking for Tomorrow's Cities* (New Haven, Conn.: Wilbur Smith and Associates, 1966), p. 87.
24 *Ibid.*, p. 104.

bus. Outside the CBD rapid transit trips dropped to 3 percent of the total. For the whole study area rapid transit, including the suburban railroads, accounted for a twelfth of all person trips and a sixth of the miles of person travel. However, 45 percent of the trips into the Loop were on rail transit and 71 percent by all forms of mass transit. Over half the subway-elevated trips were linked with bus trips, but these remained predominantly radial. The volume of circumferential transit trips by any mode was negligible. By comparison, external trips—going out of or returning to the study area—were 5.7 percent of the total vehicle trips but 18.6 percent of the vehicle-miles traveled. In short, Chicago illustrates the fundamental relationship of mass transit to automobile travel in a major metropolis; the former is valuable for trips to and from the CBD but for little else.

Detroit: Like Los Angeles, the Motor City has no rail transit or commuter railroad service; it depends entirely on movement by road. The urban area in 1967 covered 681 square miles with a population of almost 3 million.[25] It had 122 miles of freeway, occupying somewhat less than 1 percent of the land area and carrying 20 percent of the traffic. By 1980 there are to be 300 miles of freeway, taking 3 percent of the land area and handling half the traffic. The rest will move on ordinary streets, which take 30 percent of the land. The principal traffic problem was faster growth than anticipated. Traffic volumes projected for 1980 were to be realized in 1970. This complication was accentuated by delays in construction and by the necessity for design changes on older parts of the freeway system, including reconstruction of the interchange between John Lodge and Edsel Ford Expressways. Other cities have this problem also. The earliest of the Los Angeles freeways, the Pasadena Freeway, is obsolete. When it was

25 The information on Detroit is based on a report by the Technical Transportation Committee, Greater Detroit Board of Commerce, *Highway Transportation in the Detroit Region* (Detroit, 1967).

built in 1940, only a few parkways offered any practical lessons in urban freeway design. Much had to be learned from experience after the first freeways were opened.

Other needs for Detroit were listed as: ramp entry control; improvement of arterial roads offering alternative routes to the freeways; better bus movement. Basically, however, Detroit's situation is good. The city had an excellent network of broad arterial streets radiating from its CBD before the freeways were begun, and both the arterials and the freeways have up-to-date traffic control systems. The CBD therefore has good access by road, and this access has been an influential element in the renewal of downtown Detroit in recent years, manifested in the construction of new office buildings and hotels. In addition, the development of the freeways was coordinated with a program of slum clearance whereby several hundred acres were rebuilt as high-rise apartment districts supplemented by shopping centers and small manufacturing and service industries.[26]

New York: New York's transportation situation has already been comprehensively discussed. The figures in Table 14.6 add some interesting information on transportation and travel within the city itself. In particular, the relationship between mileage of freeway and the volume of traffic carried shows the characteristic pattern. Controlled-access highways constitute about 4 percent of New York City's road mileage and account for a third of the vehicle-miles traveled. The table includes only freeways in the five boroughs of New York City. When planned metropolitan freeways are completed, the network for the whole New York Region will at least match and probably surpass the Los Angeles freeway system. The benefits, however, appear likely to accrue mainly to the suburban areas unless better road access to downtown Manhattan is forthcoming—admittedly a difficult and expensive task, but not impossible. The real obstacles, in fact, are

26 *Automotive Information*, vol. 4, no. 10 (June 1967), p. 5.

Table 14.6   New York City Transportation Fact Sheet

Area

Borough	Sq. Miles
Bronx	43.1
Brooklyn	78.5
Manhattan	22.6
Queens	114.7
Richmond	60.9
Total	319.8

Population

Borough	Population (millions)
Bronx	1.5
Brooklyn	2.75
Manhattan	1.65
Queens	2
Richmond	.25
Total	8.1

Registered Motor Vehicles

Passenger cars	1,500,000
Taxis	27,000
Buses	6,500
Trucks	150,000
Motorcycles	6,500
Total	1,680,000

Length of Roads

	Miles	Kilometers
Controlled access	170	272
Other	4176	6680
Total	4346	6952

Annual Vehicle-Miles Traveled

	Miles (billions)
On controlled access	4.9
On other roads	9.8
Total	14.7

Additional Traffic Entering New York City

Per day	625,000 vehicles

Existing Mass Transit

A. Rapid transit	
Miles of route	237
Number of stations	481
Number of cars	6,700
Average weekday passengers	4.7 million

Table 14.6 (*continued*)

B. Buses	
Miles of route	832
Number of buses	4,195
Average weekday passengers	3.4 million
C. Commuter railroads	
Average weekday passengers	.5 million
D. Total daily passengers on mass transit	8.6 million

Number of Workers	
Area	Number of Workers (millions)
Manhattan CBD	2.25
Inner urban	1.04
Outer urban	.49
Total	3.77

Manhattan CBD as the Hub	
A. Area	9 sq. mi.
B. Total persons entering per day	3,400,000
C. Mode of entering persons:	
Motor vehicle	1,115,000
Subway	1,920,000
Railroad	205,000
Ferry	36,000
D. Total entering 7–10 A.M.	1,650,000
Total entering 8–9 A.M.	850,000

Source: This table was provided by the courtesy of John M. Kaiser, Assistant to the Commissioner, Department of Traffic, New York City.

not physical and financial; they are a combination of the natural objections of the people who may be dislodged, opposition on aesthetic or sociological grounds, belief by some people that a central city would be better off without motor vehicle traffic, and efforts to make political capital out of this complex of attitudes.

The story of the projected Lower Manhattan Expressway is eloquent testimony on this point. It was discussed as early as 1928 as a means of connecting the Hudson River tunnels with the East River bridges.[27] Federal and state funds would have paid

27 Roger Starr, *The Living End: The City and Its Critics* (New York: Coward-McCann, Inc., 1968), p. 63.

most of the cost, and the potential economic benefits, especially in providing direct truck access to and from the Manhattan CBD, were sizable. Yet it was never possible to reach agreement, and in 1969 the whole project was abandoned—and those who were most instrumental will also undoubtedly be the most vociferous in deploring the flight of business to the suburbs.

Other Urban Areas: City after city offers illustrations of what not only can be but also has been done, although under somewhat easier conditions than exist in New York. In Kansas City "the completion of the Intercity Freeway across downtown resulted in the rebirth of an older area which had deteriorated into a depressed 'skid row' neighborhood. The freeway was followed by urban renewal, street widenings, landscaping and new parking facilities. The neighborhood has blossomed into a new business area." [28] The result was an overall increase in land value, more than offsetting what was lost in taxable property to the freeway. Likewise in Boston the construction of the Central Expressway and the extension of the Massachusetts Turnpike were accompanied by a substantial amount of new building in the downtown area. New Haven, Connecticut, rebuilt its center about a six-lane freeway from the intersection of the Connecticut Turnpike and Interstate 91 into the heart of the city, consciously basing its urban renewal on automobile traffic.[29] Ample off-street parking has been provided, and the highway network is expected to bring 115,000 cars into the downtown area daily by 1975. This redevelopment project has generated about $170 million in new construction, and $105 million of it is private. One particularly interesting feature is a tunnel for commercial vehicles four blocks long under the retail district.

A survey of Sacramento, California, in 1967 showed 18 miles

28 R. L. Braun, "Freeways and Cities," paper presented to Educational Seminar, American Institute of Real Estate Appraisers, Washington, D.C., March 7, 1969.
29 *Automotive Information,* vol. 2, no. 1 (September 1964), p. 5.

of freeway finished or under construction, with 30 miles projected by 1972, which would be 3 percent of Sacramento's road and street mileage and would carry 60 percent of its traffic. The survey commented:

One area of concern that often arises in relation to freeway development involves disadvantages that one community might experience because of the particular location of a new freeway. Some people feel that new industry and commerce which a new freeway attracts to one area simply reflects a corresponding loss to another area. Careful analysis has shown that this is a rather static and incomplete view of what has actually happened. In spite of some selected economic and social losses that occasionally occur as freeways are built, there is almost always a net benefit to the economy as a whole. The new freeway ordinarily allows for more efficient business grouping, promotes overall cost savings, and many times causes new investment to be made that would not have been made without the new freeway. Thus, in addition to the direct benefits of improved transportation, many indirect non-vehicular benefits can be triggered by freeway development.[30]

The record is abundantly clear: for the modern metropolis an urban freeway system, properly planned, is an asset both for the metropolitan area as a whole and for the central core as well. Two elements are essential to attainment of the desired goals—"system" and "proper planning." Much of the congestion for which existing freeways have been criticized has been due to the fact that they are incomplete segments of a system. The reconstruction of downtown Pittsburgh includes making the rehabilitated Golden Triangle the hub of a freeway system. Transportation studies estimate that

a partial freeway system would deliver more traffic across a downtown cordon than either a completed system or no system at all. A completed system would increase Golden Triangle cordon crossings 16 per cent over existing levels, while a partial system would result in as much as 63 per cent rise, depending on its components. In Philadelphia it was indicated that many of the Schuylkill Expressway's problems would be relieved—if not solved—when a *full freeway system* was in operation.[31]

30 "Sacramento Survey," April 1967, published by *The Sacramento Union.*
31 Wilbur Smith and Associates, *Transportation and Parking*, p. 198.

The conclusion appears obvious: a freeway system, to be effective, should be complete.

By way of summary, these are the characteristics of urban freeways:

1. In terms of capacity, the freeway is a better investment than an equivalent or larger acreage devoted to conventional roads and streets. An acre of land used as a freeway has an average capacity of 600,000 vehicle-miles a year; as an ordinary road, about 70,000 vehicle-miles a year.

2. Even in congested central city areas and at peak hours freeways demonstrably speed up traffic.

3. Freeways are safer than ordinary roads. There is indisputable evidence on this point.

4. Control of access inhibits ribbon development and sprawl.

5. A comprehensive freeway network helps to reduce air pollution. It encourages dispersal of traffic rather than concentration, and a car moving at a steady speed emits fewer pollutants than one that is constantly stopping and starting.

6. A freeway system is actually a rapid transit system. For public transportation, freeway buses can operate as fast as rail transit (excluding commuter railroads) and with adequate capacity for all but the highest-volume travel corridors. Reserved bus lanes at rush hours and ramp metering with preferential treatment for buses can free bus movement from traffic delays. The freeway, unlike the private right-of-way, is not unused capacity at off-peak hours; 80 percent of the travel on urban freeways occurs during off-peak periods.

On the debit side are the undoubted facts that freeway planning and routing have at times been unimaginative and have been dominated by engineering and economic consideration to the exclusion of other values. These mistakes are regrettable but are also preventable in future freeway development. On balance, the advantages of urban freeways outweigh the deficiencies. They constitute a small proportion of total urban street mileage, but they are the most important single instrument for the smooth and expeditious movement of urban traffic.

IV The Road Ahead

15 Problems and Prospects

As the United States enters the 1970s, highway transportation in all its aspects poses a number of vital issues. Barring some unforeseen and drastic change in American life, motor vehicle registrations should increase from about 100 million in 1968 to 143.5 million in 1985, vehicle-miles traveled from 965 billion to 1,516 billion, annual travel per vehicle from 9,755 to 10,600 miles, and annual motor vehicle travel per person from 4,600 to 5,700 miles.[1] These are regarded as conservative estimates, based on moderate levels of economic growth. (See Figure 15.1.)

These increases will be most pronounced in urban areas, which now account for half the vehicle-miles traveled and in which highway travel doubles about every twenty or twenty-five years. No prospective development in mass transit will affect this growth rate appreciably. The Department of Transportation made a detailed analysis of two large and fairly representative metropolises, Baltimore, Maryland, and Buffalo, New York, and concluded that if transit usage to and from their CBDs could be trebled, raised in fact to a theoretical 95 percent of such trips, the result would be to reduce motor-vehicle-miles in the CBD by about 37 percent but in the entire metropolitan region by only 5 percent.[2] The effect would be to diminish downtown congestion, but the overall planned freeway needs of the two areas would not be affected to any significant extent.

This is perhaps as good a place as any to let the Department of Transportation have what ought to be the final word on "transit versus freeway":

It is clear that rail rapid transit on a separate right-of-way offers high potential for reducing peak-period congestion in dense travel corridors approaching the central business district and

1 Based on *Automobile Facts and Figures, 1969,* pp. 50–51, and *1968 National Highway Needs Report,* 90th Congress, 2nd sess., Committee Print, pp. 10–12.
2 *1968 National Highway Needs Report,* p. 27.

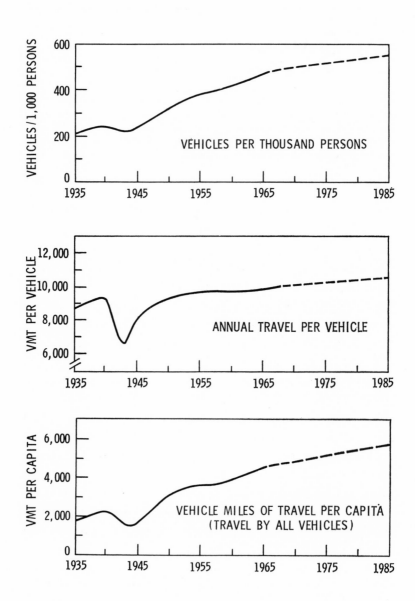

Figure 15.1 Travel forecast relationships
Source: U.S. Department of Transportation, *1968 National Highway Needs Report* (Washington, D.C.: Government Printing Office, 1968), p. 11

also within the central business district itself. Such a system will also reduce downtown parking needs. The greatest possibility of reduction of highway needs exists in the corridors specifically served by the rail lines, but even there the effect is more likely to be one of reducing the number of lanes required rather than the complete elimination of a proposed new highway.

Rail transit would attract a considerable proportion of riders from buses, which would have a significant effect on the number of highway person trips, but less on the number of highway vehicles, in proportion to the total. Not all trips are transferable to rail transit, because many trip requirements can best be met by highway travel; for example:

Trucks and other commercial vehicles (about 15 percent of all downtown trips).

Persons who use their cars in their work, such as salesmen, physicians, service and repairmen, etc.

Those who come to the downtown district from outlying areas not well served by transit.

Those who prefer to use their personal cars regardless of the availability of transit.

In any traffic corridor where there is sufficient patronage to warrant a rail transit line, usually there are also sufficient highway users to require high-capacity highways such as freeways. In such high-density corridors, it is often impracticable for reasons of cost and space to provide sufficient freeway lanes to satisfy total traffic requirements (without transit). Conversely, it is equally unrealistic to suppose that a rail transit line, even if it had sufficient capacity, could satisfy all the diverse transportation needs of the corridor. For such high-volume corridors, the provision of both rail and highway facilities is needed. Because both kinds of facilities tend to serve different components of travel, they can exist in harmony. Together, they can provide the flexibility necessary to raise the level of mobility available to our urban population.

The conclusion from this general analysis is that future urban highway needs in urban areas will be great, even though urban areas undertake extensive programs to improve mass transit, whether bus or rail, or both.[3]

Thus the impact of the highway on American life will become greater. To evaluate the prospect properly it is worth repeating what had been said before—that this is by no means an exclusively American phenomenon. In fact, the impact of highway transportation will probably be more pronounced in other parts

3 *Ibid.*, p. 28.

Table 15.1   Passenger Travel in Great Britain, 1951–1961
(in billions of vehicle-miles)

Year	Rail	Bus	Private Car
1951	24	51	32
1956	26	48	48
1961	25	43	77

Source: Based on *Traffic in Towns*, Report of the Steering Group and the Working Group appointed by the Minister of Transport (London: Her Majesty's Stationery Office, 1963), p. 12.
Figures are approximate.
Domestic air travel omitted; about 2 billion passenger-miles.

of the world where it is just beginning to approach the level of the United States and Canada. In the United Kingdom the number of motor vehicles in use rose from 2½ million in 1946 to over 10 million in 1964.[4] For the decade from 1951 to 1961 British travel patterns showed a striking change (see Table 15.1). Rail passenger travel remained at about the same level; bus travel, which was the leading mode in 1951, declined; and travel by private automobile showed a rapid growth. At the end of the decade four-fifths of all domestic passenger travel went by road. The highways carried 72 percent of the tonnage of domestic freight and 45 percent of the mileage.[5]

Japan shows an even more remarkable growth in highway transportation. In the five years from 1962 to 1967 the number of passenger cars registered rose from 700,000 to almost 3 million and the number of trucks from 2 million to 5½ million.[6] Japan has been distinctive in having more trucks than passenger cars in use. Otherwise the Japanese experience is comparable. There

4 *The Motor Industry of Great Britain, 1965* (London: Society of Motor Manufacturers and Traders, 1966), p. 85.
5 *Traffic in Towns,* Report of the Steering Group and the Working Group appointed by the Minister of Transport (London: Her Majesty's Stationery Office, 1963), p. 12.
6 Japan Road Association, *Annual Report of Roads,* 1967, p. 153.

has been a steady increase in the highway share of both passenger and freight traffic. Between 1950 and 1965 the proportion of freight traffic in Japan moving by road, measured in ton-kilometers, increased from 8 percent to 26 percent of the total freight movement, while the rail share dropped from 53 percent to 38 percent. In 1965 trucks carried 85.5 percent of the total freight tonnage. In Japan as elsewhere truck hauls are preponderantly short. For passenger travel, measured in person-kilometers, the highway share, both private car and bus, rose from 8 percent to 31.9 percent between 1950 and 1965, while railway passenger volume declined from 92 percent to 67.4 percent (the rest represents air travel).

The desire for individual mobility is universal, growing, and healthy. At the same time, the rapid growth of motorized highway transportation brings with it intensified problems of congestion, safety, and air pollution which must be faced squarely if the very real benefits of this kind of mobility are not to be seriously offset by these drawbacks—even to the extent of producing unwise and unwarranted restraints on highway movement.

Air Pollution

Pollution of the atmosphere is not new. It has existed since people lived in cities and poured out the products of combustion in concentrated form, and it has been acute since the rise of modern industrialism. European and American cities of the nineteenth century were deeply concerned with the clouds of smoke and soot that poured on them from chimneys in homes and factories, railroad locomotives, and steamboats if the city had a navigable waterfront. London's fogs have long been famous, or notorious, and they are chiefly the product of large quantities of soft-coal smoke being poured into the atmosphere. The enormous quantities of coal used in manufacturing iron and steel gave Pittsburgh its nickname of the "Smoky City." Smoke abatement measures of varying degrees of effectiveness were commonplace by the early years of the twentieth century.

Smog is a comparative newcomer to atmospheric pollution. The word was originally coined to define the combination of smoke and fog that periodically blacked out London, but it now has come to mean the chemical combination of emissions from motor vehicles, industrial plants, and burning of wastes that first became noticeable in Los Angeles during the 1940s. Dr. A. J. Haagen-Smit, then a chemist at the California Institute of Technology, identified the chemical composition of smog early in the 1950s. Although industrial wastes constitute much of the pollutants, our concern is with the share of the motor vehicle. For one thing, given adequate legislation and enforcement, industrial emissions ought to be much easier to control than the output of over 100 million motor vehicles operated under widely differing conditions and with variable standards of maintenance.

Since California, especially metropolitan Los Angeles, has the most critical problem, its experience is the most relevant, because steps taken there to curb smog emissions will certainly be effective elsewhere. Smog is an emotion-charged issue in Southern California, to the extent that the actual record is more often ignored than not. After much discussion the state legislature began in 1960 to require emission control devices on motor vehicles, aimed principally at reducing the volume of unconsumed hydrocarbons pumped into the atmosphere, since these were considered the major source of smog, especially in terms of irritation to eyes and respiratory passages. Emissions of carbon monoxides were a second important target. Unfortunately it was not appreciated until some time afterward that oxides of nitrogen were also a major villain, and techniques directed at more complete combustion so as to reduce hydrocarbon and carbon monoxide emissions had the effect of increasing oxides of nitrogen. These are also produced by industrial emissions: in the Los Angeles area 25 percent of the oxides of nitrogen come from electric generating plants, and 68 percent from motor vehicles.[7]

The result of a decade of smog control appears in Figure 15.2. From a peak in 1965 the emissions of hydrocarbons and carbon monoxide have decreased in spite of a steady increase in the number of motor vehicles. Oxides of nitrogen, on the other hand, have continued to rise in volume because of the improvement in combustion that has reduced the others. Steps to combat this source of pollution are in progress, with the prospect that by the mid-1970s air pollution from motor vehicles will be under control. The process is delayed because of the time needed to retire the older cars, which are the more prolific sources of pollutants. If all the old cars in the Los Angeles basin were to be immediately replaced by new ones, smog would be cut by at least half.[8] What has been accomplished is all the more remarkable because although California has stringent requirements for emission control on motor vehicles, for practical purposes enforcement is nonexistent. Periodic spot checks by the Highway Patrol can reach only a small fraction of the cars on California roads. There is no requirement of regular inspection to ensure that antismog devices are maintained in good working order.

Because atmospheric pollution does not recognize political boundaries, and because it was becoming a national rather than a local problem, the federal government entered the field with clean-air legislation in 1967. Other potential steps to diminish automobile-induced air pollution are in prospect, such as changes in the power plant to gas turbine, steam, electric, or fuel cell engines. As of the end of the 1960s none of these was ready for

7 Interview with Dr. A. J. Haagen-Smit, by George Getze, *Los Angeles Times*, August 14, 1969.
8 *Los Angeles Times*, February 24, 1968.

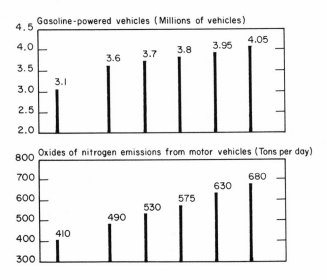

Figure 15.2   Emissions from motor vehicles, Los Angeles County

Report on pollution; graph indicates types of emissions from motor vehicles in Los Angeles County.

general use. The most likely immediate source of relief from smog lay in continued refinement of the internal combustion engine in combination with changes in automotive fuels.[9]

No responsible individual will dispute the gravity of the problem of atmospheric pollution or resist suitably conceived corrective measures. But there are no simple and inexpensive solutions —again, no "instant technology." Recriminations about past mistakes, or misdeeds, may be helpful as an outlet for emotional indignation; they may also enable politicians to drum up local

9 Elimination of lead in gasolines would diminish pollution. Experiments conducted in California using natural gas in conventional internal combustion engines seem to show a marked reduction of pollutant emission. Information on this subject comes from the Pacific Lighting System.

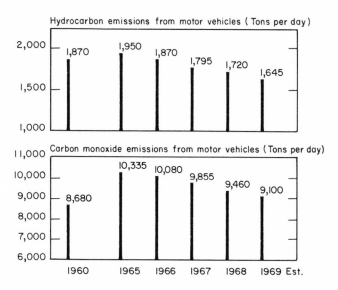

Source: *Los Angeles Times,* August 14, 1969. Copyright, 1969, *Los Angeles Times.* Reprinted by permission.

support by blaming someone else, especially if the someone else lives somewhere else; but they do nothing, literally or figuratively, to clear the air. As far as the motor vehicle's contribution is concerned, the evidence is quite conclusive that effective control is possible and is in fact on the way—except that no miraculous change will occur overnight. The automobile of today is not necessarily the automobile of tomorrow, and it would be absurd to forgo the benefits of flexible transportation merely because an existing technology has certain remediable drawbacks.

Dr. Haagen-Smit, who knows more than anyone else about pollution of the atmosphere by motor vehicles, has stated that smog in Los Angeles can and will be reduced to or below the

1940 level without giving up performance standards in motor vehicles. He says:

People are not going to stand for any reduction in the drive-ability of automomiles. The automobile of today was created over a period of sixty years and it is a marvelous instrument.

It stops, accelerates, decelerates easily and efficiently and the public won't put up with any diminution of this efficiency.

The reason it can do all these things so well is that the problems of emissions were ignored over six decades.

Now, in a few years, the industry has to rethink and redevelop the automobile so that it drives as well as it does now but doesn't pollute the atmosphere while doing it.[10]

There is also a highway factor, already referred to, in combating air pollution. If cities develop road systems and traffic control methods that facilitate the smooth flow of traffic and encourage dispersal rather than concentration—keeping vehicles out of downtown areas that do not belong there—these measures will sensibly reduce pollutant emissions.

Highway Safety

Along with air pollution, highway accidents are the greatest source of criticism of motor vehicle transportation. The record is certainly distressing. In 1965 there were over 13 million traffic accidents, which caused 49,000 fatalities and over a million disabling injuries. About 55,000 people lost their lives on American roads in 1968. Property damage is enormous, and litigation arising from automobile accidents is expensive and time-consuming, to say nothing of the fact that it is by far the worst offender in clogging court calendars. If this were the whole story, it would be a serious indictment against highway travel, but it is not. The elimination of all highway accidents is the objective to be sought, although it will probably never be completely attained. Meanwhile, the plain fact is that automobile travel in the United States has been steadily growing safer. Table 15.2 offers convincing evidence. The fatality rate per 100 million vehicle-miles is a

10 *Los Angeles Times,* August 14, 1969.

Table 15.2   Traffic Fatalities and Vehicle-Miles

Fatalities (thousands) — Vehicle-miles — Traffic fatalities — Vehicle-miles (billions)

1935 1940 1945 1950 1955 1960 1965 1969

| | All Deaths * | Deaths from Non-collision Accidents ‡ | Deaths from Collision with | | | | | | Total Death Rates | | |
			Pedestrians	Other Motor Vehicles	Railroad Trains	Street Cars	Bicycles, Animal, Animal-drawn Vehicles	Fixed Objects§	Per 100,000 Population	Per 10,000 Motor Vehicles	Per 100,000,000 Vehicle Miles
1936	38,089	9,410	15,250	9,500	1,697	269	900	1,060	29.7	13.4	15.1
1941	39,969	9,450	13,550	12,500	1,840	118	1,160	1,350	30.0	11.5	12.0
1946	33,411	8,900	11,600	9,400	1,703	174	670	950	23.9	9.7	9.8
1950	34,763	10,600	9,000	11,650	1,541	89	560	1,300	23.0	7.1	7.6
1951	36,996	11,200	9,150	13,100	1,573	46	490	1,400	24.1	7.1	7.5
1952	37,794	11,900	8,900	13,500	1,429	32	560	1,450	24.3	7.1	7.4
1953	37,955	12,200	8,750	13,400	1,506	26	540	1,500	24.0	6.7	7.0
1954	35,586	11,500	8,000	12,800	1,269	28	470	1,500	22.1	6.1	6.3
1955	38,426	12,100	8,200	14,500	1,490	15	500	1,600	23.4	6.1	6.4
1956	39,628	13,000	7,900	15,200	1,377	11	540	1,600	23.7	6.1	6.3
1957	38,702	11,800	7,850	15,400	1,376	13	540	1,700	22.7	5.7	6.0
1958	36,981	11,600	7,650	14,200	1,316	9	530	1,650	21.3	5.4	5.6
1959	37,910	11,800	7,850	14,900	1,202	6	550	1,600	21.5	5.3	5.4
1960	38,137	11,900	7,850	14,800	1,368	5	540	1,700	21.2	5.1	5.3
1961	38,091	12,200	7,650	14,700	1,267	5	570	1,700	20.8	5.0	5.2
1962	40,804	12,900	7,900	16,400	1,245	3	590	1,750	22.0	5.1	5.3
1963	43,564	13,800	8,200	17,600	1,385	10	660	1,900	23.1	5.2	5.4
1964	47,700	14,600	9,000	19,600	1,580	5	810	2,100	24.9	5.5	5.6
1965	49,163	14,900	8,900	20,800	1,556	5	800	2,200	25.4	5.4	5.5
1966	53,041	16,300	9,400	22,200	1,800	2	840	2,500	27.1	5.5	5.7
1967	52,924	16,700	9,400	22,000	1,620	3	850	2,350	26.7	5.4	5.5
1968	55,200	17,800	9,800	22,500	1,600	0	900	2,600	27.6	5.4	5.4
1969 (Prelim.)	56,400	†	9,800	23,600	1,400	—	900	†	27.9	5.3	5.3

* Totals do not quite equal the sum of the various types because the estimates were generally made only to the nearest 10 deaths, and to the nearest 50 deaths for certain types.
† Data for 1969 not comparable with previous years: Deaths from non-collision accidents 15,000; Deaths from collisions with fixed objects 5,700.
‡ Classification is according to first event. If car runs off roadway and then strikes fixed object, death is charged as run off road accident.
§ Includes deaths from collisions with fixed objects such as walls and abutments, where the collision occurred while all wheels of the vehicle were still on the road.
Source: National Safety Council, *Accident Facts*.

third of what it was thirty years ago. Looking at it another way, we can see that in this period the total number of traffic fatalities increased by 45 percent, while motor vehicle registrations increased by 350 percent and population by about 54 percent.

Comparisons with highway conditions elsewhere also come out in favor of the United States. The source of information on this matter is mainly British. In 1961 the ratio of highway fatalities to registered motor vehicles in six countries with intensive ownership and use of motor vehicles was: Italy, 1:375; West Germany, 1:430; Japan, 1:526; France, 1:935; United Kingdom, 1:1,410; United States, 1:2,000.[11]

It would of course be more informative if vehicle-miles instead of the number of vehicles had been used, since cars sitting in garages are not usually a source of accidents. Nevertheless, the disparity is great enough to make it clear that the American road is safer, and indeed the compilers of these figures comment, in typically restrained British fashion, "This is slender evidence on which to generalize, but the ratio for the United States suggests that, in some way, matters are better contrived than in Europe."

In 1965 an attorney named Ralph Nader published a book on highway accidents in which he singled out the automobile itself as the culprit. He undoubtedly performed a service by stirring up public interest in the question of safety, and one result was the enactment in 1966 of two items of federal legislation: the National Traffic and Motor Vehicle Safety Act, requiring the incorporation of safety features such as seat belts, recessed knobs, and so forth, in motor vehicles (but no legislation has been found that will induce everyone to use seat belts); and the Highway Safety Act, for developing comprehensive programs of traffic safety.[12]

11 *Traffic in Towns*, p. 19; *Statistics of Roads in Japan* (Tokyo: Japan Road Association), p. 17. The Japanese figure is for 1964.
12 *U.S. Statutes at Large*, vol. 80, pt. 1, pp. 718–730 (Motor Vehicle Safety Act); 731–737 (Highway Safety Act).

However, the emphasis that this safety crusade put on the vehicle had some unfortunate features. First, it tended to focus public attention on a single component of highway accidents. A study by Arthur D. Little, Inc., concluded that "traffic accidents are most meaningfully viewed as system failures rather than as a failure of any single component, such as the driver, the vehicle, or the environment." [13] Second, much of Nader's thrust was directed at minimizing the effects of the "second accident"—that is, protecting occupants of vehicles from the various consequences of impact after it has occurred. The goal is certainly desirable as long as it does not obscure the still greater desirability of preventing as many "first" accidents as possible. Third, the strong implication that American automobile design has consciously ignored safety is just not so. If unsafe cars were the principal cause of accidents, then the comparative accident data just cited would seem to demonstrate that American cars are considerably safer than others. In general they are. American automobiles, for example, introduced safety glass as standard equipment in the 1920s; forty years later it was still exceptional in foreign cars, unless they were intended for the American market. Finally the focus on the vehicle encourages two common but unproductive reactions: one, as with smog, to find a scapegoat (the automobile manufacturers) and assume that identifying and maybe punishing the culprit will make the problem go away; two, to decide that gadgetry will solve the problem—"instant technology" once more. It is not true that because a technological principle is understood, and perhaps even an experimental model built, it is therefore immediately possible to produce a device for everyday use. Engineers are well aware of this gap between concept and execution. So are many others who may not understand technology but do understand man—like William Shakespeare:

If to do were as easy as to know what were good to do, chapels had been churches, and poor men's cottages princes' palaces. (*Merchant of Venice,* act 1, scene 2.)

13 Quoted in *Automotive Information,* vol. 4, no. 3 (November 1966), p. 4.

Traffic safety has three components—driver, car, and road—and research into the causes of accidents has not been thorough enough to permit accurate allocation of responsibility among them. As far as the evidence goes, mechanical failures in cars are a minor factor. Human error is more important; some state highway departments, for instance, estimate that drunken driving is involved in two-thirds of the fatal accidents.[14] As far as the road is concerned, enough has been said already to show the beneficial effect of properly designed highways and well-planned traffic controls. Limitation of access, divided roadways, and grade separation add markedly to safety. A careful calculation estimates that the Interstate system will save over 9,500 lives annually by 1980.[15]

Comparable estimates for ordinary roads and streets are more difficult to make because of the multiplicity of conditions on the country's 3.5 million miles of every type of highway and the wide variety of corrective measures that can be employed. A dangerous section of road, for instance, might be completely rebuilt or merely equipped with warning signs, and traffic hazards on city streets require different treatment from those on country roads. With the conventional highway system projected to carry about 60 percent of the nation's motor vehicle traffic, it seems safe to assume that comprehensive and well-planned improvement would yield gains in safety at least equal to those of the Interstates and other freeways. As a sample, an analysis by the Michigan Highway Commission of thirty-nine sections of new and old roads showed a 73 percent reduction of traffic deaths on the new segments.[16]

Figures from Europe reach the same conclusion: driver errors and road defects are the main source of accidents. A German

14 Alfred E. Johnson, "The Traffic Safety Program in the United States," *American Highways* (April 1967), p. 6.
15 Wilbur Smith and Associates, *Future Highways and Urban Growth* (New Haven, Conn.: Wilbur Smith and Associates, 1961), p. 296.
16 *Automotive Information,* November 1963.

source placed the major cause as disregard for elementary traffic laws; on the other hand, a survey by the Inland Transport Committee of the European Economic Community led to the conclusion that the causes of accidents should be distributed: drivers' errors, 20 percent; errors by motorcyclists and pedestrians, 5 percent; defects in vehicles, 5 percent; *defects in roads, 70 percent*.[17] This is a startlingly high emphasis on roads, but it reinforces the premise that the improvement of roads is second only in importance to the improvement of drivers in the advancement of highway safety.

In the final analysis the human factor is the core of the problem of highway safety. All the safety features that are technically and economically feasible can and should be incorporated into both vehicles and roads, but when that is accomplished, the governing factor in safe driving remains the driver.

New Towns and Rebuilt Cities

One of the methods of dealing with burgeoning urban population without further uncontrolled sprawl over the countryside is to create new, comprehensively planned communities. A "New Town" in the United States is a planned community with a conscious effort to achieve a balance among residential, commercial, industrial, cultural, and recreational features. A survey dated 1968 investigated fifty-two New Towns in the United States. All were developed by private promoters (twenty-eight responded to the survey), some of whom, like Victor Gruen Associates, were consciously undertaking to apply specific theories of urban organization. A partial composite picture of them is

They are built to accommodate 65,000 people and three quarters of them claim to be multifunctional (that is, not exclusively residential and recreational but having commerce and industry also). They are built where population trends indicate a high

17 Hermann Schreiber, *History of Roads* (London: Barrie and Rockliff, 1961), p. 279.

rate of growth, with an eye toward possible available recreational uses. In fact, three quarters of them are built with a consideration for recreational or scenic water. They are built, in the average case, about thirteen miles from an already existing major urbanized area.[18]

The American New Town, in other words, is typically a variation of the expansion of Suburbia, more thoroughly planned and organized than most suburban communities. This characteristic led Robert C. Weaver, the first Secretary of the Department of Housing and Urban Development, to observe that most New Towns appeared "destined to become country-club communities for upper income families." [19] Two of the best known of these communities, Reston, Virginia, and Columbia, Maryland, have low-cost housing, but these are demonstration projects close to the national capital and with federal subsidies for the housing programs. Since 1968 federal aid, in the form of guarantees for loans, has been generally available to developers of "model communities."

Planning for New Towns in the United States is recent and fragmentary, but as far as their transportation needs are concerned, it is obvious that the highway will be the principal reliance. Some have projects for mass transit designed to reduce automobile traffic, but these are predominantly bus systems,[20] as could be expected in communities whose maximum populations are to be on the order of 100,000. New Towns should offer an opportunity for an up-to-date functional layout of streets both to facilitate internal traffic and to provide good connections with the adjoining metropolis.

American experience with New Towns is still limited. Britain,

18 See T. A. Dames and W. L. Grecco, "A Survey of New Town Planning Considerations, *Traffic Quarterly,* vol. 22, no. 4 (October 1968), pp. 556, 567.
19 *Ibid.,* p. 559.
20 A good survey of New Town transportation appears in a paper by Robert L. Morris of Alan M. Voorhees and Associates, "Transportation Planning for New Towns," presented at the 48th Annual Meeting, Highway Research Board, Washington, D.C., January 1969.

on the other hand, has been organizing them since the late 1940s, and while British conditions are not completely analogous, they are close enough to afford useful comparisons. The informative Buchanan Report gives credit to the "first generation" New Towns for being reasonably well laid out to deal with traffic but considers that inadequate allowance was made for the rapid growth of car ownership.[21] The "second generation" has faced this matter realistically. Cumbernauld in Scotland, a community of 70,000 designed as an overflow from Glasgow, planned its street system on an assumption of one car per family.[22] It concentrates its central business district on a raised deck and brings the traffic in to parking areas underneath. Thus pedestrian and vehicular movements are separated; in fact, pedestrian approaches to the business center are also separate from the streets used by vehicles. This is based on the "Radburn Plan," introduced by Clarence Stein and Henry Wright in Radburn, New Jersey, in 1928. It calls for a residential area laid out so that through traffic cannot use its streets and designed so that each house has an access street on one side and a pedestrian path on the other. The idea was not followed to any extent in the United States, probably because Americans walk less than most other people—to which the Buchanan Report adds that what walking there is in the United States "seems to be safeguarded by the comparatively mature and considerate behaviour of car drivers." [23]

The report notes with qualified approval the reconstruction of Coventry, with a large central shopping district designed exclusively for pedestrians—the principal qualification being that Coventry, one of the oldest and greatest centers of automobile manufacturing, has provided insufficiently for motor vehicle ac-

21 *Traffic in Towns,* p. 164.
22 *Ibid.,* p. 166.
23 *Ibid.,* p. 47. European visitors are frequently puzzled by the fact that in some American communities, conspicuously the wealthier suburbs of Los Angeles, a pedestrian is *ipso facto* an object of suspicion.

cess to the CBD. German cities are credited with sensitivity in restoring medieval street patterns, high quality in the design and landscaping of their new urban highways, and intelligent planning for putting street railway tracks underground or in the medians of major streets.[24]

The most interesting example of modern European city planning is Stockholm, a city of a million people which was not subjected to war damage. Much has been made by antiautomobile advocates in the United States of Stockholm's reliance on a rail transit system, supported by governmental subsidies. They ignore what the British investigators are careful to include: namely, that Stockholm has an elaborate highway network, including a considerable mileage of freeway and extensive parking facilities. The city's traffic system, in fact, assumes that rail transit will handle the commuter flow, but that there will still be a heavy volume of motor vehicle traffic.[25]

In other words, the Swedes, with the highest ratio of automobile ownership outside North America, have obviously no intention of giving up personal travel by road. They may use public transportation for trips to and from work, but for other purposes they have the same propensity as Americans to prefer the convenience of the automobile.

This British report, in fact, should be required reading for anyone concerned with urban transportation not only because of its tremendous wealth of information but also because of its balanced, dispassionate tone. It states matter-of-factly that the motor vehicle is "a beneficial invention with an assured future, largely on account of the great advantages it offers for door-to-door travel and transport." [26] As with most new technologies, disadvantages accompany the benefits, in this case increased urban

24 *Ibid.,* pp. 175–176.
25 *Ibid.,* p. 177.
26 *Ibid.,* p. 191.

congestion and air pollution. The remedy, however, is not to denounce the motor vehicle but to attack the problem rationally and have public authority determine and establish acceptable standards of performance. These might require some restrictions on the use of automobiles, but such restrictions have to be within the framework of a free society: "In Soviet Russia this [limitation of the number of vehicles on the streets] is achieved by what appears to be a deliberate restriction on the number of motor cars available for sale to the general public. We hope we may assume that this is excluded for Britain." [27] The tenor of the report is that the modern world not only can live with the motor vehicle but should; there are formidable problems to be solved, but they are all susceptible to rational and intelligent planning.

Highway Needs

The prospective expansion of highway traffic is frequently viewed, quite needlessly, with alarm. The United States, we are told, is to be covered with asphalt—or concrete, as the case may be. Actually, the United States is in a favorable position to deal with its traffic needs. If these are great, so is the country's highway capacity. By 1972 there will be 41,000 miles of Interstate highway, plus several thousand more of express highways not included in the Interstate system. Comparative figures for other industrialized countries with high volumes of traffic are: Germany (West and East), 2,500 miles of *autobahn,* most of it built in the 1930s; Great Britain, about 400 miles of motorway, begun in 1956, well designed and built except that the medians are too narrow by current American standards; Sweden, 1,200 miles; Italy, about 1,000 miles, the earliest going back to the 1920s; Japan, about 1,700 kilometers built, building, and projected; France, about 1,100 miles planned but little constructed so far.

The highway mileage of the United States has not significantly

27 *Ibid.,* Introduction, par. 29.

Table 15.3   A Comparison of Rural and Urban Highway Mileage, 1921–1965
(in five-year intervals and in thousands of miles)

Year	Rural Mileage	Urban Mileage	Total Mileage
1921	2,925	235	3,160
1925	3,006	240	3,246
1930	3,009	250	3,259
1935	3,032	278	3,310
1940	2,990	297	3,287
1945	3,012	307	3,319
1950	3,003	310	3,313
1955	3,057	361	3,418
1960	3,116	430	3,546
1965	3,183	507	3,690

Source: U.S. Department of Transportation, *Highway Statistics: Summary to 1965*, Table M-200, p. 119.

increased for half a century. (See Table 15.3.) To handle anticipated future traffic volumes, it will need qualitative improvement more than quantitative extension. For rural roads, which account for 86 percent of the total mileage and half the vehicle-miles of travel, the Department of Transportation says:

In general, there will be only a modest future growth in the extent of our national road network; it already reaches practically everywhere. In rural areas, future new road construction (as distinguished from reconstruction and improvement of existing roads, with only minor changes of alinement) will probably consist largely of arterials, including freeways, built on new locations primarily for more direct routing or because of right-of-way problems. Many of these routes will connect to the Interstate System, serving cities and other important points not on the present system. A relatively small mileage of rural land access roads will also be needed.

In addition to new major arterials, a substantial mileage of highways in rural areas will require reconstruction to higher standards and/or reconstruction of pavements worn out in service. Extensively needed are wider lanes, adequate shoulders, flatter curves and slopes, and elimination of bottlenecks, to improve traffic flow and to raise the safety quality of the rural system.[28]

28 *1968 National Highway Needs Report*, p. 15.

The mileage of rural road may indeed decrease rather than grow, because new construction will be offset by the abandonment of the old roads and the straightening of existing routes makes them shorter. Urban mileage will increase to keep pace with the growth of urbanization and the expansion of urban areas. Any estimate of the extent of this increase can at best be an informed guess, because it has to allow for imponderables such as changes in city planning, the extent and nature of the programs of urban renewal that we might undertake, and the possible effect of new transportation technologies. A reliable calculation based on projections of automobile ownership and vehicle-miles of travel concludes that over and above the completed Interstate system and such other express highways as existed in 1960, about 11,000 miles of new freeway, 5,600 of it urban, will be needed by 1980.[29] Allowing for construction of toll roads and non-Interstate freeways since 1960, the total new mileage required in this analysis is closer to 10,000 than 11,000 miles.

Additional urban freeway mileage will reduce the demand for new secondary roads and streets and may permit the elimination of some that now exist. The TOPICS program, begun in 1967, should lessen the need for major construction of arterial streets. The term means the Traffic Operations Program to Increase Capacity and Safety, adopted in 1967 to apply federal highway funds to improve urban arterials by "the systematic and comprehensive application of traffic operations and minor construction improvements in combination." The techniques are those described in the previous chapter. They can increase the capacity of existing city street networks by 10 to 15 percent, with corresponding gains in safety.

What demands do highways place on the supply of land? The answer is: substantial but a long way from insupportable. A. Q.

29 Wilbur Smith and Associates, *Future Highways and Urban Growth*, p. 211.

Mowbray states that the United States has 3.6 million square miles of land and 3.6 million miles of roads and streets, with the implication that this is an excessive proportion.[30] He gives the area of roads and their rights-of-way as 24,000 square miles, equal, as he says, to the area of West Virginia but still only two-thirds of 1 percent of 3.6 million.

It is possible to be more exact. A mile of road, on the average, takes up 6 acres of land.[31] On this basis, American roads and streets occupy about 22.1 million acres, or approximately 1.16 percent of the continental United States. Rural roads, to repeat, have adequate capacity for reasonably predictable future traffic loads. They need improvement rather than major additions. The bulk of new highway construction will fall in the one-seventh of the nation's highway mileage that is classified as urban. Approximately 1 percent of the land in the United States is urban, if we include all populated places with a thousand or more inhabitants.[32] Half of this area is in communities with population between 1,000 and 10,000.

The proportion of urban areas devoted to roads and streets falls between 20 and 40 percent, less in small towns than in large, in suburbs than in central cities, and in newly developed communities than in old. Thirty percent is a liberal average, which would give 6 million acres of urban land used for highway purposes. Urban acreage is increasing by about 400,000 acres annually, so that on the 30 percent basis 120,000 acres are being added to urban roads and streets each year. At this rate it will take fifty years to double urban highway acreage. If this is added to

30 A. Q. Mowbray, *Road to Ruin* (Philadelphia: J. B. Lippincott Co., 1969), p. 12.
31 This is calculated by the Bureau of Public Roads and includes express highways. These affect the average much less than might be expected because they constitute such a small proportion of total road mileage.
32 The figures on urban land use are based on Mabel Walker, "Land Use and Local Finance," *Tax Policy*, vol. 27, nos. 11–12 (November, December 1960), pp. 3–12.

existing national highway acreage, the total will still be less than
1.5 percent of the country's land area, and this estimate is certainly high. In new urban communities and in central city
redevelopment projects street acreages are usually not more than
20 percent. Moreover, as cities expand and as new towns are
created, some rural highway mileage is replaced by urban, so that
the national total has to be adjusted accordingly. The supply
of land is not an immediate problem; if it becomes so in the
future, the amount taken for highways will have been a minor
contributor. The principal difficulty for the time being is that
traffic is heaviest and highway needs greatest in the urban centers
where competing demands for land are also acute.

Some other points can be added. What applies to city streets
applies equally to the entire national highway network; most of
the roads would have to be there even if the motor vehicle did
not exist. They would be different in quality, but the same mileage of roads at the very least would be needed for local transport.
The motor vehicle, indeed, has made possible some economy of
land. In 1920 about 90 million acres, 27 percent of the total
harvested area and almost 5 percent of the land area of the United
States, was used to grow feed for horses and mules—apart from
the land devoted to grazing.[33] This area has decreased to less than
8 million acres—that is, by replacing the horse the automobile
has released for other purposes almost four times as much land
as is occupied by the entire highway system.

The fact that we have enough land for our present purposes
does not justify wasting it. A carefully planned highway program
will use only as much land as is necessary, but as long as the planning is well done, it need not hesitate to take the space that the
conditions demand. Inadequate roads impose a heavy social cost
in congestion, accidents, and delay, and shortsighted or penny-
pinching highway programs have repeatedly necessitated expen-

33 *Ibid.*, p. 4.

sive reconstruction in later years, using more money and more land than would have been required if provision for future needs had been made in the first place. The most difficult problems occur in large central cities where land is scarce and high-priced. In these situations the land-saving measures mentioned earlier can be explored further: using the air space over freeways or developing a multilevel structure for CBDs. Improvements in tunneling techniques offer the possibility of putting main downtown traffic arterials underground.

To sum up, the United States, indeed the entire world, faces an expansion of motor vehicle ownership and of the utilization of the highway to transport both people and goods. In order to realize to the full the potential benefits of this expansion, there has to be a candid appraisal of the problems that accompany it, and foresight in devising remedies for them. We know what the principal problems are and have made progress in developing the methods of dealing with them—technical means of reducing air pollution and of promoting safety, and designs for urban growth and redevelopment to minimize traffic congestion. To make these remedies effective demands broad cooperation between governmental authorities at all levels, manufacturers, highway builders, and the public at large. If such cooperation is achieved, then highway transportation will continue to fulfill its promise of promoting growth in the economy and freedom—individual mobility—in the society.

16 The Open Road

The total effect of motorized highway transportation on the growth and structure of present-day society is so vast and so complex that definitive measurement is out of the question. The combination of motor vehicle and paved road is one of the mightiest forces to emerge in and influence our civilization. No single study can do more than undertake to identify the principal situations where this force has made itself felt and attempt to evaluate and interpret the impacts.

The initial approach can be historical and in fact must be because the story is one of growth. Most of the varieties of growth are obvious: manufacture, ownership, and use of motor vehicles; volume of highway traffic, both passenger and freight; business enterprises supported by highway travel; industrial development and relocation based on road transport; suburban living; recreational opportunities. The statistics and the facts about all these make impressive compilations, but they are not self-explanatory. They tell what happened and how, but not why.

There is nothing automatic about the growth of modern highway transportation. It is neither an inevitable consequence of inexorable, impersonal forces, nor is it the end product of a sequence of unrelated accidents. It is the result of human activity responding to unsatisfied or insufficiently satisfied needs, and its phenomenal growth has been due to the fact that it has filled these needs better than anything else that has appeared so far.

Transportation is a service; more than that it is a public service, regardless of whether any specific transportation function is performed by public authority or private enterprise. In the broad sweep of history, the eras that have seen the greatest advances and the societies that have enjoyed growth and strength have all had good transportation. The ancient civilizations and some of the later stages of transport history were touched upon in the first chapter. More recently, the beginning of the industrial era in the Western world coincided in time with extensive road and canal building in Britain and France, followed rapidly by railroads. Whether the growth of commerce and industry stimulated better transportation facilities or better transportation stimulated the growth of commerce and industry is a question impossible to answer conclusively and is probably unimportant. It is quite obvious that economic growth on any major scale demanded the ability to move goods, and to a lesser extent people, economically and efficiently.

In the performance of this function the highway stood at a disadvantage until our own day because the vehicles were slow and inefficient. Water transportation was always cheaper for bulk shipments, and usually faster. In the nineteenth century the railroad reduced road transport to strictly local movement of both people and goods. Yet nothing ever put the highway completely out of business, because no other mode of transportation can offer the same universality of access. The road alone is capable of serving both large places and small, individual homes and farms. So when oxcarts were the only way to move goods by road, oxcarts were used—and still are used over many parts of the world. Road transport was slow and expensive, but for basic transportation needs it was irreplaceable.

The invention of the motor vehicle removed this one great limitation on road transport. It did more than that, because the motor vehicle, despite its "horseless carriage" phase, is not just a stage in an evolutionary process beginning with the oxcart, or even the chariot. It is an entirely novel form of mobility, with most of the same economic and social impacts as other modes of transportation but beyond that with distinctive qualities and characteristics to create its own unique and far-reaching impacts. The motor vehicle can and does provide mass transportation for people and bulk transportation for goods; if these were its sole functions, it would be an invaluable supplement to other forms of transportation. But these are the lesser part of what the motor vehicle has to contribute. The major part is that it offers individual, personal, flexible mobility, as nothing before it has ever done, and as nothing else now available can do. The point is summed up, to a limited degree, in a report on transportation from the Aeronautical Laboratory of Cornell University: "The automobile itself is so exasperatingly convenient that it drives the transportation inventors almost mad trying to devise competitive substitutes." [1]

There is more than just convenience involved. The mobility conferred by the automobile has benefited ordinary people most. The wealthy could afford coaches and carriages and so had some freedom of movement, although even the most luxurious coach of the preautomobile era was not only slower but clumsier and far less comfortable than the popular-priced car of today. Ordinary people seldom ranged any distance from home; if they did, they had to go by some form of public conveyance, provided it was available, or they walked. This is where the automobile has been an instrument of social revolution, first in the United States and now extending throughout the world. Perhaps this social revolution explains the distaste of so many self-appointed "elite" groups for the automobile, or more accurately for automobile ownership by people other than themselves. It is one thing to profess concern for the "common man" but quite another to have to accept him on terms of actual equality.

There is profound insight in this observation from a recent novel concerned with the 1967 *coup d'etat* in Greece: "After all, nothing upsets the status quo more than a big shot of industrial growth. You know, the maids would rather work in factories, the lower classes *start buying cars,* people put housing develop-

1 Edward M. Holmes, "Highway in Our Future," *Traffic Engineering* (May 1961), p. 34.

ments in picturesque old villages. That always burns up the old guard. Everywhere." [2]

This is not meant as an endorsement of destroying the picturesque, and most of those who clamor to preserve it would be horrified to be classified with the "old guard." Yet the village that looks picturesque to the tourist may be a slum for those who have to live in it. In this whole general attitude there is a curious affinity between the "old guard" and many of those who identify themselves as "intellectual liberals." The affinity may well arise from the fact that both groups consider themselves to be elites, better qualified to judge what is good for the common man than the common man himself and therefore entitled to impose this good regardless of how the recipient may feel about it.

In the same way that the passenger car has worked to the advantage of ordinary people, motor truck transportation has been more advantageous to small business enterprises than to large ones. Firms whose shipments do not justify railroad sidings, docks, or carload rates can utilize highway transportation and through it enjoy a freedom of location that they would not otherwise possess.

The Public Service Function

Transportation is a service and as such occupies a special place in society. Its role in an economic system is succinctly and accurately defined in this passage:

Although the achievement of an efficient and economic transportation system is a valid goal, maximum transportation efficiency in itself is not an adequate goal for national policy. The broader objective is the maximization of the efficiency of the entire national economy, of which transport is but one component. Assembly of materials, production and distribution of products, all served by transportation, are primary, and it may be that optimization of the total economy would be achieved with transport itself at less than maximum efficiency. For ex-

2 Emma Lathen, *When in Greece* (New York: Simon and Schuster, 1969), p. 21.

ample, transport operations would be more economical if shipments were larger and if their flow were steadier, but this would probably require higher investment in inventories, greater storage space requirements and other increases in the cost elements of production and distribution.[3]

On this basis, since the function of transportation is to promote the total economy and the good of society generally, the service may properly be offered as a contribution to the general welfare which need not pay its own way. Another way of stating this principle is W. W. Rostow's definition of such facilities as roads, railways, and ports as "social overhead capital."[4] Such capital equipment, he points out, is an indispensable prerequisite for initiating and sustaining economic growth, but providing it is an investment problem with special characteristics. The initial investment must be large, the returns will be long-term rather than immediate, and the benefits may accrue to the community as a whole rather than to individual investors or entrepreneurs. Consequently governments normally must take the major role in building social overhead capital. Historically, practices have varied widely, except that transportation services have seldom been offered completely free. Governments at all levels have encouraged canal and railroad building, sometimes by subsidy, frequently by direct construction and operation. We can ignore ocean and air transport, since the seas and the air come free, although even here public authority has accepted responsibility for providing harbor and airport facilities. Road building has been universally accepted as an appropriate object for the expenditure of public funds, except for the occasional resort to private construction and operation supported by tolls. (Twentieth-century toll roads in the United States are publicly owned.)

3 Reprinted by permission from *Metropolitan Transportation—1980*, pp. 3, 4, published by the Comprehensive Planning Office, The Port of New York Authority.

4 W. W. Rostow, *The Stages of Economic Growth* (Cambridge: University Press, 1960), pp. 24–25, explains the concept of social overhead capital.

It would therefore be acceptable policy for highway systems to be maintained as a cost to the society, and in the past they almost invariably have been. One of the great changes that automotive transportation has brought about, at least in the United States, is that user taxes make the highway system self-supporting. However, although balancing highway income against highway expenditures does afford a useful guide to the growth of modern road transportation, it is far from being the decisive measurement. The total impact of highway transportation extends far beyond this particular item.

The phenomenal growth in the use of motor vehicles is presumptive proof that deep-seated needs were waiting to be satisfied. The needs are universal, but the degree of satisfaction has differed —in other words, the supply of highway transportation throughout the world is uneven and has little relationship to prospective demand for it. There are wide areas that would benefit enormously from more and better roads and the vehicles to use them. One reason for this disparity is self-evident. It takes a fairly well developed industrial economy to manufacture reliable automobiles in quantity, and the building and maintenance of a good road network demands a stable government with access to the necessary resources in labor and capital. The term "access" is employed intentionally, because the capital may be procured outside and should be if the society itself cannot provide it.

Disparities in highway resources exist in the United States also, although the expansion of federal highway programs is gradually reducing them. The traveler in many parts of the South becomes aware that while the Interstate system is the same there as elsewhere, there are long stretches even of federal-aid primary road that are conspicuously inferior to their counterparts in other states. The difference is a measure of the ability of individual states to provide matching funds. There is a definite connection between the quality of the road network and the economic status of the region. The case of West Virginia has been noted previously as one in which economic advance has been retarded by poor roads, and the same consideration applies also to these other areas. The causal relationship is debatable: Are these parts of the South poor because they have inadequate roads, or do they have inadequate roads because they are poor? The circle is being broken by the Interstate and other federal highway programs. The effect of a first-class highway network on the economy of the South will be worth watching.

There is much more to enjoying the benefits of motorized highway transportation than possessing the ability to manufacture cars and construct paved roads. The human spirit comes into the picture too. The American leadership was by no means inevitable; the historical record is very clear that the United States was ten years behind Europe in the development of the automobile and more than that in the creation of a respectable highway network. The decisive difference was the insight and vision of Henry Ford, William C. Durant, and their pioneering contemporaries, who saw the possibility of "freeing the common man from the limitations of his geography" and proceeded to do it.

Perhaps conditions in the rest of the industrial world, which at that time meant Europe, were not as suitable for the same thing to be attempted. We cannot tell, because nobody tried. Until the First World War European opinion definitely classified the automobile as a luxury for the wealthy, and this attitude persisted into the 1920s and even the 1930s, long after the American example had encouraged imitation. Truck transportation is a separate category; its manifest economic advantages brought widespread and early adoption. It may be pertinent to add that when Europe accepted the concept of wide distribution of automobile ownership, its manufacturers overlooked one of the vital ingredients in the American success story—namely, that it is not enough just to produce cars cheaply. It is necessary also to create purchasing power by distributing some of the industry's profits in the form of high wages.

Obtaining the benefits of highway transportation also requires that travel be free from artificial or unnecessary restrictions. Regulations for the smooth and safe movement of traffic are indisputably essential. The unwarranted impediments are such practices as discriminatory taxes and fees imposing special burdens on "foreign" (nonlocal) traffic; traps to collect fines from visiting motorists; unreasonable border inspections; or, as in totalitarian countries, restrictions on freedom of movement. Except for this last barrier, these practices have generally diminished. Some of the credit is due to the vigorous activity of automobile clubs; most, however, is simply due to the recognition that sacrificing major benefits for petty gains is unwise. Tourist traffic especially has become an economic prize to be wooed by encouraging ease of movement by road. This applies not only to internal travel but to travel across international borders also, at least in the free world. In North America and western Europe tourists can cross frontiers with a minimum of formality and delay. Perhaps we can develop a doctrine for the road comparable to that worked out over the centuries for the seas: that the road, like the ocean, is a highway open to all who wish to pass on their lawful pursuits.

Looking Forward

In a world of accelerating change transportation has kept pace; it has, indeed, been one of the major causes of change. It is just about a century and a half since movement on land became possible at speeds beyond the capacity of the horse—specifically, the Rainhill trials on the Liverpool and Manchester Railway in 1829 demonstrated that a steam locomotive could attain an operational speed of 30 mph. The steamship did not reach this level until well into the twentieth century. The airplane, and for practical purposes the automobile, are twentieth-century innovations. In a very short span of historical time, therefore, travel habits have been radically transformed in both volume and speed. One authority on transportation goes so far as to say that change in the speed of travel may have had more to do with fundamental changes of the entire social and economic systems of the world in the past century than any other single force.[5]

This statement may claim too much for speed alone, but in conjunction with other factors it has a strong validity. One is the great increase in the total volume of movement, both passenger and freight, an increase not due simply to the fact that there are more people doing more business. In the United States passenger-miles of travel and ton-miles of freight have both risen at a higher rate since 1939 than either population or Gross National Product (see Table 16.1). Another vital contributing factor to fundamental social and economic change is the flexibility of movement offered by the automobile and the highway, and to a growing extent by air travel.

Change may not necessarily be for the better, something the advocates of change for its own sake conveniently ignore; and even when the change is recognizably good, some drawbacks are bound to accompany it. The change in our society represented by motorized highway transportation falls into this latter category. It has brought problems with it which must be acknowledged candidly and for which remedies must (and can) be found. But if a complete balance sheet on the impact of automotive transportation could be compiled, the assets would definitely outweigh the liabilities. The car and the paved road have brought economic growth with them, very well expressed by Bernard de Voto, essayist, historian, and keen observer of the American scene:

The implications of the automobile have always outrun our ability to understand them. The necessities it has created have

5 W. W. Carey, Jr., "Highway Research in Transition," *Transportation: A Service* (New York: Academy of Sciences, 1968), pp. 48–49.

Table 16.1 National Economic Trends versus Transportation Trends, 1939–1968

Year	Gross National Product* (billions of dollars)			Industrial Production (1957–59 = 100)			Population (millions)			Intercity Ton-Miles† (billions)			Intercity Passenger-Miles‡		
	Amount	(a)	(b)	Index	(a)	(b)	Amount	(a)	(b)	Amount	(a)	(b)	Amount	(a)	(b)
1939	256	100		38	100		131	100		544	100		311	100	
1940	278	109		44	116		132	101		618	114		330	106	
1941	323	126		56	147		133	102		772	142		372	120	
1942	364	142		69	182		135	103		928	171		324	104	
1943	412	161		83	218		137	105		1,031	190		296	95	
1944	442	173		82	216		138	105		1,088	200		312	100	
1945	434	170		71	187		140	107		1,028	189		348	112	
1946	382	149		60	158		141	108		904	166		427	137	
1947	379	148	100	66	174	100	144	110	100	1,019	187	100	429	138	100
1948	396	155	105	68	179	103	147	112	102	1,045	192	103	441	142	103
1949	396	155	105	65	171	98	149	114	103	917	169	90	479	154	112
1950	435	170	115	75	197	114	152	116	106	1,063	195	104	505	162	118
1951	469	183	124	81	213	123	155	118	108	1,177	216	116	571	184	133
1952	483	189	127	84	221	127	158	121	110	1,145	210	112	614	197	143
1953	505	197	133	91	239	138	160	122	111	1,203	221	118	651	209	152

Year															
1954	498	131	195	86	226	130	163	124	113	1,123	206	110	670	215	156
1955	536	141	209	97	255	147	166	127	115	1,274	234	125	713	229	166
1956	546	144	213	100	263	152	169	129	117	1,356	249	133	747	240	174
1957	553	146	216	101	266	153	172	131	119	1,336	246	131	748	241	174
1958	547	144	214	94	247	142	175	134	122	1,216	224	119	760	244	177
1959	582	154	227	106	279	161	178	136	124	1,286	236	126	765	246	178
1960	596	157	233	109	287	165	181	138	126	1,314	242	129	784	252	183
1961	608	160	238	110	289	167	184	140	128	1,310	241	129	791	254	184
1962	648	171	253	118	311	179	187	143	130	1,371	252	135	818	263	191
1963	674	178	263	124	326	188	189	144	131	1,453	267	143	853	274	199
1964	711	188	278	132	347	200	192	147	133	1,543	284	151	896	288	209
1965	756	199	295	143	376	217	195	149	135	1,638	301	161	920	296	214
1966	805	212	314	156	411	236	197	150	137	1,747	321	171	971	312	226
1967	825	218	322	158	416	239	199	152	138	1,765§	324§	173§	1,021	328	238
1968	866	229§	338	166§	437§	252§	201	153	140	1,838§	338§	180§	1,081§	348§	252§
1969(p)	890*	235	348	173	455	262	203	155	141	1,900	349	186	1,130	363	263

* Total output of goods and services in *constant 1968 dollars*. Table revised to agree with official revision of GNP for 1968.

† Includes both regulated and unregulated carriers.

‡ Includes both for-hire and private carriers, including auto.

§ Revised.

(a) Index with 1939 = 100.

(b) Index with 1947 = 100.

(p) Preliminary TAA estimate.

Source: Transportation Association of America, *Transport Facts and Trends*, 6th ed., 1969.

multiplied faster than we have kept up with them. Both our population and our wealth have increased at a greater rate than the most careful calculations had prepared us for. That fact is the most impressive evidence of the power of the American economic system. Yet it is the primary reason our highway system has grown increasingly inadequate.[6] [This passage was written in 1956.]

The social implications are combined with the economic by the economist Robert L. Heilbroner:

We are all aware in a general way of this pervasive "automobilization" of the economy. Yet it is a curious fact that when we picture the economic implications of the car, we almost always think on much too small a scale. . . .

Trucking is of course the prime example. Today rail transport has become the great bulk cargo carrier; air transport flies in the small, high value stuff; truck transport moves all the rest. Fifty-nine thousand fleets of trucks—counting only fleets with ten trucks and up—shuttle 76 per cent of the nation's total freight tonnage.

But aside from the trucking revolution, the car itself is imposing its imperious demands on merchandising. If you want to sell goods these days you have to put them where you can get to them by car, and preferably where you can get at them without even leaving your car. . . .

Yet these reflections on the impact of the automobile still fail to do justice to its quintessential contribution to our lives. This is its gift of mobility itself—not mobility as a dollar-spreading device or a mechanical substitute for personal movement, but as a direct enhancement of life, as an enlargement of life's boundaries and opportunities. This is so enormous, so radical a transformation that its effect can no longer be measured or appreciated by mere figures. It is nothing less than the unshackling of the age-old bonds of locality; it is the grant of geographic choice and economic freedom on a hitherto unimagined scale.

We can do no more than point in the general direction of the changes which mobility has wrought. We see it in the breakdown of the old factory town where workers perforce dwelt in the shadow of the mills and plants: today seven out of ten workers drive their cars regularly to work and are thereby free to live in residential rather than industrial areas. We see it in the proliferation of suburban life, a development impossible without mass automotive transportation. We see it in the great currents of internal migration, in which one family in every five changes its

6 Bernard de Voto, "The American Road," *Freedom of the American Road* (Detroit: Ford Motor Co., 1956), p. 8.

address each year in search of a better job, a better home. What this has meant, not alone in terms of wider economic horizons but in terms of wider life horizons is incalculable. . . .[7]

Against these gains might be placed the decline of central cities because of the exodus to the suburbs. Responsibility for the plight of the cities is distributed over a wide range of economic and social forces and governmental authorities, and the question of whether cities should be concentrated or dispersed has no agreed answer. The motor vehicle has made it easier for people and business to get out. It can also get some of them back in again if future urban transportation programs are geared to the realities of twentieth-century living. On the overall balance sheet the tremendous benefits of highway transportation to rural society must go far to offset the adverse effects on central cities. And in the final compilation, what quantitative value do we put on freedom of movement?

The individuality of automobile transportation is something that Americans, and others, are simply not going to give up except under a degree of compulsion completely unacceptable in a free society. Most of the plans for revised transportation policies recognize this fact and incorporate it realistically into their programs. For example, United States Senator Claiborne Pell (Rhode Island) is a staunch and persuasive advocate of high-speed ground transportation in the Northeast Corridor, and he justifies it on the eminently reasonable premise that more effective employment of rail transport in this densely populated part of the country would free the highways and the airways for the roles that they are best suited to perform.[8] He quotes Constantine Doxiadis to the effect that the main purposes of human settlements is to satisfy the inhabitants (a very vital point frequently overlooked by

7 R. L. Heilbroner, "Halfway to the Moon on Wheels," *Petroleum Today* (Spring 1960), pp. 1–3. Reprinted by permission of *Petroleum Today*.
8 Claiborne Pell, *Megalopolis Unbound* (New York: Frederick R. Praeger, 1968), p. 9.

social planners) and concludes: "I am convinced, for example, that we will have more, not fewer, individually controlled family vehicles—either the conventional automobiles we know now or their technological successors," and "There will always be a clearly defined role for individualized transportation for recreational as well as household purposes." [9] "Household purposes" covers a multitude of activities; it suggests no major limitation on the use of the automobile.

The basic feature of change is that it continues. The transportation revolution of the past century is going to go on, and no one can predict accurately what new forms of mobility will appear in the future. We may have techniques of mass transport that will avoid the rigidities of existing systems. We may, and in fact certainly will, have vehicles that can be electronically controlled in situations of high-density traffic and that have no pollutant emissions. There is a strong case for permitting the integration of transportation services—allowing the same agency, that is, to offer rail, air, water, or road transport. Such an arrangement would encourage the utilization of each mode of transportation in the conditions where it is most effective. But unless there is a radical change in our social and economic structure, people will continue to want and use transportation that will give them maximum freedom to move about and to choose where they live, work, or locate their businesses. The people we speak of are not just Americans; they are people everywhere, who have made the same choice whenever they have had the opportunity to do so.

For this purpose there is no substitute in sight for the highway and the motorized vehicle, whether "motorized" means an internal combustion engine, steam, electricity, fuel cells, nuclear energy, or sorcery. This is the paramount mode of individual, flexible, door-to-door transportation of both people and goods. If mass or bulk transportation is wanted, other agencies come

9 *Ibid.*, pp. 14–15.

into the picture, although highway transportation has a contribution in this field also.

Transportation is essential to social progress; to be exact, transportation *is* social progress because it has been throughout history the way in which not only goods and services but ideas as well were exchanged among peoples. This principle applies generally, but it applies with particular effect to movement by road. This has been the dominant method of overland travel since the beginning of history, and it is emphatically so in the United States of today. Putting artificial restraints on highway transportation can yield only economic and social stagnation. The Road and the Car together have an enormous capacity for promoting economic growth, raising standards of living, and creating a good society. The challenge before us is to implement this capacity.

Bibliography

Books

Barger, Harold. *The Transportation Industries, 1889–1946*. New York: National Bureau of Economic Research, 1952.

Bathe, Grenville and Dorothy. *Oliver Evans: A Chronicle of Early American Engineering*. Philadelphia: Historical Society of Pennsylvania, 1935.

Belloc, Hilaire. *The Highway and Its Vehicles*. London: Studio Ltd., 1926.

————. *The Road*. London: T. Fisher Unwin, Ltd., 1924.

Buchanan, C. D. *Mixed Blessing. The Motor in Britain*. London: Leonard Hill (Books) Ltd., 1958.

Bureau of Public Roads, U.S. Department of Commerce. *Highways and Economic and Social Changes*. Washington, D.C.: Government Printing Office, 1964.

Cranmer, H. Jerome. *New Jersey in the Automobile Age: A History of Transportation*. New Jersey Historical Series, vol. 23. Princeton, N.J.: D. Van Nostrand, 1964.

Dearing, Charles L. *American Highway Policy*. Washington, D.C.: The Brookings Institution, 1941.

————, and Owen, Wilfred. *National Transportation Policy*. Washington, D.C.: The Brookings Institution, 1949.

Dunbar, Seymour. *A History of Travel in America*. New York: Tudor Publishing Co., 1937.

Durrenberger, J. A. *Turnpikes*. Valdosta, Ga.: Published by the author, 1931.

Epstein, Ralph C. *The Automobile Industry*. New York: A. W. Shaw Co., 1928.

Fitch, Lyle C., and Associates. *Urban Transportation and Public Policy*. San Francisco: Chandler Publishing Co., 1964.

Friedlander, Ann F. *The Interstate Highway System. A Study in Public Investment*. Contributions to Economic Analysis, vol. 38. Amsterdam, Netherlands: North Holland Publishing Co., 1965.

Garrison, William L., and Marts, Marion E. *Geographic Impact of Highway Improvement*. Highway Economic Studies. Seattle: University of Washington, 1958.

Hart, Val. *The Story of American Roads*. New York: William Sloane Associates, 1950.

Highway Motor Transportation. Report of Subcommittee on Motor Transport of the Railroad Committee for the Study of Transportation. Washington, D.C.: Association of American Railroads, 1945.

Hilton, George W., and Due, James F. *The Electric Interurban Railways in America.* Stanford, Calif.: Stanford University Press, 1960.

Hoover, Edgar M., and Vernon, Raymond. *Anatomy of a Metropolis.* Cambridge, Mass.: Harvard University Press, 1959.

Horwood, Edgar M., and Boyce, Ronald P. *Studies of the Central Business District and Urban Freeway Development.* Seattle: University of Washington, 1959.

Jeffreys, Rees. *The King's Highway.* London: Batchworth Press, 1949.

Jordan, Philip D. *The National Road.* American Trails Series. Indianapolis, Ind.: Bobbs-Merrill Co., 1948.

Karolevitz, B. F. *This Was Pioneer Motoring.* Seattle: Superior Publishing Co., 1968.

Kirkland, E. C. *Men, Cities, and Transportation.* 2 vols. Cambridge, Mass.: Harvard University Press, 1948.

Laas, William, ed. *Freedom of the American Road.* Detroit: Ford Motor Co., 1956.

Labatut, Jean, and Lane, Wheaton J., eds. *Highways in Our National Life. A Symposium.* Princeton, N.J.: Princeton University Press, 1950.

Lang, A. Scheffer, and Soberman, Richard H. *Urban Rail Transit: Its Economics and Technology.* Cambridge, Mass.: The M.I.T. Press, 1964.

Lansing, John B. *Residential Location and Urban Mobility: The Second Wave of Interviews.* Ann Arbor, Mich.: University of Michigan, 1966.

———. *Transportation and Economic Policy.* New York: Free Press, 1966.

———, and Mueller, Eva, with Barth, Nancy. *Residential Location and Urban Mobility.* Survey Research Center, Institute for Social Research. Ann Arbor, Mich.: University of Michigan, 1964.

Leavitt, Helen. *Superhighway-Superhoax.* Garden City, N.Y.: Doubleday and Co., 1970.

Lee, J. R., and Wong, G. K. H. *An Analysis of Organized Indus-*

trial Districts. Menlo Park, Calif.: Stanford Research Institute, 1958.

Lynd, Robert S., and Helen M. *Middletown.* New York: Harcourt, Brace and Co., 1929.

————. *Middletown in Transition.* New York: Harcourt, Brace and Co., 1937.

McKain, Walter C. *The Connecticut Turnpike. A Ribbon of Hope.* Storrs, Conn.: University of Connecticut, 1965.

Mason, Philip P. *A History of American Roads.* Chicago: Rand McNally, 1967.

————. *The League of American Wheelmen and the Good Roads Movement, 1880–1905.* Ann Arbor, Mich.: University of Michigan Press, 1958.

Meyer, J. R., Kain, J. M., and Wohl, Martin. *The Urban Transportation Problem.* Cambridge, Mass.: Harvard University Press, 1965.

Mohring, Herbert, and Harwitz, Mitchell. *Highway Benefits: An Analytical Framework.* Evanston, Ill.: Transportation Center, Northwestern University, 1962.

Mowbray, A. Q. *Road to Ruin.* Philadelphia: J. B. Lippincott Co., 1969.

Mumford, Lewis. *The Highway and the City.* New York: Harcourt, Brace and World, 1963.

Owen, Wilfred. *Automotive Transportation. Trends and Problems.* Washington, D.C.: The Brookings Institution, 1949.

————. *The Metropolitan Transportation Problem.* Rev. ed. Washington, D.C.: The Brookings Institution, 1966.

————, and Dearing, Charles L. *Toll Roads and the Problems of Highway Modernization.* Washington, D.C.: The Brookings Institution, 1951.

Pell, Claiborne. *Megalopolis Unbound: The Supercity and the Transportation of Tomorrow.* New York: Frederick R. Praeger, 1966.

Port of New York Authority, Comprehensive Planning Office. *Metropolitan Transportation—1980.* New York, 1963.

Rae, John B. *The American Automobile.* Chicago History of American Civilization Series. Chicago: University of Chicago Press, 1965.

Recent Social Trends in the United States. Report of the President's Research Committee on Social Trends. New York: Mc-Graw-Hill Book Co., 1933.

Schreiber, Herman. *The History of Roads. From Amber Route to Motorway.* London: Barrie and Rockliff, 1961.

Sessions, Gordon. *Getting the Most from City Streets.* Washington, D.C.: Highway Research Board, 1967.

Smerk, George K. *Urban Transportation: The Federal Role.* Bloomington, Ind.: Indiana University Press, 1965.

Smith, Wilbur, and Associates. *Future Highways and Urban Growth.* New Haven, Conn.: Wilbur Smith and Associates, 1961.

———. *Parking in the City Center.* New Haven, Conn.: Wilbur Smith and Associates, 1965.

———. *Transportation and Parking for Tomorrow's Cities.* New Haven, Conn.: Wilbur Smith and Associates, 1966.

———. *The Motor Truck in the Metropolis.* New Haven, Conn.: Wilbur Smith and Associates, 1969.

———. *The Potential for Bus Rapid Transit.* Detroit: Automobile Manufacturers Association, 1970.

Taaffe, E. H., Garner, B. J., and Yates, M. H. *The Peripheral Journey to Work. A Geographic Consideration.* Evanston, Ill.: Transportation Center, Northwestern University, 1963.

Taylor, George R. *The Transportation Revolution.* Economic History of the United States, vol. 4. New York: Rinehart and Co., 1951.

Vernon, Raymond. *Metropolis—1985.* Cambridge, Mass.: Harvard University Press, 1960.

Willey, M. M., and Rice, S. A. *Communication Agencies and Social Life.* Recent Social Trends Monographs. New York: Mc-Graw-Hill Book Co., 1933.

Winther, Oscar O. *The Transportation Frontier: The Trans-Mississippi West, 1865–1890.* New York: Holt, Rinehart and Winston, 1964.

Wood, Frederick J. *The Turnpikes of New England and the Evolution of the Same through England, Virginia, and Maryland.* Boston: Marshall Jones Co., 1919.

Articles

Adkins, William G. "Land Value Impacts of Expressways in Dallas, Houston, and San Antonio, Texas." *Highway Research Board Bulletin* 227 (1959), pp. 50–65.

Bielak, Stanley F., and McCarthy, James F. "Highway Income, Expenditures, and Highway-User Earnings in 46 SMSA's." *Public Roads* 33, no. 9 (August 1965), pp. 185–199.

Boley, Robert E. "Effects of Industrial Parks on the Community." *Urban Land* 17, no. 10 (November 1958), pp. 3–6.

Bone, A. J., and Wohl, Martin. "Massachusetts Route 128 Impact Study." *Highway Research Board Bulletin* 227, pp. 21–49.

Bostick, Thurley A. "The Automobile in American Daily Life." *Public Roads* 32, no. 11 (December 1963), pp. 241–255.

Bowersox, Donald J. "Influence of Highways on Selection of Six Industrial Locations." *Highway Research Board Bulletin* 268 (1960), pp. 13–28.

Buhl, Walter F. "Intercity Highway Transport Share Tends to Vary Inversely with Size of Plant." *Highway Research Record*, no. 175 (1967), pp. 9–14.

Cherniak, Nathan. "A Statement of the Urban Transportation Problem." *Transportation* 5, Washington, D.C., United Nations Conference on the Application of Science and Technology for the Benefit of the Less Developed Areas (1963).

Church, Donald E. "Impact of Size and Distance on Intercity Highway Share of Transportation of Industrial Products." *Highway Research Record*, no. 175 (1967), pp. 1–8.

Dean, Edwin B. "Practicalities in Motel Development." Community Builders Council, Fort Lauderdale, Fla., *Urban Land* 19, no. 10 (November 1960), pp. 3–4.

Doxiadis, Constantine. "Toward the Ecumenopolis." *Rotarian* 112, no. 3 (March 1968), pp. 19–23.

Dutton, Davis. "Traffic Fatality Rates. A Downtrend for California." *Westways* 59, no. 10 (October 1967), pp. 35–36, 56.

Fogarty, Frank. "Trailer Parks: The Wheeled Suburbs." *Architectural Forum* 111, no. 1 (July 1959), pp. 127–130.

Hamilton, Williams F., II, and Nance, Dana K. "Systems Analysis of Urban Transportation." *Scientific American* 221, no. 1 (July 1969), pp. 19–27.

Herr, Philip B. "The Regional Impact of Highways." *Urban Land* 19, no. 2 (February 1960), pp. 3–8.

Hilton, George W. "The Decline of Railroad Commutation." *Business History Review* 36, no. 2 (Summer 1962), pp. 171–187.

———. "Rail Transit and the Pattern of Modern Cities: The California Case." *Traffic Quarterly* (July 1967), pp. 379–393.

Hoover, Edgar M. "Motor Metropolis: Some Observations on Urban Transportation in America." *Journal of Industrial Economics* 13, no. 3 (June 1965), pp. 177–192.

Hoyt, Homer. "Changing Patterns of Urban Growth." *Urban Land* 18, no. 4 (April 1959), pp. 1, 3–6.

———. "The Status of Shopping Centers in the United States." *Urban Land* 19, no. 9 (October 1960), pp. 3–6.

———. "The Changing Patterns of Land Economics." Urban Land Institute, *Technical Bulletin* 60 (1963).

Hunter, Robert F. "Turnpike Construction in Antebellum Virginia." *Technology and Culture* 4, no. 2 (Spring 1963), pp. 177–200.

Kanwit, E. L., and Eckartt, A. F. "Transportation Implications of Employment Trends in Central Cities and Suburbs." *Highway Research Record* 187, pp. 1–14.

Kennedy, Charles J. "Commuter Services in the Boston Area, 1835–1860." *Business History Review* 36, no. 2 (Summer 1962), pp. 153–170.

Koltnow, Peter G. "The Los Angeles Commuter: Going Farther, Faster." *Westways* 59, no. 9 (September 1967), pp. 17–19.

Lemly, James H. "Changes in Land Use and Value along Atlanta's Expressways." *Highway Research Board Bulletin* 227 (1959), pp. 1–20.

McConochie, William R. "Exclusive Lanes for Express Bus Operation in Cities of One to Three Million." *Urban Land* 22, no. 11 (December 1963), pp. 3–5.

Moses, Leon N., and Williamson, Harold F., Jr. "The Location of Economic Activity in Cities." *American Economic Review* 57, no. 2 (May 1967), pp. 211–222.

———. "Value of Time, Choice of Mode, and Subsidy Issue in Urban Transportation." *Journal of Political Economy* 71, no. 3 (June 1963), pp. 247–264.

Newcomb, Robinson. "Urban Land Use Shifts to Low Gear." *Appraisal Journal* 32, no. 3 (July 1961), pp. 376–382.

Pereira, William L. "Transportation: What's Ahead for Southern California." *Westways* 59, no. 11, pp. 3–5, 48–50.

Reinsberg, Max. "The Heyday of Highway Benefits." *I.C.C. Practitioners' Journal* 30 (June 1963), pp. 1143–1168.

Seifert, William W. "The Status of Transportation." *Proceedings of the IEEE* 56, no. 4 (April 1968), pp. 385–395.

Shaler, N. S. "The Common Roads." *Scribner's Magazine* 6, no. 4 (October 1889), pp. 473–483.

Spilhaus, Athelstan. "The Experimental City." *Rotarian* 112, no. 3 (March 1968), pp. 27–29, 54.

Stroup, R. H., and Vargha, L. A. "Economic Impact of Secondary Road Improvements." *Highway Research Record,* no. 16 (1963), pp. 1–13.

Witheford, David K. "Airports and Accessibility." *Traffic Quarterly* 23, no. 3 (April 1969), pp. 275–289.

Wunderlich, Gene. "Costs of Communicating by Transportation." *Journal of Economic Issues* 1, no. 3 (September 1967), pp. 199–210.

Public Documents

State of California, Department of Public Works. *The California Freeway and Expressway System. 1968. Progress and Problems. Summary Report.* Sacramento, Calif., 1969.

U.S. Congress. *Third Progress Report of the Highway Cost Allocation Study.* 86th Cong., 1st sess., House Document no. 91. Washington, D.C.: Government Printing Office, 1959.

U.S. Congress. *1968 National Highway Needs Report.* 90th Cong., 2nd sess., Committee Print. Washington, D.C.: Government Printing Office, 1968.

U.S. Department of Housing and Urban Development. *Tomorrow's Transportation. New Systems for the Urban Future.* Washington, D.C.: Government Printing Office, 1968.

Unpublished Sources

Davis, J. Allen. "Raids on the Gas Tax." Photocopied. Los Angeles: Automobile Club of Southern California, 1960.

"The Dynamics of Urban Transportation." A National Symposium Sponsored by Automobile Manufacturers Association, Inc. Photocopied. Detroit, 1962.

Fehan, J. P. "The Influence of Massachusetts Route 128 on the Travel Patterns of Workers at the New England Industrial Center, Needham, Mass." Bachelor's thesis, Massachusetts Institute of Technology, 1959.

McElhiney, Paul T. "The Freeways of Metropolitan Los Angeles. An Evaluation in Terms of Their Objectives." Ph.D. thesis,

School of Business Administration, University of California at Los Angeles, 1959.

Moses, Leon N., and Williamson, Harold F., Jr. "The Location of Economic Activity in Cities." Ms. Transportation Library, Northwestern University, Evanston, Ill., March 1966. A different version of this paper was published in *The American Economic Review* and is cited under "Articles."

Index